The Social Licence for Financial Markets

David Rouch

The Social Licence for Financial Markets

Reaching for the End and Why It Counts

David Rouch
London, UK

ISBN 978-3-030-40219-8   ISBN 978-3-030-40220-4   (eBook)
https://doi.org/10.1007/978-3-030-40220-4

This Palgrave Macmillan imprint is published by the registered company Springer Nature Switzerland AG.
The registered company address is: Gewerbestrasse 11, 6330 Cham, Switzerland

This book is dedicated to the part of each of us that desires justice, in the hope that it will grow, and to all who have fostered it in me, especially my parents Vic and Esmée

Foreword

The progress that David has made in defining a framework for social licence in financial markets is considerable, and it is a privilege to write the Foreword to this important book.

Almost seven years ago, when I returned to the UK, the process of repairing the balance sheets of the banks was well-advanced. However, the process of repairing the balance sheet of society still had a long way to go.

It was clear that social capital—the links, shared values and beliefs that encourage responsibility not just for self but for others—in finance had been badly depleted by the crisis. Many in the City were defensive and demoralised. Many in the country were angry and aghast. The breakdown in that trust stemmed from a fracture in the relationship between finance and society, the loss of *social licence*, a lack of purpose.

When I added my voice to calls for a more inclusive capitalism, I had hoped to open up a discussion on the importance of social licence for the financial sector and how to rebuild social capital so that individual virtue and collective prosperity could flourish.

So what values and beliefs are needed to refocus finance on its core purpose and reconnect with the communities and customers it serves? To succeed, *dynamism* is essential. To align incentives across generations, a *long-term perspective* is required. For markets to sustain their legitimacy, they need to be not only effective but also *fair*. Nowhere is that need more acute than in financial markets; finance has to be *trusted*. And to value others demands *engaged citizens* who recognise their obligations to each other. In short, there needs to be a sense of society.

These beliefs and values are not necessarily fixed; they need to be nurtured. Unchecked market fundamentalism can devour the social capital essential for the long-term dynamism of capitalism itself. To counteract this tendency, individuals and their firms must have a sense of their responsibility for the broader system.

All ideologies are prone to extremes. Capitalism loses its sense of moderation when the belief in the power of the market enters the realm of faith. In the decades prior to the crisis, such radicalism came to dominate economic ideas and became a pattern of social behaviour.

Market fundamentalism—in the form of light-touch regulation, the belief that bubbles cannot be identified and that markets always clear—contributed directly to the financial crisis and the associated erosion of social capital.

Ensuing events have further strained trust in the financial system. Many supposedly rugged markets were revealed to be cosseted:

- major banks were too-big-to-fail: operating in a privileged heads-I-win-tails-you-lose bubble;
- there was widespread rigging of benchmarks for personal gain; and
- equity markets demonstrated a perverse sense of fairness, blatantly favouring the technologically empowered over the retail investor.

We simply cannot take the capitalist system, which produces such plenty and so many solutions, for granted. Prosperity requires not just investment in economic capital, but investment in social capital. It is necessary to rebuild social capital to make markets work. We can help to create an environment in which financial market participants are encouraged to think of their roles as part of a broader system. By building a sense of responsibility for the system, individuals will act in ways that reinforce the bonds of social capital and inclusive capitalism.

In doing so, we need to recognise the tension between pure free market capitalism, which reinforces the primacy of the individual at the expense of the system, and social capital which requires from individuals a broader sense of responsibility for the system. A sense of self must be accompanied by a sense of the systemic.

In this book David considers how to do this. He starts by posing a crucial question: are financial markets solely about making money? David's response is a resounding no. He explores how firms must use just means to achieve just ends. David emphasises that the importance of self-interest and financial return does not contradict the concept of human dignity, which is realised through positive reciprocity.

David sets out a vision for how to build social capital, through strengthening *positive reciprocity* between the financial world and society, by re-establishing a relationship where the financial world and society have mutual regard of each other's needs and can justifiably trust each other. In order to achieve that, David has outlined a formalised framework for thinking about social capital, starting from first principles of what drives human behaviour. He also offers an extended set of solutions, particularly nested within regulation and policy.

Financial reform is already making progress. Globally systemic banks are simplifying and downsizing. Some are de-emphasising high-profile but risky businesses that benefited employees more than shareholders and society. Authorities are working feverishly to end too-big-to-fail. The structure of compensation is being reformed so that horizons are longer and rewards better match risk. Regulation is hard-wiring the responsibilities of senior management. And new codes are seeking to re-establish finance as a true profession, with broader societal obligations. A welcome addition to these initiatives would be changes to the hard and soft infrastructure of financial markets to make them dynamic and fair.

All of us, the firms in the financial sector, their regulators and their advisers are responsible for building and maintaining the social capital that markets need to thrive. This book will prove an invaluable read to financial actors, academics and politicians and to anyone else seeking to understand how to focus finance for good. Through this book, David gives us all a call to action, and we must answer it and give it the attention it deserves.

December 2019   Mark Carney
London, UK   Governor of the Bank of England

Acknowledgements

I would like to thank Jeremy Anderson, Bill Blair, Paul Bowden, Ed Brooks, James Featherby, Nicholas Granger, Brian Griffiths, Mari Jones, Mark Kalderon, Adrian Pabst, Harry Readhead, Peter Rouch, Costanza Russo, Nick Segal, Peter Selby, Lodewijk van Setten and Annabel Sykes for their help and comments in the course of writing this book. It is written in a personal capacity. However, I am very grateful to colleagues at Freshfields and my clients for discussions and insights over many years on aspects of what follows. Tula Weis and Lucy Kidwell at Palgrave Macmillan have been a fantastic editorial team, sensitively applying the tiller at the right moments, being accommodating with timetable extensions and keeping me to my word limits.

I could not have predicted before I started quite what impact writing a book has on those who are closest. My wife, Abigail, has been through it all with me, from long absences while I was incarcerated in my study to mealtime discussions about whatever I happened to be mulling. Her patience, lively observations, humour and steadfast support have been enormously appreciated. One cause of timetable extension was the riotously wonderful arrival of our baby boy, Daniel, in the middle of 2019. He has been a source of much sleeplessness, but also delight and inspiration as I wrote the final chapters. I hope that the contents will help influence for the better world he and his generation will one day come to inherit.

Responsibility for what follows is mine alone.

13 December 2019
London, UK

Contents

Start Here: The Fast Track   xix

1   The Great Re-evaluation: Reaching for an End   1
   Fast Track   1
   1.1   The Purpose of This Book—the Social Licence for Financial
       Markets   7
      1.1.1   Risk Warning   10
      1.1.2   Definitions: Which Financial Markets?   11
   1.2   Financial Market Narratives and the Great Re-evaluation   13
      1.2.1   Economic Man Revisited   15
      1.2.2   Shareholder Value Revisited   17
      1.2.3   The 'Invisible Hand' Revisited   19
      1.2.4   Alternative Frameworks in Practice   20
   1.3   Conclusion   25

Part I   In the Beginning, an End   35
   Fast Track   35

2   People, Firms, Markets, Behaviour   37
   Fast Track   37
   2.1   Desire and Desired Ends   41
      2.1.1   Desire   41
      2.1.2   Emotions   43

2.2	Beliefs About the World—Meaning	44
	2.2.1 Meaning in Financial Markets	46
	2.2.2 The Meaning of Money	46
	2.2.3 The Meaning of Language	47
2.3	Habit and Reason	49
	2.3.1 Models, Schemas and Narratives	49
2.4	People in Markets—the Group Dimension	51
	2.4.1 Individuals Conforming with Group Standards—'Norms'	52
	2.4.2 Authority, Power and Obedience	56
	2.4.3 The Impact of Legal Structures on Individual Behaviour	56
2.5	Markets and Firms 'Behaving'—the Continuing Role of Individuals	57
	2.5.1 Markets and Firms as Legal Structures	58
	2.5.2 Markets and Firms—the Organic Perspective	59
2.6	A Note on Technology	60
2.7	Conclusion	61
3	**The Ends of Desire in Financial Markets**	**69**
	Fast Track	69
3.1	Markets, Red in Tooth and Claw?	74
	3.1.1 Money as an End	74
	3.1.2 One Step Beyond: Others	75
	3.1.3 Other-Regarding Behaviour: Bad for Financial Markets?	81
3.2	The Ends of Desire	82
	3.2.1 Introducing the 'Altruistic Gene'	84
	3.2.2 Self-Interest	86
	3.2.3 Kind Regards: Altruism	88
	3.2.4 The Desire for Dignity and the Role of Mutuality	91
	3.2.5 Financial Desire and Financial Self-Interest	94
3.3	Reciprocity, Positive Reciprocity and Broad-Based Mutuality	96
3.4	Conclusion	98

Part II   The Social Licence and Justice   111
　　　　　Fast Track   111

4   The Social Licence for Financial Markets   113
　　Fast Track   113
　4.1   Introducing the Social Licence   115
　4.2   Why Talk of a Social Licence for Financial Markets Makes
　　　　Sense   118
　4.3   'Mere' Metaphor?   123
　4.4   Who Gives the Licence?   124
　4.5   To Whom Is the Licence Given?   127
　4.6   What Are the Terms of the Licence?   128
　　　　4.6.1   Authoritative Sources for the Terms of a Social
　　　　　　　　Licence   129
　　　　4.6.2   The Social Licence for Financial Markets—
　　　　　　　　Aspirations and Desired Ends   133
　4.7   How Do We Know if a Social Licence Has Been Given?   139
　4.8   What Does It Mean?   141
　　　　4.8.1   Markets and Society   142
　　　　4.8.2   Conflict and Consensus   143
　　　　4.8.3   Is the Social Licence for Financial Markets a Form
　　　　　　　　of Social Contract?   144
　　　　4.8.4   Is Social Licence the Same as 'Legitimacy'?   146
　4.9   Conclusion   146

5   Realising Justice: the Role of Written Standards   163
　　Fast Track   163
　5.1   Norms, Behavioural Norms, Written Standards, the Social
　　　　Licence and Justice   168
　5.2   Types of Written Standard and Their Relationship with a
　　　　Social Licence   169
　　　　5.2.1   The Originators of Written Standards   170
　　　　5.2.2   The Subjects of Written Standards   176
　　　　5.2.3   Written Structural and Behavioural Standards   176
　　　　5.2.4   Written Behavioural Standards and the Role of
　　　　　　　　Aspiration   179
　5.3   Conclusion   190
　　Appendix   191
　　　　The Written Standards Map   191

Part III In the End, a Beginning   221
      Fast Track   221

6 Behaviour—Change in Practice   223
  Fast Track   223
  6.1 The Power of Narratives—Minds and Hearts   227
  6.2 The Resonance of the Social Licence   229
  6.3 Focusing Motivation   230
      6.3.1 Direct Appeal to Other-Regarding Desires—Salience   231
      6.3.2 Making Social Space   233
      6.3.3 Empathy, Trust and Shared Identity   234
  6.4 Framing   235
      6.4.1 Wall Street, Community or Social Licence?   236
      6.4.2 Financial and Economic Priming   237
      6.4.3 Crowding Out/Crowding In   238
  6.5 Formation—Character and Culture   240
      6.5.1 How Are Financial and Economic Narratives
            Formative?   241
      6.5.2 Habitus: How Greater Recognition of a Social
            Licence Can Influence Formation   244
  6.6 Written Standards   246
      6.6.1 The Social Licence and the Substance of Written
            Standards   247
      6.6.2 The Social Licence and Following and Complying
            with Written Standards   250
  6.7 Conclusion—'Social Control' and Individual Choice   255

7 Policy Implications   273
  Fast Track   273
  7.1 The Salience of the Social Licence   279
      7.1.1 Publicly Connecting Policy and Regulation with the
            Social Licence   279
      7.1.2 Cross-Sector Work to Test and Articulate the Terms
            of the Social Licence   280
      7.1.3 Financial Firm Purpose and the Social Licence   282
      7.1.4 Financial Firm Reporting   285
      7.1.5 Professional Advice   287

7.2 Consistent Alignment of Policy, Law and Regulation with
     the Social Licence   288
     7.2.1 Regulatory Purpose   289
     7.2.2 Policy Decisions and Cost-Benefit Analysis   290
     7.2.3 Legal Assumptions Concerning the Aspirations of
            Investors/Shareholders   292
     7.2.4 Finance and Investment Versus Speculation   293
     7.2.5 Supplementing Individual Accountability and
            Remuneration—Culture and Character Formation   299
     7.2.6 Enforcement and Restorative Justice   300
7.3 Conclusion—Incommensurate Values and Measurement   303

8 Conclusion—Not an End, but a Beginning   313

Postscript: The Social Licence in a Time of Pandemic   315

Bibliography   329

Index   357

Start Here: The Fast Track

This book is about getting financial markets to work well and sustainably. It is about the social solidarity needed for them to do that. It is about how what Mark Carney, then Bank of England governor, has called the *social licence for financial markets* can help financial markets to create that social solidarity, rather than destroy it. It is about the practical impact of common narratives and the mental models individuals and groups use as they make their way through life. It is about the account of financial life advanced by recognition of a social licence for financial markets—one very different from the usual account of markets as places of unrestrained self-interest. It is about individual, institutional and systemic behaviour change, not imposed by regulatory fiat but emerging out of the very substance of market relationships.

While I was writing this book, Keith Baker died. Keith was a major influence on my early life. He was my history teacher. He embodied so much that is good: he was committed to his students, interested in their ideas and concerns, patient and generous with his time, unfailingly enthusiastic and supportive, and wise. He also had a great sense of fun. He arrived at my school in the 1960s, long before I turned up, and stayed until he retired from teaching. He was fully engaged with the cultural and intellectual mainstream, but he had found a place where he was content to serve, and serve he did. He was not alone in that.

Keith's world was dominated by giving. He inhabited, if you like, an economy of gift. His was a culture in which what you did was not because of an expectation of return, and it showed in his relationships and their outcomes. I don't mean exam grades. I mean what others were inspired to do.

A different relationship: vox pops and surveys consistently highlight a deep fracture between the financial sector and the societies in which it exists. This is at the very time when we need the relationship to work: financial firms are being called upon to help humanity address some of its most pressing challenges, from climate change to environmental and social sustainability more broadly. Capitalism in one form or another is the only realistic option for meeting a host of human needs. Yet inflamed feelings towards the financial sector risk prejudicing its ability to help meet those needs and feed discontent towards social and political institutions. It is time for change throughout the financial ecosystem. But change must help us to realise desired ends, not undermine those ends or, indeed, our efforts to realise them.

Whether that happens depends on the behaviour of us all. Change has to result in greater *positive reciprocity* within the multitude of financial market relationships: not just positive reciprocity in the more conventional sense of a relationship that benefits the parties concerned, but reciprocity that is also positively orientated towards those affected by their activities more widely. In other words, market relationships need to function in a way that supports the social solidarity on which market activity ultimately relies.

There is also a need for *greater urgency*. Addressing the fracture and helping humanity deal with the many challenges it faces are linked. But the response so far has not found its mark. The period after 2008 witnessed one of the most intense financial sector regulatory reform processes ever. Those changes have made a big difference: look no further than the change in bank balance sheets to see that. However, the usual toolkit of laws and regulations has been powerless to heal the fracture between the financial sector and surrounding society. Work on bank culture and sustainable finance promises much, but has yet to provide the framework and the language needed to chart a new course. Meanwhile, too much funding continues to flow to economic activities that are not sustainable, and not enough to what is. The prospect of more structural upheaval in the finance sector, driven by advances in technology, makes the need for good coordinates even greater, and even more urgent.

Markets are not school rooms—not, at least, of the kind in which Keith worked. But what if we could somehow infuse the economy of exchange with more of the energy and positive reciprocity of Keith's 'economy of gift', not by imposing lots of new rules, but by recognising the existence of a different story about what's going on in financial life? Is there another story? It might seem fanciful: as one senior banker said to me recently, 'these guys are really only interested in money'. But perhaps one is not as far away as we might think.

If you want to find ways of addressing the fracture, and of making financial markets more effective at supporting human wellbeing—the realisation of people's intrinsic value in practice—this book is for you. It is relevant to individual firms; those who run, advise and regulate them; politicians and those who make policy; and those with an academic interest. It seeks to identify a practical response and encourage multi-disciplinary work, drawing in market participants especially. I come to this as an international regulatory lawyer who has spent two and a half decades giving advice in most sectors of the financial markets. That period has spanned the growing financialisation of the global economy, the most recent crisis and subsequent reform and social fall-out. I have worked with many major international financial institutions and with people in all of the categories above. Others will bring their own expertise and experience.

The book covers some areas in depth and not everyone will have the chance to read it end to end. So, there is a **Fast Track**. Each chapter starts with a short summary split into two sections: **Speed Read** (the key messages of that chapter) and **So What?** (its main implications). The Fast Track is easy to follow. You will find the relevant sections listed in the Contents pages and they appear in highlighted text boxes throughout the book. Use them to decide where you want to dig into the underlying content.

But to get things started, here's the nub of it.

§   Particularly in the West, where the breakdown of trust is most serious, the relationship between finance and the societies in which it operates has come to be defined by narratives of fracture promoted by public figures from Donald Trump in the US to Jeremy Corbyn in the UK. They cast financial sector greed as a major source of social ills, and their claims are not groundless. These narratives feed off the public's experience of the financial crisis and subsequent austerity. They also build on another set of greed stories which cast financial life as the relentless pursuit of self-interest: stories of *The Wolf of Wall Street* genre. That message is echoed in key economic models that have long been used to understand and influence financial and economic life, such as 'economic man', shareholder value and the 'invisible hand' of the market.

§   But there is a big problem. These narratives only capture half the truth. They leave out the significant extent to which a different value, that of human dignity, is also at work in financial life—and if that sounds odd to you, it's evidence of how powerful the narratives are. The reality gap is serious because narratives are more than 'just' stories. They influence perceptions and shape behaviours. Perhaps they lie behind some of the behaviours that have lent the narratives of social fracture their credibility.

§   So, is there a different story to be told? Back to the social licence for financial markets: what is it? I argue that the licence is not simply a metaphor or theory, but draws attention to what can be seen operating in practice. Recognising that it's there is a little like noticing the musical themes in an opera such as Puccini's *Tosca*; once you spot them, you realise that they keep recurring and structure the whole piece. You can't un-hear them after that; you never listen to *Tosca* in the same way again. Are financial markets really only about money? The social licence for financial markets gives a radically different account.

›   The idea of a licence makes sense, among other things, because of the extent to which markets depend on their social context. It is partly expressed in law and regulation and other statements of social expectation for financial markets. However, recognition of a social licence also reaches beyond these things by drawing attention to aspirations about the purpose of financial activity—its *ends*—that are present in markets and beyond them, even if those ends are not always realised in practice. It is, then, both an observation about the relationship between finance and society *and* an expression of aspiration about how it could be at its best.

›   From that aspirational perspective, the licence can be understood as a freedom given to financial market participants by those in the societies in which they carry on business: a *freedom to pursue just ends by just means in financial markets*, where justice is a situation in which the *human dignity* of market participants and those affected by their activities can be experienced most fully. This end is dependent on *broad-based mutuality*: a generalised mutual regard in social relations. It connects with the goal of social and environmental sustainability. Pursuing it can provide a basis for justified trust in the finance sector, as well as social solidarity.

›   Indeed, the licence can be treated as granted to the extent that those in society have given their justified trust to financial operators, trust based on solid reasons for believing that those in financial markets will carry on business in a way that is consistent with the licence.

›   So, recognition of a social licence reaches past stale narratives of finance as a conflictual pursuit of financial self-interest; these narratives do not adequately represent reality and have strait-jacketed aspiration in financial life. But recognition of a social licence is not about doing away with financial exchange; exchange is integral to realising human dignity. Nor does it involve denying self-interest or the importance of financial return. Rather, it embraces all these things in a reciprocal balance with desire for the wellbeing of others.

›   In going beyond the 'usual toolkit' of laws and regulations, the social licence nonetheless focuses on an end similar to theirs: justice. The context it provides for law and regulation is important given their prominent role in financial markets.

§   Why should the recognition of this licence make a difference? Consider the earpieces that musicians wear when they perform at rock concerts.

Without them, all the musicians can hear is a huge amount of noise, and they end up playing against each other. With the earpieces in, they can hear the overall sound the band is making—much as the audience will hear it—and that helps them to *feel their way* to an outstanding group performance. Similarly, paying attention to the social licence has the potential to help reorientate the individual relationships that comprise the wider relationship between finance and society, by strengthening positive reciprocity.

§   How exactly? In three broad ways. Firstly, by *focusing desire* on relational over financial goods, so 're-purposing' market activity and the usual toolkit of law and regulation applied to it, thereby influencing what end goals get pursued and how. Secondly, by *framing* market decisions in relational as well as financial terms, so influencing the *meaning* they have for those involved as they *reason* about how to achieve their desired ends, again impacting behavioural outcomes. (Put crudely, so that the Wall Street Game becomes a bit more like the Community Game.) And, thirdly, influencing the development of individual and group *habits* (or 'norms' of behaviour and thinking) over time in ways that reflect the valued ends and meanings highlighted by recognition of a social licence: the *formation of character and culture*. A surprising amount of life is driven by habit—'making the tea' mode—so this is crucial. Formation of habit is going on all the time in financial markets and beyond, largely unrecognised. The key question is, to what end? There is a need to make the unseen seen and to become more intentional about it.

§   What about policy measures? In a sense, the significance of the social licence lies beyond policy, in its potential to affect the very substance of financial market relationships. However, policy steps can help, and Chap. 7 provides some examples, not as a comprehensive reform programme, but as a starting point for thinking about what policy difference it makes. They fall into two broad categories.

›   Firstly, steps to make the recognition of a social licence (the aspirations and meanings it embeds) more *salient* in financial relationships. These include, for example, regular and consistent reference to it in policy and regulatory communications (including in work on finance culture and sustainable finance), cross-sector work to test and articulate its terms and encouragement of financial institutions to articulate and report on how they seek to align their activities with its end goal.

›   Secondly, steps to ensure that law and regulation and other policy measures are consistently aligned with the reality thrown into relief by recognition of a social licence. Examples include making the end goal of the licence more explicit in statements that set the objectives of regulators;

reviewing the criteria used in addition to cost-benefit analysis in assessing the desirability of regulatory intervention; revisiting the duties of directors and institutional investors to include an assumption that the underlying owners of financial instruments care about environmental and social impact as well as financial return; strengthening the distinction between narrowly speculative financial activity and investment and finance directed at broader ends; and making restorative justice (such as engagement in community financial service programmes) available to firms facing enforcement, as an alternative to sanctions.

There has been much hand-wringing in recent years over the loss of trust in commercial organisations and within society more widely. This has been accompanied by growing discussion about the need for companies to have a sense of purpose beyond financial return. Indeed they do need a sense of purpose: purpose is an aspired end in corporate form which gives meaning because of the way people seek to organise reality around it. However, more is needed to address current challenges. It cannot be *any* purpose, and these challenges are *systemic*, extending to all involved in financial markets.

The social licence for financial markets speaks to the *financial ecosystem* as a whole and points towards justice as an *ultimate end*. It incorporates but transcends financial return. Greater recognition of the licence is not a panacea, but it can provide a set coordinates for charting a course towards that end, a language to use in pursuing it and ways of realising it, including a different approach to law and regulation. More importantly still, it advances a narrative with the potential to reach beyond rational self-interested calculation, into the substance of relationships as they are lived, felt and understood in practice.

Recognising that is a *beginning* in the project of healing the current fracture. And, as it happens, the very word 'finance' already directs us that way. It is derived from the French words 'fin', 'finer' and 'finance'. These carry the sense of an end, but not simply a monetary end. It is an end that involves the use of money in reinstating or maintaining a relationship, such as the settling of a dispute or debt or the payment of a fine or ransom. Finance, then, speaks of an activity that reaches beyond monetary ends towards relational goods.

So, this is a call to action. Shortly after the onset of the financial crisis, Alan Greenspan accepted that 'I made a mistake in presuming that the self-interests of organisations … were such that they were best capable of protecting their own shareholders and their equity in the firms.'[1] He realised that he needed to re-evaluate, and a process of re-evaluation—ultimately, of what ends we value or desire—has been underway ever since. The recognition that financial markets operate subject to a social licence is an end of that beginning. Whether you run or work in a financial firm, advise or regulate one, are a politician or make policy, or have an academic interest, it is now time to pursue its end goal.

London, UK   David Rouch

Note

1. Alan Beattie and James Politi, '"I made a mistake," admits Greenspan', *Financial Times*, London, 23 October 2008.

1

The Great Re-evaluation: Reaching for an End

Fast Track

Speed Read

More than a decade after the global financial crisis, the relationship between finance and wider society remains fractured, and social solidarity (the social cohesiveness on which human wellbeing depends) is under strain. This is just when financial firms are being called upon to help humanity address some of its most pressing challenges, from climate change to environmental and social sustainability more broadly. The break is serious. It inflames wider mistrust of business activity and political regimes. Capitalism in one form or another is the only realistic option for organising and sustaining much of the economic activity on which society relies, but it rests to a large degree on social solidarity. The need to heal the relationship is therefore urgent.

Relationship strain has been framed by narratives of fracture, promoted by public figures from Donald Trump in the US to Jeremy Corbyn in the UK. These narratives cast financial sector greed as a major source of social ills and feed off the experience of the financial crisis and subsequent austerity. They also build on another set of stories about greed in financial life: stories of *The Wolf of Wall Street* genre. That basic message of relentless financial self-interest is echoed in key economic models used to understand and influence economic life: the idea of 'economic man' as a rational maximiser of his own (usually financial and material) utility; shareholder value (the idea that the purpose of a company is to maximise financial return to its shareholders); and the idea that an 'invisible hand' guides self-interest in markets to the most beneficial outcome for all. Little wonder that people have concluded that finance is about the conflictual pursuit of money, and little wonder if sometimes it is.

(continued)

© The Author(s) 2020
D. Rouch, *The Social Licence for Financial Markets*,
https://doi.org/10.1007/978-3-030-40220-4_1

(continued)

But there is a big problem. At best, models of this sort only capture half the truth. They leave out the significant extent to which regard for the interests of others is at work in financial life. If that sounds odd, it is evidence of how powerful the narratives are. The reality gap is highly problematic because models and narratives like these are more than 'just' stories. They impact perceptions and shape behaviours. Perhaps they lie behind some of the behaviours that have lent the narratives of social fracture their credibility.

A re-evaluation is under way, and gathered pace following the 2008 crisis. Among other things, it has involved attempts to adjust or supplement these key economic models to reflect the other-regarding aspirations people really bring to markets. Yet, we still lack a framework within which to navigate the systemic challenges before us. Current work on culture *in* financial firms and sustainable finance is promising, but seems to struggle to break free of the assumptions behind the old economic models. Too much funding continues to flow to economic activities that are not sustainable, and not enough to what is. Meanwhile, social fracture remains in spite of one of the most intensive regulatory reform processes the financial world has ever seen. Reform has achieved much, but the usual regulatory tools have not yet healed the fracture.

This is the context for growing attention to what Mark Carney, then Bank of England Governor, has suggested could be lost: the 'social licence for financial markets'. Can the observation that financial markets operate under a social licence help in tackling the multitude of challenges? This book answers, 'yes'. It also explains why. It takes a narrative to beat a narrative. The recognition of a social licence advances a radically different account of financial markets: one much closer to reality; one with the potential to engage with a deeply held human desire for **justice** and to displace the damaging delusion that finance is about little more than a conflictual pursuit of money.

Social solidarity, on which the wellbeing of financial markets and everyone else depends, is based in large part on a **broad-based mutuality**—a generalised mutual regard in social relations—among those in the relevant society. Financial market relationships can contribute to this where they display **positive reciprocity** and damage it where they do not. The expression 'positive reciprocity' is used here not in the conventional sense to describe a situation where the immediate parties to a relationship are mutually regarding of the needs of each other, but also where reciprocity is orientated in a way that is positive for those affected by their relationship more widely. It involves a balancing of needs that can be thought of, like the social licence, in terms of justice. Those who cooperate to manipulate a market may display reciprocity, but the wider impact is not positive. That is not positive reciprocity.

There is already positive reciprocity in financial markets. However, strengthening it in a way that can help to address current challenges goes well beyond 'business as usual'. It requires fundamental behaviour change. Financial market behaviour takes place within and emerges from chains of relationships. It is never 'neutral'. At some level, each act either advances or undermines aspired ends. If behaviour is to change, it needs to happen in the way these multiple relationships are lived, felt and understood in practice. There is a need to transform their very character and that involves influencing the way the parties to them relate. You cannot micro-regulate for that.

(continued)

(continued)

What is the role of the recognition of a social licence for financial markets in that? This book gives an answer in three stages.

- Part I does important groundwork. Since the objective is behaviour change, it looks at how individuals, firms and markets come to behave as they do and what motivates them.
- Part II unpacks the substance of the social licence for financial markets, also looking at its relationship with law and regulation, some of the main tools for influencing financial market behaviour.
- Part III explores the potential for greater recognition of the social licence to make a difference in practice by influencing the substance of market relationships. It also gives examples of how policy can help.

The principal focus is financial markets. However, the need to look at their social context is never far behind. To put the point at its sharpest, when financial markets go wrong, is that no more than at least some of those in the wider societies in which they operate deserve—for example, because of the social expectations placed on markets? It is equally important not to lose sight of the enormous contribution that financial markets already make to social wellbeing, from savings to payments, and from insurance to investment.

So What?

Responding to current challenges requires a more realistic way of seeing and talking about finance because that, in turn, impacts how finance is *done*: one more closely aligned with reality and the aspirations that people have for financial activity; one that recognises the presence of positive reciprocity in financial life and can help to strengthen it; one that can provide a framework within which to approach the task of addressing current challenges, and a language to use in doing so; one that can inject a greater sense of urgency; and one that reaches beyond rational calculation, to how relationships are experienced *in practice*.

The observation that financial markets operate in some sense subject to a social licence has the potential to provide a basis for that, as this book goes on to explain.

'Few trends could so thoroughly undermine the very foundations of our free society as the acceptance by corporate officials of a social responsibility other than to make as much money for their stockholders as possible.'[1]

The foundations of our free society look less than stable at present, but it is not clear that the reason was an outbreak of social responsibility. Milton Friedman, who originally issued this stark warning, has nonetheless been making a celebrity come-back. His first appearance was as the high priest of what is often called 'neoliberal economics'. His second is as its chief whipping boy. Writing the preface to the 2002 republication of his book, *Capitalism and Freedom*, Friedman could celebrate the advance of the free market and the decline of centrally planned economies. The first edition, written in 1962 in a world polarised by the Cold War, called for economic freedom as a basis for political liberty. By 2002 the Soviet Union was long gone; the world had changed.

By then, Western capitalism had also developed a new feature, together with globalisation, now commonly associated with neoliberalism. It had become highly financialised. The trend continued thereafter. By 2007, after 40 years of rapid growth, the financial sector had a greater role in the UK, the US and the other advanced economies, measured as a share of GDP, than ever before.[2] Friedman did not live long enough to see that process grind to its calamitous halt with the onset of the global financial crisis in 2008. However, his friend Alan Greenspan did.

Greenspan had retired as the chairman of the United States Federal Reserve shortly before the crisis started and, for him, it prompted an immediate re-evaluation of what had shortly before been economic orthodoxy. As he said in October 2008 before a Congressional hearing, 'I made a mistake in presuming that the self-interests of organisations … were such that they were best capable of protecting their own shareholders and their equity in the firms'.[3] He was not alone. Much of the academic and practising economic establishment also discovered it had been mistaken,[4] together with the multitude of those who had come to rely on their view of the world: policymakers, politicians, think tanks, business people, financiers, journalists, consultants, lawyers, accountants. In the words of one senior British civil servant, 'This was a monumental, collective, intellectual error.'[5] A particular set of assumptions had become deeply embedded in the way the world was understood and lived in. It took an enormous shock to begin to realise that things might be different. An assumed reality was now in question.

The questions have not stopped. Indeed, the process of reassessment continues to gather momentum, breadth and emotional intensity. At a popular level, it is seen in a steady flow of surveys, vox pops and anecdotes suggesting that there is a severe fracture between the financial world and the societies in which it operates, especially in the West.[6] The UK's Parliamentary Commission on Banking Standards noted the strain in 2013 when it spoke of, 'a profound loss of trust born of profound lapses in banking standards',[7] as did the Bank of England in preparatory work for its Open Forum in November 2015.[8] Likewise, the Australian Royal Commission enquiry into financial sector misconduct, reporting in 2019, noted that conduct has, 'Very often … fallen short of the kind of behaviour the community … expects …'[9] Social trust has been damaged. Bankers were never the most popular members of society, but this has been described as possibly one of the greatest challenges the financial sector now faces.[10]

The anger and loss of trust also feeds a wider systemic discontent.[11]

Perhaps the most significant political development of our time is the populist rage of disgruntled people who are no longer confident that the country in which they live is in tune with their values, and who think they have experienced less than their share of overall prosperity.[12]

So much so that the 2017 UK Conservative Party Manifesto proclaimed that, 'We do not believe in untrammelled free markets. We reject the cult of selfish individualism. We abhor social division, injustice, unfairness and inequality.'[13] The symbolism could not have been more powerful. The party of UK Prime Minister Margaret Thatcher (with US President Ronald Regan, at the vanguard of the introduction of Friedman's brand of economics during the 1980s) had joined in. The Great Recession has turned into a Great Re-evaluation of the role and purpose of financial and economic activity in the societies it affects.[14]

Senior business people increasingly recognise the magnitude of what is happening.[15] Yet, day-to-day, it can still sometimes seem as if the business and financial worlds are largely impervious to it. Of course, business has gone through significant changes, not least in regulation. The increasingly populist outcome of elections and referenda in recent years has also made its mark, from Donald Trump to Brexit, as has growing concern about environmental sustainability. Yet much of life appears to go on regardless. The immediate can be absorbing, and social spaces such as the workplace bring their own sets of expectations. Even now, businesses can appear to proceed as if the turmoil is simply another risk to be managed, rather than addressing more fundamental questions about whether they might be partly responsible and need to change.[16]

But get people out of their immediate context, and a different picture emerges. On the one hand, there is a sense of bewilderment, particularly among senior management. In the words of one CEO, 'I'm not sure I understand what problem we're trying to solve and who we are solving it for. Are we solving it so that we all, as companies, survive? Are we solving it for our shareholders? Are we solving something for society?'[17] What is the desired end? On the other, there can also be an unmistakable sense of aspiration for business and finance to do more to address current challenges. Sometimes, that finds a more public voice: authentic social purpose, '… comes down to values … I don't mean values like honesty and integrity: if you haven't got them, you shouldn't be in business. It comes down to what you want to stand for as a business.'[18] It comes down to the ends you value.

And here lies the irony. At the very point at which the relationship between the financial world and the societies in which it operates is perhaps more fractured than ever before, humanity needs the relationship to work as never before. Financial institutions are being called upon to help deliver on some of humanity's most pressing challenges, from addressing climate change, to wider issues of social, environmental and economic sustainability, including supporting individual financial self-sufficiency as state welfare systems struggle. The finance sector is a crucial part of the answer. Indeed, there are significant business opportunities since, 'Every single social and global issue of our day is a business opportunity in disguise.'[19] For example, the funding to meet the word's sustainable development needs has been estimated to be US$5–7 trillion annually, and there are hopes that the private sector will be able to cover a substantial portion of that.[20]

There has certainly been progress on a number of fronts. For example, sustainable finance activity has grown very noticeably in the last couple of years,[21] and there has been considerable work in many firms to improve their culture. However, the growth in sustainable finance is falling far short of what is needed.[22] Meanwhile, the President of the New York Federal Reserve commented in June 2019 on the lack of progress on finance culture.[23] Observations from the UK's Financial Conduct Authority suggest something more mixed.[24] However, in the view of the head of the UK's Banking Standards Board, 'I think the honest thing to say would be that some progress was being made, but ... we would ... be foolish to go any further than that.'[25]

On top of this, the apparent deficit in social trust shows few signs of reducing: trust, which is so critical to adequately addressing these challenges, as well as underpinning a host of other goods;[26] trust, on which the financial development that supports economic growth depends, for example, in willingness to take investment risks.[27]

Commercial and financial exchange is, and remains, the only serious way of providing what is needed, at scale, to sustain life materially. It is also a source of wider relational and social benefits including, potentially, social trust. However, it can also destroy that trust and damage social solidarity—the social cohesiveness on which human wellbeing depends. It is therefore essential that it works, and works well. The financial sector has long addressed human needs, much of it continuing to do so even in the depths of the financial crisis. In the words of the UK's Fair and Effective Markets Review, set up in 2013 to assess market abuse in the fixed income, currency and commodities ('FICC') markets, these markets, 'lie at the heart of every aspect of the global economy'.[28] From the FICC markets to markets for products for retail customers, financial markets are a vast source of social wellbeing, ranging from financing investment and growth and helping companies manage their risks, through to enabling people to save for future needs, protect themselves from uncertainty, spread their spending or simply make payments. It is important to be clear about that, and not detract from the good faith efforts of many within the sector, day-in, day-out, to serve clients and customers. But the current challenges are nonetheless serious. There are significant tensions, and a financially charged global economy continues to channel too much funding towards economic activity that is not sustainable and insufficient to what is. The current response is falling short.

And there is a further complexity. All of this comes at a time when the financial world is in flux. Some global financial groups are now so large as to rival many of the states in which they operate, so that it has become plausible to see the international economy as a series of interlocking bank balance sheets as much as inter-related national economies.[29] At the same time, new forms of technology, including artificial intelligence, look set to transform the way finance operates. Old certainties have begun to dissolve, whether the essence of money in the face of cryptocurrencies, the boundary between financial institutions and technology giants or the question of what activity falls within and beyond the financial services regulatory perimeter and who gets to decide (witness discussion around Facebook's announcement of its new Libra currency).[30] Coordinates are needed to chart a course through, as are ways of positively influencing financial activity outside the regulated space.[31]

1.1   The Purpose of This Book—the Social Licence for Financial Markets

And so to the purpose of this book. Its focus is on how we respond and, in particular, the role of what Mark Carney, then Governor of the Bank of England, has called the 'social licence for financial markets'. Whether you are a trader, director, lawyer, campaigner, regulator, academic, politician or policymaker, I hope you will approach finance differently as a result of what you read here. I have worked with people in all of these groups during my legal career. However, the daily pressure of market practice leaves little scope for grappling with how the immediate task might fit into the broader context of challenges and opportunities such as these. That is not too surprising. Markets are ruthlessly practical places and look for results, not words. Yet the discussion I want to take forward here is intended to be deeply practical.

Successfully addressing current challenges and realising opportunities inevitably comes back exactly to that: *practice*—how all of the relevant parties *behave* from here. There is a need for greater urgency in tackling current challenges. There is a need for healing in the relationship between finance and the societies in which it operates. That, in turn depends on greater *positive reciprocity* in the relationships that comprise financial markets; positive reciprocity, not in the conventional sense of a relationship that only benefits the immediate parties to it, but reciprocity that is also positively orientated towards those in the chains of relationships their activities affect; reciprocity that also supports the wider outcome of social solidarity on which markets themselves rely. Market relationships must be a source of broad-based mutuality, as well as drawing on it. All of this boils down to behaviour.

There is a common assumption that the way to change behaviour is to regulate it with rules: laws, regulations, codes. You encounter it a lot as a lawyer. Rules are certainly important, especially in the financial sector, and later chapters come back to them. But they also have limits. Massive rules-based financial sector regulatory reform in recent years has undoubtedly made a difference: look no further than the changing composition of bank balance sheets to see that. Yet evidence of fracture suggests that something more serious is afoot, which the usual tool-kit of rules and regulations is powerless to resolve. The recognition that financial markets operate subject to a social licence does not involve ditching the tool-kit. However, it does mean approaching current challenges and opportunities in a radically different way: one that takes better account of the aspirations people really bring to financial markets; one that can reach into the very substance of the multiple relationships that make up those markets, changing the way they function from the inside out; one that reflects how the narratives or mental models that people apply to financial markets affect the behaviour that results.[32]

Narratives loom large in the current fracture between finance and wider society, and they have clearly influenced popular behaviour. The sense of division is embedded in a series of narratives, including those about the damage that financial institutions have inflicted, and their continuing power:-

> 'Do I consider myself part of the casino capitalist process by which so few have so much and so many have so little by which Wall Street's greed and recklessness wrecked this economy, no, I don't'.[33]

> 'Globalization has made the financial elite, who donate to politicians, very, very wealthy.'[34]

> 'Their greed plunged the world into crisis and we're still paying the price…'[35]

We could call them the *narratives of fracture*, and they are obviously myopic. They ignore the fact that finance does not exist in a vacuum—that, like the classic exam question about whether the Sarajevo bullet caused the First

World War, a much broader range of factors lay behind the 2008 financial crisis including macroeconomic fluctuations, regulatory policy, political expediency and popular culture.

However, narratives have to be credible to stick. These are credible, among other things, because of the experience of the financial crisis and austerity, the perception that key individuals have not been held accountable, and because of the way some in the financial sector have behaved and remunerated themselves since: because of how people are seen to have behaved.[36] But they are also credible because they were prefigured by a further set of narratives presenting financial and economic life as an individualistic pursuit of financial self-interest; narratives that lead to the conclusion that financial crisis and scandal is exactly what you would expect from finance. In their popular form, these could be described as the *Wolf of Wall Street* genre of financial narratives.[37] Yet behind them lies a further set of narratives that are based on similar assumptions in the form of economic models and theories, most notably the idea of 'economic man', shareholder value and the 'invisible hand'.[38] More on those later. They have been advanced as a way of understanding how finance and the economy works, and shaping both. But accounts such as these not only provide a basis for narratives of fracture.[39] If it is right that mental models of how the world works influence behaviour, they may also lie behind some of the behaviour on which the narratives of fracture are based.

Here is the point: addressing current challenges and realising opportunities is not simply about making more legal and regulatory rules. It is about re-writing the script or, more correctly, recognising that there is a more accurate narrative about financial markets, which now needs to be told. Rules have their place, but you cannot ultimately legislate for a sense of urgency. Nor can you force people to have a healthy relationship or to be trustworthy. These have to develop naturally within the very substance of relationships: the way they are lived, felt and understood by the parties to them. The desires and beliefs that are brought to bear on relationships have a key role here: what ends are valued and what the relationships mean to those involved. The narratives within which relationships get contextualised are important in shaping both.[40]

What follows will argue that this is one of the main ways in which greater recognition of a social licence can make a difference: by establishing a more accurate account of what is really going on and expressing an aspiration for what it can be at its best. Its account is quite different from that of prevailing narratives. Of course, we are not used to the idea of financial markets operating under a 'social licence'. It is not our habitual way of seeing things. However, look, and its traces are there, like an archaeological crop pattern in a field of corn. It highlights something that is right in front of us, even though we may not presently see it. Talk of a social licence is not theoretical, but is an observation about reality. It reflects the embeddedness of finance in society and, in contrast with Friedman's words at the start of this chapter, draws attention to aspirations for finance reaching far beyond individual or institutional financial self-interest. It reflects a desire to realise the sort of human value that, ultimately, cannot be measured in financial terms. It does not disregard the immense power of money or of financial self-interest, but embraces both within that broader end.

Greater recognition of a social licence for financial markets is not a panacea. However, it has the potential to reach to the core of market relationships because of the way it addresses the *desired ends* that people pursue through them and the *meaning* that is placed on them. It can also provide a powerful framework within which the relationship between finance and society more broadly can be understood, navigated and strengthened, and a language to use in doing so. Because of that, this book will argue that recognition of a social licence has an important role in helping to meeting the challenges and realise the opportunities outlined above.

The book is in three parts. After sketching out in Part I a framework for understanding how human behaviour works individually and in groups, and what drives it in financial markets in particular, it goes on to look at the social licence in more depth in Part II. Part III then considers the practical implications. However, before doing that, the remainder of this chapter looks more closely at some of the more notable narratives that get applied to financial life: what they say; their current re-evaluation; and how some of the initiatives that have been taken to address current challenges are still influenced by them, in particular, in the areas of sustainable finance and culture in financial institutions. These initiatives are significant, but they have yet to provide the framework and language we need to deal with the challenges identified above. That is perhaps because they have not yet adequately addressed the question of 'why'—to what end?

But before any of that, a risk warning and a definition.

1.1.1   Risk Warning

This book is a view from the market. It trespasses into a number of heavily populated specialist areas. However, things do not get interesting unless you take risks. So, here is the risk warning. Many of the topics covered here, such as justice, are subjects on which industrial quantities of ink have been spilt, breath expended, experiments undertaken and library shelves filled. The question of why humans behave as they do, and whether they could do better, has occupied minds since the beginning of recorded history and probably beyond. This book does not attempt to review that earlier work, or to advance a new theory. Rather, it seeks to identify a few basic coordinates and suggest some linkages between them in order to begin to show how greater recognition of a social licence has the potential to make a significant positive impact. It generally seeks to avoid going beyond positions that command a reasonable level of consensus. However, since views diverge on just about every topic covered, that is not always possible or desirable. If I am stepping out into multiple minefields of learning, market practice and expertise, it is in the hope that doing so can help to open a path which others can extend.

Importantly, I come to this as someone who has spent two and a half decades in practice providing legal and regulatory advice in most sectors of the financial markets. That period has spanned the process of financialisation, mentioned earlier, the most recent crisis and subsequent reform and social fallout. Working out how to realise the full potential of financial markets is necessarily a multi-disciplinary exercise. Economist Jean Tirole has, for example, noted the importance of the human and social sciences nourishing each other in developing ways to help ensure that the economy serves the common good.[41] He mentions anthropology, law, economics, history, philosophy, political science and sociology, and excellent work is being done. But one important group is missing from the list: those actually involved in markets. For some of the reasons already alluded to, engaging market participants in a dialogue of this sort is always going to be challenging, but it is also critical if academic and policy work is to avoid progressing in a parallel universe. As noted, the key challenge here is to affect the very substance of market relationships *in practice*: the way the parties to them relate. With that in mind, what follows is a perspective based on experience in practice. In the interests of advancing a dialogue, it seeks to engage across all of the constituencies just mentioned.

1.1.2 Definitions: Which Financial Markets?

A market is a context in which buyers and sellers come together to transact, normally involving an element of competition which affects market prices. That context can be tightly defined. For example, it might be restricted to a particular physical or virtual place where transactions are governed by established rules, such as the New York Stock Exchange. Other markets are defined by little more than the commodity bought and sold, such as the property market. This book uses the word in both senses, but focusing on *financial* markets.

Financial markets are distinct because of the 'commodity' transacted in. The commodity is financial—it concerns 'finance'. Finance essentially refers to the raising, provision or management of money, including arrangements helping people store and use it when needed (such as payment systems). Another type of financial transaction involves using derivative contracts, among other things, to provide financial protection from the adverse consequences of an uncertain future event, such as the default of a counterparty, or currency movements. Insurance contracts also provide risk protection, but for a much broader range of risks. They might not ordinarily be regarded as 'financial' contracts. However, they involve a monetary claim on the insurer and insurance companies managing their funds are deeply involved in financial market activity, so insurance is included in what follows.

Financial transactions can involve money directly (for example foreign currency exchange or cash loans). Alternatively, they can be in what are often called 'financial instruments' or 'financial assets'. These are legal claims on others, such as a bond or a derivative contract, the value of which is denominated in monetary terms. Particularly when financial markets concern financial assets, the transactions can be seen not just as monetary transactions, but also transfers of risk: the risk that the claim represented by the relevant instrument will turn out to be not as valuable as thought, for example, because of changes in the creditworthiness of the person against whom the claim can be made. While money and monetary claims are central to financial markets, so is managing these risks—the risk that you will not get your money.

So, money is a defining feature of financial markets, and it is important to be clear from the start that it is completely different from the subject matter of other markets. Its pervasiveness in economic and social life makes it more like a language than a commodity. Indeed, we say that 'money talks'. It is fundamental to what it is to be human. Its value resides in claims that people have against each other, whether in its power to secure behaviour on the part of someone else who needs it, or because of its relationship with the productive activities of others; for example, the value of a bond depends upon the financial success of the issuing company, and a mortgage, the earning potential of the borrower. These features make money an incredibly powerful symbol. It is a commodity like no other. This distinguishes financial market activity from all other sorts of commercial activity. People sometimes talk about money as if it is somehow 'neutral'. Far from it.

This book will refer to anyone who transacts in a financial market directly or as an intermediary as a *market participant*. Market participants therefore include private individuals and companies who may need to access financial products and services, but also financial firms and their staff. The immediate focus of what follows is the UK financial markets, but its significance is by no means restricted to the UK or to the financial markets alone.

1.2   Financial Market Narratives and the Great Re-evaluation

It is time now to look more closely at the narratives that get told about financial life. As noted, popular narratives have given voice to a fracture between the financial world and society. They seem to have been prefigured by a further set of common stories about how financial self-interest and greed drive financial life: the *Wolf of Wall Street* genre of narratives. Similarly, some of the most influential economic models used to understand and shape financial and economic life assume that financial and material self-interest is what motivates market participants.

These earlier narratives and models deserve a closer look because, as discussed, they cast light on the fracture. First, they lend credibility to the narratives of fracture. However, secondly, mental models of how the world works, 'how things are', influence behaviour (see Chaps. 2 and 6). These narratives and economic models are likely to have influenced the way people have approached financial life. They may therefore also lie behind some of the behaviour on which the narratives of fracture are based.

What follows concentrates on three economic models in particular: the idea of *economic man* ('*homo economicus*') assumed to be acting rationally to maximise his own utility (usually treated as a matter of financial or material self-interest); the concept of *shareholder value* asserting that the purpose of a company is to maximise financial return for its shareholders; and the *invisible hand*, referring to the belief that markets comprised of participants pursuing their rational self-interest in competition allocate resources efficiently, and so unintentionally realise social goods. Economic man concerns individuals, shareholder value the activities of firms and the invisible hand what happens when they get together in markets—an economic trinity. Economic man and the invisible hand have a theoretical significance for economists that shareholder value does not. Shareholder value is more overtly normative.

Material and financial self-interest are indeed powerful motivations. That is one reason why these models are compelling. Superficially, the models also seem to connect with other narratives in evolutionary biology, such as 'the selfish gene' (see Sect. 3.2.1).[42] On the face of it, none of them leaves much room for the positive reciprocity needed to address current challenges and opportunities. However, what follows highlights how, both in their origins and in the way they are being reassessed, there is evidence of a much broader set of aspirations directed at economic and financial activity—aspirations that seem more other-regarding and hence more consistent with positive reciprocity and justified trust.[43] Something has got lost in the telling and needs to be rediscovered.

With the exception of 'shareholder value', you do not often hear people in financial markets referring to these models by name. Nonetheless, the assumptions behind them have been influential.[44] They were, after all, part of the worldview that led Mr. Greenspan and many others to make their mistake in the run up to 2008. They have had a significant influence on policymaking, for example: in legislation,[45] in the form of cost-benefit analysis[46] and in the way competition authorities and other regulators approach regulating markets and market participants.[47] They influence the way companies are run[48] and their executives are remunerated.[49] They have shaped financial market practice itself, for example, in the form of modern portfolio theory.[50] To *The Economist*, shareholder value is the biggest idea in business.[51] Meanwhile, the concept of the invisible hand has been described as, 'one of the Great Ideas of history … [a] most important legacy to … all economics.'[52]

But all three models involve a common sense gap. What you see in practice is not what you would expect if everyone was as self-interested as these narratives suggest. A truth is hiding in plain sight and has been there all along: economic life involves extensive other-regardingness. What follows highlights the way in which that truth is increasingly showing through in the way people approach these models (see Sects. 1.2.1, 1.2.2 and 1.2.3 below). Yet how far that changing perspective has made its way into the financial markets that have previously been affected by models like these is less clear. Section 1.2.4 looks at two examples of attempts to change financial market practice: sustainable finance and work to influence the culture of financial institutions. In each case, there seems to be a struggle to integrate the self-regard assumed by economic models and the broader reality of other-regardingness. In contrast, subsequent chapters will show how recognition of a social licence can provide an integrative framework, conceptually and in practice.

1.2.1   Economic Man Revisited

'Economic man' was never intended as more than a theoretical model for economists. He is often thought of as Adam Smith's creation, but owes little to him. Smith certainly saw an important role for self-interest in explaining business relationships. As he famously observed in *The Wealth of Nations*, it is the butcher, baker and brewer's regard for their own interests that makes it possible to trade with them to put supper on the table. But this, he said, is because we cannot rely upon their benevolence 'only'; Smith recognised that motivations other than self-interest are also involved, but alone are not sufficient to explain business life, since providers of goods and services also have legitimate needs to meet.[53]

Yet, contemporaries understood even this account as a fiction for the purposes of Smith's theory.[54] The opening words of his other great work, *The Theory of Moral Sentiments* reflect that: 'How selfish soever man may be supposed, there are evidently some principles in his nature, which interest him in the fortune of others, and render their happiness necessary to him, though he derives nothing from it, except the pleasure of seeing it.' This 'compassion' is one of a number of 'original passions of human nature', the presence of which, he said, is 'too obvious to require any instances to prove it.'[55]

So where did this rational self-seeking economic man come from? The first iteration was advanced by John Stewart Mill in his *On the Definition of Political Economy* in 1836, explicitly for the purpose of defining the study of economics. This individual was dominated by a 'desire to possess wealth' and later evolved in the hands of late nineteenth century economist William Stanley Jevons into a mathematised 'calculating man' desiring wealth as a means to enjoyment or utility from its consumption. This model of economic man, increasingly assumed to be making rational choices in pursuing his preferences, has remained influential in one shape or form ever since.[56] Many who have used it knew that assumptions were being made to facilitate economic analysis and that reality was more complex.[57] Nonetheless, defining and studying economic activity in this way carried the dangerous implication that other motivations are somehow not essential to what goes on in markets.

Unsurprisingly, therefore, by the 1970s, some were expressing concern about how far use of the model had become detached from reality, and the possible policy implications.[58] Dissatisfaction continued to grow, gaining added impetus as a result of the events of 2008. The result has been two broad areas of work.

First, psychologists and behavioural economists (building particularly on research by Daniel Kahneman and Amos Tversky) have focused on the assumption of rationality, attempting to make the model more realistic by incorporating behavioural pre-dispositions that are known to affect rational processes at the point at which an economic decision is made. We may not be able to discern our best interests. The decisions we make are affected by the way they are framed, our aversion to loss, our tendency to privilege short over long-term benefit, to apply shortcuts when presented with too much information, our over-optimism, our selective memory, and so on.[59] However, this work leaves the underlying assumption of economic man as an individual rational actor largely intact with policy attempts to address these behavioural 'kinks' operating as 'nudges' to get people back onto a rationally self-interested track.[60]

A second stream of work, more significant for current purposes, concerns the assumption of self-interest, and that the preferences of economic man are fixed. It has made extensive use of behavioural game theory.[61] There are various strands but, very broadly, they draw attention to the fact that, in practice, people behave in ways that are other-regarding as well as self-regarding, and that their preferences are not simply a given, but change, including as a result of social interaction.[62] A substantial body of anthropological and sociological work has long recognised the social embeddedness of economic activity and the way in which it is influenced by and influences culture.[63] So, economics is making up ground here. Economic sociologists, in particular, question the primacy that has been given to material and financial self-interest in explaining market activity. As elsewhere, humans in financial markets do not operate as socially atomised units, neatly predictable, much as with the laws of physics. Financial activity is not just about markets and transactions, and the laws that regulate them. These may not even by the principal part of it. Rather, financial behaviour grows out of and is based on a series of individual and institutional relationships in which the values involved extend far beyond financial values. Values of this sort influence activity at every level of financial markets, '…from the selection of economic goals to the organization of relevant means to achieve them'.[64]

Economic man is a myth and is being re-evaluated. Recognition of a social licence offers a framework for working through the implications for financial markets.

1.2.2 Shareholder Value Revisited

The pattern is similar for shareholder value. Like *homo economicus*, the motivations and aspirations reflected in early accounts of shareholder value were more nuanced than popular usage might suggest. It is easy not to get past the arresting title of Friedman's famous 1970 *New York Times* article, 'The Social Responsibility of Business is to Increase its Profits', often seen as having launched the shareholder value concept even though he did not call it that.[65] But look more closely, and he describes that responsibility as being, 'to conduct the business in accordance with [the shareholders'] desires, which generally will be to make as much money as possible while conforming to the basic rules of society, both those embodied in law and in ethical custom.'[66] So, the desires of shareholders are only 'generally' to make money, and their financial desire is circumscribed by law and 'ethical custom'. This crucial observation was left undeveloped by Friedman. However, clearly, other-regarding aspirations made an almost unavoidable appearance in his thinking alongside financial self-interest. And, significantly, that reference is getting picked in the current process of re-evaluation.[67]

Logically, the reference to ethical standards must reach beyond 'enlightened self-interest' ('doing well by doing good') to situations where doing the right thing carries a price tag. Otherwise, why bother to mention it—everything would simply reduce to making a profit. Understood this way, the pursuit of profit should lead to good social outcomes as long as shareholders' sense of right and wrong pays due regard to the needs of others, and the directors reflect that in the way they run the business.

However, as with economic man, that is not the version of shareholder value that subsequently emerged. Instead, it came to be associated with a relentless prioritisation of financial return for shareholders, especially short-term return. If shareholders are assumed to resemble profit-obsessed economic man, perhaps that is unsurprising. Whether the concept of shareholder value has been the cause or a rationalisation or both, there is a perception that shareholders' short-term financial interests have been privileged in the running of listed companies.[68] The financial sector has been seen as a key source of pressure to do so.[69] There are various reasons for wanting to maintain a company's share price, certainly not just dogged adherence to an economic doctrine, such as the risk of a takeover and the way executive remuneration is structured. This, in turn, can have an important impact on corporate activity.[70] Nonetheless, the idea of shareholder value has clearly been part of the mix.[71]

Yet shareholder value has increasingly been questioned in ways that reflect a much broader set of aspirations for the positive impact companies should have beyond shareholders' pockets. This is unsurprising if humans do not take after economic man after all. Even as Friedman was writing, others were advancing alternative views on corporate purpose, such as business management expert Peter Drucker.[72] However, especially since the mid-1980s, there have been growing efforts to identify ways of recognising and addressing the broader social impacts of business activity. The most significant is stakeholder theory, essentially, based on the idea that a company exists to serve the interests of all who may be affected by what it does.[73] This has had notable impact. For example, in the UK, it was reflected in an amendment to the Companies Act 2006, requiring company directors to have regard to the interests of various groups other than shareholders in discharging their duty to seek the success of the company.[74] Further, as noted above, during August 2019, the US Business Roundtable published a Statement on the Purpose of a Corporation essentially moderating its previous commitment to shareholder value by setting out 'commitments' to a range of stakeholders in the interests of 'inclusive capitalism'. Other similar frameworks include corporate social responsibility, responsible business, responsible investment, sustainable business, sustainable investment and 'triple bottom line accounting'.[75] All of these seek in some way to integrate into corporate decision-making the wider interests of those affected by a company's activities.

There has also been growing attention to the issue of 'corporate purpose' as something that goes beyond making money. Larry Fink (CEO of multi-trillion dollar investment manager BlackRock) has described corporate purpose as, 'a company's fundamental reason for being – what it does every day to create value for its stakeholders' (note, 'stakeholders' not just 'shareholders'), urging the companies in which BlackRock invests on behalf of its clients to identify theirs and pursue it.[76] Pursuing a purpose of this sort will commonly be consistent with positive long-term financial performance, that is, long-term shareholder value. However, some recognise that it might not always be.[77] Either way, corporate success, and hence corporate purpose, is increasingly no longer seen in terms of value for shareholders alone. So much so, that the first two principles of the UK's Corporate Governance Code, with which UK listed companies must 'comply or explain' was amended in 2018 to state that:

A. A successful company is led by an effective and entrepreneurial board, whose role is to promote the long-term sustainable success of the company, generating value for shareholders and contributing to wider society.

B. The board should establish the company's purpose, values and strategy, and satisfy itself that these and its culture are aligned.'[78]

It seems unlikely that this will be the end of the matter.[79]

1.2.3   The 'Invisible Hand' Revisited

Like economic man, the economic concept of an invisible hand evolved from the work of Adam Smith, especially his well-known observation that, by participating in economic activity, a person:

> generally … neither intends to promote the publick interest … he intends only his own gain, and he is in this, as in many other cases, led by an invisible hand to promote an end which was no part of his intention … By pursuing his own interest he frequently promotes that of the society more effectually than when he really intends to promote it.[80]

However, again, the contemporary idea of the invisible hand, at least in its more popular forms, bears only limited resemblance to Smith's. First, as discussed, it is questionable whether Smith really considered humans engaging in economic activity as solely driven by self-interest. Secondly, his principal interest in the 'invisible hand' is not to affirm the role of self-interest, but an end reaching beyond it—the public interest and social good. He does not equate the 'invisible hand' with self-interest, but with a benign force that can work through it; something that exists beyond self-interest. Thirdly, he shows some reserve in the claims he makes for the outcomes that pursuing self-interest produces: it promotes the interests of society only 'frequently', and the results are 'not always the worse for society'.

Consistent with this, it is clear that few people really approach markets on the assumption that participants will act in a way that is solely self-interested. Indeed, they depend upon them not to be. More on that in Chap. 3. It is also clear that people have an aspiration that markets should, 'promote … [the interests of] … society more effectually' than sometimes they do—in other words, their aspirations for markets seem to involve an element of other-regardingness since they concern social outcomes.

It is recognised that markets, self-interested or otherwise, do not always produce results consistent with those desired outcomes. The limitations of markets are well-known. In particular, market mechanisms are not good at providing or maintaining what economists refer to as 'public goods'[81] since, being public, access cannot be excluded and therefore priced (e.g. national defence). However, that does not mean that markets are not essential to them. Further, markets give rise to what economists call 'negative externalities'. These are the harmful side effects of an economic activity the cost of which is borne by those who are not parties to the activity because it is not factored into the cost of production and therefore borne privately by the parties to the transaction.[82] Environmental damage from economic activities is a prime example. Externalities are evidence for the power of self-interest in markets; competitive self-interest tends not to address them unless it turns out to be in someone's interest to do so. They get labelled as instances of 'market failure', where there is a case for government intervention to correct the problem. However, it follows from the above that participants in markets do not behave in an exclusively self-regarding way (see Chap. 3), and the market has only failed by reference to some wider standard of wellbeing that is, at some level, other-regarding. Talk of 'failure' suggests an aspiration for markets to meet that standard.

In short the metaphor of the invisible hand has, once again, become a myth;[83] one that adds little by way of explanation, but provides, '…a social justification for the primacy of self-regard'.[84]

1.2.4   Alternative Frameworks in Practice

The three economic models considered above are inadequate as an account of how humans really engage in financial activity, but may nonetheless have been shaping it. Both in their origins and in the way they are being reassessed, there is abundant evidence that aspirations brought to bear on economic life are not just narrowly self-interested but also other-regarding. However, that is not reflected in the way these models are often conceived of. Nor do they provide an adequate way of recognising the potency of this aspirational mix.

There is a similar issue with some of the frameworks currently being advanced to help address the sort of challenges discussed earlier, in particular, galvanising the finance sector to address environmental and social sustainability and the related task of healing the fracture between the financial world and the societies in which it operates. Initiatives on sustainable finance are the most obvious example of the first. Attention to banking culture is an example of the second. In each case, work tends to be premised on assumptions of self-interest among financial market participants, much as with the economic models considered above, even though other-regarding attitudes are also clearly at work. The frameworks and language used sometimes seem inadequate in drawing on other-regarding aspirations, or providing a way of combining the two. As subsequent chapters will show, the recognition of a social licence has the potential to provide a framework for holding these ends together and a language for navigating the difference.

Sustainable Finance

As noted, sustainable finance activity has grown significantly in recent years. But what is sustainable finance? What is being sustained—finance, or something else? Is the goal simply sustaining it, or more? And for how long, to what end, and from whose perspective? The United Nations Sustainable Development Goals ('SDGs') adopted in November 2015 purport to answer some of these questions,[85] and some finance firms have begun to reflect them in their sustainability activities. However, there is a tension at the heart of the SDGs, and it concerns the balance between, on the one hand, harnessing the power of material self-interest in the pursuit of wealth and development and, on the other, the desire to address environmental and social needs more widely. For example, Goal 8 sets a target for growth of, 'at least 7 per cent gross domestic product growth per annum in the least developed countries', but only talks of an, 'endeavour to decouple economic growth from environmental degradation'.

This tension has existed since before the UN Commission on Environment and Development which published the report, *Our Common Future* (also known as the *Brundtland Report*) in 1987.[86] That report first defined sustainable development as development that meets the needs of the present without compromising the ability of future generations to meet their own needs. Until then, there had been a divergence between those who saw development in terms of economic growth, and those concerned about its environmental and social impact. The Brundtland Report did not resolve the tension, but put the emphasis on the possibility of a 'win-win' by calling for 'economic growth – growth that is forceful and at the same time socially and environmentally sustainable'.[87] Economic growth became part of the solution.[88] Potentially, indeed it is. But in its current form it is also part of the problem.[89] And since economic activity and consumption is funded through and by the finance sector, it is the same for finance. Indeed, that is where sustainable finance comes in.

The European Commission has described sustainable finance as the process of taking due account of environmental and social considerations in investment decision-making, leading to increased investments in longer-term and sustainable activities.[90] Environmental considerations refer to tackling climate change, as well as avoiding environmental degradation more broadly, while social considerations cover, among other things, inequality, inclusiveness, labour relations, investment in human capital and communities. This is largely consistent with the way the expression is used in the market, but leaves many of the questions above unanswered. The advantage of that is that 'sustainability' can provide a loose framework within which those pursuing a set of potentially conflicting interests can meet and identify a shared agenda. However, the danger is that issues that drive the need for a sustainability initiative in the first place do not get adequately articulated and addressed. In particular, there is a risk that the fear of denying material and financial self-interest trumps the possibility of drawing on other-regarding aspiration based on valued ends that transcend what is financial.

It is not feasible here to track this tension through the vast body of policy and industry work on sustainable finance. However, two discussions in which I was involved help to illustrate the point.

The first was among a small group of business people, policymakers and representatives from NGOs who were preparing for an event on sustainable finance. During the conversation, one person remarked that, if business and finance has to change in order to address the challenges of environmental damage, logically, that cannot be good news for everyone. For example, who at present would want to have made a substantial long-term investment in a single use plastics business? Probably not the owners of Nelson Packaging which found itself in difficulties following the introduction of a charge for disposable plastic carrier bags in English supermarkets in 2016.[91] A silence followed the remark. It seemed as if talk of sustainability as a potential source of damage to business rather than an opportunity was a taboo. It was as if the terms of the discussion had been set by assumptions similar to those of the economic models discussed above; the priority of satisfying material and financial self-interest had to be respected even though many in the room were almost certainly also motivated by broader other-regarding aspirations.

The second discussion involved a senior EU legislator. During 2018, the European Union published its ambitious Sustainable Finance Action Plan, intended to redirect the European financial sector towards ends that are 'sustainable' (a concept the European Union is seeking to define more fully, starting with climate change objectives).[92] The discussion concerned how policymakers' ambitions can best be realised. The talk was largely of economic incentives. Given the power of self-interest to drive behaviour, that is clearly important. But is there no possibility that people's other-regarding aspirations might also be a source of change, particularly in areas where self-interest and state-based enforcement run out? Each time the topic was raised, the sub-text of the response was along the lines of, 'that's interesting; anyway, as I was saying about incentives.' The assumptions involved in the economic models run deep. Indeed, a review of some of the key international publications on sustainable finance shows a preponderance of words like 'incentive' and the need to manage economic risk (i.e. not suffer financial loss) in the context of discussion of how to change current practice.[93]

Drawing on material and financial self-interest to engage the financial sector to address challenges like climate change clearly makes sense, for example, through greater disclosure of climate risk in the financial system, stronger risk management practices and greater clarity on what investments are sustainable.[94] Yet, the sustainability discussion itself is also evidence that powerful non-financial and other-regarding aspirations are also at work. This is captured most forcefully in the language of the United Nations Sustainable Development Goals: 'All countries and all stakeholders … are resolved to free the human race from the tyranny of poverty and want and to heal and secure our planet. We are determined to take the bold and transformative steps which are urgently needed to shift the world onto a sustainable … path.'[95] Unsurprisingly perhaps, some have criticised them for their breadth.[96] However, clearly, there is a profound aspiration for ends that go beyond what is economic, and it is questionable to what extent material and financial incentives will be sufficient alone to realise them. A way is needed to embrace material and financial self-interest within, and draw more effectively on, these wider other-regarding aspirations.

Culture in Finance

There are similar tensions in work to improve culture in financial firms which, as noted earlier, seems to be making patchy progress. The work recognises that, to change behaviour, it is necessary to get to its 'root cause'. Since culture essentially describes the way an institution 'is', including how those within it behave, attention has focused on the need to shape culture in order to influence behaviour. Regulators and firms have a different but overlapping agenda here. Regulators are principally interested in behaviours that could prejudice regulatory objectives and, more widely, destroy public trust in the financial sector. Firms are more focused on franchise preservation and enhancement (including energising staff), and avoiding regulatory infringements as part of that. However, in each case, the underlying objective is for firms and their staff to behave in a more other-regarding manner that does not conform to the narrowly self-interested assumptions of the economic models.

Work on the culture of financial firms is nonetheless strongly influenced by assumptions that echo those of the models. For example, attempts to motivate firms to address their culture often appeal to controlling 'misconduct risk'—among other things, the firm's self-interest in avoiding damage.[97] There is also considerable regulatory emphasis on the need to incentivise behaviours consistent with the desired culture,[98] improving incentives being seen by some as, 'the most direct way to improve culture and conduct'.[99] Incentives are important, but they depend on manipulating self-interest with external rewards and punishment, rather than attempting to strengthen other-regarding aspiration; the risk is that that they result in compliance more than the right sort of culture change and that the desired behaviours end once the incentives are removed. More recently, staff at the New York Federal Reserve have been developing the concept of cultural capital, treating 'sound culture' as an intangible asset.[100] Good culture is an asset, and this is a promising initiative. However, the language is telling since, again, it seems to carry the implication that culture needs to be 'sold' to financial institutions on the basis of self-interest, like building up assets on their balance sheet.[101]

Nonetheless, a review of speeches by senior US and UK regulators on culture change in financial institutions in the period up to June 2019 suggests a growing recognition that appeals to self-interest alone are not enough; that it may be necessary to gear culture change to a broader sense of mission or purpose that engages aspiration. At the time of writing, the UK Financial Conduct Authority is embarked on a project looking at 'the case for creating purposeful cultures', in particular the link with 'healthy outcomes' for consumers, markets and firms.[102] Significantly, comments from both the Chief Executive of the Financial Conduct Authority, the Chairman of the SEC and others have begun to link culture with the 'public interest'.[103] Exactly what is meant by the public interest is not clear—for example, whether it is anything more than a utilitarian 'greatest good for the greatest number'. However, it nonetheless seems to appeal to a sense of other-regardingness on the part of institutions and their staff and, perhaps, to reach in a similar direction to talk of a social licence for financial markets (see Chap. 4). This emphasis on public interest seems more marked in the UK. Yet, even in the UK, the two themes of private and public interests are not teased out in a way that addresses the relationship between them, an area in which recognition of a social licence has much to contribute. For example, Andrew Bailey, while CEO of the Financial Conduct Authority, stated that, 'Firms are part of … society, as such they have public interest duties.' Yet he still noted that the role of regulation is, 'to create the right incentives', adding that regulators can also 'prompt and persuade'.[104] Further, it is unclear how far talk of a 'duty' to serve the public interest also involves a recognition that there may already be a desire to do so. Likewise, in industry discussion of culture it is fairly common to hear words like 'integrity' and 'ethics' (as in corporate codes), which seem to indicate a recognition of the need somehow to draw on internally generated other-regardingness. However, their substance and their relationship with self-interest are rarely unpacked.

1.3   Conclusion

The observation that financial markets operate subject to a social licence has emerged in the context of the current re-evaluation of, among other things, the role of finance and what motivates it. It has the potential to provide a valuable framework and language to use in working through that re-evaluation in the context of financial markets, both in theory and, importantly, in practice, influencing the aspirations and beliefs that animate market activity.

Part II will look at the idea of a social licence for financial markets more closely and, Part III, how it can be expected to change behaviour in practice. However, before that, it is necessary to do important groundwork by considering some of the key drivers of behaviour in financial markets, since recognition of a social licence would need to influence these if it is to help the financial world respond to the challenges outlined earlier. That is the purpose of Part I.

Notes

1. Milton Friedman, *Capitalism and Freedom* (40th anniversary edition, University of Chicago Press 2002), 133.
2. Adair Turner, *Between Debt and the Devil – Money, Credit and Fixing Global Finance* (Princeton University Press 2016), 20.
3. Alan Beattie and James Politi, "I made a mistake,' admits Greenspan', *Financial Times*, London, 23 October 2008.
4. See, for example, *IMF Performance in the Run-up to the Financial and Economic Crisis: IMF Surveillance in 2004–2007*, International Monetary Fund Independent Evaluation Office, 2011; *The Turner Review: A Regulatory Response to the Global Financial Crisis*, Financial Services Authority, 2009.
5. George Parker, 'Veteran of Treasury Battles tots up a decade's wins and losses', *Financial Times*, London, 14 April 2016.
6. For example, see *2019 Edelman Trust Barometer, financial services* (Edelman 2019), and research by Edelman over many years at https://www.edelman.com/research/edelman-trust-barometer-archive (accessed 14 October

2019); *GlobeScan Radar 2016: Finance eBrief* (GlobeScan 2016) available at: https://globescan.com/wp-content/uploads/2017/07/GlobeScan_Radar_2016-Finance_eBrief.pdf (accessed 14 October 2019); John Authers, 'Finance, the media and a catastrophic breakdown in trust', *FT Magazine*, London, 4 October 2018. Trust levels may have improved as compared with just after the financial crisis, but they remain low.

7. *Changing Banking for Good*, Report of the Parliamentary Commission on Banking Standards, First Report of Session 2013–2014, Volume I: Summary, and Conclusions and Recommendations, HL Paper 27-I, HC 175-I, June 2013.

8. See video of Open Forum Breakout Session 1, Panel 2: https://www.youtube.com/watch?v=dUE_opd01lA (accessed 21 November 2019).

9. *Royal Commission into Misconduct in the Banking, Superannuation and Financial Services Industry, Final Report*, Commonwealth of Australia, 2019, 1.

10. *Challenges for financial markets*, speech by John Cunliffe, Deputy Governor Financial Stability, Bank of England, 3 November 2016.

11. For example, according to the *2019 Edelman Trust Barometer* global report, only one in five of those asked believed that the system is working for them.

12. John Kay, *Other People's Money: Masters of the Universe or Servants of the People?* (Profile Books 2015), 306. See also Martin Wolf, 'The Price of Populism', *Financial Times*, London, 24 October 2018.

13. Conservative Party Manifesto (2017) 9, https://s3.eu-west-2.amazonaws.com/conservative-party-manifestos/Forward+Together+-+Our+Plan+for+a+Stronger+Britain+and+a+More+Prosperous....pdf (accessed 14 October 2019).

14. The current re-evaluation is much broader than this. However, the fracture between the financial world and society has played a significant role.

15. For example, in August 2019, the US Business Roundtable published a statement on the purpose of a corporation setting out 'commitments' to a range of stakeholders in the interests of 'inclusive capitalism': https://opportunity.businessroundtable.org/ourcommitment/ (accessed 14 October 2019). See also the *World Economic Forum Global Risks Report 2019* (World Economic Forum 2019), 13–14, and the 2019 annual letter from the CEO of BlackRock, Larry Fink, to the CEOs of companies in which BlackRock invests client funds, https://www.blackrock.com/corporate/investor-relations/larry-fink-ceo-letter (accessed 5 November 2019).

16. See, for example, *CEOs' curbed confidence spells caution*, 22nd Annual Global CEO survey (PWC 2019) available at https://www.pwc.com/ee/et/publications/CEOSurvey/22nd_Annual_Global_CEO_Survey_Report.pdf (accessed 29 July 2019); Philip Stephens, 'Populism is the true legacy of the global financial crisis', *Financial Times*, London, 30 August 2018.

17. Interview with an unnamed CEO of a company described as a 'major corporate', reported in Nik Gowing and Chris Langdon, *Thinking the Unthinkable* (John Catt Educational Ltd 2018).
18. Mark Wilson, then CEO of Aviva, speaking at the Saïd Business School, Oxford University, 1 February 2018, https://www.sbs.ox.ac.uk/news/mark-wilson-leading-legacy (accessed 14 October 2019).
19. Management expert Peter Drucker as reported by David Copperrider, 'Sustainable Innovation', *BizEd*, 1 July 2008, available at https://bized.aacsb.edu/articles/2008/07/sustainable-innovation (accessed 9 November 2019).
20. *World Investment Report 2014 – Investing in the SDGs: An Action Plan*, United Nations Conference on Trade and Development, 2014. See also Bertrand Badré, *Can Finance Save the World* (Berrett-Koehler Publishers, Inc. 2018); *Rethinking Impact to Finance the SDGs*, United Nations Environment Programme Finance Initiative, November 2018.
21. See for example, *Sustainable Finance Progress Report*, United Nations Environment Programme Inquiry into the Design of a Sustainable Finance System, March 2019; *The State of Sustainable Business 2018, results of the 10th annual survey of sustainable business leaders* (Globescan and The Business of a Better World, 2018) available at https://www.bsr.org/files/event-resources/BSR_Globescan_State_of_Sustainable_Business_2018.pdf (accessed 14 October 2019).
22. *Sustainable Finance Progress Report*, United Nations Environment Programme Inquiry into the Design of a Sustainable Finance System; Ben Caldecott, 'Banks need to get ahead of climate change, or else', *Financial Times*, London, 30 June 2019.
23. *Banking culture: the path ahead*, remarks by John C. Williams, President and Chief Executive Officer, Federal Reserve Bank of New York, 4 June 2019. See also *Reform of culture in finance from multiple perspectives*, remarks by Kevin J. Stiroh, Executive Vice President, Federal Reserve Bank of New York, 26 February 2019.
24. *Realising the benefits of purposeful leadership*, speech by Jonathon Davidson, Director of Supervision – Retail and Authorisations, Financial Conduct Authority, 1 November 2018; *Senior Managers and Certification Regime Banking Stocktake Report*, Financial Conduct Authority, 5 August 2019.
25. Dame Colette Bowe, Chairman of the Banking Standards Board, response to question 3, House of Commons Treasury Committee, Oral Evidence: The Work of the Banking Standards Board, HC 1715, 13 November 2018. *Banking on Conduct and Culture: A Permanent Mindset Change*, Group of Thirty, November 2018 conveys a similar message.
26. Robert D. Putnam, *Bowling Alone: The Collapse and Revival of American Community* (Simon & Schuster 2001), 134 et seq.; Francis Fukuyama, *Trust: The Social Virtues and the Creation of Prosperity* (Simon & Schuster

1995); Yann Algan and Pierre Cahuc, *Inherited Trust and Growth*, American Economic Review, 2010, Vol. 100(5), 2060–2092; *Strengthening culture for the long term*, remarks by William C. Dudley Former President and Chief Executive Officer Federal Reserve Bank of New York, 18 June 2018.

27. Luigi Guiso, Paola Sapienza and Luigi Zingales, 'Civic Capital as the Missing Link', in *Handbook of Social Economics Vol. 1A*, eds. Jess Benhabib, Alberto Bisin and Matthew O. Jackson (North-Holland 2011), 472–3; Karl V. Lins, Henri Servaes and Ane Tamayo, *Social Capital, Trust, and Firm Performance: The Value of Corporate Social Responsibility During the Financial Crisis*, Journal of Finance, 2017, Vol. 72(4), 1785–1824.

28. *How Fair and Effective are the Fixed Income, Foreign Exchange and Commodities Markets*, Fair and Effective Markets Review, Consultation Document, HM Treasury, Bank of England and Financial Conduct Authority, October 2014, 6. The Appendix provides more detail on why these markets matter.

29. *Globalisation: real and financial*, speech by Hyun Song Shin, Economic Adviser and Head of Research of the BIS, BIS 87th Annual General Meeting, quoted by Adam Tooze, *Crashed: How a Decade of Financial Crises Changed the World* (Allen Lane 2018).

30. *Committee Democrats call on Facebook to halt cryptocurrency plans*, US House Committee on Financial Services, 2 July 2019, available at https://financialservices.house.gov/news/documentsingle.aspx?DocumentID=404009 (accessed 26 July 2019); Dirk A. Zetzsche, Ross P. Buckley and Douglas W. Arner, *Regulating Libra: the Transformative Potential of Facebook's Cryptocurrency and Possible Regulatory Responses*, University of New South Wales Law Research Series [2019] UNSW Law Research Paper No. 47.

31. Jason G. Allen and Rosa M. Lastra, *Border Problems II: Mapping the Third Border*, 1 January 2018, UNSW Law Research Paper No. 18–88; Saule T. Omarova, *New Tech v. New Deal: Fintech as a Systemic Phenomenon*, Yale Journal on Regulation, 2019, Vol. 36(2), 735–793.

32. Karla Hoff and Joseph E. Stiglitz, *Striving for Balance in Economics: Towards a Theory of the Social Determination of Behavior*, Journal of Economic Behavior and Organization, 2016, Vol. 126, 25–57. Different disciplines distinguish between concepts, such as models, narratives, stories, world views, scripts and schemas. Distinctions are important, and some are picked up in subsequent chapters. However, the word 'narrative' is used broadly in what follows to describe ways of explaining how various events and facts are connected, usually involving a sense of movement from a beginning towards an end.

33. Bernie Sanders quoted by Barney Henderson, 'Bernie Sanders causes searches for 'socialism' to spike on Merriam-Webster', *The Telegraph*, London, 14 October 2015.

34. Donald J. Trump, Remarks on trade, 28 June 2016, quoted by Amy Skonieczny, *Emotions and Political Narratives: Populism, Trump and Trade*, Politics and Governance, 2018, Vol. 6(4), 62–72.

35. Jeremy Corbyn, quoted by Jim Pickard, 'Corbyn lashes out at financial sector "speculators and gamblers"', *Financial Times*, London, 1 December 2017.

36. See, for example, 'Runaway bankers: the sequel', *Private Eye* no. 1501, London, 26 July–8 August 2019.

37. *The Wolf of Wall Street* (Paramount Pictures 2013). A film about greed and corruption surrounding the rise and fall of stockbroker Jordon Belfort.

38. While they are models, they can also be seen as a form of story about the way people and companies engage in markets and how markets work. See, for example, Frank Pasquale, *Two Narratives of Platform Capitalism*, Yale Law and Policy Review, 2016, Vol. 35(1), 309–318.

39. Skonieczny, *Emotions and Political Narratives*.

40. Hoff and Stiglitz, *Striving for Balance in Economics*. See further in Chap. 6.

41. Jean Tirole, *Economics for the Common Good* (Princeton University Press 2017), 122. See also *The complexity of culture reform in finance*, remarks by Kevin J. Stiroh, Executive Vice President, Federal Reserve Bank of New York, 4 October 2018.

42. Simon Blackburn, *Ruling Passions* (Oxford University Press 1998), 144; John Gowdy and Irmi Seidl, *Economic Man and Selfish Genes: The Implications of Group Selection for Economic Valuation and Policy*, The Journal of Socio Economics, 2004, Vol. 33, 343–358.

43. Chapter 3 returns to how both self-interest and, probably, altruism can motivate behaviour that addresses others' needs. References in this book to 'other-regarding' aspirations and behaviours should be read in that light.

44. See, for example, Donald MacKenzie, *An Engine, Not a Camera: How Financial Models Shape Markets* (MIT Press 2006); Fabrizio Ferraro, Jeffrey Pfeffer and Robert I. Sutton, *Economics Language and Assumptions: How Theories Can Become Self-fulfilling*, Academy of Management Review, 2005, Vol. 30(1), 8–24; Dale T. Miller, *The Norm of Self-interest*, American Psychologist, 1999, Vol. 54(12), 1053–1060.

45. For example, in the competition objectives of the UK financial services regulators: sections 1B, 1E and 2H, Financial Services and Markets Act 2000.

46. Robert Baldwin, Martin Cave and Martin Lodge, *Understanding Regulation: Theory, Strategy, and Practice* (2nd edn, Oxford University Press 2012), 315; *How we Analyse the Costs and Benefits of our Policies*, Financial Conduct Authority, July 2018.

47. Tirole, *Economics for the Common Good*, 122.

48. Colin Mayer, *Firm Commitment* (Oxford University Press 2013).

49. Robert J. Rhee, *A Legal Theory of Shareholder Primacy*, Minnesota Law Review, 2018, Vol. 102, 1951–2017, 1980; Edward B. Rock, *Adapting to the New Shareholder-Centric Reality*, University of Pennsylvania Law Review, 2013, Vol. 161(7), 1907–1988, 1917; Alex Edmans, Xavier Gabaix and Dirk Jenter, *Executive Compensation: A Survey of Theory and Evidence*, European Corporate Governance Institute Finance Working Paper No. 514/2017, July 2017.

50. MacKenzie, *An Engine, Not a Camera*.
51. 'Shareholder value – the enduring power of the biggest idea in business', *The Economist*, London, 31 March 2016.
52. James Tobin, *The Invisible Hand in Modern Macroeconomics*, Cowles Foundation Discussion Paper No. 966, Cowles Foundation for Research in Economics at Yale University, January 1991.
53. Adam Smith, *An Inquiry into the Nature and Causes of the Wealth of Nations* (Liberty Fund edn, 1981), I.ii.2, 26–27.
54. Mary S. Morgan, *Economic Man as Model Man: Ideal Types, Idealization and Caricatures*, Journal of the History of Economic Thought, 2006, Vol. 28(1), 1–27, 3.
55. Adam Smith, *The Theory of Moral Sentiments* (Liberty Fund edn, 1982), I.i.I.1, 9.
56. Morgan, *Economic Man as Model Man*.
57. Morgan, *Economic Man as Model Man*; Amartya Sen, *Rational Fools: A Critique of the Behavioral Foundations of Economic Theory*, Philosophy & Public Affairs, 1977, Vol. 6(4), 317–344.
58. Amartya Sen op. cit., 322.
59. Tirole, *Economics for the Common Good*, 122 et seq.
60. Richard H. Thaler and Cass R. Sunstein, *Nudge: Improving Decisions About Health, Wealth, and Happiness* (Penguin Books 2009).
61. Samuel Bowles, *The Moral Economy: Why Good Incentives Are no Substitute for Good Citizens* (Yale University Press 2016), 43 and Appendix 2 summarises the sort of experiments that have been used.
62. See, for example, Hoff and Stiglitz, *Striving for Balance in Economics*; Samuel Bowles, *Endogenous Preferences: The Cultural Consequences of Markets and Other Economic Institutions*, Journal of Economic Literature, 1998, Vol. 36(1), 75–111; Samuel Bowles and Sandra Polanía-Reyes, *Economic Incentives and Social Preferences: Substitutes or Complements?* Journal of Economic Literature, 2012, Vol. 50(2), 368–425; George A. Akerlof and Rachel E. Kranton, *Identity Economics: How Our Identities Shape Our Work, Wages, and Well-being* (Princeton University Press 2010); Margit Osterloh and Bruno S. Frey, 'Motivation Governance', in *Handbook of Economic Organization: Integrating Economic and Organization Theory* ed. Anna Grandori (Edward Elgar 2013); Joseph Henrich, et al., *Foundations of Human Sociality: Economic Experiments and Ethnographic Evidence from Fifteen Small-scale Societies* (Oxford University Press 2004).
63. The relationship between humans and economic activity was a preoccupation of Émile Durkheim, Karl Marx and Max Weber, founding fathers of sociology. More recently, the development of economic sociology has highlighted the embeddedness of economic activity in social relations: Mark Granovetter, *Economic Action and Social Structure: The Problem of Embeddedness*, American Journal of Sociology, 1985, Vol. 19(3), 481–510;

Alejandro Portes, *Economic Sociology: A Systematic Enquiry* (Princeton University Press 2010).

64. Portes, *Economic Sociology*, 14.

65. Milton Friedman, 'The Social Responsibility of Business is to Increase its Profits', *New York Times Magazine*, New York, 13 September 1970. The article said much the same as his 1962 book *Capitalism and Freedom*. The expression 'shareholder value' emerged some time later, and was developed by Alfred Rappaport, *Creating Shareholder Value: The New Standard for Business Performance* (The Free Press 1986). The idea was elaborated upon by Michael C. Jensen and William H. Meckling in an article that became highly influential in business management circles: *Theory of the Firm: Managerial Behavior, Agency Costs and Ownership Structure*, Journal of Financial Economics, 1976, Vol. 3(4), 305–360.

66. Friedman, *The Social Responsibility of Business is to Increase its Profits*.

67. *Transforming culture in financial services*, speech by Andrew Bailey while Chief Executive of the Financial Conduct Authority, 19 March 2018.

68. So much so that in 2012 the UK government launched a public consultation on the issue: *The Kay Review of UK Equity Markets and Long-Term Decision Making*, Final Report, July 2012.

69. See, for example, *The Kay Review of UK Equity Markets and Long-Term Decision Making*; *Call for advice to the European Supervisory Authorities to collect evidence of undue short-term pressure from the financial sector on corporations*, European Commission, 1 February 2019, https://ec.europa.eu/info/publications/190201-call-for-advice-to-esas-short-term-pressure_en (accessed 24 October 2019).

70. Kay, *Other People's Money*; Mayer, *Firm Commitment*, 89 et seq.

71. For a US perspective, Edward B. Rock, *Adapting to the New Shareholder-Centric Reality*, 1917.

72. Peter Drucker, *Management: Tasks, Responsibilities, Practices* (Heinemann 1974).

73. R. Edward Freeman, *Strategic Management: A Stakeholder Approach* (Pitman 1984); Samuel F. Mansell, *Capitalism, Corporations and the Social Contract: A Critique of Stakeholder Theory* (Cambridge University Press 2013).

74. Section 172(1), Companies Act 2006.

75. Triple bottom line accounting emerged in the 1990s and seeks to provide a way of measuring a company's social and environmental performance in addition to its financial performance.

76. *Purpose & Profit*, Larry Fink's 2019 letter to CEOs, https://www.blackrock.com/corporate/investor-relations/larry-fink-ceo-letter (accessed 24 October 2019). See also, Andrew Edgecliffe-Johnson, 'Beyond the bottom line: should business put purpose before profit?', *Financial Times*, London, 4 January 2019.

77. Colin P. Mayer, *Prosperity: Better Business Makes the Greater Good* (Oxford University Press 2018), 6.
78. *The UK Corporate Governance Code*, Financial Reporting Council 2018.
79. *Principles for Purposeful Business: How to Deliver the Framework for the Purpose of the Corporation* (British Academy 2019).
80. Smith, *An Inquiry into the Nature and Causes of The Wealth of Nations*, IV.ii.9, 456.
81. Economists think of public goods as a commodity or service the benefits of which are not depleted if an additional user is introduced, and from which it is difficult to exclude people even if they are unwilling to pay for the good.
82. Externalities are not all bad. Economists also talk of positive externalities, such as the skills a person develops at work which can be deployed more widely in their community.
83. Warren J. Samuels, *Erasing the Invisible Hand: Essays on an Elusive and Misused Concept in Economics* (Cambridge University Press 2011); Gavin Kennedy, *Adam Smith and the Invisible Hand: From Metaphor to Myth*, Econ Journal Watch, 2009, Vol. 6(2), 239–263; Avner Offer, 'Regard for Others', in *Capital Failure: Rebuilding Trust in Financial Services*, eds. Nicholas Morris and David Vines (Oxford University Press 2014), 162; Kaushik Basu, *Beyond the Invisible Hand: Groundwork for a New Economics* (Princeton University Press 2011).
84. Offer, *Regard for others*, 162.
85. See https://www.un.org/sustainabledevelopment/sustainable-development-goals/ (accessed 25 September 2019).
86. *Our Common Future: Report of the World Commission on Environment and Development* (Oxford University Press 1987).
87. Ibid., Foreword.
88. Ben Purvis, Yong Mao and Daren Robinson, *Three Pillars of Sustainability: In Search of Conceptual Origins*, Sustainability Science, 2019, Vol. 14(3), 681–695.
89. *Global Warming of 1.5°C*, Intergovernmental Panel on Climate Change, October 2018; Will Steffen et al., *The Trajectory of the Anthropocene: The Great Acceleration*, The Anthropocene Review, 2015, Vol. 2(1), 81–98.
90. *Action Plan: Financing Sustainable Growth*, Communication from the European Commission, COM(2018) 97 final.
91. 'Plastic Bag Manufacturer goes bust "due to 5p charge"', *BBC News*, 1 March 2016, https://www.bbc.co.uk/news/uk-england-manchester-35694164 (accessed 24 October 2019).
92. *Action Plan: Financing Sustainable Growth*, European Commission; *Financing a Sustainable European Economy, Taxonomy Technical Report*, EU Technical Group on Sustainable Finance, June 2019.
93. David Rouch, *The Language of Sustainable Finance, Economics and Aspiration*, 2019, available at SSRN: https://ssrn.com/abstract=3544781

94. *Remarks given during the UN Secretary General's Climate Action Summit 2019*, speech by Mark Carney, Governor of the Bank of England, 23 September 2019.

95. *Transforming our World: The 2030 Agenda for Sustainable Development*, Resolution adopted by the General Assembly on 25 September 2015, preamble.

96. See, for example, 'The 169 commandments', *The Economist*, London, 26 March 2015.

97. *Strengthening Governance Frameworks to Mitigate Misconduct Risk: A Toolkit for Firms and Supervisors*, Financial Stability Board, 20 April 2018 (which is also concerned with wider systemic risks created by misconduct); *Misconduct risk, culture and supervision*, speech by Kevin J. Stiroh, Executive Vice President, Federal Reserve Bank of New York, 7 December 2017; *The evolving first line of defense*, speech by Michael Held, Executive Vice President and General Counsel, Federal Reserve Bank of New York, 17 April 2018. See also more generally, David Rouch, *Economics and Aspiration in Language used by Regulators When Discussing Culture in Finance*, 2019, available at SSRN: https://ssrn.com/abstract=3544778

98. Based on a review of speeches by senior US and UK regulators in the period to June 2019 on culture change in financial institutions (see Rouch, *Economics and Aspiration in Language used by Regulators When Discussing Culture in Finance*). See, for example, *The importance of incentives in ensuring a resilient and robust financial system*, remarks by William C. Dudley, President and Chief Executive Officer Federal Reserve Bank of New York, 26 March 2018.

99. *Strengthening culture for the long term*, Dudley.

100. *Reform of culture in finance from multiple perspectives*, Stiroh. See also Nava Ashraf and Oriana Bandiera, *Altruistic Capital*, American Economic Review, 2017, Vol. 107(5), 70–75.

101. See, for example, *The importance of incentives in ensuring a resilient and robust financial system*, Dudley.

102. *Business Plan 2019/20*, Financial Conduct Authority 2019.

103. *Transforming culture in financial services*, Bailey; *The evolving first line of defense*, Held; *Observations on culture at financial institutions and the SEC*, Jay Clayton Chairman of the SEC, 18 June 2018; *Strengthening culture for the long term*, Dudley; *The future of financial conduct regulation*, speech by Andrew Bailey while Chief Executive of the Financial Conduct Authority, 23 April 2019.

104. *Transforming culture in financial services*, Bailey.

Part I

In the Beginning, an End

Fast Track

There is a need for greater finance sector urgency in helping humanity address some of its most pressing sustainability challenges. Yet the relationship between finance and wider society is fractured and needs healing. Regulatory rules are not enough to get this to happen: building a championship-winning football team does not start with hours of coaching on the minutiae of the rules of football. Somehow, there needs to be a deeper change in the very substance of the many relationships that make up the wider relationship between finance and society—in the way they are lived, felt and understood by the parties to them. Financial markets are a form of ecosystem. Because of the many interdependencies, change needs to happen in a coordinated way.

In view of this, Part I does important groundwork by looking at two things.

- First, how individuals, firms and markets come to behave as they do (Chap. 2). These are the processes that greater recognition of a social licence must influence if it is to be a source of behaviour change.
- Secondly, how these processes can be seen playing out in practice in financial markets, especially what motivates people (Chap. 3). If greater recognition of a social licence is to make a practical difference, it must engage with behaviour and motivations as they are.

2

People, Firms, Markets, Behaviour

Fast Track

Speed Read

Can greater recognition of a social licence for financial markets help in addressing the challenges identified in Chap. 1? Doing so requires behaviour in financial markets that is systemically and credibly more other-regarding in a way that goes beyond the immediate financial goals of transactions.

To begin to assess whether recognition of a social licence can help, this chapter looks at what causes people, firms and markets to behave as they do. It sketches out some of the key aspects of human behaviour that are susceptible to influence by the time people enter financial markets (as compared with, for example, those that are ingrained as a result of early life experiences).

Behaviour results from people pursuing the ends they **desire**, and how they **reason** about the world as they believe it to be (the **meaning** it holds for them) in working out how to realise their desires.

- A desire can be thought of as the experience of wanting something that is **valued**. There are essentially **two sorts of desire**, and the distinction is important for what follows. Some desires are '**instrumental**'; what is desired is an instrument in realising a greater desired end—'I want a car, so I need to earn some money'. Then there are '**intrinsic**' desires. With these, the desired end is valued for itself, not as a step in realising a further desire; the end is an **ultimate end** such as, 'I want to feel valued'. So, intrinsic desires lie behind instrumental desires. Any attempt to change behaviour needs to engage with both, but especially intrinsic desires.
- The **beliefs** people hold about what the world **means** also affect their behaviour—these meanings are a sort of raw material on which desires come to

(continued)

© The Author(s) 2020
D. Rouch, *The Social Licence for Financial Markets*,
https://doi.org/10.1007/978-3-030-40220-4_2

(continued)

bear. Job titles have meaning for people; because of that, some people pursue their desire for recognition by trying to secure one. However, desires can also affect the way this sense of meaning evolves. That is because the meaning things develop is influenced by how they can help in reaching desired ends: is it just a rock, or is it a diamond in an engagement ring; is it just a piece of paper, or a bank note; is it just a number on a screen, or does it have a dollar sign in front of it? In financial markets, one of the most powerful sources of meaning is **money** so, up to a point, the financial narratives considered in Chap. 1 are correct. Decisions based on the meaning of money structure markets, and the lives of those within them. The meaning of money is far from neutral. An even more powerful source of meaning in markets, as elsewhere, is **language**. **Laws and regulations** are a particular sort of language which is especially important in structuring the world of financial markets. Because of that, subsequent chapters come back to their relationship with the social licence. Meanings such as these usually involve some element of **social consensus**; most obviously, language does not work if people do not agree on what words mean.

Over time, consistently repeated behaviours and ways of looking at things can become **habits**. Habits drive behaviour without most people realising, indeed, they probably drive most behaviour. Even thoughtful, reasoned behavioural decisions often rely upon habitual ways of thinking and behaving, such as the habitual belief that a flight of stairs will get you from one floor to another; we might think about why we want to visit someone, but not about using the stairs to get there. Meaning could be thought of, in a sense, as a group's habitual way of looking at things. Habits therefore join desires and beliefs about meaning as key drivers of behaviour.

These factors operate not just for people as **individuals** but also for **groups**. And the way they work for individuals is influenced by the groups people are a part of. Behaviour becomes aligned with, or is at least affected by, group expectations and practices: group **norms**. This happens, for example, because of a person's desire to belong; they develop an identity by reference to the group. Again, the development of group norms and beliefs is fundamentally affected by the goals of the group, its desired ends, and the need to make sense of its environment in pursuing them. So, a person's behaviour can vary depending on the groups the person belongs to: company staff, firm's running club, team of traders.

Financial markets are complex **ecosystems** of individuals and groups, which means that the processes mentioned above operate within a dense behavioural network. One of the defining features of financial markets is the presence of huge international financial firms operating through a multitude of subsidiary companies across multiple jurisdictions. These legal structures carry additional meanings (such as the idea of limited liability) that affect the behaviour of the groups of people assembled using them. A person can be in multiple groups at the same time, ways of behaving can pass between groups and the behaviour of individuals and groups is affected by what goes on in other groups. To make a practical difference, greater recognition of a social licence needs to influence each part of this ecosystem; the level of inter-dependence between the different parts means that change needs to happen in a coordinated way.

(continued)

(continued)

Financial markets are highly automated, and increasingly use forms of artificial intelligence. Does that make a difference? Certainly: it profoundly affects how markets and those within them behave. The full impact of AI, in particular, is yet to be felt and looks set to transform the sector. Nonetheless, the behavioural elements sketched out in this chapter remain key. Indeed, concepts of belief and desire figure prominently in attempts to model AI. Systems ultimately have to be designed and created, and operated and controlled by people.

So What?

If greater recognition of a social licence for financial markets is to make a practical difference, it must be able to influence the things discussed in this chapter in a way that generates greater positive reciprocity, and it must do so throughout the financial market ecosystem.

The date: November 2009. The place: Sotheby's New York. A work of art is up for auction: Andy Warhol's '200 One Dollar Bills', depicting a huge 20-by-10 grid of dollar bills. It is estimated to sell for between US$8–12 million, but the final sale price is a stunning US$43.8 million. The global economy is experiencing the worst crisis in living memory. At times last year, it almost seemed as if trust in money itself would collapse. Against that backdrop, for the art market to rebound quite like this is quite a surprise.[1]

Two hundred dollars. Except that these dollars were different from the sort in the auctioneer's wallet. Cut one out and hand it over at a coffee shop and it would not get you very far, unless the vendor recognised its provenance. However, an auction at Sotheby's was another matter. The image on the paper was essentially the same as an ordinary dollar bill, but not the behaviour induced. What accounts for differences like these? What drives behaviour? It is a key question in looking at the potential impact of greater recognition of a social licence for financial markets. Addressing the challenges and realising the opportunities outlined in Chap. 1 depends on how market participants, users and regulators *behave* from here on. There is a need for greater urgency. There is also a need to strengthen positive reciprocity in the relationships that comprise financial markets; an orientation of those relationships in a way that supports the social solidarity on which markets themselves rely. That cannot be imposed by law. It relies on change in the very substance of the multiple relationships that go to make up that wider relationship, involving the parties living, feeling and understanding them in a different way. Can the recognition that financial markets operate subject to a social licence help to deliver?

To begin to answer that, it is necessary to start by identifying some of the key drivers of human behaviour. That is the purpose of this chapter. It picks out four in particular. If greater recognition of a social licence is to make a practical difference, it needs to impact each of them: first, desires to achieve a particular outcome or end (see Sect. 2.1, below); secondly, beliefs about what things mean, such as money or works of art (see Sect. 2.2, below); thirdly, habit (see Sect. 2.3, below); and fourthly, the way individual behaviour is influenced by groups and social context, including the legal structures established to pursue common aims (see Sect. 2.4, below). Clearly, these factors are deeply interrelated. However, the first two are especially important. They influence individual and group behaviours directly but, over time, the resulting behaviours also get embedded in habits of thinking, seeing and behaving, so forming individual character and group culture.

Mention of groups is a reminder that financial markets resemble a form of ecosystem, comprised of multiple groups of individuals and firms interacting. Financial system outcomes ultimately result from the behaviour of individuals. However, the groups those individuals belong to and the interaction between groups affects their behaviour so that it is possible to talk about *group outcomes* as well as individual behavioural outcomes. Most obviously, the behavioural outcome of a group of people organised through a financial firm is entirely different from the same number of people acting individually. So, in addition to considering individual behaviour, this chapter also looks at what it means for a market or a firm within that market to 'behave' (see Sect. 2.5, below).

Because of this complex ecosystem, attempts to change financial market behaviour need to be system-wide, with each part of the system adjusting in relationship with the others.[2] Recognition of a social licence concerns the financial market ecosystem as a whole and each of its parts, with the potential to have a coordinating effect throughout.

Financial markets are increasingly automated. The trend will continue. It is likely to result in further significant structural change in the sector, which is another reason why the coordinates provided by the social licence could be so valuable. Because of that, in closing, this chapter considers briefly how the role of information technology and electronic trading alters the behavioural position (see Sect. 2.6, below).

Human behaviour is multi-layered; a complex interplay of biological, individual, familial and social factors.[3] Intellectual and physical features circumscribe what is possible, childhood experiences affect behaviour in adult life and so on. This chapter does not get into all that. Instead, it covers elements of human behaviour that are more susceptible to influence by the time people come together in financial markets. That is where recognition of a social licence has the greatest potential to impact behavioural outcomes. Even so, what follows is still inevitably high-level and will use shorthand in places.

2.1   Desire and Desired Ends

There are some consistently recurring themes in the way people have tried to explain how humans behave, and what it means to live well. However, three are particularly prominent: they concern passion, reason and habit. The first emphasises how 'passion' impels or motivates people towards a certain end: 'Reason is, and ought only to be the slave of the passions, and can never pretend to any other office than to serve and obey them.'[4] So said Scottish enlightenment philosopher David Hume. In other words, it is passion that drives someone to act; reason alone cannot produce action.[5] A word like 'passion' can get used as a catch-all, but two elements are particularly relevant here: desire and emotion. The second set of explanations focuses on the way rational thought-processes are deployed in deciding and then, potentially, motivating what to do. This approach tends to be associated with philosophers such as Immanuel Kant, who saw reasoning as fundamental in determining what it is to live well and motivating decisions consistent with that (tending to privilege reason over passion). Thirdly, other accounts emphasise the role of habit in driving certain ways of thinking and acting.[6] So, for Aristotle, 'It makes no small difference ... whether we form habits of one kind or another ... it makes a very great difference, or rather *all* the difference.'[7] Likewise, for David Hume, 'Habits, more than reason, we find, in everything, to be the governing principle of mankind.'[8]

As noted, these three elements are recurring themes. However, most accounts of human behaviour have some role for each, even if the relationship between them varies.[9] They are not rigid categories, and most behavioural steps probably involve all of them in some way. Indeed, neuroscientific evidence seems to confirm that, with desire and habit playing a particularly important role.[10] Subsequent sections will pick up on the role of reason and habit, but what of the motivating power of desire?

2.1.1   Desire

The narratives discussed in Chap. 1 make a strong connection between financial markets and desire in the form of financial self-interest. In a financial market context, desire usually has an object, a goal, a valued outcome—an end.[11] It motivates a person to secure that end. It affects what they do and the way they do it—their behaviour. You want a particular financial return. I want to help you, so I design a derivative that I think will generate it for you. Except that I also want to make a lot of money, so I design the derivative in a way that maximises my return in ways that will not be visible to you. Desires are at work throughout the chain.

But what is desire? It can be thought of as a combination of feeling, thinking and, usually, acting. Features commonly associated with desire tend to include at least: an end that a person believes is in some way good; that person being prepared to take steps that he or she believes will help to realise the end; that person anticipating some sort of pleasure or satisfaction in the end being realised, or dissatisfaction if it is not. The end is something that is *valued*, and desire is a motivating feeling of aspiration towards it. A desired end is a source of perceived value. Chapter 4 will suggest that talk of a social licence is connected with ends people value.

Taking this a step further, it is possible to distinguish between two sorts of desire: *intrinsic* and *instrumental*.[12] This distinction is important to what will follow, so it is worth pausing on it. Both sorts of desire can be seen at work in financial markets. Intrinsic desires are foundational. They address an end that is wanted for itself: an end that is not wanted simply to achieve some other end. For individuals, the most obvious intrinsic desire is for personal wellbeing. However, it is plausible that there are others, such as an aspiration for others' welfare, for example, for a loved one's recovery from illness, for famine victims to be fed or, at the most general level, for justice to prevail.[13] This distinction between self-interest and others' interests as intrinsic desires is also important for what follows. The next chapter will return to it.

Intrinsic desires lie behind instrumental desires. Instrumental desires are, essentially, things it would be desirable to achieve to bring the world into line with what is intrinsically desired. Instrumental desires, then, are directed at an end that is not wanted for itself, but as a step towards achieving some other end. For example, a trader might have an instrumental desire to reach a year-end target, with the instrumental desire of securing a bonus, with the instrumental desire of buying a house in the country, because the trader associates that with an intrinsic desire for wellbeing. In each case, achieving the immediate goal is instrumental to the ultimate end (even if the ultimate end is not consciously acknowledged at the time). The distinction between intrinsic and instrumental desires may not always be clear-cut. For example, there could come a point where the meaning of money is so closely entwined with a trader's sense of who they are, that steps taken to possess it are not just instrumental, but become effectively an expression of intrinsic desire—an end in itself. Again, the next chapter will pick up on this.

Importantly, just because an end, such as the wellbeing of others, is desired does not necessarily mean that a person will act to realise it. Among other things, the differing strength and salience of desires leads to prioritisation. For example, an investment adviser might want to serve a client well, but could still end up advising them to take a less beneficial course of action because it benefits the adviser in some way.[14] Greater recognition of the social licence for financial markets may be important here because of its potential to strengthen the salience of some desires in relation to others (see Sect. 6.3).

2.1.2 Emotions

If desires motivate people in financial markets, where does that leave emotions? Surely they are a key motivator as well, most visibly in the panic of a bank run or the 'irrational exuberance' of the stock markets.[15] For current purposes, it is helpful to draw out two features of emotions.

First, if desire is a sense of aspiration towards a valued end, emotions often involve evaluating current circumstances against that end.[16] Emotions of this sort are based, among other things, on conscious and non-conscious beliefs about the world—beliefs about what it means (see Sect. 2.2 below). They help make people aware of the extent to which current circumstances (at least as they believe them to be) are consistent with a desired end. For example, a person with a valued goal (such as winning a business pitch) may experience frustration where they perceive another person's behaviour to be detrimental to the attainment of the goal. Returning to the populist narratives of fracture discussed in Chap. 1, research has often linked anger to the perception that a situation is unjust or unfair.[17]

Secondly, many emotions are related to changes in motivation to act. Based on a desired end, emotions can heighten or reduce motivation to act to achieve that end. Emotions of this sort produce a physical reaction that signals the need to act to realise the desired end, mobilising resources in response. For example, the move from mild irritation to anger is often connected with steps to remedy a perceived injustice arising from a behavioural line-crossing, in particular by punishing the behaviour.[18] The widespread anger that led to former RBS CEO, Fred Goodwin, being stripped of his knighthood following RBS's near collapse is a case in point.[19]

So, the impact of emotions on behaviour depends on a person's assessment of what a given set of circumstances means, the extent of divergence between that assessment and a desired end state and the importance to the person of the relevant end. The assessment need not be accurate to motivate action; for example, it may be based upon an inadequate understanding of the situation, like the collective mistake about economic models discussed in Chap. 1. However, where an assessment is inaccurate, the resulting action may not realise the person's desired end, or may even undermine it. Think of the, probably apocryphal, story of Sir Isaac Newton, who lost a fortune in the bursting of the South Sea Bubble in 1720, having failed to apply the principle to rising markets that what goes up must come down.[20] History has been repeating itself more recently in the froth of the cryptocurrency markets. The phenomenon of market panics is a reminder that these assessments are not made in isolation; people can be swept along by the 'emotions of the crowd', but more of groups in a moment.

2.2   Beliefs About the World—Meaning

This leads on to how a person's beliefs about his or her circumstances—what those circumstances mean—can influence behaviour. The dollar bill in a person's wallet and Andy Warhol's dollars look essentially the same, and both have a value that can be measured in monetary terms. But that is where it ends. People take them to mean something quite different. The enormous dollar value attaching to Warhol's work reflects that: a representation of money, but traded at prices vastly exceeding the money it depicts.

Differences like these are neither isolated nor static. The meaning ascribed to something can change over time, and the meaning of one thing can affect the meaning of others. As meaning changes, so do patterns of behaviour. Apply a financial measure to a work of art and you affect what it means and how people respond to it. Conversely, part of Warhol's purpose in 1962 in creating his work was to say something about the meaning of dollars. He presented reality, including art, covered by dollars: a symbol of US power and a ticket to satisfy desires. Yet, by the time of the auction, dollars were defining art in a different way. The original meaning of the piece was changing. The status of the dollar was faltering, rocked among other things by the onset of the 2008 financial crisis. Against that backdrop, the work acquired a certain irony. But there was a further irony. The auction of Warhol's piece marked the start of a ten-year period of rising prices and accelerating financialisation in the art market. The high-end art market would increasingly be driven by investment activity, with the involvement of the very industry that had only just sent art prices into a dive.[21] One reason for that was the wealthy attempting to diversify their assets.[22] What was their desired end? In part, they wanted to protect themselves from a change in the meaning of money. There was a risk of inflation, undermining its power, which made the meaning of art look suddenly attractive. Changes in meaning have behavioural consequences. They alter how people pursue their desired ends.

What do these beliefs about the meaning of the world consist of? Broadly, beliefs arise where a person has an attitude towards a particular thing or state of affairs which the person would regard as true. We encountered them in Chap. 1, in the stories that get told about financial markets. It is worth highlighting three features of beliefs of this sort. First, they concern the world that presents itself to the person who holds the belief, both the natural world (of seas, mountains and the like) and the social world (of what humans make, such as money, governments, football teams and so on). These beliefs are a form of memory that stores the sense people make of the information around them. Secondly, they are not always consciously present to people, even when relevant to a particular decision: I believe that a combination of gravity and a flight of stairs will enable me to realise my purpose of getting from one floor of my office building to a colleague on another floor, but would never pause to think about it before setting out. So, there is a sense in which many of these beliefs are habitual and held 'in practice'. Thirdly, in a social context at least, their power derives from the fact that they are collective. Dollars do what they do not just because of what one person believes, but because that belief is shared *and* all of us believe that it is shared. The meaning rests on a consensus about what money is and how it can be used.

Where do these beliefs come from? Up to a point, this brings us back to desired ends.[23] Seeking to realise a desired end involves a process of imagining and testing different possible accounts of the mass of information that presents itself, by reference to that end. The meaning with the 'best fit' emerges.[24] Something like this happens when lawyers advise on the meaning of a piece of legislation; the alternative possibilities are imagined and tested, and the most appropriate selected. This sense-making process happens within parameters, such as the physical reality of the natural world or, in the case of the law, the letter of the legislation—you cannot deny gravity, and a lawyer cannot ignore what is there in print. However, within that, making meaning is fundamental to being human. That may make the search for meaning sound like a conscious, deliberative process. However, much of this field of beliefs is not consciously learnt. Like language, and in large part through language, meaning gets absorbed in and through observing the social world, for example, as trainees join financial institutions and watch how people interact. A process of learning and imitation is involved as we draw on the meaning-making of others in our community who have gone before. The group context is critical (see Sect. 2.4, below).

2.2.1 Meaning in Financial Markets

Financial markets are dense networks of meaning. In a sense, they are 'webs of significance' spun by humans in which we and our institutions are suspended.[25] That spinning takes place, as people pursue their desired ends, but the resulting meaning, in turn, creates the context for the pursuit of those ends. Given the profound impact of beliefs about meaning on behaviour, it is worth pausing to identify some of the dominant sources of meaning in the financial world. There are many possible candidates, but what gives an overarching sense of the meaning of what is going on? One of the most significant sources, as in other spheres of life, is narratives; narratives and other mental models are a particularly powerful way in which humans make sense of reality and communicate that meaning (see Sect. 2.3, below, and Chap. 6). The narratives discussed in Chap. 1—narratives of fracture between finance and society, financial narratives of the *Wolf of Wall Street* genre and the economic models—highlight two further meaning sources particularly: the meaning of money and the meaning of language. The recognition of a social licence for financial markets is relevant to both. It concerns the meaning and role of money, and effectively advances a new language about financial markets. In doing so, it draws attention to a radically different account of what is going on (see Chap. 4).

2.2.2 The Meaning of Money

The power of the meaning of money has already emerged as an important theme in Chap. 1. It is obviously central to financial market behaviour. However, it also affects the very structure of markets and financial firms and shapes the lives of those within them.

Markets revolve around money. They move it from those with a surplus to those who can pay to use it. Financial firms hold money for others, borrow it and lend it on; they transact in money and in legal claims of one person on another (such as bonds) expressed in monetary terms; they help others to do so; they value assets and risks by reference to money; they assess the likelihood that money invested will yield more money or be lost; they help people use money to manage their risks. Firms reward staff using it. Money is not just a means of buying things. It operates as a symbol and measure of power and value, and so is a key basis of comparison between businesses (ask any fund manager) and individuals (ask those involved in bonus processes). As noted in Chap. 1, money is not 'neutral'. It has a significant bearing on the structures that get created to carry on business, the teams that are put in place and the lives of those within them. A succession of reports on failures in financial institutions in recent years attests to the destructive power of money to define and shape firms and people.[26] That is one reason for the detailed regulatory rules that now govern staff remuneration in financial firms.[27]

Yet the meaning of money itself emerges, in part, from market activity; money would not have developed without markets or markets without money. Markets shape the meaning of money, for example, through the emergence of cryptocurrencies. In turn, market activity is based on what markets have helped to shape. In this sense institutions and those within them are both meaning makers and meaning made; they shape and are shaped, among other things, by the meaning of money.

2.2.3 The Meaning of Language

But perhaps the most significant meaning source, in markets as elsewhere, is language—the language used to carry on business, to describe and regulate financial transactions, to operate markets and financial firms and to rehearse narratives about what is going on. Language shapes market realities at every level. Although finance has become increasingly electronic, it still relies on the ability to communicate. Language is part of the very substance of how people think about the world and seek to express its meaning.[28] Syme, in George Orwell's *Nineteen Eighty-Four*, recognises the depth of the relationship, even if he overstates it:

> Don't you see that the whole aim of Newspeak is to narrow the range of thought? In the end we shall make thoughtcrime literally impossible, because there will be no words in which to express it. Every concept that can ever be needed will be expressed by exactly *one* word, with its meaning rigidly defined and all its subsidiary meanings rubbed out and forgotten.[29]

Language is also relational. Communication occurs within relationships. It is part of their essence. Language is vital to the way relationships grow and develop. Meaning emerges from its use, and the language used by one person can influence the behavioural decisions of others. In that sense, using language does not just make meaning, but also people (see Chap. 6, Sect. 6.5).[30] As with beliefs more generally, the meaning in language is largely absorbed rather than formally learnt, and lies beyond the conscious.

Different kinds of language carry different sorts of meaning. Chapter 1 has already touched on the meaning advanced by language in narratives. But there is also another kind of language which powerfully shapes financial markets and those within them—legal language. In spite of the limits of the regulatory tool-box, highlighted in Chap. 1, the extensive role of law and regulation in financial market activity means that it will remain significant in any attempt to change market behaviour.

Because of that, Chap. 5 looks at its connection with talk of a social licence for financial markets. However, for now, note how, more than any other sort of business, finance and investment is a legally defined exercise. A financial firm will normally be established as a company (a legal construct); it will need to be 'authorised' to do business (another legal construct); its activities must comply with legal rules (more law); most financial business involves dealing in legal claims, entering into legal obligations or helping others to do so (a derivative is a form of legal agreement, a bond is too, and so on). Offer shares to the public and the prospectus must comply with legal requirements. Property rights are defined by law, as is the process for dealing in them if the owner becomes insolvent; the winding up of Lehman Brothers involved a massive exercise in identifying everyone's legal claims.

Importantly, legal language does not just describe what already exists in financial markets or provide a way of enforcing rights. It has a unique linguistic power to make something socially true simply by saying it, such as by providing for limited liability companies. It changes the meaning of what is going on and, in doing so, alters behaviour.[31] For example, law is used to categorise kinds of activity so that one sort is regulated differently from another and, as a result, has to be conducted differently. If you are a UK banking group and accept deposits from private individuals, your group structure will be different from banks that do not. You will have to establish a separate banking company to hold their money (known as 'ring-fencing').[32] Likewise, the Act of Parliament which establishes the regulatory framework for financial services in the UK, the Financial Services and Markets Act 2000, is based on a legal categorisation of each sort of financial activity (from insurance and banking to investment management and broking). Different rules then apply to the way in which each activity is carried on.[33] Legal language changes what it means to engage in those activities and consequently shapes the structures within and by reference to which activity takes place, and the lives of those involved.

2.3   Habit and Reason

The interaction between desires and beliefs about the meaning of the world can be thought of as shaping behaviour through two basic mental processes.[34] If the social licence for financial markets is to be a source of behaviour change, it needs to influence both.

The first process is 'bottom-up'. It is deliberative, conscious and reasoned. It involves a person accumulating relevant information about a situation, assessing what it means and deciding how to act to realise a desired end. Deliberation of this sort requires effort. Consequently, it is more likely to happen where a situation really demands it, for example, because it is novel or unfamiliar, technically challenging, requires planning or involves overcoming some sort of habit. A lot of decisions in financial markets are just like that.

However, a second process is also at work which is more 'top-down', automatic and less conscious, and this accounts for a great deal more of what is going on in financial markets. It is closely related to habit. Essentially, it involves relying on 'behavioural models' in determining how to act in a given situation. Rather than building up a complete picture of a situation to use in making a decision, the person defaults to relying on a basic framework for dealing with situations of that sort, gaps in knowledge being filled by using previous experience, rules of thumb and assumptions.[35] My descent of the stairs to visit a colleague is 'top-down' in more ways than one. Most behaviour tends to rely to some degree on these more habituated, top-down processes, as has long been recognised. Top-down processing influences more deliberative behaviour as well, since bottom-up processing will often partly rely on more automatic processes. For example, even the most cautious lawyers do not generally pause to weigh up the precise meaning of every word before using it in a contract (otherwise, they would not get past the first clause) and most investment managers will pay little regard to the meaning of money in managing a portfolio of shares.

2.3.1   Models, Schemas and Narratives

The influence of behavioural models on behaviour in the 'top-down' process seems to happen in two stages, each taking place with potentially little conscious control. Step one, the person perceives certain things about a situation, assesses their significance by reference to, among other things, memories of similar situations, and then uses this to categorise the situation. So, this step is closely connected with the perceived meaning of the situation for that person and their desired goals. For example, financial advisors hoping to sell investment products often distinguish between professional investors and retail clients in this way, so placing the conversation they are about to have in one category or the other. However, a person may also categorise by reference to their own various identities—for example, work as compared with family or non-work identities.

At step two, a form of behavioural model for situations of that type is thought to come into play, following categorisation. So, in the case of professional/retail categorisation, the associated models are likely to affect how business is done (the sort of products sold, the way they are sold, the risks disclosed, the language used, and so on). Different disciplines talk about these behavioural models in various ways and they may not all be describing exactly the same thing.[36] However, psychologists use the concept of 'schemas' or 'schemata'.[37] Schemas involve an organised framework of knowledge: an arrangement of inter-related beliefs, meanings, expectations and rules, based in part on the memory of multiple previous experiences that the person concerned will apply where that framework is perceived as relevant to a given situation. Which schema gets applied in a given situation will depend on the goal of the person concerned.[38] Other factors may also come into play; for example, schemas that are habitually used or more salient in the memory may be more accessible.[39]

Schemas related to action are goal-orientated (they operate by reference to a desired end) organising accumulated knowledge to enable people to interpret and respond to situations they encounter. For example, someone walking into the offices of a client categorises the situation differently from arrival at a friend's house for dinner. As a result, they will run a different 'script' for approaching encounters in that setting; they will apply a set of assumptions and understandings about the purpose and meaning of the interaction and how it ought to run to secure an appropriate outcome.[40] This will affect the nature and result of the interaction. Mix up the scripts, and things might go wrong; for example, offence as a result of undue formality with a friend or over-familiarity with a client.

Chapter 1 identified a need for behaviour change. One way of approaching that in the context of top-down processing is to try to influence which schemas get selected in the first place. But what about the schemas themselves? If they are so influential, can they change and, if so, how? A feature of schemas is indeed their adaptability. As with beliefs and language, to a significant degree, schemas are not consciously learnt, but tend to be absorbed from the social environment as people grow and interact. They can adjust incrementally over time. In particular, schemas can mature to reflect a person's experience of their social environment, encoding new information. They may also change more fundamentally if an environment turns out to be different from how it was thought to be; for example, the sort of shock experienced by Mr. Greenspan at the outbreak of the financial crisis, discussed in Chap. 1.[41]

From this brief outline, it seems reasonable to suppose that greater recognition of a social licence for financial markets could have an important influence on both bottom-up and top-down processes in financial markets. That is because of the meaning it advances of financial market activity, and the aspirations it seems to embed (see Chap. 4). Both seem relevant to deliberative reasoning, categorisation and, if schemas adjust over time, the development of schemas themselves. Chapter 6 looks in more detail at its potential to influence each of these.

What about the sort of narratives and associated economic models discussed in Chap. 1? Are these schemas? These concepts are not tightly defined, so there may be an overlap between them.[42] However, it may be more helpful to think of narratives of this sort as proving a broader framework of meaning within which various schemas are contextualised—much as just described in the case of a social licence for financial markets. Again, Chap. 6 will return to this.

2.4   People in Markets—the Group Dimension

Individuals do not act in isolation. As noted earlier, financial markets are an ecosystem of individuals and groups—places of social interaction. These groups also shape individual behaviour. That is one reason why groups emerge: groups enable people to pursue goals they cannot realise on their own. But groups also have a more profound impact on individual behaviour, recognised in talk about the need to improve culture in financial institutions.

Section 2.2, above, looked at how people's beliefs about the meaning of the world shape their behaviour. Meaning of this sort does not arise spontaneously. It involves some level of group consensus. Language is intelligible because there is a common understanding about what it means. Money has the power it does, because it is accepted by a group. Similar processes of definition are at work in the groups that comprise financial markets. These processes shape those within the group, and their behaviour. In this sense, the desires people have, their beliefs about meaning, and the models and frameworks they apply in determining how to behave are not entirely their own.[43] The inter-relationships involved are highly complex. What follows is no more than an outline of three ways in which group participation affects individual behaviour that are particularly relevant here: first, how individuals come to conform their behaviour with group standards (Sect. 2.4.1, below); secondly how group power structures can determine individual behaviour (Sect. 2.4.2 below); and thirdly, the impact of legal structures on individual behaviour (Sect. 2.4.3 below). In each case, greater recognition of a social licence has the potential to influence the way they operate (see Chap. 6).

But first, what sorts of groups are involved in financial markets? Groups may develop within a particular market (the fellow traders you have a drink with after work), or industry sector (for example, through trade associations). Individuals will also usually be employees—in a relationship with their firm and other staff. Those employers are often large international financial firms. Indeed, these firms are one of the defining features of modern financial markets. Large international firms can be looked at in two ways, each of which is relevant to understanding the impact of a person's social context on their behaviour: legal and organic. First, they are legal structures, comprised of a holding company and multiple subsidiary companies, each operating in a different jurisdiction and employing staff locally. The structure operates according to a hierarchy of legal control, cascading down from the parent company. But, secondly, these legal structures are also a way of organising an organic network of relationships; the business of a firm is essentially in the hands of groups of staff working together through business divisions and less formal associations. The emergence of large international firms means that influences on people's behaviour now transcend the circumstances in any single company, jurisdiction or political system and cannot be controlled by any individual.[44]

The myriad of different groups, and frequent cross-membership between them, means that what happens in one group influences another. It is because of this ecosystem that any process of behaviour change in financial markets must necessarily operate at many different levels.

2.4.1 Individuals Conforming with Group Standards—'Norms'

Commonly accepted standards of behaviour and beliefs about meaning in a group are often referred to as 'social norms'. When you go to a coffee shop, you expect everyone to behave in a particular way, and you do the same yourself. If a fire alarm goes off while you are there, another set of commonly assumed behaviours will come into play. Social norms have been defined in various ways and, as usual, views diverge on precisely what they are.[45] However, in their broadest sense, they are standards that are shared by a group and can commonly be perceived as guiding behaviour within it. That loose definition covers a range of finer distinctions. Chapter 5 returns to some of these. As with commonly accepted meanings, people are often not conscious of group norms influencing their behaviour and consequently the resulting behaviours may simply be experienced as 'normal'. Indeed, norms have been described as a grammar of social interaction because of the way, like language, they are absorbed and determine interaction within the group.[46] It is impossible to live in a group and not be influenced by them.

This means that much human behaviour 'follows' rules, but not in the way people often think. It is not a case of 'there is a law, therefore I act', first because little of life is covered by legal rules and, secondly, even when there are legal rules, people rarely consciously comply with them. Most people do not need a law against murder to prevent them from strangling someone who pushes in front of them at the checkout, but then people rarely do push in because of the social norm of queuing. Social norms can be much more powerful in driving behaviour than laws and regulations (see Sect. 6.6).

Two aspects of how individuals come to follow norms need attention here: where do the norms come from and, once the norms are there, why do people conform to them?

The Origin of Norms

Broadly, norms emerge as groups of people seek to negotiate the circumstances they face. Norms are therefore related at some level to two things: first, people's goals (or desired ends) in charting a way through the reality that confronts them and, secondly, the process of defining or giving that reality meaning, so removing uncertainty.[47]

Starting with the first, the relationship between a group's goals and the norms that emerge is obvious, especially in business settings. Businesses involve a network of formal and informal operating standards, all trained on achieving the goals of the organisation, from induction processes for new recruits to appraisals and quality-control testing. Academic studies show something similar.[48] It is one reason why there is so much interest in the question of company purpose at the moment (see Chap. 1).

The other way norms emerge—in ordering or giving meaning to people's circumstances—should also be familiar to those in business. As lawyers know well, legal rules are often introduced to reduce uncertainty by defining relationships and rights more precisely. For example, the EU Settlement Finality

Directive[49] and the EU Financial Collateral Directive[50] seek to reduce uncertainty over the treatment of payments, securities transfers and collateral (such as securities delivered as collateral for a derivative transaction), among other things, when a party to a transaction becomes insolvent. They do it by clarifying the legal status of different parts of a transaction and hence their social meaning. However, this function is not confined to legal norms. Academic studies suggest that a wider process of sense-making is ongoing in groups. Take, for example, work building on a series of experiments by psychologist, Muzsafa Sherif.[51] In Sherif's experiments, individuals' assessment of how far a spot of light was moving in a darkened room converged by reference to those of the rest of the group; in a sense, then, the group seems to have been defining reality. Once the standard had emerged, it continued to influence group members' assessments even when they were taken out of the group.

Indeed, it follows from examples already considered—language, money, auctions, laws, financial markets, regulators and so on—that the meaning of the social world is, in large part, socially determined (i.e. in some way established by groups) because of how it emerges and is carried and acted out in social practices. This process of meaning-making, sometimes referred to as 'social construction', operates within parameters.[52] However, a process of making sense is ongoing and is closely related to the norms that emerge.[53]

Why Do Individuals Conform with Group Norms?

Three reasons tend to predominate in answers to that. First, individuals sometimes adopt norms for the same reason as groups do; they may help to address an individual's sense of uncertainty in situations they are unfamiliar with.[54] People often consult financial services lawyers to find out 'what market practice is' on various aspects of the regulatory regime; in other words, what is the norm? They use this information to decide how to act. Back in 1936, John Maynard Keynes came up with his own take on this in financial markets. He memorably described how the investment process can come to resemble a beauty contest, so that it is more of an exercise in attempting to second-guess the effect of investor group-think than assessing fundamental underlying value.[55]

Secondly, compliance with group norms is generally necessary to progress within a group.[56] Following group norms that coordinate activity may be the easiest way to function, for example, by not driving on the wrong side of the road. However, divergence from group norms can also be socially 'punished'.[57] A series of experiments by psychologist, Solomon Asch seems to point to this.

Subjects were shown a picture of three lines and asked to decide in various group settings which of them matched the length of a base-line. By introducing 'stooges' into the groups who deliberately provided an incorrect response, Asch demonstrated the considerable impact of a majority judgement on that of an individual, even when the judgement was clearly wrong. Not being aligned with the majority carried a risk of social sanction through losing respect.[58]

Thirdly, a person may develop a sense of attachment to a group and wish to identify with it by adopting its norms. This may be partly driven by a basic need of individuals to be able to evaluate and thereby validate opinions they hold. Indeed, a person's selection of which groups to join may be influenced by the person's assessment of the proximity between their own beliefs and attitudes, and those of the group, with the tendency to compare decreasing as the divergence becomes greater.[59] So, a process of self-selection goes on in relation to group membership, highlighting why the current emphasis in business upon diversity and challenge is so important to address 'group think'. Either way, the group's norms get adopted because it is a group the individual trusts and wants to be part of—much as a finance employee might follow the internal arrangements put in place to ensure that the business achieves its goals.

These three reasons for adopting group norms can interact. For example, people sometimes comment on how fast trainees in a financial institution learn the behavioural ropes. This happens at a point when they are likely to have the highest level of uncertainty about what is expected of them, but are most keen to be accepted. However, having decided that the firm concerned 'fits' with who they are, they are already predisposed to adopt the standards applied in the group. In all of this, an individual's desired ends, and their need to find meaning in pursuing them, clearly have an important role.

What does this step of conforming to group norms involve in practice? Essentially, internalisation or compliance. With internalisation, a person adjusts his or her beliefs and attitudes to be consistent with those of the group. It has been suggested that this involves the integration of the norm into the individual's narratives or schemas, discussed above, so that they get applied on future occasions.[60] By contrast, compliance is where only a person's publicly expressed attitudes and behaviours are aligned with group norms, not those they hold privately. They 'comply' as a result of experiencing some form of social force. The use of the word 'compliance' will immediately resonate with anyone in the finance sector; all financial firms are required to have a compliance department the role of which is to ensure that regulatory rules are followed. Compliant behaviour may cease once the force is withdrawn. However, where norms have been internalised, a person may continue to follow them even after leaving the group and, significantly for the prospects of behaviour change in financial institutions, especially where they have been internalised in an organisational setting.[61] This 'stickiness' of internalised norms suggests that attempts to change behaviour need both to address negative norms that have become internalised and to foster the internalisation of positive norms.

2.4.2   Authority, Power and Obedience

Talk of enforced compliance leads on to how authority and power operate in groups to influence behaviour. Power structures develop within groups: individuals and sub-groups whose power rests on their relationship with a wider group, but whose beliefs, desires and values may not be fully aligned with the group. As noted, in large financial firms, systems of relationships that shape behaviour do not necessarily emanate from the board of individual group companies, but are more organic, operating across the group. Power can be based on various factors, but a common feature in practice is the ability of particular individual or group to win business for the institution.

The powerful effect of authority on behaviour was famously demonstrated by psychologist Stanley Milgram. Milgram's series of experiments involved random members of the public[62] being instructed by a person they thought was a scientist to administer what they believed were electric shocks of an increasingly severe and ultimately fatal magnitude to another individual who, unknown to them, was an actor.[63] A disturbingly high percentage were prepared to administer shocks that would have been fatal had they not been fake. A range of factors may have been behind this including not just a perception of the coercive power of the scientist, but also their legitimacy and expertise.[64] Relationships such as these are important determinants of individual behaviour, sometimes because of the way they can affect perception of group norms[65] (for example, the divisional head giving voice to the group's expectations) and sometimes in ways that are more connected with the exercise of power (for example, a business head setting a financial target).

2.4.3   The Impact of Legal Structures on Individual Behaviour

Finally, the legal structures used by groups to pursue their desired ends can also affect individual behaviour. A prime example is the limited liability company. It was regularly suggested following 2008 that financial businesses would have been run more prudently had they been carried on through partnerships, where the members could not benefit from limited liability.[66] Indeed, many UK banks may have been slow to adopt limited liability status when originally introduced in the mid-nineteenth century precisely for this reason. They wanted to emphasise to depositors that the bank's owners stood personally behind deposits and would therefore be more prudent in running the bank.[67]

Another example results from the way legal obligations in financial markets tend to apply to companies more than individual staff. As a result, responsibility for compliance can become dissipated among the company's officers and other agents since the rules do not apply to any of them individually. Where that happens a company's veil of incorporation creates not only limited liability for members but also, potentially, a sense of limited individual responsibility among officers and staff.[68] It took the 2008 crisis and a string of subsequent scandals for this to receive greater regulatory attention in the UK. As a result, UK regulators introduced what is known as the 'Senior Managers Regime' for directors and other senior staff in UK financial firms. Essentially, this seeks to counter the dissipation of responsibility by placing identified senior managers under a direct regulatory duty to ensure that UK regulatory requirements are complied with in their part of the firm.[69] Similar thinking lies behind US Department of Justice prosecutorial guidelines that focus attention on the role of individuals in the context of prosecuting corporate crime.[70]

2.5 Markets and Firms 'Behaving'—the Continuing Role of Individuals

So far, the focus has been on *individual behaviour*. However, the social licence for financial markets concerns markets. What does it mean to talk about markets and firms that deal in them 'behaving'? Is it the same as individual behaviour and, if so, in what sense?

This can be considered from two perspectives: first, the behaviour of markets and firms *as legal structures* (see Sect. 2.5.1, below), and secondly, the *group behaviour* of people that are brought together using those structures (see Sect. 2.5.2, below). Ultimately, the behaviour of both markets and companies comes back to the behaviour of individuals alone and in groups. If greater recognition of a social licence for financial markets is to influence markets or the companies that operate in them, that must be the prime focus. However, as just noted, legal and group settings do have an important impact on individual behaviour. To influence behaviour, the recognition of a social licence therefore needs to have an impact at this level of the financial ecosystem as well.

2.5.1   Markets and Firms as Legal Structures

Starting with markets as legal structures, people sometimes talk about markets as if they behaved like humans. 'Do financial markets care about a blue wave, red wall or gridlock?' ran a *Financial Times* headline shortly before the close of polling in the US midterm elections in November 2018.[71] Markets caring? How? We tend to anthropomorphise markets, for example, by talking about their 'invisible hand' (see Chap. 1). But markets are clearly not people. They are places where financial firms come together to trade. In most cases, these markets have some level of legal definition: we assign them to legal categories such as 'recognised investment exchange'; those who operate them usually have to be authorised; and there are rules for those who deal in them.[72] However, these legal structures do not have a mind to reason with and cannot hold beliefs or experience emotions and desires. Talk of markets having human qualities, such as 'caring', only makes sense as shorthand for the collective sentiments of those who participate in them.

Likewise, as a legal matter, most firms are established as companies. Like the legal structure of a market, a company as a legal construct does not have the ability to feel or reason. Because of this, for example, people have struggled with the idea of companies having moral agency and whether they have a distinct role in political processes.[73] So, what is it for a company to 'behave'?

In the UK, companies are incorporated under the Companies Act 2006 and are treated as an artificial legal person (whereas individuals are 'natural persons'). In other words, a company has a legal identity which is distinct from its members, officers and staff.[74] This is how limited liability for a company's shareholders is established. What does it mean to talk about this legal structure deciding or acting to achieve something? The answer the English courts have developed is, essentially, to treat the company as acting through natural persons. This has the merit of being consistent with what happens in practice: companies can only act through humans. In particular, the courts look to the board of directors and those operating under their authority or, in limited cases, another person who can be treated as the 'directing mind and will' of the company for the relevant purpose.[75] Where this happens, the knowledge, decisions and activities of the person or group of people concerned on behalf of the company are attributed to the company.

In a sense, therefore, individual behaviour also becomes the behaviour of the company.[76] Because of this, the behavioural sketch for individuals above is also relevant to corporate and market behaviour.

2.5.2 Markets and Firms—the Organic Perspective

However, markets and firms are more than legal structures. Legal structures provide a framework for gathering groups of people to pursue ends specific to that group. The impact of a group, especially when concentrated through a legal structure, is greater than its parts; it is not just an aggregate of the individual behaviours. Rather, it involves, first, coming together to pursue a desired end which cannot be achieved by individuals alone, and, secondly, some level of common intention about that end and the framework for pursuing it.[77] Several people dealing in shares on the stock market are performing similar activity, but it is not shared as it would be if they were all working together on a project, such as mounting a takeover of a listed company. That is something 'we' do together, and the difference between the two activities is recognised in the codes that govern takeover activity.

This need to facilitate group activity was partly behind the creation of English limited liability companies culminating in the Companies Act 1862; individuals cannot marshal the resources to achieve a goal like building railways, but companies can.[78] Legal structures can concentrate and augment the behavioural effect of a group, so much so in the case of global financial firms that many are now regulated as 'globally systemically important banks' (or 'G-SIBs') because of the material risk their collapse would pose to financial stability.[79] The goals of an enterprise, the legal structure used and behavioural outcomes are closely related. However, behind this nonetheless remains a group of people.

So, in understanding what it means for markets or financial firms 'behave', it is also necessary to bear in mind the workings of these groups. Financial firms are not just legal vehicles, but also 'organic' human structures. Technically, each subsidiary company in an international financial firm is an autonomous legal unit, run by its directors and subject to the control of a chain of shareholders running up to the holding company. However, in practice, their business is generally 'matrix managed': centrally managed group-wide divisions operate through the subsidiary companies. For example, a global head of share trading may be based in a company in London or New York, but have strategic responsibility for equities traders in local subsidiary companies across the world; traders are just as likely to take instructions from this global head as they are the directors in the company that employs them. While the legal network of individual subsidiary companies is not ignored, the use of matrix management reflects the essentially human structure of the enterprise, sometimes represented diagrammatically in the form of an 'organogram'.

From this 'organic' perspective, individual behaviours still remain key in determining behavioural outcomes. However, the *effect* of those behaviours is changed through group membership. Again, therefore, if recognition of a social licence is to make a difference in financial markets, it must exert an influence at this group level as well.

2.6   A Note on Technology

Finally, what about the impact of technology on this? As noted in Chap. 1, rapid technological development is likely to drive major structural change in the finance sector in the years ahead. However, finance is already highly IT dependent—so much so that people in financial firms sometimes tell you that their firm is little more than an IT company wrapped in a banking licence. That is an exaggeration, but not much. If IT plays such an extensive role, is it still relevant to talk about individual and group behaviour?

It is indeed essential to appreciate how far trading activity has moved from face-to-face or even telephone dealing, and is continuing to change fundamentally with the advance of 'intelligent computing'.[80] In practice, a considerable proportion of market trading is now controlled by computers, often applying algorithmic trading strategies, sometimes enhanced using forms of artificial intelligence. For example, a computer may be programmed to 'learn' from previous trading patterns, such as increasing market volatility, and adjust its trading activity accordingly. Estimates vary, but most tend to put computerised trading in shares in the New York and London markets at well over half of all trades, and trading in other forms of financial instruments is moving the same way.

These trading systems can sometimes interact with each other in unpredictable ways, leading to unexpected trading patterns. For example, they may have led to higher levels of volatility in some markets.[81] Most famously, they were behind the so-called Flash Crash in US equities on the afternoon of 6 May 2010 when the S&P plunged by over 8% in half an hour and then rebounded just as fast. This is all largely unseen by most people outside financial markets,[82] and is challenging even for many in financial firms, let alone their regulators, to stay ahead of. However, the important point to bear in mind for now is that financial firms are still run by people, as are many forms of financial market transaction. And even where trading activity is channelled through electronic systems, there is usually still significant human involvement at some level—not least in the process of designing, building and continuing to operate electronic strategies. It is still therefore necessary to focus on the various drivers of individual and group behaviour discussed above to assess how greater recognition of a social licence could positively influence behavioural outcomes.

2.7 Conclusion

This chapter has been no more than a sketch. However, where it points is this: ultimately, behaviour of and in financial markets comes down to individuals in relationships and groups pursuing desired ends based on their beliefs about the circumstances before them.

Desire both towards ultimate ends ('intrinsic desire') and the steps needed to reach those ends ('instrumental desire') is a motivating force. It operates by reference to the world as it is understood: its meaning as it is articulated through language and as it is believed to be and as experienced in the form of emotion. Some behavioural decisions rely heavily on reason, for example, in deciding which desires to pursue and in assessing how to realise them. More commonly, however, behaviour is driven by less conscious, more habitual, processes involving a rough and ready categorisation of situations and the application of pre-set narratives, models scripts or schemas for situations of that sort as a way of navigating the situation. Consistently repeated behaviours tend to become habitual: the interaction of desire, meaning and reason is therefore important not just to short-term behaviours, but also in the longer-term. Resulting behaviours can become matters of individual, institutional and systemic habit.

Individual beliefs, desires and emotions emerge in dialogue with others. In addition, they find common expression: there are common goals; there is the emotion of the group; we reason with ourselves, but we also reason with others and shared understandings emerge. As a result, individual behaviours are shaped by the groups to which people belong. However, group outcomes are also different from the aggregate of behaviours of individuals left to their own devices. People are shaped by group but, in turn, shape it and others. This shaping frequently occurs at a non-conscious level, the subterranean result of day-to-day activity.

The groups people belong to in financial markets overlap. The composition, history and circumstances of each group are unique and each group has its own goals. Each is a context in which people will encounter end goals and meanings that are those of that group and different from those of another. Individuals are involved in an iterative process with members of their group or groups in working out how to realise individual and group ends. Sometimes common understandings of meaning and group norms are explicitly agreed. More often, they simply emerge and are absorbed without group members being conscious of it. They can become embedded in personal mental models for how to behave.

Legal structures make possible the coordination and concentration of individual and group behaviours, but also influence them. Legal structures facilitate particular forms of cooperation over others, affect what ends it is possible to desire and create a framework of meaning within which desires are pursued. In doing so, they shape not just individual behaviour, but also 'corporate behaviour' and 'market behaviour'. Over time, these behaviours become habituated in the form of corporate and market cultures.

The recognition of a social licence for financial markets is relevant throughout this chain, and to each part of the complex financial ecosystem. Among other things, that is because it advances an account of the meaning and end goal of all financial activity, and provides a framework for reasoning about it and a language to use in doing so. However, before looking at what it has to say, it is important to establish what desired ends and meanings are seen at work in financial markets in practice. That is relevant both in understanding the substance of the social licence, but also the reality it has to influence to make a positive difference. It is the subject of the next chapter.

Notes

1. Roger Kamholz, 'Andy Warhol and "200 One Dollar Bills" ', Sotheby's, 3 November 2013 https://www.sothebys.com/en/articles/andy-warhol-and-200-one-dollar-bills (accessed 15 October 2019).
2. Barbara Rogoff, *The Cultural Nature of Human Development* (Oxford University Press 2003); Hazel Rose Markus and Shinobu Kitayama, *Cultures and Selves: A Cycle of Mutual Constitution*, Perspectives on Psychological Science, 2010, Vol. 5(4), 420–430.
3. Robert Sapolsky, *Behave: The Biology of Humans at Our Best and Worst* (Bodley Head 2017).
4. David Hume, *A Treatise of Human Nature*, eds. David Norton and Mary Norton (Oxford University Press 2001), Book 2, Part 3, Section 3, 226.
5. Views diverge significantly on what motivates people to behave well. For some, reasoned moral judgements motivate action. It may be possible to call this motivation a desire, but the desire flows from reason. This contrasts with the idea that action is motivated by pre-existing desires. The debate lies beyond the scope of the current exercise. Either way, the ends of desires, however they emerge, are important to what will follow.

6. See the characterisation of the different approaches to moral motivation provided in Timothy Schroeder, Adina L. Roskies and Shaun Nichols, 'Moral Motivation', in *The Moral Psychology Handbook*, eds. John M. Doris, et al. (Oxford University Press 2010).

7. Aristotle, W. D. Ross and Lesley Brown, *The Nicomachean Ethics* (Oxford University Press 2009), Book II.1.

8. David Hume, *The History of England*, Vol. V, chapter L (Phillips, Sampson and Company 1856, Michigan Historical Reprint Society), 4.

9. They have also featured in work on artificial intelligence, for example, in the form of the Belief-Desire-Intention ('BDI') model for programming 'intelligent agents'. As the name suggests, the model emphasises beliefs and desires operating through rational processes. See, for example, Philippe Caillou, et al., 'A Simple-to-use BDI Architecture for Agent-based Modeling and Simulation', in *Advances in Social Simulation 2015*, eds. Wander Jager, et al. (Singer 2017).

10. Schroder, Roskies and Nichols, *Moral Motivation*.

11. As compared, for example, with the experience of beauty in the form of a landscape.

12. Nomy Arpaly and Timothy Schroeder, *In Praise of Desire* (Oxford University Press 2014), 6 et seq.

13. C. Daniel Batson, *Altruism in Humans* (Oxford University Press 2010).

14. Stephen Stich, John M. Doris and Erica Roedder, 'Altruism', in *The Moral Psychology Handbook*, eds. John M. Doris, et al. (Oxford University Press 2010), 151.

15. *Central banking in a democratic society*, remarks by Alan Greenspan, Chairman of the Federal Reserve Board, 5 December 1996.

16. Jesse J. Prinz and Shaun Nichols, 'Moral Emotions', in *The Moral Psychology Handbook*, eds. John M. Doris, et al. (Oxford University Press 2010); Richard Lazarus, *Emotion and Adaptation* (Oxford University Press 1991).

17. Prinz and Nichols, *Moral Emotions*.

18. Ibid., 125.

19. 'Former RBS boss Fred Goodwin stripped of knighthood', *BBC News*, 31 January 2012, https://www.bbc.co.uk/news/uk-politics-16821650 (accessed 15 October 2019).

20. The precipitate fall in value of stock in the South Sea Company which had risen from £130 at the beginning of 1720 to nearly £1,000 by June. Julian Hoppit, *The Myths of the South Sea Bubble*, Transactions of the Royal Historical Society, 2002, Vol. 12, 141–165.

21. *Deloitte and ArtTactic Art and Finance Report* (Deloitte and Art Tactic 2016) available at https://www2.deloitte.com/content/dam/Deloitte/global/Documents/Finance/gx-fsi-art-finance-report-2016.pdf (accessed 15 October 2019); Georgina Adam, 'Boom amid the bust: ten years in a turbulent art market', *Financial Times,* London, 27 July 2018.

22. For example, see *Why Should Art be Considered an Asset Class* (Deloitte 2011), available at https://www2.deloitte.com/content/dam/Deloitte/lu/Documents/financial-services/artandfinance/lu-art-asset-class-122012.pdf (accessed 15 October 2019); *Deloitte and ArtTactic Art and Finance Report*.

23. Michael F. Steger, 'Meaning in Life', in *The Oxford Handbook of Positive Psychology*, eds. Shane J. Lopez and C.R. Snyder (2nd edn, Oxford University Press 2009).

24. Clifford Geertz, *The Interpretation of Cultures* (Basic Books 1973), 77; Iain McGilchrist, *The Master and His Emissary: The Divided Brain and the Making of the Western World* (Yale University Press 2012), 166.

25. Geertz, *The Interpretation of Cultures*, 5.

26. Including: *The Run on the Rock*, House of Commons Treasury Committee, fifth report of session 2007–08, HC 56–I; *The Financial Crisis Inquiry Report: Final Report of the National Commission on the Causes of the Financial and Economic Crisis in the United States*, The Financial Crisis Inquiry Commission, January 2011; *The Failure of the Royal Bank of Scotland*, Financial Services Authority Board Report, December 2011; *'An Accident Waiting to Happen': The Failure of HBOS*, Parliamentary Commission on Banking Standards, fourth report of session 2012–13, 7 March 2013, HL Paper 144, HC 705; *Salz Review: An Independent Review of Barclays' Business Practices*, April 2013, especially 8.13–8.24 available at https://online.wsj.com/public/resources/documents/SalzReview04032013.pdf (accessed 8 November 2019); *Changing Banking for Good*, Report of the Parliamentary Commission on Banking Standards, First Report of Session 2013–14, 12 June 2013, HL Paper 27-I, HC 175-I and HL Paper 27-II, HC 175-II; *Royal Commission into Misconduct in the Banking, Superannuation and Financial Services Industry, Final Report*, Commonwealth of Australia, 2019.

27. See, for example, articles 75 and 92–96, Directive 2013/36/EU of the European Parliament and of the Council of 26 June 2013 on access to the activity of credit institutions and the prudential supervision of credit institutions and investment firms.

28. The debate about whether it is even possible to think without language falls outside the current scope.

29. George Orwell, *Nineteen Eighty-Four* (Penguin Books reprint 1988), 44.

30. In the context of the concept of a social licence to operate, see Richard Parsons and Kieren Moffat, *Constructing the Meaning of Social Licence*, Social Epistemology, 2014, Vol. 28(3–4), 340–363.

31. Jeff Hass, *Economic Sociology: An Introduction* (Routledge 2007), 14–15.

32. Part 9B, Financial Services and Markets Act 2000.

33. Financial Services and Markets Act 2000 (Regulated Activities) Order 2001. For the underlying rules see, in particular, the Prudential Regulation Authority Rulebook and the Financial Conduct Authority Handbook.

34. Different disciplines approach this point in various ways. One of the most well-known is Daniel Kahneman's distinction between 'fast' and 'slow' thinking or, in the language of psychology, System 1 and System 2; Daniel Kahneman, *Thinking Fast and Slow* (Allen Lane 2011). See also Paul DiMaggio, *Culture and Cognition*, Annual Review of Psychology, 1997, Vol. 23, 263–287.

35. Donald A. Norman and Tim Shallice, 'Attention to Action: Willed and Automatic Control of Behavior', in *Consciousness and Self-regulation, Vol. 4: Advances in Research and Theory*, eds. Richard A. Davidson, Gary E. Schwartz and David Shapiro (Plenum Press 1986); David Rumelhart and Andrew Ortony, 'The Representation of Knowledge in Memory', in *Schooling and the Acquisition of Knowledge*, eds. Richard C. Anderson, Rand J. Spiro and William E. Montague (Lawrence Erlbaum Associates Inc. 1977), 99–135, 128.

36. Vanessa E. Ghosh and Asaf Gilboa, *What is a Memory Schema? A Historical Perspective on Current Neuroscience Literature*, Neuropsychologia, 2014, Vol. 53, 104–114; Karla Hoff and Joseph E. Stiglitz, *Striving for Balance in Economics: Towards a Theory of the Social Determination of Behavior*, Journal of Economic Behavior and Organization, 2016, Vol. 126, 25–57.

37. There are thought to be different sorts of schemas. The following is particularly focused on those that concern action.

38. Norman and Shallice, *Attention to Action: Willed and Automatic Control of Behavior*; Richard Cooper, Tim Shallice and Jonathan Farringdon, 'Symbolic and Continuous Processes in the Automatic Selection of Actions', in *Hybrid Problems, Hybrid Solutions*, ed. John Hallam (IOS Press 1995).

39. John Bargh, Wendy Lombardi and E. Tory Higgins, *Automaticity of Chronically Accessible Constructs in Person X Situation Effects on Person Perception: It's Just a Matter of Time*, Journal of Personality and Social Psychology, 1988, Vol. 55(4), 599–605.

40. Roger C. Schank and Robert P. Abelson, *Scripts, Plans, Goals and Understanding: An Inquiry into Human Knowledge Structures* (Lawrence Erlbaum Associates 1977), 36 et seq. They distinguish between scripts and plans, the former concerning the appropriate sequence of events in a given context and the latter the possible actions to achieve a goal (70). However, both will be treated as schemas for current purposes.

41. Ghosh and Gilboa, *What is a Memory Schema?*

42. Ibid.

43. The sociological debate over how far individuals retain their autonomy or whether it just gets subsumed within the 'group mind' lies largely outside the scope of the current exercise, but Chap. 6 returns to it, especially Sect. 6.6.

44. Nonetheless, the Financial Services Authority report on the bailout of the British bank RBS in 2008 is a reminder of how important individuals can still be: *The Failure of the Royal Bank of Scotland*, Financial Services Authority, 26. Indeed, recognition of this was behind the introduction of the UK's 'indi-

vidual accountability' regime for senior managers of financial firms (see Sect. 2.4.3, below).

45. Christina Bicchieri, *The Grammar of Society: The Nature and Dynamics of Social Norms* (Cambridge University Press 2006), 1–42; Geoffrey Brennan, et al., *Explaining Norms* (Oxford University Press 2013), 15–39.

46. Bicchieri, *The Grammar of Society*.

47. Brennan, et al., *Explaining Norms*, 133–175.

48. Lester Coch and John R. P. French, *Overcoming Resistance to Change*, Human Relations, 1948, Vol. 1(4), 512–532; John Van Maanen, 'The Smile Factory: Work at Disneyland', in *Reframing Organizational Culture*, eds. Peter J. Frost, et al. (Sage Publications 1991); Richard A. Guzzo and Marcus W. Dickson, *Teams in Organizations: Recent Research on Performance and Effectiveness*, Annual Review of Psychology, 1996, Vol. 47(1), 307–338; Gregory A. Janicik and Caroline A. Bartel, *Talking About Time: Effects of Temporal Planning and Time Awareness Norms on Group Coordination and Performance*, Group Dynamics: Theory, Research, and Practice, 2003, Vol. 7(2), 122–134.

49. Directive 98/26/EC of the European Parliament and of the Council on settlement finality in payment and securities settlement systems.

50. Directive 2002/47/EC of the European Parliament and of the Council on financial collateral arrangements.

51. Muzafer Sherif, *A Study of Some Social Factors in Perception*, Archives of Psychology, 1935, No. 187, 23–46.

52. The expression 'social construction' is used sparingly in this book, among other things, because it could be taken to suggest that the process is planned and consciously controlled. That is sometimes the case. However, it would be misleading to suggest that it is the norm or that it is limitless. Nonetheless, the idea of social construction is helpful because it makes clear that much of 'reality' emerges from a process of human interaction in practice and is not external to it, even if it is partially derived from physical realities.

53. There is a wider debate about the relationship between norms and meaning which it is not necessary to get into here.

54. Morton Deutsch and Harold B. Gerrard, *A Study of Normative and Informational Social Influences Upon Individual Judgement*, Journal of Abnormal and Social Psychology, 1955, Vol. 51(3), 629–636.

55. 'It is not a case of choosing those [faces] which, to the best of one's judgement, are really the prettiest, nor even those which average opinion genuinely thinks the prettiest. We have reached the third degree where we devote our intelligences to anticipating what average opinion expects the average opinion to be.' John Maynard Keynes, *The General Theory of Employment, Interest and Money* (Royal Economic Society/Macmillan Press 1976 reprint), 156.

56. Deutsch and Gerrard, *A Study of Normative and Informational Social Influences Upon Individual Judgement*.

57. See, for example, Ernst Fehr and Urs Fischbacher, *Social Norms and Human Cooperation*, Cognitive Sciences, 2004, Vol. 8(4), 185–190.

58. Solomon E. Asch, *Opinions and Social Pressure*, Scientific American, 1955, Vol. 193(5), 31–35.

59. Leon Festinger, *A Theory of Social Comparison Processes*, Human Relations, 1954, Vol. 7(2), 117–140.

60. Bicchieri, *The Grammar of Society*, 82.

61. Lynne Zucker, *The Role of Institutionalization in Cultural Persistence*, American Sociological Review, 1977, Vol. 42(5), 726–743.

62. They were all men, but it is not clear that gender makes a difference to how participants respond: Thomas Blass, *The Milgram Paradigm After 35 Years: Some Things We Now Know About Obedience to Authority*, Journal of Applied Social Psychology, 1999, Vol. 29(5), 955–978.

63. Stanley Milgram, *Behavioral Study of Obedience*, The Journal of Abnormal and Social Psychology, 1963, Vol. 67(4), 371–378; Stanley Milgram, *Obedience to Authority: An Experimental View* (Tavistock Publications 1974).

64. Blass, *The Milgram Paradigm*, 958 et seq.

65. Giovanna d'Adda, et al., *Do Leaders Affect Ethical Conduct*, Journal of the European Economic Association, 2017, Vol. 15(6), 1177–1213.

66. For example, the point came up in the work of the UK Parliamentary Commission on Banking Standards: see *Changing Banking for Good*, First Report of Session 2013–14, Volume II: Chapters 1 to 11 and Annexes, together with formal minutes, HL Paper 27-II HC 175-II, June 2013, paragraph 810 et. seq.

67. John D. Turner, *Banking in Crisis: The Rise and Fall of British Banking Stability, 1800 to the Present* (Cambridge University Press 2014), 124–125.

68. Ian Maitland, 'How Insiders Abuse the Idea of Corporate Personality', in *The Moral Responsibility of Firms*, eds. Eric W. Orts and N. Craig Smith (Oxford University Press 2017), 106.

69. The relevant rules appear in various sections of the Prudential Regulation Authority Rulebook and Financial Conduct Authority Handbook. In the case of the former see, for example, Allocation of Responsibilities, Conduct Rules and Senior Management Functions in relation to CRR Firms.

70. US Department of Justice, Justice Manual 9-28.010, Foundational Principles of Corporate Prosecution.

71. Colby Smith, 'Do financial markets care about a blue wave, red wall or gridlock?', *Financial Times*, London, 5 November 2018.

72. See, for example, Title III of Directive 2014/65/EU of the European Parliament and of the Council of 15 May 2014 on markets in financial instruments.

73. See for example, Orts and Smith, *The Moral Responsibility of Firms*; Andrew Crane, Dirk Matten and Jeremy Moon, *Corporations and Citizenship* (Cambridge University Press 2008), 17 et seq.

74. Section 16, Companies Act 2006; *Salmon v A Salmon & Co Ltd* [1897] AC 22.
75. *Meridian Global Funds Management Asia Ltd v Securities Commission* [1995] 2 AC 500 is the leading case on the civil law position. The court expressed some caution about using the concept of a 'directing mind and will' and attributing human characteristics to companies.
76. There is a technical legal distinction between the acts of the board, which are treated as being the acts of the company, and the acts of agents, which are treated as being on behalf of the company. It is not necessary to go into that here.
77. John R. Searle, *The Construction of Social Reality* (Free Press 1995), 23 et seq.; Michael E. Bratman, 'The Intentions of a Group', in *The Moral Responsibility of Firms*, eds. Eric Orts and Craig Smith (Oxford University Press 2017).
78. John D. Turner, 'The Development of English Company Law Before 1900', in *Research Handbook on the History of Corporate and Company Law*, ed. Harwell Wells (Edward Elgar 2018).
79. The list is maintained by the Financial Stability Board.
80. *Artificial Intelligence and Machine Learning in Financial Services: Market Developments and Financial Stability Implications*, Financial Stability Board, 1 November 2017.
81. Robin Wigglesworth, 'Volatility: how 'algos' changed the rhythm of the market', *Financial Times*, London, 9 January 2019.
82. With notable exceptions, for example, Michael Lewis, *Flash Boys: A Wall Street Revolt* (W. W. Norton & Company 2014).

3

The Ends of Desire in Financial Markets

Fast Track

Speed Read

Chapter 2 highlighted the power of desires and beliefs about the meaning of the world to drive behaviour. For greater recognition of a social licence to make a practical difference in addressing the challenges and opportunities identified in Chap. 1, it must engage effectively with the prevailing desires and frameworks of meaning in financial markets in a way that strengthens positive reciprocity. What are they?

Chapter 1 identified a common set of narratives that cast financial markets as places where people and firms pursue money. There is an obvious sense in which this is true, and necessarily so. The clue is in the name: finance. Financial markets revolve around handling and generating money and they perform an essential role in doing so. The meaning of money is a potent force in shaping markets and the lives of those within them.

But look for a moment at market reality, and it is obvious that these narratives are a gross caricature, to the extent that it would be embarrassing to mention it had not their account become so prevalent. Something is hiding in plain sight.

In reality, day-to-day behaviour in financial markets is characterised by high levels of belief in, and regard for, the needs of others. Not everyone to the same degree, and not all of the time, but most to some degree and for some of the time. For example, take what is often treated as the defining relationship in financial markets: the contract. Contracts could be seen as a sign of mistrust. (Why else involve lawyers?) And yet, no contract can ever fully document a relationship, even the highly detailed ISDA documentation, which is commonly used for bespoke derivative transactions. For contracts to work in practice, they must be underpinned by and sustained with trust. Trust is given and earned

(continued)

(continued)

over time through relationships in which both parties benefit. It is a **reciprocal** process. But the degree to which trust is built up also depends on the quality of a much broader set of relationships going far beyond the parties themselves. Trust is more like a **gift** than an economic exchange, even in an economic context; it is given voluntarily, with no assurance of valuable consideration in return; it involves generosity towards the person trusted.

But the presence of outwardly other-regarding behaviour does not necessarily reveal what motivations lie behind it. For example, earning trust could be driven by self-interest—what you have to do to accumulate money as efficiently as possible. Isn't self-interest still the best way to explain even other-regarding behaviour? After all, the evolution of life itself is apparently driven by a 'selfish gene'. This question is important. If desires are a key driver of behaviour and the objective is behaviour change, then it is essential to understand which ones we are dealing with.

Taking the selfish gene in the room first, it turns out (from no higher authority than the person who first coined the term) that it is, in reality, an 'altruistic gene'; it can provide a basis for other-regarding behaviour. More importantly, however, evolutionary biology only takes us so far if we want to understand the psychological motivation of people in financial markets.

Chapter 2 distinguished between instrumental desires (desiring something that is a stepping stone to achieving a greater end) and intrinsic desires, which are particularly important because of the way that instrumental desires cascade from them. An intrinsic desire concerns an ultimate end. Realising it is not a means to satisfying any other desire. There are various candidates for what these ultimate desired ends might be for those in financial markets, but two of the most plausible are **personal wellbeing (or self-interest)** and the **wellbeing of others (or altruism)**. Pursued to their extreme, both self-interest and altruism can be destructive, of the other or the self, respectively. However, **wellbeing**—the experience of **human dignity** in practice—involves a balance.

Experiencing dignity may require money, but is not a financial value. It is the value that is intrinsic to being human. That is how the Universal Declaration of Human Rights approaches it. That intrinsic value can be experienced more or less fully in practice. However, it cannot be fully experienced in isolation. It involves, among other things, the regard of others. But for those others to treat a person with dignity, they need to have experienced it themselves. There is, then, a **mutuality** in experiencing dignity. Indeed, since people exist in a network of relationships, the mutuality needs to be **broad-based**.

How does this square with the common belief that the desired end of those in financial markets is to make money? Money is instrumental in realising human dignity, especially in a developed economy. However, where it becomes so intimately tied up with what is thought necessary to realise a person's dignity or a firm's success—where personal or institutional value is understood or felt in monetary, more than human, terms—financial self-interest can operate as if it were an intrinsic desire and money as an ultimate end. In practice, that's not how people function in markets for much of the time. However, countless episodes, most recently in 2008 and what followed, confirm what happens when it is. Trust and social solidarity are destroyed and the experience of dignity diminished.

(continued)

(continued)

Mutuality and reciprocity are integral to financial life. Indeed, the instances of LIBOR rigging that were widely publicised in the aftermath of the financial crisis involved both. However, the result was commonly viewed as destructive, not **positive**. That is because mutuality and reciprocity was limited to the narrow ends of those involved—a kind of you-scratch-my-back-and-I'll-scratch-yours reciprocity. **Positive reciprocity**, as the expression is used here, is different. It involves an orientation of market relationships that goes beyond their immediate transactional ends and has wider positive results. It can provide a basis for strengthening the broad-based mutuality on which human wellbeing and social solidarity rest, as do markets themselves. That is the orientation that needs to be emphasised within the multitude of relationships that comprise financial markets if the challenges and opportunities outlined in Chap. 1 are to be addressed. It requires, in part, a clearer sense of ends for financial market relationships that transcend their immediate financial goals.

So what?

Financial markets already display positive reciprocity. However, there is also reciprocity that is not positive in the sense used here. A key challenge is therefore to strengthen the first and reorientate the second, rather than introduce something new. As noted, used here, positive reciprocity describes an orientation of financial relationships beyond immediate financial ends, which can benefit those in the wider chains of relationships their activities affect. The financial narratives and models discussed in Chap. 1 emphasise financial self-interest and short-term financial ends. They are subject to re-evaluation. This has been the context for the observation that markets operate subject to a social licence. Recognition of a social licence casts light on exactly this issue of ends; ends that embrace financial return, but also reach beyond it.

Can the recognition that financial markets operate subject to a social licence help with the reorientation? To answer that, the first step is to understand what recognition of a social licence consists of. Part II addresses that. Part III then looks at its potential to help in practice.

Consider four scenarios:

1. Saturday 3 June, 2017. Terrorists drive a van at pedestrians on London Bridge. A young nurse, named Kirsty Boden, runs to the aid of the wounded and is stabbed to death by the attackers. Her family say that, 'Helping people was what she loved to do …'[1] A representative of the National Health Service says that, 'Her courage and selflessness reflect all that is best about the NHS and will not be forgotten.'[2] They are not.
2. Two men sit in a room, The first asks, 'What do you think motivates the traders in your team?' The second responds, 'Making money.' The first man presses him: 'Is there anything else?' The second thinks for a moment and replies, 'No. Really – they're not interested in anything else.' The first man pauses. 'Is that what motivates them when they're with their families?' he asks. The second replies, 'Of course not!' The first goes on: 'So how can

you be so sure that they don't bring some other motivation to work?' 'Hum,' says the second.

3. A woman and a man are talking. 'What is the purpose of business?' the man asks. 'To make money,' the woman replies. 'To make money,' the man echoes. 'Is that all?' The woman replies without hesitation, 'Yes – making money.' There is a silence. 'Well,' says the man, 'can you think of anything else business might be there to do?' There is a longer silence. The man continues: 'If you compare, say, Ford and BT, would you come to the conclusion that they *only* exist to make money?' 'Oh,' says the woman.

4. A senior executive at a large financial firm welcomes the latest group of graduate recruits. 'The bank is here to make money,' she says. 'We have chosen you because we think *you* want to make money.' The recruits say nothing. 'Our experience,' continues the executive, 'is that those who want to become rich help the company to become rich, and that is why we have chosen you.'

In my line of work, I sometimes encounter a reality gap. There is a disparity between how people and firms are *assumed* to be and how they really are. The assumptions concern the ends and meaning of financial activity, similar to those found in the financial narratives and economic models of Chap. 1. The discussion of behaviour in Chap. 2 made plain how both desired ends and meaning shape behaviour, and it is therefore possible that these assumptions about behaviour are, at least in part, causing people to act in a certain way.

The second and third scenarios, depicted above, reflect discussions I myself have had with City professionals in seminars and elsewhere. There was no scientific method at work in these discussions. While I tried to be neutral, it is always possible that I inadvertently posed questions in a way that provoked this response. It is possible, too, that the context had some effect on the assumptions involved in these conversations. More mixed perspectives may now be emerging, especially among younger City workers.[3] But I have had conversations like these sufficiently often to know that how they run can usually be predicted, and they start with the assumption that the purpose of business and of those who work in business is to make money. The day-to-day conduct of some of the people with whom I have spoken—at least in the cases in which I have known the other person well—would not confirm this assumption. And yet this is how they freely describe the motives of others. The time taken to arrive at the final 'Oh' or 'Hum' varies, but it can be surprisingly long.

Kirsty Boden did not work in the City, but in its shadow, at Guy's Hospital, south of the River Thames. Her tragic story contrasts starkly with the conversations described above. But, manifestly, people are not divided neatly into those who desire to help others, and those whose sole desire is financial gain. Likewise, there are different sorts of organisation, but these do not fall into two categories: those committed to the betterment of human wellbeing and those devoted to making money. In practice, much of life, business life included, is lived in a way that quite clearly takes account of the needs of others. A truth is hiding in plain sight.[4] What, then, is really going on? And what does engagement in financial markets suggest about the ends people desire and the meaning that financial activity has for them?

These are crucial questions. After all, addressing the challenges and taking advantage of the opportunities described in Chap. 1 necessarily involves behaviour change and the desired ends and beliefs about meaning of those whose behaviour must change will drive that change in behaviour. Financial markets are not like the National Health Service: they have a different function. Nonetheless, what is now needed in financial markets is greater regard for the needs of others within those markets and outside them. In other words, there is a need for greater positive reciprocity in the many relationships that exist in and comprise financial markets: a reorientation of those relationships so that their ends are not just narrowly transactional. This must happen in a way that supports the wider objective of building the social solidarity on which markets themselves rely. That, in turn, will provide a basis for justified social trust.

But the starting point is to recognise the extent to which this positive reciprocity and social solidarity already exist. Chapter 1 described conversations of a different nature with City people—conversations that suggest a desire for change. In business settings especially, these sorts of conversations can seem hesitant. Perhaps those concerned do not realise that they are not alone. The framework of the social licence for financial markets has the potential to provide us with a way of recognising, understanding and balancing this mixture of motivations, and coordination for those (who are perhaps the majority) who want things to be different.

With that in mind, Sect. 3.1 challenges the common idea that financial markets are hot-beds of financial self-interest by examining market behaviour in practice. It acknowledges the importance, but potentially destructive power of financial self-interest. But it also explores behaviour that serves the interests of others, and considers whether, ironically, that too is sometimes damaging. The perception that financial self-interest *and* other-regarding behaviours can be harmful, suggests that there is a desired outcome that has not been realised.

In view of that idea, Sect. 3.2 centres on what *motivates* market behaviour. It examines the self-interested desire for personal wellbeing and the altruistic desire for the wellbeing of others. It explores the way in which both can be considered in terms of intrinsic human value (human dignity) or financial value. Finally, Sect. 3.3 considers whether it is plausible to think that financial markets can be a source of the broad-based mutuality on which the experience of dignity rests, and how ultimate desired ends are fundamental in determining whether the outcome of mutuality and reciprocity in financial markets is positive. The Mafia are, after all, great reciprocators, but the outcome of their reciprocity is not positive.

3.1   Markets, Red in Tooth and Claw?

In the popular financial narratives of Chap. 1, financial markets are places of Darwinistic conflict between traders in pursuit of financial returns, where only the fittest will survive. There is something in this. However, consistent with the discussion of economic models described in Chap. 1, in reality, you see lots of other-regarding behaviour in financial markets too. Yet, there is also an irony. Although this other-regarding behaviour might be considered beneficial, other-regardingness can sometimes also be damaging.

3.1.1   Money as an End

Clearly, finance is about making money, and the desire to do so has been an extraordinary force for human good, in terms of goods and services provided, livelihoods nourished and material poverty eliminated. Financial markets fund economic activity. Necessarily, therefore, they revolve around money, and the towering architecture of international regulation reflects the importance of what they do with it.

Yet history is also replete with cases of unbridled financial desire causing significant damage.[5] The Wolf of Wall Street genre is informed by them and is part of a tradition stretching back past Trollope's searing novel The Way we Live Now (written shortly after the collapse of British bank Overend, Gurney & Co in 1866). More emerged in the context of the financial crisis of 2008.

For example, the UK Parliamentary Commission on Banking Standards, considering the reasons for the failure of British bank HBOS plc, focused on its aggressive target of moving from a return on equity of 17% in 2001 to 20% in 2004, accepting more risk across all divisions.[6] Likewise, the UK regulator's report on the failure of the Royal Bank of Scotland questioned whether it was, 'overly focused on revenue, profit and earnings per share rather than on capital, liquidity and asset quality, and whether the Board designed a

CEO remuneration package which made it rational to focus on the former.'[7] Similar connections were made elsewhere. For example, the Australian Royal Commission on financial sector misconduct noted that, 'in almost every case, the conduct in issue was driven not only by the relevant entity's pursuit of profit but also by individuals' pursuit of … remuneration…'[8]

Financial desire also drove market abuse. The UK's Fair and Effective Markets Review was set up in 2013 following a series of attempts by a number of finance sector staff around the world to manipulate interest rate and other financial indices to benefit themselves and colleagues.[9] The force of financial desire was obvious from communications between those involved.[10] This was potentially damaging to clients and the wider economy, and undermined confidence in financial markets.

Scenario 4 at the start of this chapter is part of an induction speech given to graduate trainees by a senior staff member of one of the large UK banks in the early 1990s. It conjures up a world similar to the financial narratives of Chap. 1, echoing the conversations reported in scenarios 2 and 3 above. Twenty years later, the bank was involved in these scandals. It may do things differently now. However, induction programmes are a key moment, when businesses seek to instil a sense of the goals and standards of their organisation (see Sect. 2.4.1). This bank made no bones about it. The purpose of the business was to make money. A trainee could safely assume that getting rich was a key motivation for their fellow trainees and others in the bank, and that making money was the way to get on.[11] If this sort of thing was common over the intervening period, it is easy to see how finance was set on a course that produced the sort of results just described.

3.1.2 One Step Beyond: Others

But concentrating on the sort of narratives discussed in Chap. 1, and on financial scandals, can mask another sort of behaviour. In practice, whether you look at individuals, companies or markets, financial life is not simply an endless pursuit of money. There is also behaviour that takes account of the needs of others, be they colleagues, employers, clients, trading counterparties more widely or the communities in which individuals and firms carry on business ('other-regarding behaviour').[12] Indeed, but for the strength of assumptions about self-interest, it is so obvious that it is almost embarrassing to mention it.

Individuals

Clearly, individuals fall along a spectrum in their other-regardingness. However, much individual behaviour appears other-regarding, whether team work, serving clients, supporting a distressed colleague or celebrating their life events, raising money for charity or otherwise. Academic studies in various work settings have found the same: behaviour apparently intended to benefit others, not just as an indirect consequence of pursuing financial goals.[13] Take employee volunteering programmes run by many City institutions, where staff are given time off to work on projects addressing community needs. Some see them as corporate window dressing, but, even if that is right, it implies something about those looking through, including staff and potential staff. From experience, it certainly appears as if wanting to help people is a key reason for volunteering. Again, academic work seems to confirm it.[14] Salary and prestige is obviously a factor in job selection. However, for many, that is not all of it, none more than recent graduates: 'Young workers are eager for business leaders to be … making a positive impact in society…'[15]

Firms

There is also extensive other-regarding behaviour among financial firms. After all, their business depends on providing 'goods' or 'services' for remuneration and accumulating trust and goodwill. Indeed, many financial relationships are particularly trust-dependent, either because of the complexity of financial products or because of the services firms provide, such as holding cash, and investing and safeguarding client assets. English law characterises investment management and custody relationships as 'fiduciary' because of that, applying an additional legal duty of loyalty to the service provider. But the law is there to create a remedy if trust is abused more than being the basis of trust.[16] Trust creates opportunities for dishonesty, but most of the time they are not taken.

Returning to community engagement programmes, they have become prominent in the corporate landscape in the last twenty years.[17] More recently still, financial firms have started to publish statements of 'corporate purpose' presenting their business in a broader context, beyond shareholder returns.[18] A review of the websites of 22 of the largest banks in the London financial market as at January 2019 revealed a diversity of approaches.[19] All had some form of statement of purpose. Unsurprisingly, most referenced the needs of customers. However, two thirds also expressed some sort of desire to make a positive difference to society or local communities. Again, some dismiss this as 'brand management'. Certainly, there is artificiality where purpose statements ignore financial objectives, which are so obviously important for finance firms. Contrast them, for example, with firms' annual reporting. The activities of brand consultants can lend weight to that impression:

> ... **companies looking to build their competitive agility need to find new ways to stand out.**
>
> Brand purpose provides the differentiation that many seek ...[20]

But this developing emphasis on wider objectives has not happened on a whim. Experience suggests that statements of this sort are likely to have complex origins, with other-regardingness being part of the mix. Further, emphasis on purpose responds to changing social expectations; societies in which financial firms' directors and staff are also involved. Attitudes have moved significantly over the last decade, the August 2019 publication by the US Business Roundtable of its Statement on the Purpose of a Corporation, mentioned in Chap. 1 (Sect. 1.2.2), being one of the more striking milestones. A recent statement from HSBC's Group Head of Strategy raises some questions, but captures something of this:

> A sustainable global economy starts with individual acts of conscience and responsible corporate citizenship. But taking on the climate and social issues that continue to affect people all over the world requires more. To drive fundamental change, individual action must evolve into institutional transformation – where Environmental, Social and Governance (ESG) becomes not simply a moral imperative, but a business imperative as well.[21]

Financial Markets

Other-regardingness is also plain in the two relationships that most define financial markets: transactional, and investment and financing relationships. That may sound odd given the extent of market standardisation and electronic trading, especially since some financial markets are restricted to sophisticated firms that could be expected to need little consideration from others. So, it needs unpacking.

Transactional Relationships

Taking transactional relationships first, how do these really work in practice? To answer that, it is helpful to begin with the experience of a senior commodities trader at a well-known City firm who recently described to me the way she sees trading relationships work in practice.[22] Where trading involves standardised derivatives contracts, she thought that little else matters than the price (but what follows will test that); 'Screen trading is more brutal', and dealing 'less empathetic'. However, where transactions are not standardised, establishing good working relationships with counterparties is important. The best involve trust because, for example, you may need to make yourself vulnerable by revealing aspects of your commercial position to achieve the best deal for both. Trust enables the parties to 'open up', allowing a 'quality of conversation'. Trust develops incrementally over time; traders you have dealt with long-term get more trust than others. Initially, she said that the underlying objective on all sides would always be to secure the best deal for one's own firm; other-regarding behaviour there might be, but 'there is always a calculation'. However, in discussing the origin of trust, it was less clear that it is exclusively the result of both parties consistently looking to their own interests. The trust you are given may play a part as much as the trust you give, as if there may be an element of generosity and reciprocity that goes beyond a simple commercial calculation. In the course of a long relationship, one party may help another where commercially possible and subject to the duty to one's firm. The other may return the favour later on a similar basis. Vulnerability offered is not abused. A relational history emerges and even a sense of friendship. In these lies the emergence of trust.

In fact, 'Virtually every commercial transaction has within it an element of trust…'[23]—a willingness to act on a belief that the other party will not act exclusively in its own interests, but will take some account of the interests of the other. Ironically, the very step often assumed to reflect the lack of trust is powerful evidence of the opposite: the practice of recording commercial agreements in legal contracts. Contracts are indeed legally enforceable, but in practice performance of most of them depends to a significant degree on trust. Among other things, that is because few contracts are ever really 'complete'. Economists have long been interested in this element of 'incompleteness'. However, they have tended to approach it as a risk that needs managing, theorising about how various economic phenomena (such as firms) emerge to deal with the uncertainty.[24] This assumes an element of mistrust. But, coming back to the obvious being overlooked, incompleteness as evidence of other-regardingness that supports trust has received less attention.[25]

When drafting most contracts it is simply not feasible precisely to record every aspect of the parties' agreement (see Sect. 6.6). The essence of the agreement would just get lost in a sea of defined terms and detail. The parties would also think it ridiculous. Indeed, it might even be taken as a sign of mistrust, undermining the commercial relationship. So, legal drafting may sometimes deliberately, even if unconsciously, leave space for other-regardingness to do its work.[26] Of course, there has to be a base level of contractual certainty or the courts will not enforce the agreement.[27] But courts are a blunt tool. In reality, there is usually a point at which parties have to trust each other to behave reasonably in resolving disagreements rather than litigating, otherwise, nothing would happen. Trust is essential. In practice, in spite of contractual incompleteness, disputes are relatively rare. When they do happen, a contract often operates as a framework for resolution, rather than a manual for telling the parties exactly what to do, or providing a basis for litigation (although the possibility of litigation can help to focus minds).[28]

Something of this is seen in industry standard derivatives documentation, known as 'ISDAs',[29] and a number of other industry standard contractual arrangements, such as those used for stock lending and repurchase transactions.[30] ISDAs are 'master agreements' under which individual 'over the counter' (or relatively bespoke) derivatives deals are entered into. They use various mechanisms for resolving uncertainties later in the relationship, treatment of which cannot be agreed in advance. For example, the parties can appoint a 'calculation agent' to make determinations, such as valuations that are relevant to the commercial value of derivatives entered into under the arrangement. In practice, the calculation agent is usually one of the parties, underscoring the element of trust.[31]

But these are longer-term customised trading relationships. The commodities trader, mentioned above, perceived lower levels of other-regardingness in standardised, short-term trading relationships. There is indeed a difference between the two. However, it may not be as stark as we might imagine. First, even short-term trades often take place in the context of wider institutional relationships; for example, most large firms maintain lists of brokers they are prepared to deal with, selection being based partly on their previous experience of those firms. Secondly, the contracts, while generally not as complicated, are nonetheless incomplete and therefore still involve a degree of trust.

Taking the issue of short-term standardised trading a step further, what of transactions resulting from electronic trading (see Chap. 2)? Computers cannot have regard for themselves or others since they lack consciousness. However, the environment in which electronic systems are developed and maintained can nonetheless involve significant other-regardingness,[32] and market participants rely upon the firms operating these arrangements to do so in ways that support an orderly market. The legal framework for markets is evidence of the last of these. For example, European financial market legislation requires firms to have robust systems and controls to ensure that algorithmic trading or high-frequency algorithmic trading techniques do not create a disorderly market and cannot be used for abusive purposes.[33] These rules are evidence, not of a lack of other-regarding behaviour, but that trust exists (because firms generally do seek to avoid disrupting markets and abusing the trust of other market participants) and needs to be sustained. In the words of the European Commission, establishing a High-Level Expert Group on Artificial Intelligence, 'New technologies are based on values' and for AI to take off in the EU an, 'environment of trust and accountability around the development and use of AI is needed'.[34] Electronic trading does not turn markets into a 'neutral space' where trust and other-regarding values no longer matter. They just come into play in a different way.

But other-regarding behaviour is not just inherent in transactional activity; many of those transactions also have an other-regarding *purpose*. An obvious example is transactions in pension fund assets, one of the largest sources of wealth behind market activity. Pension assets are generally managed by investment managers to fund retirement income for pension scheme beneficiaries who are not a party to any transactions entered into by the investment manager. A key purpose of the transactions is nonetheless to serve beneficiaries' needs.[35]

Finance and Investment Relationships

There is also other-regarding behaviour in financing and investment relationships. Currently, it is perhaps most clear in the growth of 'sustainable finance' and 'ESG investing'. These concern the integration of the environmental, social and corporate governance credentials of investee firms into finance and investment decisions.[36] A consistent theme in discussions with asset management clients during 2018–2019 has been the interest of their own clients in ESG investing. It has been estimated that, by the start of 2018, approximately $30.7 trillion of assets in five major world markets were being managed by reference to sustainability criteria, a 34% increase in two years.[37] The figures should be treated with caution, since they mask a wide variety of investment approaches. However, the trend is clear. Much of it is driven by investors' desire to manage their investment risk, for example, where the value of an investee firm could fall as a result of environmental factors (i.e. financial self-interest). Current discussion of the potential investment fallout from a precipitate transition away from carbon-based energy is a case in point.[38] Risks of this sort also lie behind some of the heightened regulatory attention.[39]

But is sustainable and ESG investing about more than protecting or enhancing financial return? There have always been some potentially financially attractive investments that would simply be assumed off-limits, or have become off-limits, such as slavery. However, some pension funds have started to become more intentional in seeking to achieve positive social and environmental goals as well as financial return in managing their assets. Take, for example, an agreement between 73 Dutch pension funds managing combined assets of €1178 billion to do just that.[40] A key motivation for ESG investing is the belief that it offers the best long-term financial returns. From that perspective, any wider benefit is incidental. However, some at least, also want to advance environmental and social goods.[41]

Pension funds are not alone. A succession of headlines and ESG fund launches during 2017 and 2018 suggests that, increasingly, investors do not just want a financial return; they want to earn it by investing in companies they regard as addressing social and environmental challenges or not contributing to them.[42] Again, some of them may simply see 'ESG' as a new asset class, promising above average returns. But a review of the growing number of studies by financial firms and policymakers strongly suggests that many investors want their investment to make a positive social or environmental difference.[43] Academic research reveals the same.[44] Some investors may even be willing to risk investment return to pursue a positive environmental and social impact. In the words of HSBC, 'As the market continues to shift, we believe incorporating ESG factors will become the norm and impact the choices people make about who they do business with and how they invest.'[45]

3.1.3 Other-Regarding Behaviour: Bad for Financial Markets?

But just as unbalanced financial self-interest can cause substantial damage, so can other-regarding behaviour. The attempts to manipulate LIBOR, mentioned above, are an example.[46] Those involved were other-regarding between themselves, but had little regard for other market participants or society more broadly. This is a reminder of two things. First, as discussed in Chap. 2, individual behaviour takes place in and is shaped by the groups people join; behaviour can be other-regarding within a group and support the group's desired ends, but damaging for those outside it.[47] Secondly, it follows that the *ultimate* goal of other-regarding behaviour—what is intrinsically desired—is critical to its outcome.

It is instructive to see how market participants reacted to this issue of the relationship between group interests and the ultimate ends of financial markets in the aftermath of the LIBOR and similar scandals, not least because it is further evidence of other-regardingness. Their views were sought as part of the UK's The Fair and Effective Markets Review.[48] Essentially, they seem to have recognised that financial market activity has ultimate ends that transcend the more immediate objectives of any individual or group within the market. The idea that financial markets have a desired end was implicit in the name of the Review: 'effective' to what end and 'fair' to what standard? Ultimately, the Review defined effectiveness by reference to positive outcomes that lie beyond markets themselves: effective FICC markets are those that, 'allow end-users, borrowers, end-investors and their intermediaries to undertake transactions in a predictable way and in support of the broader non-financial economy.' Meanwhile, fairness was defined in a market-facing manner, essentially, by reference to the need for those participating in markets to balance their own interests with the interests of other market participants.[49] In each case, then, the definition involves recognising the needs of others, the first by reference to society and the second the market.

Few financial institutions commented on the proposed definitions of 'fair' and 'effective' in detail, but none questioned them in substance.[50] Some firms may have made comments through industry associations, especially if they wanted to avoid publicly challenging the definitions. However, responses from industry associations did not seem to raise material concerns with the proposed definitions either. Key associations, such as the Association for Financial Markets in Europe, the British Bankers Association, ISDA and the Investment Association, appeared largely to agree with them, presumably reflecting the feedback from their members.[51] The Review concluded that the definition, 'was well received by a wide range of key stakeholders, including end-users, market participants, national and international authorities, public interest groups and leading academics.'[52]

3.2   The Ends of Desire

This chapter has highlighted two ironies. First, the knee-jerk view of industry insiders on market behaviour is often similar to the financial narratives discussed in Chap. 1 but, in practice, their own behaviour is frequently other-regarding. Secondly, although other-regarding behaviour is generally considered positive, taking LIBOR manipulation as an example, other-regardingness within a group can have disastrous consequences more widely. Financial self-interest can be a powerful source of good, but can destroy if not sufficiently balanced by other-regardingness. Yet the wrong sort of other-regardingness can do the same.

So, self-interested behaviour should sometimes be encouraged and other-regarding behaviour discouraged. But when and how? As to 'when', the answer turns on what is ultimately motivating the behaviour—the end at which the behaviour is directed—and the extent to which that corresponds with wider aspirations for financial markets. The second half of this chapter looks at motivation within financial markets. Chapter 4 will consider wider aspirations for financial market activity in looking at the idea of a social licence for financial markets. Part III will consider 'how'.

Chapter 2 discussed how desires drive behaviour, distinguishing intrinsic desires (those directed at an ultimate end) from instrumental desires (where something is desired to help in achieving that ultimate end). Instrumental desires cascade from intrinsic desires, so intrinsic desires are the principal interest here, and the most obvious intrinsic desires to focus on in the light of Sect. 3.1 are self-interest (a desire for one's own *wellbeing*), and a desire for others' *wellbeing* regardless of the impact on the self (or 'altruism').[53]

The willingness to be other-regarding varies between individuals.[54] However, from the perspective of the need to address the challenges and opportunities discussed in Chap. 1, the question of motivation is relevant to, essentially, whether people need to be motivated to respond by appeals to self-interest or an aspiration for others' wellbeing, or a mixture of both.[55] And yet this dichotomy between self-interest and altruism risks being a diversion. That is because, in practice, there may be a point at which wellbeing of the self and wellbeing of the other begin to merge, so that personal wellbeing cannot be realised without also realising a desire for the wellbeing of others.

John Donne, living in seventeenth century London, not far from where a host of financial institutions now stand, captured something of this:

No man is an island, entire of itself; every man is a piece of the continent, a part of the main; if a clod be washed away by the sea, Europe is the less, as well as if a promontory were, as well as if a manor of thy friend's or of thine own were; any man's death diminishes me, because I am involved in mankind, and there-fore never send to know for whom the bell tolls; it tolls for thee.[56]

This speaks of a profound inter-dependency, in which a person's wellbeing is intimately tied up with the wellbeing of others, both in individual relationships and in communities. Growing attention to the idea of human dignity, for example, in the context of the Universal Declaration of Human Rights, with its emphasis on the inherent value of each person, suggests that, intuitively at least, the ultimacy of this more relational human end is well-recognised. However, financial narratives of the sort discussed in Chap. 1 emphasise a different sort of value; one measured financially.

What follows therefore looks in turn at self-interest, altruism and how, in practice, the desire for wellbeing involved in each can be understood in terms of intrinsic human value (or human dignity), or financial value. Section 3.3 then considers whether the reciprocity displayed in financial markets can be a source of the kind of relational goods that underpin dignity, not just financial return.

But before any of that, it is necessary to deal with the selfish gene in the room, since there is a popular belief that evolutionary biology long ago settled this question of whether self-interest drives all human behaviour, and it is not correct.

3.2.1   Introducing the 'Altruistic Gene'

Given the title of his book, *The Selfish Gene*, it is unsurprising that Richard Dawkins is often associated with the idea that humans are essentially selfish. A biological block-buster, it is now sold as part of the Oxford Landmark Science series, underscoring its totemic significance. Jeff Skilling, former CEO of Enron, was among those drawn to it. Renowned for his Darwinistic approach to business, *The Selfish Gene* was apparently one of his favourite books.[57] Perhaps he felt it confirmed him in some of the management practices that led Enron to disaster. As discussed in Chap. 2, beliefs about the meaning of the world have behavioural impacts.[58]

In any event, Dawkins is now concerned both about what Skilling made of it[59] and that he may have misled us. In the Introduction to the 30th Anniversary Edition, he sought to clarify his position. Rather than calling his book *The Selfish Gene*, he suggests that, '… I should perhaps have gone for … *The Altruistic Vehicle* … [or] *The Cooperative Gene…*'[60] Genes cannot act 'selfishly' or 'unselfishly' because they are not 'selfs'. Genes can only be part of what it is to be a self, such as a human. By describing genes as selfish, Dawkins was resorting to metaphor. He had tried to make this clear in the first edition. His book, he said, was not about whether people acting altruistically are really doing it for self-interested or other-regarding reasons.[61] His focus was on how natural selection operates at the level of genes, not individual organisms or the groups they join. He wanted to show how genes lie behind natural selection: how genes 'behave' so that the likelihood of their being passed on is maximised.

Some might see this as a fine distinction. Since genes are part of 'selfs' (such as humans) their survival depends on the behaviour of the organism they are part of. Indeed, Dawkins shows signs in *The Selfish Gene* of experiencing this very tension. Take the following passage, often quoted as evidence of Dawkins' commitment to a selfish view of humans:

> Be warned that if you wish, as I do, to build a society in which individuals coop-
> erate generously and unselfishly towards a common good, you can expect little
> help from biological nature. Let us try to teach generosity and altruism, because
> we are born selfish.[62]

In the midst of a full-throated affirmation of the primacy of human selfish-ness, he gives voice to a quite different aspiration: 'I wish to build the common good.' It echoes Jean Tirole's *Economics for the Common Good*:[63] an aspiration about the way things should be between members of a community that is good for all. Where did that aspiration come from? According to Dawkins, not from 'biological' nature, and yet the aspiration is clearly there. Intentionally or not, Dawkins seems to recognise a bigger picture. Claiming that 'we are born selfish' was apt to confuse, as Dawkins has since acknowledged.[64]

Biologists recognise the 'manifest existence of cooperation and related group behaviour such as altruism and restraint in cooperation' that can be seen in nature.[65] It is sometimes called 'biological altruism'. Biological altru-ism seems to present a challenge to the idea of natural selection. Why would genes that predispose an organism to behave 'altruistically' simply not die out over time? Various theories have been advanced to explain it, generally by seeking to show how other-regarding behaviour is still based on the 'self-interested' activity of genes. These include 'kin selection'[66] and 'reciprocal altruism'[67] and, more recently, 'costly signalling'[68] and 'indirect reciprocity'.[69]

But do theories like these somehow set the parameters within which altru-ism could develop in humans? Do they mean that all altruistic desires must somehow be derived from 'self-interested' genetic behaviour? It is an unre-solved question, but there is reason to think that they do not.[70] Other theories have been advanced about selection processes that might explain this broader range of cooperative behaviours, one of the most notable being 'cultural group selection'. This is based on the idea that groups with strong cooperative ten-dencies are more likely to survive, with the possibility over millennia of culture-gene co-evolution (where genes that predispose towards cooperation in successful groups get selected, because the groups survive).[71] But looking beyond these too, theories of natural selection do not really address what psychological states might lie behind other-regarding behaviours. Indeed, most of the organisms covered by theories of natural selection generally do not appear to have psychological desires in the human sense. Further, human desires also operate by reference to a world of social meaning which is uniquely human (see Chap. 2).

In sum, evolutionary theory supports the idea that there is a process by which genes that can predispose towards other-regarding behaviour are selected. Further, it does not appear to be incompatible, as a matter of psychology, with the emergence of desires that are other-regarding or altruistic. So, it is now time to look more closely at psychological motivation.

3.2.2 Self-Interest

Even if evolutionary biology leaves room for the possibility of altruistic desires motivated by something other than self-interest, that does not mean that they exist. So, could self-interested desires motivate all market behaviour, other-regarding behaviour included? Many have answered 'yes' to that, few more firmly than English seventeenth century philosopher Thomas Hobbes. For him, 'All society … exists for the sake of either advantage or of glory, i.e. it is a product of love of self, not love of friends.'[72] The same assumption has essentially been made in much academic economics (see Chap. 1). A plausible case can be made.

The idea of self-interest is surprisingly difficult to pin down. Utilitarianism initially treated it as a matter of maximising pleasure and minimising pain. However, it is perhaps better understood as a desire for personal wellbeing. One well-known attempt to describe it was Abraham Maslow's hierarchy of needs: physical survival is at the base and 'self-actualisation' (broadly, being everything you are capable of) at the top.[73] However, there are influential alternatives, such as Self-Determination Theory which regards people as having three basic psychological needs: for competence, relatedness and autonomy.[74]

For current purposes, a simpler approach is to treat this desire for wellbeing as comprising three elements: first, a desire to gain something associated with personal flourishing (such as finding meaning in life, being valued, wealth, social power, or some sort of self-reward, such as being healthy or feeling good); secondly, a desire to avoid what diminishes personal flourishing (such as feelings of meaninglessness, worthlessness or guilt, financial loss, or reputational loss through public censure); and, thirdly, perhaps, a desire to reduce negative feelings evoked by another's distress.[75]

It is obvious that desires such as these can motivate other-regarding behaviour in financial markets. Examples are plentiful. Services are rendered to others, for remuneration. Lunches are offered, in the hope of future business. Referrals are made, in anticipation of a return favour. Favours are returned, in the hope of further favours, or because people feel guilty if they do not. You want your colleagues' esteem? Champion a charitable initiative. Make it a marathon and get fit too. It's all about me, not about you. Except that, in some of these cases, my self-interest *is* about you as well. That is because the behaviour relies on the expectation of a reciprocal response.

It is similar at company level. Treat the client nicely so they give us more work. Do not invest in companies with poor environmental standards; we may lose value. Encourage employee volunteering; clients want evidence of it when we pitch for their business. We provide a good working environment for staff; it makes them more motivated. We must improve our gender balance; clients expect it. '#MeToo moments', compensation claims and regulatory sanctions damage our business. Make sure that staff treat colleagues properly, avoid dubious business events and do not breach regulatory rules: 'we need to manage risks to our business' (a common refrain). Again, some of these involve expectations of reciprocity, where satisfying self-interest depends not just on treating the other well, but on the anticipation of a positive response.

In these and many more ways, self-interest motivates other-regarding behaviour in financial markets, and it is an important source of individual, relational and social goods. Frequently, that behaviour depends upon anticipated reciprocation. Sometimes the reciprocation may be commercially self-interested, sometimes it may be based on social expectations (or norms of reciprocity) so that reciprocation maintains esteem,[76] and sometimes it may be based on a sense of gratitude.[77] This combination of self-interest and reciprocity is clearly important in realising the positive outcomes of cooperation (see Sect. 3.3 below).

But other-regardingness, reciprocal or otherwise, motivated by self-interest also has shortcomings if the objective is the sort of behaviour change needed to address the challenges identified in Chap. 1. For example, there may be other-regarding behaviour within a group, as in the case of LIBOR manipulation, but if the objective is realising financial self-interest above all, it can still be destructive; ultimate desired ends remain important. Further, if only self-interest is motivating other-regarding behaviour, it may not last once it is no longer in a person's interest to cooperate. It may also be challenging and expensive to incentivise, requiring extensive regulatory and management intervention. Relying on self-interest in this way may even undermine other-regarding motivations (see Sect. 6.4.3).[78]

3.2.3   Kind Regards: Altruism

However, there are good reasons to think that other-regarding behaviour is sometimes based on altruism. Altruism could be described as an intrinsic desire to further the welfare of another person for their own sake, regardless of the impact on oneself. The end of altruism is the wellbeing of another based on 'no strings attached' giving, or gratuity. The kind of reciprocal response normally associated with altruism is gratitude; a desire to give something back or 'pay it forward'. Altruism may, then, both cause and result from feelings of gratitude.

But gratitude is unlikely to be the only source of altruism. One influential body of work has looked at the link between altruism and empathy. Empathy can be thought of as 'other-orientated emotions elicited by and congruent with the perceived welfare of someone in need.'[79] It is an emotional response based on assessing a person's situation against what might be in their interests and seems to result from detecting a gap between a person's circumstances and what is consistent with their wellbeing.[80] Feelings of empathy can therefore emerge from taking another's perspective. They can be strengthened, among other things, by observing or imagining another's emotional state.[81] This suggests that actual or imaginative relatedness can be an important source of empathetic concern. Recognition of a social licence is potentially relevant to this question of relatedness (see Sect. 6.3.3).

It is reasonably clear that feelings of empathy and other-regarding behaviour are connected. But, as just discussed, other-regarding behaviour can result from self-interest. Can empathetic emotion trigger an *altruistic* desire for the wellbeing of another person, resulting in other-regarding behaviour? Work by Daniel Batson and others suggests that altruism may indeed sometimes be involved. They have undertaken a series of carefully crafted experiments over a period of nearly twenty years, designed to test whether any of the types of self-interest, described above, appeared to be motivating other-regarding behaviour, or whether altruism was a more plausible explanation. The experiments are too numerous to detail here.[82] However, Batson and his colleagues have concluded that, 'It seems impossible for any known egoistic explanation of the empathy-helping relationship—or any combination of them—to account for the research evidence... To say that we are capable of altruistic motivation is to say that we can care about the welfare of others for their own sakes and not simply for our own.'[83]

This may overstate the strength of the experimental evidence to date. Self-interested desires, individually or in combination, might still lie behind even altruistic behaviour of the sort identified by Batson. However, this body of work presents a serious challenge to those who see all human behaviour as ultimately motivated by individual self-interest.[84] It has also attracted neuro-scientific support.[85] So, as things stand, it is far from clear why self-interest should be privileged over the intuitively more probable explanation that some other-regarding behaviour may be motivated by intrinsically other-regarding desires.

But the focus of Batson's work has been on altruism towards individuals, whereas the challenges identified in Chap. 1 principally concern the communities in which financial markets operate. Self-interest can drive other-regarding behaviour in this wider context. What of altruism? First, where altruistic motivation is based on feelings of empathy, there is a question about whether sufficient proximity exists between those in financial markets and the needs of people in those communities for empathy to arise. However, it may be better to see this as a matter of degree; the strength of motivation might not be the same, but that does not necessarily mean it is absent, and heightening the sense of connection might strengthen it. Indeed, there is some evidence to suggest that empathy induced altruism can extend beyond a person's immediate group and towards those who are not similar to them or with needs they have not themselves experienced.[86] Yet Batson sounds a note of caution about the power of altruism to motivate a response to what he calls 'abstract needs', such as climate change or social unrest—needs, then, not dissimilar to some of those identified in Chap. 1. 'Not only is it difficult to evoke empathy for such needs, they often cannot be effectively addressed with a personal helping response. They must be addressed in political arenas, through institutional and bureaucratic structures.'[87]

However, note that Batson's comment reflects the fact that people do *want* to address needs of this sort. As well as the various self-interested motivations already identified, could a sort of wider altruism also be involved in this? Quite possibly. There has been growing attention over the last twenty-five years to 'public service motivation', looking at what motivates those like civil servants who go into public service. It explores an orientation towards society and the wider public.[88] Some of this may be self-interested, for reasons already discussed. However, while work on the concept may need refinement, it consistently highlights motivation among public sector employees variously described as 'service motivation', 'altruism', 'helping others' and 'prosocial motives'.[89] Significantly, one criticism of this work is that 'public service motivation' seems insufficiently distinguished from more commonly held feelings of altruism directed towards a community, and nor is it obviously restricted to those who work in public sector entities; there is evidence for it in private sector entities too.[90] The possibility of public service motivation in the private sector has not received the same attention as in the public sector, and it may not be as strong. For example, private sector staff seem to value economic rewards more highly than public sector staff.[91] Nonetheless, studies of political motivation more generally seem to echo the presence of broader other-regarding aspirations,[92] as do studies on work motivation, vocation and the desire for work to be meaningful.[93] Further, manifestly, a desire to see justice done for others as well as oneself can also be motivating. This has made justice the subject of centuries of philosophical reflection, but it has also attracted attention from other disciplines, for example, the 'justice motive' in the case of psychologists.[94] Notions of justice have also been advanced to explain transactional behaviour in dictator games that is not narrowly self-interested.[95] While experimental evidence testing the precise nature of these aspirations remains relatively limited,[96] it is therefore reasonable to think that a form of altruism, or a desire to see people treated justly, may also have a role in motivating people to address broader human needs, not just those in their immediate circle.

But altruistic motivation does not guarantee positive outcomes either for the person experiencing it or for others. For the altruist, their altruism could become destructive if is not balanced by self-interest; in an extreme case, it would involve the subjection of their needs to those of others and 'altruistic burn-out'. Similarly at an institutional level, a company that took no account of its own interests would not survive long. In each case, the wellbeing of the self needs attention if the wellbeing of the other is also to be served.[97] Further, the example of LIBOR manipulation is a reminder that altruistic motivation can be damaging if it is directed at the wrong sort of ends. Recognition of a social licence concerns the aspired ends of financial activity and provides a possible framework for finding a balance, as Chaps. 4 and 6 will explain. However, as a preliminary, it is necessary to look more closely at what wellbeing of the self and the other consist of, and how this relates to financial self-interest—the end of financial markets advanced by narratives of the sort discussed in Chap. 1.

3.2.4   The Desire for Dignity and the Role of Mutuality

The idea of human dignity has become highly influential in recent decades as an aspiration in guiding public debate, policy and law, especially following the recognition in the Universal Declaration of Human Rights that, 'the inherent dignity and … the equal and inalienable rights of all members of the human family is the foundation of freedom, justice and peace in the world'.[98] It has since been introduced into a range of international instruments and national constitutions, and the human rights regime is increasingly important in a business context. Can this goal help in understanding what, intuitively at least, may lie behind the desire for wellbeing, whether for oneself or for others, and the balance between the two? What follows argues that it can.

The basis and substance of the concept of human dignity, and whether it is so broad as to lack any substance at all, are contested.[99] In-depth treatment (including the growing body of dignity-based human rights law and theory) falls outside the scope of this book.[100] The focus here is on the fact that an aspiration to realise human dignity has been so clearly and consistently identified in practice, the nature of the basic concept and its relationship with desires for wellbeing. That alone is a big topic, so the following is inevitably a sketch. However, taking the Universal Declaration as one of the most authoritative invocations of human dignity, it is possible to identify two senses of the word 'dignity': first, dignity as something inherent to what it is to be human and, secondly, dignity as something that humans come to realise in practice.[101] The second could be seen as the lived experience of the first.

The underlying basis for dignity in the first sense remains subject to considerable discussion. Again, it is not feasible to go into that here. However, for current purposes, the important point is that it has been recognised in practice in the Universal Declaration and a range of similar contexts and concerns the intrinsic value of a human being. Immanuel Kant is often associated with dignity in this sense—that humans are ends in themselves, for which no substitute can be found.[102] Since he wrote in German, he spoke of *Würde* rather than 'dignity'. Fairly obviously, that is connected with the idea of worth. It was English translators who chose the word 'dignity', recognising that Kant was trying to make clear that human worth is entirely different from economic worth.[103] Significantly for the recognition of a social licence, which involves an aspiration about the *ends* of financial activity, Kant was at pains to distinguish between this inherent value of human beings and instrumental economic value, and hence a market price, in the context of what he described as 'the kingdom of ends':

> In the kingdom of ends everything has either a **price** or a **dignity** [intrinsic value]. What has a price can be replaced with something else, as its *equivalent*; whereas what is elevated above any price, and hence allows of no equivalent has a dignity [intrinsic value].

> What refers to general human inclinations and needs has a *market price*; … but what constitutes the condition under which alone something can be an end in itself does not merely have a relative worth, i.e. a price, but an inner worth, i.e. dignity.[104]

In other words, the intrinsic value of a person cannot be traded in like commodities or investments that have a price. The value of a person transcends economic measures. It is an end in itself. Significantly, given his role as one of the founding fathers of modern economics, Adam Smith also gestures towards something like human dignity, again distinguishing it from economic value, in his *Theory of Moral Sentiments*.[105] Unlike Kant, his approach is based not so much on human capacity to reason but, '…the general fellow feeling which we have with every man merely because he is our fellow-creature.'[106] Significantly, for the preliminary connection made in Chap. 1 between the social licence for financial markets and justice, Smith's view of the human person is also closely connected with his understanding of justice.[107]

The second sense of the word 'dignity' in the Declaration describes something that needs to be realised in practice. How so if dignity is already intrinsic to humans? One way of approaching this is to take this second use of the word 'dignity' as describing a situation in which a person can experience dignity in the first sense (i.e. their intrinsic human value), both in terms of the way they are treated and the person they become; it involves a sense of self-worth and being valued *by others*, and living in conditions consistent with that.

Something of this is reflected in the way dignity crops up in human rights law. The underlying principle is that the rights are needed to tackle situations where people are not able to enjoy their intrinsic human dignity.[108] Since, people are so affected by their social environment, the quality of their relationships—those relationships affected by financial markets and otherwise—must have an impact on this. Indeed talk of human rights only makes sense in the context of relationships. The Universal Declaration makes just this kind of connection. For example, Article 22 links dignity with a person's social, economic and political environment and the development of their personality:

> Everyone, as a member of society, … is entitled to realization, through national effort and international co-operation … of the economic, social and cultural rights indispensable for his dignity and the free development of his personality.

Article 23, meanwhile, talks of 'an existence worthy of human dignity'.

The idea of human dignity as something needing to be realised in experience does not involve denying intrinsic human dignity. Rather, it recognises that people experience their inherent value only imperfectly. So, one way of thinking about personal wellbeing is to see it as describing the extent to which a person experiences their intrinsic dignity. That depends in practice on the quality of their relationships with others, both individuals and institutions. However, the value that others are capable of offering is also likely to depend, in turn, upon the extent to which their own dignity has been realised in practice. There is a profound mutuality about it. There are obvious ways in which individual wellbeing depends on the wellbeing of others—not just in terms of others' ability to provide materially (goods and services, healthcare, defence and so on), but also because a person's consciousness turns a good deal on the perspective of the other, which is, in turn, affected by the other's experience. The 'self' of self-interest and the self that is the subject of altruism are 'relational selves'; an individual's personality, and hence their behaviour, is partially the result of interaction with 'significant others', such as family and friends,[109] and with others more generally, especially in social groups.[110] Each person's experience of dignity depends upon a broad-based mutuality of valuing.

Putting this in a financial market context the experience of dignity could be described as emerging, in part, from pursuing ends that are worthy of respect by oneself and others, and in ways that are worthy of respect.[111] In other words, a person's experience of dignity relies upon having their value recognised by others in the right way. Establishing this kind of respect involves more than earning capacity as a measure of value. It can include recognition of skill, expertise and technical proficiency. However, looking even beyond these, the fact that the child trafficker or money launderer has mastered their art does not dignify them, except perhaps among a confined group of fellow practitioners. The ends to which effort is directed, and the meaning an activity therefore has for those engaged in it and for others, are also critical in realising human dignity, both for the self and for others. And the visceral negative reaction most people have to activities such as child trafficking[112] suggests that there is a relationship between the impact of an activity on the dignity of others and this sort of respect.[113]

Political philosopher Michael Rosen seems to recognise something of this when, talking of dignity, he says that, 'In failing to respect the humanity of others we actually undermine the humanity in ourselves...'[114] Few activities are as destructive of dignity as child trafficking, but no activity is neutral and it is a matter of degree. 'Wanting to help others, acting on that desire, and feeling that we have made a difference is one of the most meaningful parts of working life …'[115] At a profound level, the quality of our relationships with others (the dignity we accord to them and they accord to us) is integral to our own sense of wellbeing as well as theirs.

3.2.5   Financial Desire and Financial Self-Interest

Previous chapters have touched on the powerful role of money in financial markets. How might the desire to make money relate to an intrinsic desire to experience dignity and accord it to others? In one sense, money is an instrument that can be used to make something happen. Financial self-interest might therefore be expected always to be an 'instrumental' desire, not 'intrinsic'. It might be expected always to be focused on getting money to achieve something that can help to realise some other desired end, and, ultimately, wellbeing (or dignity) for oneself or the other. But is there anything more to it than that?

The intense debate over banker remuneration following the financial crisis confirms, first, that the desire for money is a powerful motivation for those in finance, secondly, that their employers assume it to be so, and use it to get staff to do what they want and, thirdly, that regulators assume the same and use it to pursue regulatory objectives. Remuneration matters. In the words of the UK Parliamentary Commission on Banking Standards:

> … The opportunity quickly to earn huge amounts creates strong incentives to obtain them. Sadly, such incentives have often led to behaviour … which contributed to many of the failures in banking. …
>
> … PWC concurred that this "feedback loop between pay and performance reinforced a certain cycle of behaviour".[116]

Chapter 2 looked at how money carries meaning so that it could almost be seen as a sort of language. It symbolises something. It is not just a token of exchange. It is also a symbol of stored value and power and consequently gets used to measure both. The desire for money as a token of exchange is inevitably instrumental, and that clearly lies behind some of the intense focus on financial reward in financial markets. However, it is not the only motivation; the broader range of meanings carried by money is also in play. For example, for an individual, money as a form of stored power can become a symbol of status. As a measure of value it can also provide a way of ranking personal worth as compared with others and defining personal success, as anyone who has had to meet an annual revenue target will confirm.

It is similar at company level. Financial performance is treated as a signal of institutional success, defining the way a firm is perceived, in turn, affecting investment and business decisions and competition. Some would say that it has become *the* defining signal (see Sect. 1.2.2). As discussed above, firms may have edged towards defining their purpose by reference to non-financial factors, but financial return remains key in the way they measure themselves and are measured. A great deal rests on what money says about business organisations. As noted in Chap. 2, there is also a symbiotic relationship between individual desires and group purposes. The purpose of the group is shaped by the financial desires of those involved in it, and group membership affects the way individual desires get expressed. This symbolic power of money is, then, extremely important for individuals and firms in financial markets, and the two feed off each other.

So, while financial self-interest involves a desire to obtain an instrument of exchange, a sense of personal worth, security and power may also be tied up with it or, in a corporate context, a desire to signal success, prestige and potency. Market language sometimes reflects this intrusion of financial value into human value, for example, the tendency in private banks to refer to clients as 'high net worth' and 'ultra-high net worth' (echoing the language of UK financial services regulation[117]). This interaction between the multiple meanings of money and the more intrinsic aspirations of individuals is hinted at in work by PWC and the London School of Economics. They found that an overriding concern for financial services executives is whether their pay is comparable against their peer group, suggesting that they need to be paid at a level they consider to be 'fair' within the company and as compared with those working in competitors. Other than that, 'it almost becomes irrelevant how much they are paid'.[118] Other studies seem to tell a similar story.[119]

The desire to obtain money is about much more than buying power. Success in getting and accumulating it can influence how people and business institutions understand their status, value, success and power and how they feel about themselves. It may also result in the objectification of others, resulting in people being seen as means to an end.[120] Looking at this in terms of the distinction between instrumental and intrinsic desire, where the meaning of money becomes integral to a sense of personal and corporate worth, identity and meaning—where having it is so mixed up with an understanding of what it is to experience wellbeing or dignity—financial desire seems no longer instrumental but almost intrinsic. What is desired is conceived of as if it was an end in itself and drives the actions of those pursuing it accordingly.

3.3 Reciprocity, Positive Reciprocity and Broad-Based Mutuality

The discussion of human dignity, above, suggested that, ultimately, realising wellbeing, either for the self or the other, does not resolve into a simple duality of self-interest and altruism. Rather, it involves a broad-based mutuality: a sharing of value between parties in which each person's ability to give value to others also depends upon their own experience of being valued within their wider network of relationships. Because of that, the mutuality on which wellbeing depends needs to be broad-based. As is clear from this chapter, financial markets are certainly places of mutual giving and receiving; of positive reciprocity in the conventional sense. However, is it realistic to think that they could be a source of broad-based mutuality of this wider sort? For that, they also need to be places of positive reciprocity in the sense that expression is used in this book, to describe an orientation of market relationships beyond their immediate ends which is also positive for the broader networks of relationships that are affected by them.

Mutuality can be seen in various contexts, including in healthy friendships. Friendship involves giving as much as receiving; something people pursue together which can inseparably enrich those involved.[121] Even if friendship is no more than an expression of self-interest, what does that consist of if it is so dependent on another's wellbeing? Wanting a friend's wellbeing seems to involve a mutuality of neither party being 'entire in his or herself'. There is an ongoing process of reciprocity within the relationship, or perhaps reciprocities in which people give something of themselves to each other. Sometimes it is the sort of reciprocity involved in self-interested cooperation and sometimes the gratitude-based reciprocity discussed above in the context of altruism, and sometimes perhaps a hybrid.[122]

Hobbes, in the quote above, clearly recognised the existence of friendship even if, unlike Donne, he discounted it as something that underpins human society. But is it possible to draw a firm line separating friendship, or the kind of mutuality you see in friendship, from economic and civil relationships? While he distinguished between friendship and other sorts of relationship, Aristotle thought not: 'Friendship seems too to hold states together…', he says in his *Nicomachean Ethics*.[123]

Centuries later, sociologist Robert Putnam has spoken of the touchstone of 'social capital'[124] being a norm of, 'generalized reciprocity', which also involves an element of open-ended giving: 'I'll do this for you now, without expecting anything immediately in return and perhaps without even knowing you, confident that down the road you or someone else will return the favour.'[125] He regards it as short-term altruism and long-term self-interest, but, based on the discussion of those two motivations above, perhaps that is too sharp a distinction. Short-term self-interest and long-term altruism may also be involved.

Turning, more specifically, to commercial relationships, French anthropologist Marcel Mauss also seems to have identified the possibility of something similar. In his famous study of a number of non-industrialised people groups, *The Gift*, he drew attention to the prevalence of gift exchange in social relations, including economic relations. As he says of one such group, there is, '… a constant 'give and take'. … a continuous flow in all directions of presents given, accepted, and reciprocated…'[126] The gift-giving he identified was not free of obligations, including material and economic obligations. However, it involved the exchange of something more than material wealth.[127] Mauss went on to highlight the continuing presence of this broader relational exchange in the economic relationships of French twentieth century society:

> … man … has not been a machine for very long … The producer who carries on exchange feels once more – he has always felt it, but this time he does so acutely – that he is exchanging more than a product of hours of working time, but that he is giving something of himself – his time, his life.[128]

In other words, he is giving intrinsic human value. The presence of a general, but not universally held, predisposition towards reciprocity, and the element of gift in economic exchange has been identified experimentally and in practice, and harks back to the discussion of incomplete contracts and trust in Sect. 3.1.[129] However, these processes do not necessarily result in healthy relationships, or wider benefits to those beyond them. The outcome depends upon the end at which they are directed.[130]

Nonetheless, together, these observations would suggest that financial market relationships should not be seen simply in terms of what is exchanged, even non-financially, between the immediate parties. There is also a need to recognise the wider network of relationships they affect and, in turn, on which transactions and the parties to them depend. From that perspective, market relationships do indeed have the potential to be a source of broad-based mutuality. Consistent with that, there has been a growing recognition that commercial and financial transactions are not simply about monetary and material exchange, but depend upon and are a vital source of wider relational goods:[131] economic exchange draws on broader mutuality but can also affect the mutuality on which it relies.

The different cultural expectations in which economic actors are socialized, the need for sociability and the quest for approval, the webs of reciprocity expectations created by repeated interaction are all factors that affect not only the social framework within which economic transactions occur, but also the very nature of the latter.[132]

The activities of those involved in attempting to manipulate LIBOR and other indices look to have been reciprocal, but not in a way that would generally be regarded as *positive*, since those involved apparently had little regard to wider outcomes. It was not the sort of reciprocity that would strengthen broad-based mutuality. *Positive reciprocity*, in the sense used in this book, depends on the ends being pursued. It involves an orientation of market relationships in a way that does not just benefit the immediate parties (which is the conventional way of thinking about positive reciprocity), but also helps to realise wider goods on which broad-based mutuality and individual wellbeing rely, as do markets. Because of that, it is important to find ways of strengthening that orientation within the multitude of relationships that comprise financial markets. In part, that requires a clearer sense of ends of market activity that transcend immediate transactional financial goals, such as the pressing human needs discussed in Chap. 1. Greater recognition of a social licence for financial markets has a potential role to play (see Chap. 6).

3.4   Conclusion

If people really thought that humans pursue only self-interest, they would behave very differently. In practice, however, they assume and display a desire for the wellbeing of others and themselves both in financial markets and beyond. This might be the product of self-interest, but probably also involves altruism or, systemically, commitment to the public good or justice. Wellbeing can be thought of as an experience of a person's human dignity, or intrinsic value, and their experience of it depends to a significant degree on the extent to which others in their network of relationships have also experienced it. The realisation of that value relies upon broad-based mutuality which, in turn, depends upon relationships that are positively reciprocal.

Not all reciprocity is positive. Reciprocity can be destructive, both for the self and for others if self-interest and other-regardingness are not balanced. Discovering that balance in practice depends, in part, upon the ends being pursued. Obtaining money is an end. It can be desired and used instrumentally, out of self-interest or altruism, in ways that enhance or detract from human dignity. However, when the symbolic meaning of money becomes equated with human wellbeing, the risk is that human worth is reduced to something measured by money rather than being served by it. Behaviour motivated by this limited understanding of wellbeing can detract from positive reciprocity and undermine social solidarity, the very solidarity on which markets rely. Because of the financial values they assume, financial narratives and models of the sort discussed in Chap. 1 create a risk of precisely that. However, they are now being re-evaluated: the question of what ends are valuable is being reassessed. It is in this context that recognition of a social licence for financial markets has emerged. It speaks to exactly this issue of valued ends, but draws attention to a different sort of value from that of the financial narratives in Chap. 1. It is to the social licence that Part II now turns.

Notes

1. Helen Horton and Eleanor Steafel, '"Selfless and heroic"' Australian nurse Kirsty Boden died while running to help injured on London Bridge, say grieving family', *The Telegraph*, London, 6 June 2017.
2. Nicola Merrifield, 'Tributes pour in for nurse killed in terror attack', *Nursing Times*, London, 6 June 2017.
3. *Deloitte 2018 Millennial Survey*, Deloitte 2018, available at https://www2. deloitte.com/content/dam/Deloitte/global/Documents/About-Deloitte/gx-2018-millennial-survey-report.pdf (accessed 16 October 2019). Thirty-nine per cent of millennials surveyed identified one purpose of business as promoting social wellbeing. Sixty-three per cent nonetheless stated that remuneration was very important in deciding who to work for. Seventy-five per cent believed businesses focus on their own agenda rather than considering wider society.
4. The observation is not new. See for example, Dale T. Miller, *The Norm of Self-interest*, American Psychologist, 1999, Vol. 54(12), 1053–1060; Fabrizio Ferraro, Jeffrey Pfeffer and Robert I. Sutton, *Economics Language and Assumptions: How Theories Can Become Self-fulfilling*, Academy of Management Review, 2005, Vol. 30(1), 8–24; Lynn Stout, *Cultivating Conscience: How Good Laws Make Good People* (Princeton University Press 2011); Yochai Benkler, *The Penguin and the Leviathan: How Cooperation Triumphs Over Self-interest* (Crown Business 2011).
5. Charles P. Kindleberger and Robert Z. Aliber, *Manias, Panics and Crashes: A History of Financial Crises* (5th edn, Palgrave Macmillan 2005).
6. 'An Accident Waiting to Happen': *The Failure of HBOS*, Parliamentary Commission on Banking Standards, fourth report of session 2012–2013, 7 March 2013, HL Paper 144, HC 705.

7. *The Failure of the Royal Bank of Scotland*, Financial Services Authority Board Report, December 2011.
8. *Royal Commission into Misconduct in the Banking, Superannuation and Financial Services Industry, Final Report*, Commonwealth of Australia, 2019, 1–2.
9. *How Fair and Effective are the Fixed Income, Foreign Exchange and Commodities Markets?* Fair and Effective Markets Review, Consultation Document, October 2014, HM Treasury, Bank of England and Financial Conduct Authority, 9.
10. Lina Saigol and Gina Chon, 'Libor: the email trail', *Financial Times*, London, 25 September 2013.
11. Reported to the author by one of the trainees who was sufficiently struck to remember it nearly 30 years later.
12. Dan Awrey, William Blair and David Kershaw, *Between Law and Markets: Is There a Role for Culture and Ethics in Financial Regulation?* Delaware Journal of Corporate Law, 2013, Vol. 38(1), 191–245. The literature variously describes behaviour of this sort as 'pro-social', 'altruistic' or 'ethical'. 'Other-regarding' is used here as a way of referring to what can be seen in practice at an individual and social level, without at this stage looking at the question of motivation (on which, see below).
13. See, for example, Mark C. Bolino and Adam M. Grant, *The Bright Side of Being Prosocial at Work, and the Dark Side, Too: A Review and Agenda for Research on Other-oriented Motives, Behavior, and Impact in Organizations*, The Academy of Management Annals, 2016, Vol. 10(1), 599–670; Philip M. Podsakoff, Scott B. Mackenzie and Nathan P. Podsakoff eds., *The Oxford Handbook of Organizational Citizenship Behavior* (Oxford University Press 2018); Lea Cassar and Stephan Meier, *Nonmonetary Incentives and the Implications of Work as a Source of Meaning*, Journal of Economic Perspectives, 2018, Vol. 32(3), 215–238.
14. Recognising that a range of motives may be involved such as skill acquisition and sociability: Jessica B. Rodell, et al., *Employee Volunteering: A Review and Framework for Future Research*, Journal of Management, 2016, Vol. 42(1), 55–84.
15. *2018 Deloitte Millennial Survey*; see also *FCA Transforming Culture Conference 19 March 2018, Event Summary and Next Steps*, Financial Conduct Authority 2018, 5.
16. *Bristol & West Building Society v Mothew (t/a Stapley & Co)* [1996] 4 All ER, 712–713.
17. Rodell, et al., *Employee Volunteering: A Review and Framework for Future Research*; Cassar and Meier, *Nonmonetary Incentives and the Implications of Work as a Source of Meaning*.
18. See, for example, 'Banking on purpose—Adding value', *The Banker*, London, January 2017; Leonie Roderik, 'Why bank brands are taking a more purposeful approach', *Marketingweek.com*, 25 January 2017.

19. David Rouch, *Statements of Corporate Purpose of Key Global Financial Institutions and Social Aspiration*, 2019, available at SSRN: https://ssrn.com/abstract=3544793

20. So says Accenture, https://www.accenture.com/gb-en/insights/strategy/brand-purpose?c=strat_glb_globalconsumerp_10446585&n=psgs_generi c_1218&gclid=EAIaIQobChMIhNebyM2u4AIVZ7vtCh3NFQOZEAAY ASAAEgK4g_D_BwE (accessed 16 September 2019).

21. https://www.gbm.hsbc.com/insights/sustainable-financing/sustainable-financing-and-esg-investing-report (accessed 18 January 2019).

22. She was aware that the conversation would inform this book and has reviewed what follows.

23. Kenneth J. Arrow, *Gifts and Exchanges*, Philosophy and Public Affairs, 1972, Vol. 1(4), 343–362, 357.

24. Oliver Hart, *Incomplete Contracts and Control*, American Economic Review, 2017, Vol. 107(7), 1731–1752.

25. But see Samuel Bowles, *Endogenous Preferences: The Cultural Consequences of Markets and Other Economic Institutions*, Journal of Economic Literature, 1998, Vol. 36(1), 75–111, 77 et seq.; Edward Lorenz, *Trust, Contract and Economic Cooperation*, Cambridge Journal of Economics, 1999, Vol. 23(3), 301–315; Ernst Fehr and Simon Gächter, *Fairness and Retaliation: The Economics of Reciprocity*, The Journal of Economic Perspectives, 2000, Vol. 14(3), 159–181; Ernst Fehr, Susanne Kremhelmer and Klaus M. Schmidt, *Fairness and the Optimal Allocation of Ownership Rights*, The Economic Journal, 2008, Vol. 118, 1262–1284.

26. Fehr and Gächter, *Fairness and Retaliation*, 176 et seq. They suggest that the presence of reciprocity (among other things, in response to the generosity of the contracting counterparty) 'may give rise to a world of incomplete contracts', 160.

27. For example, *Scammell v Ouston* [1941] AC 251, 268–269.

28. Mark Granovetter, *Economic Action and Social Structure: The Problem of Embeddedness*, American Journal of Sociology, 1985, Vol. 91(3), 481–510, 496 advances this as evidence of how commercial transactions rely upon a broader network of social relations.

29. ISDA standard for the International Swaps and Derivatives Association. Most non-standard derivatives transactions are subject to the terms of the 1992 ISDA multicurrency—cross-border master agreement or the 2002 master agreement. Copies can be obtained from ISDA.

30. Whereby, very broadly, one party transfers investments to another on the basis of an agreement that they will be transferred back at a future date. In return, the other party pays over a cash amount, subject to an agreement that it will be repaid at the time the investments are returned. In each case, the parties enter into a master agreement under which a series of transactions will take place, agreed on a case-by-case basis, often over many years.

31. Employment contracts are another example. These cannot record everything expected of an employee. Rather, there is a basic description of their role and, usually, some sort of requirement to exercise diligence, skill and care in discharging it. After that the arrangement relies on an understanding that, whether out of self-interest or otherwise, the employee will perform. See Fehr and Gächter, *Fairness and Retaliation*, 168.

32. Yochai Benkler, *The Wealth of Networks: How Social Production Transforms Markets and Freedom* (Yale University Press 2006).

33. See Recital 64 and Articles 17, 31 and 48 of Directive 2014/65/EU of the European Parliament and of the Council on markets in financial instruments.

34. Communication from the Commission on Artificial Intelligence for Europe, European Commission COM(2018) 237 final, section I and at paragraph 3.3.

35. Not all transactions have such an obvious other-regarding element (especially where trading is principal-to-principal), but examples are plentiful.

36. The following focuses on ESG investing as an example, but there are others.

37. *2018 Global Sustainable Investment Review*, Global Sustainable Investment Alliance, 2018.

38. For example, *Too Late, Too Sudden: Transition to a Low-Carbon Economy and Systemic Risk*, Reports of the Advisory Scientific Committee, No.6/February 2016, European Systemic Risk Board.

39. *Enable, empower, ensure: a new finance for the new economy*, speech by Mark Carney, Governor of the Bank of England, 20 June 2019.

40. See https://www.imvoconvenanten.nl/pensioenfondsen/news/2018/12/convenant-pensioenfondsen?sc_lang=en (accessed 16 October 2019).

41. Max M. Schanzenbach and Robert H. Sitkoff, *The Law and Economics of Environmental, Social and Governance Investing by a Fiduciary*, Harvard Law School Discussion Paper 971, September 2018. It seems implicit in their discussion of the US legal treatment of ESG investing that a mixture of motives may be involved.

42. 'Sustainable investing joins the mainstream', *The Economist*, London, 25 November 2017; Jennifer Thompson, 'Battle to recruit ESG specialists intensifies', *Financial Times*, London, 15 October 2018; Attracta Mooney and Peter Smith, 'As the climate changes, ESG investing powers into the mainstream', *Financial Times*, London, 18 November 2018.

43. David Rouch, *Survey Evidence for the Role of Other-regarding/Sustainability Aspirations in Addition to Financial Objectives in the Investment Process*, 2019, available at SSRN: https://ssrn.com/abstract=3545242. These surveys tend to rely on peoples' expressed preferences so may not accurately reflect what they would do in practice. However, some of the academic work in the footnote that follows helps to correct for that.

44. *Walking the Talk: Understanding Consumer Demand for Sustainable Investing*, University of Cambridge Institute for Sustainability Leadership, 2019; Rob

Bauer, Tobias Ruof and Paul Smeets, *Get Real! Individuals Prefer More Sustainable Investments*, February 2019 (available at: https://ssrn.com/abstract=3287430); Lei Delsen and Alex Lehr, *Value Matters or Values Matter? An Analysis of Heterogeneity in Preferences for Sustainable Investments*, Journal of Sustainable Finance and Investment, 2019, Vol. 9(3), 240–261; Gunnar Gutsche and Andreas Ziegler, *Which Private Investors Are Willing to Pay for Sustainable Investments? Empirical Evidence from Stated Choice Experiments*, Journal of Banking and Finance, 2019, Vol. 102, 193–214; Samuel Hartzmark and Abigail B. Sussman, *Do Investors Value Sustainability? A Natural Experiment Examining Ranking and Fund Flows*, forthcoming in the Journal of Finance.

45. HSBC Sustainable Financing and Investment Report (HSBC 2018) https://www.gbm.hsbc.com/insights/sustainable-financing/sustainable-financing-and-esg-investing-report (accessed on 16 January 2019).

46. See also Granovetter, *Economic Action and Social Structure*, 492; Alejandro Portes, *Economic Sociology: A Systematic Enquiry* (Princeton University Press 2010), 38 et seq.; Bolino and Grant, *The Bright Side of Being Prosocial at Work, and the Dark Side, Too*, 28 et seq.

47. See further, Wieke W. Scholten and Naomi Ellemers, *Bad Apples or Corrupting Barrels? Preventing Traders' Misconduct*, Journal of Financial Regulation and Compliance, 2016, Vol. 24(4), 366–382.

48. See Sect. 3.1.1 above.

49. See 'Why the FICC markets matter', in *How Fair and Effective are the Fixed Income, Foreign Exchange and Commodities Markets?*, Fair and Effective Markets Review, and 'What do 'fair' and 'effective' mean?', in *The Fair and Effective Markets Review*, Final Report, Fair and Effective Markets Review, HM Treasury, Bank of England and Financial Conduct Authority, June 2015, 18–20.

50. Public comments are available at https://www.bankofengland.co.uk/paper/2015/how-fair-and-effective-are-the-fixed-income-foreign-exchange-and-commodities-markets-responses (accessed 20 September 2019).

51. They did raise a number of important concerns about how fair and effective markets can be achieved including, among other things, the need to maintain market liquidity and the risks of inappropriate regulation. However, these tend to assume the basic definition advanced by the Review.

52. *The Fair and Effective Markets Review*, Final Report, Fair and Effective Markets Review, 18.

53. Other sorts of intrinsic desire may also be involved, such as aesthetic desire. However, they fall beyond the scope of the current exercise.

54. Ernst Fehr and Herbert Gintis, *Human Motivation and Social Cooperation: Experimental and Analytical Foundations*, Annual Review of Sociology, 2007, Vol. 33, 43–64 observe that in experimental games some subjects consistently appear 'completely self-regarding'.

55. It also has major moral philosophical implications which are not addressed explicitly here.

56. John Donne and Anthony Raspa, *Devotions Upon Emergent Occasions* (Oxford University Press 1987), Meditation XVII, 87 (spelling updated).

57. Bethany McLean and Peter Elkind, *The Smartest Guys in the Room: The Amazing Rise and Scandalous Fall of Enron* (Penguin 2004), xix, 31, 54 et seq., *Enron: The Smartest Guys in the Room* (HDNet Films 2005) at 21 minutes.

58. As Dawkins notes in the preface to the second edition, if you 'push novelty of language and metaphor far enough you can end up with a new way of seeing' which can change the direction of science. It does not stop at science. Richard Dawkins, *The Selfish Gene* (40th Anniversary edn, Oxford University Press 2016), xxi.

59. Richard Dawkins, *The God Delusion* (Black Swan 2016), 246.

60. Dawkins, *The Selfish Gene*, x.

61. Ibid., 5.

62. Ibid., 3–4.

63. Jean Tirole, *Economics for the Common Good* (Princeton University Press 2017).

64. Dawkins, *The Selfish Gene*, ix.

65. Robert Axelrod and William D. Hamilton, *The Evolution of Cooperation*, Science, 1981, Vol. 211(4489), 1390–1396, 1390.

66. William D. Hamilton, *The Genetical Theory of Social Behaviour*, Journal of Theoretical Biology, 1964, Vol. 7, 1–52.

67. Robert L. Trivers, *The Evolution of Reciprocal Altruism*, The Quarterly Review of Biology, 1971, Vol. 46(1), 35–57; Axelrod and Hamilton, *The Evolution of Cooperation*.

68. Amotz Zahavi, *Altruism as a Handicap—The Limitations of Kin Selection and Reciprocity*, Journal of Avian Biology, 1995, Vol. 26(1), 1–3.

69. Martin A. Nowak, *Five Rules for the Evolution of Cooperation*, Science, 2006, Vol. 314, 1560–1563.

70. Stephen Stich, John M. Doris and Erica Roedder, 'Altruism', in *The Moral Psychology Handbook*, eds. John M. Doris, et al. (Oxford University Press 2010), 154–169; Herbert Gintis, et al., 'Moral Sentiments and Material Interests: Origins, Evidence, and Consequences', in *Moral Sentiments and Material Interests: The Foundations of Cooperation in Economic Life*, eds. Herbert Gintis, et al. (MIT Press 2005); Robert Kurzban, Maxwell N. Burton-Chellew and Stuart A. West, *The Evolution of Altruism in Humans*, Annual Review of Psychology, 2015, Vol. 66, 575–599.

71. Much of this has developed from the work of Robert Boyd and Peter J. Richerson. It has been much supplemented and remains subject to debate and refinement: Peter J. Richerson, et al., *Cultural Group Selection Plays an*

Essential Role in Explaining Human Cooperation: A Sketch of the Evidence, Behavioral and Brian Sciences, 2016, Vol. 39, 1–68.

72. Thomas Hobbes, *On the Citizen*, edited and translated by Richard Tuck and Michael Silverthorne (Cambridge University Press 1998), I:2, 24.

73. Abraham H. Maslow, *Motivation and Personality* (Harper & Row 1954).

74. Richard M. Ryan and Edward L. Deci, *Self-determination Theory: Basic Psychological Needs in Motivation, Development and Wellness* (The Guilford Press 2017).

75. Batson, *Altruism in Humans* (Oxford University Press 2011), 70.

76. B. Douglas Bernheim, *A Theory of Conformity*, Journal of Political Economy, 1994, Vol. 102(5), 841–877; Robert Akerlof, *Value Formation: The Role of Esteem*, Games and Economic Behavior, 2017, Vol. 102, 1–19; Geoffrey Brennan and Philip Pettit, *The Economy of Esteem* (Oxford University Press 2004), 72.

77. David DeSteno, et al., *Gratitude as Moral Sentiment: Emotion-Guided Cooperation in Economic Exchange*, Emotion, 2010, Vol. 10(2), 289–293.

78. Samuel Bowles, *The Moral Economy: Why Good Incentives Are No Substitute for Good Citizens* (Yale University Press 2016).

79. Batson, *Altruism in Humans*, 11.

80. Ibid., 33 et seq.

81. Dennis L. Krebs, *Empathy and Altruism*, Journal of Personality and Social Psychology, 1975, Vol. 32(6), 1134–1146; Frédérique De Vignemont and Tania Singer, *The Empathic Brain: How, When and Why?* Trends in Cognitive Sciences, 2006, Vol. 10(10), 435–441, 437–438.

82. For Batson's own description, see Batson, *Altruism in Humans*, Part II.

83. Ibid., 160.

84. Stich, Doris, and Roedder, *Altruism*.

85. Indrajeet Patil, et al., *Neuroanatomical Basis of Concern-based Altruism in Virtual Environment*, Neuropsychologia, 2018, Vol. 116, 34–43.

86. Batson, *Altruism in Humans*, 193–194.

87. Ibid., 195.

88. Wouter Vandenabeele, Adrian Ritz and Oliver Neumann, 'Public Service Motivation: State of the Art and Conceptual Cleanup', in *The Palgrave Handbook of Public Administration and Management in Europe*, eds. Edoardo Ongaro and Sandra van Thiel (Palgrave 2018).

89. Barry Bozeman and Xuhong Su, *Public Service Motivation Concepts and Theory: A Critique*, Public Administration Review, 2015, Vol. 75(5), 700–710; Vandenabeele, Ritz and Neumann, *Public Service Motivation*.

90. Bozeman and Su, *Public Service Motivation Concepts and Theory*; Stephanie Moulton and Mary K. Freeney, *Public Service in the Private Sector: Private Loan Originator Participation in a Public Mortgage Program*, The Journal of Public Administration Research and Theory, 2011, Vol. 21(3), 547–572.

91. Marc Buelens and Herman van den Broeck, *An Analysis of Differences in Work Motivation Between Public and Private Sector Organizations*, Public Administration Review, January/February 2007, Vol. 67(1), 65–74.

92. Leif Lewin, *Self-interest and Public Interest in Western Politics* (Oxford University Press 1991).

93. Bryan J. Dik and Ryan D. Duffy, *Calling and Vocation at Work: Definitions and Prospects for Research and Practice*, The Counselling Psychologist, 2009, Vol. 37(3), 424–450; Ryan D. Duffy and Bryan J. Dik, *Research on Calling: What Have We Learned and Where are We Going?* Journal of Vocational Behaviour, 2013, Vol. 83(3), 428–436; Ruth Yeoman, et al. eds., *The Oxford Handbook of Meaningful Work* (Oxford University Press 2019); Adam M. Grant, *Relational Job Design and the Motivation to Make a Prosocial Difference*, Academy of Management Review, 2007, Vol. 32(2), 393–417.

94. See generally, Dale Ross and Michael T. Miller eds., *The Justice Motive in Everyday Life* (Cambridge University Press 2002).

95. Claudia Dalbert and Sören Umlauft, *The Role of the Justice Motive in Economic Decision Making*, Journal of Economic Psychology, 2009, Vol. 30(2), 172–180; Helena Lopes, *From Self-Interest Motives to Justice Motives: The Challenges of Some Experimental Results*, American Journal of Economics and Sociology, 2008, Vol. 67(2), 287–314. See also Fehr and Gintis, *Human Motivation and Social Cooperation*, highlighting findings that 'reciprocal fairness' and 'equity aversion', in addition to self-interest, are behind what they call 'strong reciprocity'.

96. Robyn M. Dawes, Alphons J. C. van der Kragt and John M. Orbell, 'Cooperation for the Benefit of Us – Not Me, or My Conscience', in *Beyond Self-interest*, ed. Jane J. Mansbridge (University of Chicago Press 1990); Batson, *Altruism in Humans*, 218 et seq.; Carolyn L. Hafer and Laurent Bègue, *Experimental Research on Just-world Theory: Problems, Developments, and Future Challenges*, Psychological Bulletin, 2005, Vol. 131(1), 128–167.

97. Jane J. Mansbridge, 'On the Relation of Altruism and Self-interest', in *Beyond Self-interest*, ed. Jane J. Mansbridge (University of Chicago Press 1990).

98. Preamble to the Universal Declaration of Human Rights, first paragraph.

99. Michael Rosen, *Dignity: Its History and Meaning* (Harvard University Press 2012); Christopher McCrudden, 'In Pursuit of Human Dignity: An Introduction to Current Debates', in *Understanding Human Dignity*, ed. Christopher McCrudden (published for the British Academy by Oxford University Press 2013).

100. Even the 600 page *Cambridge Handbook of Human Dignity* eschews what it describes as a 'futile attempt at completeness': Thomas Pogge, 'Dignity and Global Justice', in *The Cambridge Handbook of Human Dignity: Interdisciplinary Perspectives*, eds. Marcus Düwell, et al. (Cambridge University Press 2014), xx.

101. Pogge, *Dignity and Global Justice*.
102. Immanuel Kant, *Groundwork of the Metaphysics of Morals*, translated and edited by Mary Gregor and Jens Timmermanm, revised edition (Cambridge University Press 2012), 4:428. He used it as a basis for his framework of duties and rights based on 'categorical imperatives'. It is not intended to explore that here, simply to highlight his understanding of the substance of the idea of dignity and situate it as part of a continuum.
103. Remy Debes, 'Introduction', in *Dignity: A History*, ed. Remy Debes (Oxford University Press 2017)
104. Immanuel Kant, Groundwork, 4:434–4:435 (insertions in square brackets added).
105. Remy Debes, *Adam Smith on Dignity and Equality*, British Journal for the History of Philosophy, 2012, Vol. 20(1), 109–140.
106. Adam Smith, *The Theory of Moral Sentiments* (Liberty Fund edn 1982), II. ii.3.10, 90.
107. Jesse Norman, *Adam Smith: What He Thought and Why It Matters* (Allen Lane 2018), 199; Stephen Darwall, *Sympathetic Liberalism: Recent Work on Adam Smith*, Philosophy and Public Affairs, 1999, Vol. 28(2), 139–164; Charles L. Griswold, JR., *Adam Smith and the Virtues of Enlightenment* (Cambridge University Press 1999), 238; Remy Debes, *Adam Smith on Dignity and Equality*.
108. Importantly, in its original context, the Declaration was principally concerned with protecting the person and institutions of social solidarity against the state rather than the enforcement of rights between individuals. Further discussion of why that is significant lies outside the scope of the current work.
109. Susan M. Anderson and Serena Chen, *The Relational Self: An Interpersonal Social-cognitive Theory*, Psychological Review, 2002, Vol. 109(4), 619–645.
110. There is a debate over which influences are the most powerful in shaping personality (see, for example, Constantine Sedikides and Lowell Gaertner, 'The Social Self: The Quest for Identity and the Motivational Primacy of the Individual Self', in *The Social Mind: Cognitive and Motivational Aspects of Interpersonal Behavior*, eds. Joseph P. Forgas, Kipling D. Williams and Ladd Wheeler (Cambridge University Press 2001). The point here is to highlight the apparently close connection between the other and the self.
111. Randy Hodson, *Dignity at Work* (Cambridge University Press 2001), 3–4. See also Adam M. Grant, *Giving Time, Time After Time: Work Design and Sustained Employee Participation in Corporate Volunteering*, Academy of Management Review, 2012, Vol. 37(4), 589–615, 594–595 and Brent D. Rosso, Kathryn H. Dekas and Amy Wrzesniewski, *On the Meaning of Work: A Theoretical Integration and Review*, Research in Organizational Behavior, 2010, Vol. 30, 91–127. They do not talk of 'dignity', but the factors they identify as relevant to the desire for work to be meaningful highlight the close inter-relationship between self and other. On the way in

which self-esteem is dependent on the attitudes of others, see Bernheim, *A Theory of Conformity*; Akerlof, *Value Formation: The Role of Esteem*; Brennan and Pettit, *The Economy of Esteem*.

112. See for example, Kiril Sharapov, *Understanding Public Knowledge and Attitudes Towards Trafficking in Human Beings*, Research Paper, Part 2 (Center for Policy Studies, Central European University 2015).
113. Adam M. Grant, *The Significance of Task Significance: Job Performance Effects, Relational Mechanisms, and Boundary Conditions*, Journal of Applied Psychology, 2008, Vol. 93(1), 108–124.
114. Rosen, *Dignity*, 157–158.
115. Bolino and Grant, *The Bright Side of Being Prosocial at Work, and the Dark Side, Too*, 52.
116. *Changing Banking for Good*, Report of the Parliamentary Commission on Banking Standards, First Report of Session 2013–14, Volume II: Chapters 1 to 11 and Annexes, together with formal minutes, HL Paper 27-II HC 175-II, June 2013, paragraphs 112 and 113.
117. For example, Article 48 of the Financial Services and Markets Act 2000 (Financial Promotion) Order 2005 which refers to 'certified high net worth individuals'.
118. *Pay: What Motivates Financial Services Executives?*, PWC 2012, available at https://www.pwc.com/gx/en/financial-services/publications/assets/pwc-pay-what-motivates-financial-services-executives.pdf (accessed 28 October 2019), 20–21.
119. See for example James Wade, Charles O'Reilly and Timothy Pollock, *Overpaid CEOs and Underpaid Managers: Fairness and Executive Compensation*, Organization Science, 2006, Vol. 17(5), 527–544; Luis Gomez-Mejia and Robert M. Wiseman, *Reframing Executive Compensation: An Assessment and Outlook*, Journal of Management, 1997, Vol. 23(3), 291–374.
120. Xijing Wang and Eva G. Krumhuber, *The Love of Money Results in Objectification*, British Journal of Social Psychology, 2017, Vol. 56(2), 354–372.
121. Obviously, where there is an imbalance, they can also be destructive.
122. Joel Sobel's concept of 'intrinsic reciprocity' seems to reflect this, although it is still ultimately based on self-interest: Joel Sobel, *Interdependent Preferences and Reciprocity*, Journal of Economic Literature, 2005, Vol. 43(2), 392–436. Luigino Bruni advances a different categorisation of various sorts of reciprocity, but sees them essentially growing from self-interest and altruism: *Reciprocity, Altruism and the Civil Society: In Praise of Heterogeneity* (Routledge 2008).
123. Aristotle, W. D. Ross and Lesley Brown, *The Nicomachean Ethics* (Oxford University Press 2009), Book VIII, 1155a22.

124. Given the divergent ways in which the expression 'social capital' is understood and defined, this book generally avoids using it. However, it is taken here to mean a form of social solidarity or mutuality.

125. Robert D. Putnam, *Bowling Alone: The Collapse and Revival of American Community* (Simon & Schuster 2001), 134.

126. Marcel Mauss, Mary Douglas and W. D. Halls, *The Gift: The Form and Reason for Exchange in Archaic Societies* (Routledge Classics edn 2002), 37.

127. Ibid., 42.

128. Ibid., 98, 99.

129. Fehr and Gintis, *Human Motivation and Social Cooperation*; Alex Bryson and Richard B. Freeman, *The Role of Employee Stock Purchase Plans – Gift and Incentive? Evidence from a Multinational Corporation*, British Journal of Industrial Relations, 2019, Vol. 57(1), 86–106; Kévin André, et al., *Beyond the Opposition Between Altruism and Self-interest: Reciprocal Giving in Reward-based Crowdfunding*, Journal of Business Ethics, 2017, Vol. 146(2), 313–332.

130. Note also experimental evidence suggesting that the ability to punish unduly self-interested behaviour also has a role in supporting socially cooperative results: Fehr and Gintis, *Human Motivation and Social Cooperation*. Detailed discussion of the relationship between punishment and reciprocity falls outside of the scope of the current work. However, it is important, connecting it, for example, with the themes of justice and law and regulation.

131. See for example, Granovetter, *Economic Action and Social Structure*; Alejandro Portes, *Economic Sociology*, 27 (but note his caution about the (mis)use of the expression 'social capital'); Bruni, *Reciprocity, Altruism and the Civil Society*; Jean Tirole, *Economics for the Common Good*; *Good Work: The Taylor Review of Modern Working Practices*, 2017.

132. Portes, *Economic Sociology*, 18.

Part II

The Social Licence and Justice

Fast Track

There is a need for healing in the relationship between finance and wider society and for greater urgency in addressing humanity's many challenges. This requires behaviour change throughout the financial ecosystem. An effective response depends upon how all of us behave from here.

Part I outlined key drivers of behaviour in financial markets and beyond. With that groundwork complete, Part II considers the observation that financial markets operate subject to a social licence; what it highlights about the relationship between finance and wider society, especially where that is relevant to addressing current challenges.

- Chapter 4 looks at why it makes sense to talk of financial markets being subject to a social licence and what the licence consists of.
- Chapter 5 deals with the relationship between the social licence and law, regulation and other sets of written standards (such as a conduct codes and statements of good practice) that are used to influence behaviour.

Part III will go on to connect this with the discussion in Part I by looking at how recognition of a social licence can make a difference in practice.

4

The Social Licence for Financial Markets

Real markets are resilient, fair and effective. They maintain their social licence.
—*Building real markets for the good of the people*, speech by Mark Carney, Governor of the Bank of England, London 10 June 2015.

Fast Track

Speed Read

Does the observation that markets operate subject to the licence of society make sense and, if so, what sort of licence is it? What sort of account of financial markets does recognition of a social licence advance?

Talk of a social licence does make sense. It is not 'mere' metaphor. It identifies something that can be seen operating **in practice**. Most obviously, in almost any jurisdiction, finance firms must be authorised (or 'licensed') by regulators to carry on business. But, beyond that, it also makes sense because of the extent to which finance is socially contingent. For example, the 'raw materials' of financial markets (such as money and investments) are social constructs. Similarly market participants rely on social constructs to carry on business (such as the limited liability company, the gift of the state), and upon social frameworks (such as education systems and defence). Indeed, market activity would be impossible in the absence of social solidarity and deep social consensus (including, at the most basic level, about the meaning of language and money). There is also considerable evidence beyond the financial sector that businesses both regard them-

(continued)

This chapter builds on David Rouch, 'The Social Licence for Financial Markets, Written Standards and Aspiration' in *Edward Elgar Handbook on Law and Ethics in Banking and Finance*, eds. Costanza Russo, Rosa M. Lastra and William Blair (Edward Elgar 2019).

© The Author(s) 2020
D. Rouch, *The Social Licence for Financial Markets*,
https://doi.org/10.1007/978-3-030-40220-4_4

(continued)

selves, and are seen, as being subject to a 'social licence to operate'. Indeed, some financial institutions refer publicly to their social licence to operate.

A licence is a permission giving someone freedom to do something.

- Which societies give this permission to financial markets? Since law and regulation is so fundamental to financial activity, much more so than other sorts of commercial activity, it is reasonable to view the licensing societies as those capable of generating financial law. Without law, financial activity could not exist in anything like its current form. Most obviously, these societies correspond with nation states. However, regions (such as the EU) and even international bodies (such as the United Nations) generate forms of financial law and regulation, so licensing societies can be identified at these levels too. That is important, given the international character of many financial markets.
- To whom is the licence given? Since markets are largely constituted by those who participate in them, it can be regarded as given to the firms and individuals who carry on business in financial markets.
- How do you know if the licence has been given? Discussion of the licence repeatedly connects it with public trust. On that basis, it can be regarded as given to the extent that the public have placed **justified trust** in financial market participants—justified, because the trust needs to be based on trustworthy behaviour, otherwise it will not be sustained. Trust of this sort is systemic. An abuse of trust by one participant can damage it for all, even for institutions beyond the finance sector, so undermining social solidarity. And as mistrust migrates through the system, it can return to damage those who first caused it. Trust is easier to lose than to gain, but the strengthening of trust can work in reverse.
- What are the terms of the licence? Most obviously, they are likely to include law and regulation. But the social licence reaches beyond law and regulation just as it does statutory licensing regimes; otherwise, why not just say that finance must be carried on in accordance with law and regulation? There are also various other sources of statements of social expectation about financial markets, such as regulatory guidance, parliamentary committees, industry and professional codes of conduct and commentary from NGOs and other 'civil society' bodies.

However, ultimately, the social licence is not about a set of carefully crafted written rules or standards. Relationships don't work that way. Rather, it is an observation of practice, and identifies a set of aspirations that are present in financial life and beyond (even if not fully realised in practice). It advances an account of the role of financial markets in the societies in which they operate, both as it is and as it could be at its best.

- It recognises an **aspiration**, or **desire**, both about how financial market activity should be carried on and the outcomes it should produce—**its ends**. In that sense, it can best be thought of as the grant of **a freedom to pursue just ends by just means in financial markets**. Justice in this context could be thought of as a situation in which the relationship between the different groups within, or which are affected by, financial markets is such that the **dignity** of each person in those groups is most fully realised. Financial returns are an important part of

(continued)

(continued)

realising dignity, but only a part. Among other things, realising human dignity connects with the goal of social and environmental sustainability.

- Recognition of the licence is also relevant to the other key driver of behaviour discussed in Chap. 2—the **meaning** of the social world on which people base decisions as they pursue their desires. Talk of a social licence suggests that society is prior to markets, but in a way that emphasises mutuality between the two. Trust and freedom are given to market participants in the use of what, in many cases, society makes available to them in the hope that the result will be mutually beneficial: a relationship based on consensus over conflict. And as to that result, it places financial ends in the context of realising relational goods (especially justice), however important financial ends may be. From this perspective, market decisions cannot simply be defined by the **meaning of money**, since everything that happens in markets is also tied up with **intrinsic human value**.
- It is a 'social licence', not 'social contract'. This distances it from the hypothetical thought experiments favoured by some political philosophers which tend to assume a society of contracting individuals who are largely self-interested and often in conflict (echoing the financial narratives in Chap. 1), but also from the idea that the relationship is defined by commercial exchange.

So What?

So far, so ideal. But the question remains why the insight provided by recognition of a social licence would make any practical difference. We generally use laws and regulations and other written standards (such as conduct codes) to control behaviour in financial markets. In spite of their shortcomings, are they not still the best option?

Rules of this sort are certainly still relevant. Indeed they can be seen as part of a social licence. Because of that, the next chapter looks at the way the two are connected.

However, as noted in Chap. 1, the usual tool-kit of laws and regulations has not yet generated the urgency needed in tackling current sustainability challenges or healed the relationship between the financial world and the societies in which it operates. Part III therefore looks at the potential for the account of financial markets advanced by recognition of a social licence to reach into the substance of market relationships to change them from within.

4.1   Introducing the Social Licence

The Governor of the Bank of England's annual Mansion House speech is a notable event in the City of London's calendar. The Governor generally uses it to give a view on the state of the finance sector and share policy thinking. In as much as any speeches make an impact across the UK financial markets, this is usually one of them. However, those reading the *Financial Times* on the morning of 11 June 2015 will have remained ignorant of one aspect of the previous night's speech, so significant to the Governor, Mark Carney, that he referred to it on five occasions—the social licence for financial markets. The *Financial Times* did not mention it once.[1]

Talk of a social licence for financial markets has only emerged relatively recently.[2] Some banks have begun to recognise that they operate under a social licence,[3] and it has been suggested that large institutional investors are subject to a 'social licence to operate'.[4] However, wider engagement has so far been limited when compared, for example, with intense industry and media attention to some parts of the post-crisis regulatory reform agenda.[5] Why is that? Some might be tempted to dismiss the idea of a social licence for financial markets as 'mere metaphor', forgetting that the use of a metaphor tends to confirm the existence of its primary subject. Others might consider the concept too theoretical. However, governors of the Bank of England cannot generally afford themselves the luxury of theoretical flights of fancy, not in their public role at least. The *Financial Times* certainly did not accuse the Governor of that on the morning of 11 June 2015. There is also a third, more intriguing, possibility. Perhaps the Governor's remarks on the social licence did not attract more attention because they were largely congruent with the way many who heard or who have read the speech see the world. They might not have used the expression 'social licence', but perhaps they nonetheless recognise the reality it describes—one of a relationship between society and those who engage in market activity within it, with the activities of the latter in some sense contingent on the former. This third possibility is the departure point for what follows: talk of a social licence for financial markets seems to refer to something that can be seen operating in practice and to draw on commonly held aspirations that are relevant to the future relationship between financial activity and the communities in which it takes place.

Yet, even if the idea of a social licence has resonance, that does not mean it is well understood or that the relationship it describes is in good health. The relationship is troubled, and the Governor was advancing the idea of a social licence to help address precisely that; the need for market behaviour to change so that the relationship is nourished. Can the recognition of a social licence for financial markets help? Part I of this book looked at what drives human behaviour individually and in groups. It highlighted the power of people's desired ends to shape behaviour when they are brought to bear on the world as people believe it to be—the meaning the world has for them. Together with Chap. 1, it also looked at how narratives and behavioural models can influence those beliefs and the way this interaction plays out. How might greater attention to a social licence for financial markets affect the way these behavioural drivers operate? To begin to answer that question, we need to establish what the recognition of a social licence suggests about the desired ends and meaning of financial activity and what sort of account of financial activity it advances. That is the aim of this chapter. Part III of this book will look at the practical implications.

Before starting, it is important to note that the definition and application of a concept described as 'social' cannot be confined to particular individuals or groups. The process therefore needs to extend beyond this book. There is relevant work across a range of policy fora and academic disciplines and within financial services firms, but it has not yet generally been connected with the idea of a social licence for financial markets and there is still some way to go in bringing the streams together. There has also been extensive attention to something called the 'social licence to operate' ('SLO') in a number of other industry sectors. Discussion of a social licence for financial markets has not made much reference to this, but there are connections between the two, so this chapter will return to the SLO later. Crucially, attempts to understand the nature of any 'social' licence and to change financial behaviour, need to involve those on the ground, both in the markets and in the communities in which they operate.[6] That is ultimately where practice emerges and behaviour changes. The recognition of a social licence for financial markets can provide a context for that very process.

This chapter is organised as follows. It starts by answering the question, why is it meaningful to talk of a social licence for financial markets? It goes on to look at who might be granting the licence, to whom, its possible terms and particularly the desired ends that seem to lie behind it, and how it is granted.[7] Finally, given the power of desired ends interacting with beliefs to shape behaviour, it asks what account of the purpose and meaning of financial activity is being advanced by talk of a social licence.

But first, what is a licence? Licences are ubiquitous in public law contexts:[8] driving, marriage, gaming, premises for the sale of alcohol, operating a scrap metal business, even playing background music require licences. Indeed, so many activities are licensed in the UK that there is a dedicated Government website to help firms work out which ones they need.[9] The English courts have defined licences as follows:

> … a licence … is … a permission granted to a person to do some act which but for such permission it would be unlawful for him to do … There are … different types of licence. A man may grant another a licence to use the grantor's property in some particular way. Or a statute may authorise the granting of a licence to carry on some trade or business which the statute does not allow to be carried on without such a licence. But whatever … the type of licence, the presumption is that it is purely personal privilege …[10]

However, the word 'licence' is not restricted to the law. The sense of a licence as a permission giving someone freedom to do something they would not otherwise be able to do reflects wider English usage. The Oxford English Dictionary defines 'licence' as a formal permission from a constituted authority to do something, but also as liberty to do something, permission, or liberty of action conceded or acknowledged. The word can also carry the sense of an abuse of freedom, disregard of law or propriety or licentiousness. Clearly, this second sense is the opposite of what is involved in talk of a social licence. However, both concern a freedom: the grant of a freedom and its abuse. On this basis, the social licence for financial markets is the grant of some sort of freedom to financial markets by 'society'. Does that sound basically plausible?

4.2   Why Talk of a Social Licence for Financial Markets Makes Sense

Is it at all meaningful to talk about a social licence for financial markets? In other words, do financial markets operate, in some sense, with the permission of the communities in which they are situated? Is some sort of 'social consent' involved? Particularly in broadly democratic societies, if we can see government at some level representing the interests of the community, the answer is 'yes'.[11] Most obviously, it is not possible to engage in financial business in most jurisdictions without being authorised to do so by a government agency: this is commonly referred to by those in the market as being 'authorised' or 'licensed'. In many parts of the financial market, there are also regulatory regimes for market operators, such as the London Stock Exchange, requiring them to be recognised before they can provide trading facilities. These licences and approvals do not attach to whole markets, but are nonetheless necessary for a market and its infrastructure to function: no market operator and no participants, no market.[12]

   Further, the corporate vehicles through which market activity is generally conducted are the gift of the state, vesting the benefit of limited liability on their shareholders. This can be thought of as a form of licence:

> Today it almost seems to have been forgotten that the word "Limited" was intended as a red danger flag … That this should be so is a tribute to the morality of the English commercial community and indicates the very small extent to which they have abused the privileges of incorporation. Nevertheless, the possibilities of abuse are plain … In this respect freedom may have amounted to license – and a remarkably cheap license at that.[13]

The privilege extends beyond the benefit of limited liability. The state gives the means of their association, the company, the legal power to define social relations, both within the company (for example, in contracts with its employees) and outside it.

But the recognition of a social licence identifies something more than legal arrangements, otherwise there would be no need to refer to it. So, is there a broader sense in which it is meaningful to talk of markets being licensed? Contrary to the financial narratives discussed in Chap. 1, and as became clear in Part I, financial market activity is intricately connected with chains of human relationships reaching deep into the communities in which it takes place. Finance is not simply a process of interaction between multiple atomised individuals (or machines) involving nothing but isolated transfers of money and investments. Rather, these transactions are embedded in numerous relationships on which they depend, for which they have implications and from which their meaning is derived. This is one of the key insights of economic sociology and a major area of study.[14] It is not simply that finance depends upon social infrastructure, such as education, health, defence and social welfare systems, although it does and that, in itself, gives good reason to talk of society's licence. It is also part of the very substance of the vast networks of relationships which more or less directly depend upon or are affected by financial markets. What happens in financial markets to some extent relies on the health of these. Given the systemic nature of finance, these networks of relationships ultimately extend to entire communities. Those communities hope to derive a benefit from finance. However, finance can also do them great damage, whether economically or to the networks of relationships on which social solidarity depends. Communities could not be expected to countenance an activity regardless of that. Again, this suggests that it is reasonable to see financial activity as being conducted, at some level, with the permission of the communities in which it takes place.

This underlying sense of consent to pursue commercial activity became clear in Australia during 2018 as a result of a vigorous public debate over a proposal by the ASX Corporate Governance Council to amend Principle 3 of the Australian Corporate Governance Principles and Recommendations and associated guidance to refer to companies (so, not just financial institutions) needing to maintain a 'social licence to operate'. The fact that there was a debate at all demonstrates the presence of something to talk about. Before looking at what was said, it is helpful to give some background on the concept of a social licence to operate so as to understand what lay behind the debate. The expression 'social licence to operate' has not so far been applied generally to financial markets and has accumulated a certain amount of conceptual baggage in other industry sectors.

The observation that business needs to have an SLO originally emerged from the business community where it reflected experience, not theory. It is often taken to have been coined in 1997 in the mining sector as a way of describing how mining companies needed to manage their relationship with communities affected by their activities. Not doing so could result in commercial projects being impeded as a result of social pressure. Talk of an SLO, then, reflected a recognition that mining businesses rely in some way on social consent. This issue is particularly sharp for extractive industries given the visible harm they can cause, so it is not surprising that the insight emerged there first.

Interest in the idea of an SLO has grown rapidly since then, particularly in the last five or six years.[15] It has also been taken up in other industry sectors, for example, in relation to oil and gas pipelines, renewable energy, farming, water use, ports, retailing, aquaculture, forestry and pulp and paper manufacturing.[16] It is commonly noted that the SLO defies easy definition. In its original use, the main focus of the SLO was the management of a company's relationship with the local community most immediately affected by specific commercial projects. Over time, the SLO concept has come to take in wider risks from consumer boycotts, adverse publicity and legal and regulatory challenge, which can have direct commercial impacts, but also undermine a company's standing with governments and regulators. It can be thought of, then, as what is needed to secure, 'the ongoing acceptance and approval of a [project] by local community members and other stakeholders that can affect its profitability.'[17] Commercial self-interest (or less charitably, window dressing[18]) lies behind much of this, and a substantial body of theory and practice has emerged on steps needed to manage the relationships involved.[19]

More recently the SLO concept has evolved (but without replacing the original use of the expression) so that it is also sometimes used to describe the relationship between a business and society more broadly, and the need for businesses to operate in accordance with wider social expectations.[20] Superficially, this may appear closer to the idea of a social licence for financial markets. However, the Bank of England's Governor did not use the expression 'social licence to operate' in his speech and certainly did not seem to be proposing a market-wide public relations exercise. Especially given the background to the SLO in managing relations with communities affected by specific projects and the differences between finance and the sectors the SLO has been applied to so far, we should be wary of assuming that it and the social licence for financial markets are one and the same. That said, the two are not entirely unconnected; it is clear that behind all uses of the expression 'social licence to operate' lies a recognition that some sort of social consensus is needed to pursue business activity.

The ASX Corporate Governance Council SLO proposal concerned business generally, not just mining, and was not tied to specific projects. It is therefore particularly instructive for current purposes to look at what those commenting publicly in the consultation process made of it.[21] Those representing company directors strongly opposed the amendments. Some responses from the legal community also expressed misgivings. However, most other responses either did not comment on the proposal, seem to have taken the existence of a 'social licence' as read, or expressly supported it. Express supporters included, among others, major institutional shareholders (presumably holding shares in companies managed by the directors who opposed the proposal) and professional services firms such as PWC and KPMG (advisors to the same companies, but also providing assurance services on some aspects of the 'social licence'). Significantly, even those who were uncomfortable with the proposal did not generally deny that there is such a thing as a 'social licence to operate' for business.[22] Indeed some of their responses assumed it. Rather, they focused, not unreasonably, on the potential for conflict with directors' legal duties, the fact that the concept is not well defined and could create legal uncertainty, and the way it can be used by special interest groups to force 'shopping list' agendas on companies.[23] In the light of the consultation, the ASX Corporate Governance Council withdrew the proposal, substituting wording that left the position open.[24] However, the debate they provoked seems to confirm that, intuitively, the idea of a 'social licence' makes sense. There have been similar debates in Canada.[25]

Taking this sense of consent (or licence) based on business dependency on society one step further, Chap. 2 highlighted the way financial activity relies on and uses a series of social constructs such as money and language. These emerge in part from financial activity itself, but they are 'carried' by the communities in which it takes place. Indeed, one of those constructs is the word 'finance' itself. Why does it mean what it does? The very meaning of the world on which financial activity depends is based in large measure upon an implicit social consensus. If there were not some underlying consensus about the meaning of language, market activity would be impossible (see Sect. 2.2.3). It is the same with the 'raw materials' of financial business, such as money, shares and debt. These are not natural resources, but concepts created by human communities, underpinned by productive human activity and law and regulation. They emerge from repeated social and economic exchanges, which, in turn, rely on and are given greater definition by community institutions, especially the state, all of which involve some level of social consensus (see Sect. 2.2.3). Indeed, 'The rule of law presupposes the coming together of commitment to common values …'[26] In turn, social stability itself relies upon the same constructs and can therefore be damaged if they are undermined. Financial market participants are part of that process of generation and dependency, but only a part. Likewise the state.

Statutory licensing recognises the social importance of these cultural constructs, both the benefits that can accrue when they are used well and the damage that can ensue when they are not. In the words of the United States Financial Crisis Inquiry Commission in 2011, the events emerging from the 2008 financial crisis, 'were … a fundamental disruption … that wreaked havoc in communities and neighborhoods across this country.'[27] In the light of the narratives of fracture discussed in Chap. 1, this turns out to have been remarkably prophetic. So, for example, a banking licence is, among other things, a licence to create money (through the process of fractional reserve banking), the meaning of which is culturally determined and is fundamental to financial markets and social life more widely. However, the process of creating money can also alter its meaning; create too much by extensive lending to purchase assets at increasingly inflated prices, and you have asset inflation so that the value of money declines: bad news for those without assets and growing inequality between them and those that have. Go too far, and trust in money itself begins to fail. A failure of trust in money then has broader social consequences, witness the recent history of the Euro and the European Union.[28] The legal licence reflects an understanding that the 'raw materials' of financial markets are precious because of the way they are embedded in human relationships and that they need to be handled accordingly.

The idea of a social licence may incorporate statutory licensing regimes. However, like contracts (see Sect. 3.1.2), laws are incomplete. They are made in a social context and rely for their effectiveness upon social consensus and trust. Ultimately talk of a social licence reaches beyond statutory licensing regimes: the expression being used is 'social licence for financial markets' not simply, for example, authorisation under section 19 of the UK Financial Services and Markets Act 2000.[29] Indeed, that is the very point of the social licence; it reaches beyond law and regulation to the social solidarity on which law and regulation also relies.[30] Like markets, government is a social activity, but government does not encompass or comprehend the communities it serves. Indeed, like markets, there is a sense in which the machinery of state also relies upon social order, order that can be damaged if finance does not work well. From that perspective, statutory licensing can be seen as a token of something broader: a recognition that ends sought by those involved in financial activity and those of the communities within which that activity takes place are in some way inter-dependent and at some level shared; an understanding that the health of society and financial markets relies upon a broad-based mutuality, and that both can be damaged if participants in markets do not operate in a way that recognises the interests and expectations of the communities in which they are located.[31]

This is not the result of a detached, rational calculation by either element in the relationship. It has been a dialogic process, perhaps as old as humanity itself. The contemporary financial services licensing and company law regimes made a relatively late entry into pre-existing financial markets, but rules on lending appear in some of the world's earliest extant legal texts.[32] Financial activity and steps by societies to regulate it have grown up cheek by jowl over centuries based on the recognition of its broader benefits and risks, and its dependence on ordered relationships—relationships, among other things, protected from the damage that financial activity can do them. In view of that inter-dependency and the fact that financial activity is socially contingent, it makes sense to talk of society in some way 'licensing' financial markets.[33]

However, we can also look at this the other way round because, as noted in Chap. 1, there are signs that this permission or consent is in danger of being withdrawn. Talk of a social licence for financial markets has emerged from mounting evidence of fracture in the relationship between the financial sector and society, where a perception has emerged that financial activity is conducted in a way that does not recognise broader interests and, indeed, has damaged them. Permissions and privileges, giving financial market participants the licence or freedom to do things, depends to some degree on justified trust. There may be reliance on financial markets, but there is a sense that trust is being withheld (see Chap. 1, and Sect. 4.7 below). The need to re-establish it is pressing.

4.3   'Mere' Metaphor?

Social licences for financial markets cannot be acquired in the same way as a driving licence. Even if they could, it is not clear how a market as a whole could acquire one as compared with the multiple participants that comprise the markets. The social licence for financial markets is therefore partly metaphor. It uses the two concepts of 'society' and 'licence' to try to understand and influence the relationship between participants in financial markets and the societies in which they operate.

People often talk of 'mere' metaphor as if metaphor somehow does not count. That is not correct. Much human understanding develops using metaphor, effectively comparing or associating something that is not well understood with something else that is. This echoes the way in which commercial practice develops. For example, when commercial lawyers are advising a client who wants to do something novel, they will often look for situations in the past that resemble what the client wants—'it's a bit like X and it also has some features of Y…' The experience of X and Y are then used in helping the client navigate a way through what is new, helping them articulate their reality in legal form. The re-evaluation discussed in Chap. 1 involves looking again at reality, but it also reflects a complex new reality of increasingly strained social relations. If the social licence metaphor is sound, and for the reasons discussed, it seems to make sense, it can be a powerful way of getting to grips with this. The sort of account of reality that it advances—its meaning—is sketched out at Sect. 4.8 below.

However, as we have also seen, talk of a social licence reaches beyond metaphor; it does not just illuminate reality, but expresses it too. There is, in fact, a licensing regime for those who participate in financial markets, and societies create laws and regulations that stipulate some of the terms on which firms are permitted to carry on business. These are not the extent of it, but they can be seen as simultaneously part of the primary subject of the metaphor and the substance of the metaphor itself. Talk of a social licence for financial markets, then, seems to be operating at more than one level and goes beyond metaphor.

Having established the basic credibility of the concept, it is time to look at the elements more closely. If there is a social licence for financial markets, who is giving the licence, to whom, what are its terms and how can you tell if it has been given?

4.4   Who Gives the Licence?

It follows from the idea that the social licence for financial markets is 'social' that the licence is somehow given by 'society'. It is not necessary to stray here into detailed debates about what is 'society', and especially not the statement by Margaret Thatcher, regularly quoted out of context, that there is no such thing.[34] However, some basic definitions are helpful. Society has been described as, 'the structured social relations and institutions among a large **community** of people which cannot be reduced to a simple collection or aggregation of individuals', and 'community' as 'a group of people living in a particular locality, who have a certain shared interest, who engage in systematic **interactions** with one another.'[35] A community, '… is constituted by a shared sense of problem, by common concerns and common ambitions.'[36] It comes together around commonly desired ends. So 'society' is not the same as the 'state' (the political power structure governing a particular locality), even though states commonly emerge from societies and are involved in granting legal financial services licences. In view of the multi-jurisdictional nature of most financial services groups, described in Chap. 2, it is not clear that references to a social licence can be entirely confined to a 'society' located in any one jurisdiction. Nonetheless, in identifying a community that is capable of granting a social licence for financial markets, it seems reasonable to take the approach that the relevant community needs to have the institutions necessary to generate financial services law, not least because of the fundamental importance of law and regulation in the way financial services business is constituted, organised and conducted (see Sect. 2.2.3).

The most obvious sort of communities that satisfy this criterion are those associated with a financial law making nation state.[37] However, other groups of people also generate forms of financial services law and might also be seen as 'societies' for these purposes, most obviously those corresponding to regional political unions such as the European Union and, based for example on the presence of international law, even a form of global community.[38] In the case of the second of these, significantly, the SLO concept has made its way into the United Nations human rights regime. In particular, the United Nations 'Protect, Respect and Remedy' Framework describes the responsibility on business organisations to respect human rights as, 'part of what is sometimes called a company's "social licence to operate"', linking this to the, 'courts of public opinion – comprising employees, communities, consumers, civil society, as well as investors…'[39] The SLO concept in the narrower sense of consent to a mining project has also recently been considered in ICSID arbitral proceedings, although the Tribunal concluded that it is not clearly defined in international law.[40] Based on proceedings currently underway, its appearance in international investment law arbitration looks likely to grow in the years ahead.[41]

Global financial institutions function at all of these geopolitical levels in pursuing their ends, using their global power to influence nation states or regions, whether through the threat of moving their business elsewhere or otherwise.[42] The implication of approaching the social licence in this multi-layered way is that these firms may also need a social licence at each of these levels. That might seem like a recipe for confusion. However, what follows will suggest that underlying principles, or values, ultimately unite all of them. The multi-jurisdictional character of international financial groups underscores the importance of recognising the multiple levels at which a social licence may be granted.

Who are the members of these societies? The individuals comprised in the relevant community. Importantly, that includes the individuals who work in the finance sector (although international mobility in some parts of the sector may weaken their connection with the society where they are working at any given time).[43] Whether it is also correct to see financial firms themselves as members of the societies in which they are incorporated is a moot point. Chapter 2 looked at how financial firms are normally established as companies which are treated as 'legal persons'. For that reason among others, there are those who argue that they should be treated as 'corporate citizens'.[44] Broadly, citizenship is a legal status given to people within a specific state or political unit (such as the EU) denoting their relationship with it and carrying certain rights and responsibilities.[45] Even if it is correct to regard companies as citizens, citizenship is therefore distinct from being a member of a society, although the two are not entirely unconnected. Citizens or not, financial services groups will have been actively involved in any significant process of regulatory reform you care to think of, and they also seek to shape the attitudes of those within the communities in which they carry on business (not least, as clients and consumers). Corporate entities are therefore deeply implicated in social processes. However, harking back to the discussion of corporate behaviour in Chap. 2, in assessing whether companies can be thought of as members of a society that grants a social licence, it seems more accurate to look to the social membership of the individuals and groups of individuals assembled using corporate vehicles rather than the legal forms themselves.[46]

Identifying the 'social' in 'social licence' in this way begins to establish a distinction between the social licence for financial markets and the SLO concept. First, as already noted, the SLO (particularly in its original form) has commonly been linked to specific local communities affected by particular industrial projects (rather than society associated with some sort of national or international political structure). Secondly, there are differences of approach even where SLO is understood in a less localised, project-specific way. In this broader context, it has been suggested, for example, that the SLO in reality involves multiple social licences being given by different groups within the same society.[47] Talk about a company needing to identify its various 'stakeholders' in establishing its SLO seems to point in a similar direction, stakeholders being understood as those who can affect or who are affected by the pursuit of a company's objectives.[48] This perception of multiple consents within a given society may partly have grown from the origins of the SLO in describing the need to obtain consent to a mining project from each of the groups affected by it. Certainly, the 'multiple licences' approach is helpful in making clear the numerous interests and complexity of the dialogues involved, and the inter-dependencies between them. However, it risks diminishing the consensual nature of talk about a licence that is 'social'. Describing a licence as 'social' suggests that it is not for any individual or single group within a society to determine whether or not the licence has been given or to seek to apply some sort of veto. Indeed, concerns about the 'social licence to operate' in the Australian and Canadian debates discussed earlier seem in part to respond to fears of exactly that sort: that interest groups had been pressing their claims in a way that disregards the very need for social consensus of which the social licence seems to speak. The currently polarised political discourse across much of the West might lead some to despair of ever achieving such a thing as social consensus. However, the idea of a social licence for financial markets can provide a helpful framework for developing just that.

4.5   To Whom Is the Licence Given?

To 'financial markets'. But what does that mean in practice? This point was picked up in Chap. 2, Sect. 2.5. Markets are, at one level, legal structures: they do not have a mind to reason with and cannot hold beliefs or experience emotions and desires and it is not easy to see how they can be licensed to do or not do things. They are, however, a framework within which firms and individuals come together to transact. Those transactions are fundamental to what makes the market. In view of that, it seems reasonable to suppose that the social licence for financial markets principally describes a permission given to the firms and individuals that transact in financial markets. It could also be seen as extending to the companies and individuals who operate and facilitate those markets and their infrastructure.

Financial firms are also legal structures, but not in the same way as markets. Again, as discussed in Chap. 2, international financial services firms are generally groups of limited companies, each treated as 'legal persons'. Because of that and because the legal licensing regime attaches to firms, it seems reasonable to regard those firms as being given a social licence as much as the individuals comprised in the groups of people that are assembled using them. As such, they can be seen as having 'public interest duties'.[49]

The individuals (even if not the firms) to whom the licence is given are also part of the society that grants it. On that basis, society is licensing some of its own members. As noted, many large financial groups comprise vast international networks, spanning multiple societies. However, as discussed above, it is also possible to think of a social licence for financial markets being given in multiple social contexts, whether state, regional or global. As already noted and discussed further below, it is reasonable to suppose that similar values, or desired ends, may lie behind licences at all of these levels.

4.6   What Are the Terms of the Licence?

If some sort of permission has been given, what are its terms? In a sense, that is the wrong question to ask. Recognition of a social licence involves an expression of aspiration and an observation about social reality—something that can be seen operating *in practice*—more than an attempt to describe specific licence terms.

However, as an observation of practice, at least in a broadly democratic society, one would expect the terms of the licence to be reflected, in part, in the law and regulations applied to financial market activity.[50] Indeed, given the extent to which financial markets are constituted and sustained by law and regulation (see Sect. 2.2.3), legal rules could be expected to be a particularly important element of any licence. As noted already, it is generally necessary to be legally licensed to conduct financial services activities. Those licences are given by regulators acting, in some sense, on behalf of society.[51] Those licensed are expected to carry on business in accordance with the laws and regulations society makes through its institutions of government and courts to order the role of financial markets in social life. These can be seen as part of a social licence and, given their importance, Chap. 5 comes back to them in more detail.

But recognition of a social licence also seems to reach beyond the black letter of law and regulation to the social relationships that lie behind both markets and legal rules, and the shared end goals of the community on which those relationships depend. Were that not so, it would only be necessary to talk of people pursuing purposes defined by law in the manner prescribed by law.[52] The relationship addressed by the social licence is that between society as a whole and those of its members that engage in financial market activity. That is expressed, in practice, in a myriad of individual and group relationships.[53] Since relationships are living and irreducible to an inventory of rules, we should not expect to be able to provide an exhaustive statement of specific social licence terms. There is a sense in which 'social licence' can be seen as 'an intangible construct associated with acceptance, approval, consent, demands, expectations and reputation.'[54]

Nonetheless, it is possible to do two things beyond looking at law and regulation. First, we can try to identify authoritative sources for expressions of social expectation in practice for how financial market participants should operate, other than law and regulation. The statements that emerge from those sources can help to give a better sense of its terms. Secondly, it is also possible to ask what values lie behind the social licence for financial markets (i.e. the 'normative' content of the social licence for financial markets), since, ultimately, talk of a social licence seems to express an aspiration for relationships that run in a way consistent with certain valued end goals. The idea that financial activity needs to be licensed suggests some valued end behind the licensing. What is the ultimate purpose for which the permission is being given? What valued or desired ends does it reach towards? If desired ends are important in driving behaviour, as discussed in Part I, it is vital to be clear about what they are. Clarity about desired ends is also important for another reason. If the social licence for financial markets is not grounded in some common conception of the desired ends lying behind it, attempts to apply it in practice are likely to proceed at cross-purposes,[55] among other things, causing legal uncertainty (see Sect. 7.1.2).

4.6.1 Authoritative Sources for the Terms of a Social Licence

The idea that the social licence for financial markets is 'social' suggests that understanding its scope needs to involve a process of listening and dialogue within the relevant community. However, the recent experience of political pollsters in Western election processes should make us cautious about thinking we can hear with precision what a community is really saying at any given time; even more that we can discern a consensus on complex matters, such as the terms of the UK's withdrawal from the European Union. The interplay between local, regional and global communities and changing circumstances means that attitudes are constantly in flux. In part, that results from the shaping of preferences and culture by firms in the very markets that are being licensed, as a moment's reflection on the impact of marketing in contemporary life confirms.[56] There is also an emotional dimension to the expectations of a community, introducing additional instability.[57] Further, there is no single 'voting chamber' where the voice of society can be heard. Media comment is not an accurate representation of the terms of the licence, not least because the media do not speak with one voice.[58] The expression of beliefs, attitudes and values has become increasingly fragmented. Consistent with this, the terms of an SLO are notoriously difficult to pin down,[59] giving rise to the sort of concerns voiced in the Australian debate discussed earlier. Those seeking to identify the terms of a company's SLO seem to struggle with the same challenges.[60]

In addition, the complexity of financial market activity presents particular barriers to developing a social consensus given the technical knowledge needed to make judgements; even specialists can struggle to discern what is prudent. Inevitably, many decisions have to be made by technicians so there is a point beyond which it is not realistic or desirable to expect the social licence to be tightly prescriptive. Trust has to be part of it. But trust to do what? The discussion of underlying values at Sect. 4.6.2 below (i.e. the normative content of the social licence), seeks to get to the root of that, and suggests that there may be some important areas of consensus. However, in the gap between consensus about ultimate ends and the relative consensus that emerges in the form of black letter law, it is inevitably necessary to be more tentative about precisely what a social licence for financial markets might involve. It is particularly here that the process of dialogue and listening must come into play. That raises the further question of where and how? The following four suggestions of fora in which social expectations are formed and expressed ought to avoid the charge of being too speculative.

First, since the purpose of regulators is, in some sense, to pursue the public interest,[61] the practical behavioural understandings that emerge from the relationships between regulators and the regulated arguably reflect at some level the terms of a social licence. These may be partially articulated in writing, for example, in the form of regulatory guidance and statements of supervisory practice. However, the process of regulatory supervision also involves many judgements and compromises as a result of which standards of acceptability get set, for example, as to the level of Pillar 2 regulatory capital that it is appropriate for firms to hold[62] or how many non-executive and independent non-executive directors financial groups should have on the boards of significant subsidiaries. There is also a sense in which standards emerge based on what the regulator is 'thought to want'. Discussions take place between industry associations and firms and regulators, there are supervisory dialogues, there are speeches and consultations in which regulatory commentary is given, regulatory guidance is issued, and so understandings of what is and is not acceptable emerge.[63]

Secondly, the governmental machinery of democratic societies tends to generate statements about what is considered appropriate or just that are not necessarily reduced to law or regulation, or even writing. These have some claim to be expressing the substance of a social licence. Examples include the proceedings of the United States National Commission on the Causes of the Financial and Economic Crisis, mentioned earlier, the Australian Royal Commission into Misconduct in the Banking, Superannuation and Financial Services Industry, mentioned in Chap. 1; the UK's House of Commons Treasury Committee (the remit of which is, among other things, to examine the administration and policy of the UK regulatory authorities, which draws it into commenting on the activities of the regulated); the UK's Parliamentary Commission on Banking Standards, a commission appointed by the House of Commons and the House of Lords to report on professional standards and culture in the UK banking sector, which published its report in June 2013; and the work of the European Union High-Level Experts Group on Sustainable Finance formed by the European Commission in 2016 to advise on enhancing sustainable finance within the European Union.[64]

Thirdly, a case can also be made for industry, professional and corporate codes as potentially articulating the terms of a social licence.[65] This is particularly so where they respond to wider social expectations so that they could be seen as a statement of the originator's understanding of the terms of a licence,[66] are part of an attempt to avoid public sector regulation,[67] or the code has in some way been 'enlisted' in the regulatory project.[68] Indeed, codes of this sort are sometimes introduced with the encouragement of central banks and regulators.[69] The Global FX Code and the UK Money Markets Code have been described as 'one form of licence'.[70] Codes of this sort have a particularly important role at a global level where international regulatory structures are weak.[71] Notably, discussion of the SLO emphasises the place of the company seeking a licence in defining and obtaining its own social licence in discussion with various interest groups. In a similar way, company reporting (particularly non-financial reporting) and 'corporate social responsibility' programmes could to some extent be seen as reflecting the company's understanding of the terms under which it is expected to operate.[72] However, industry and corporate codes are made and CSR programmes are run by private actors, not on behalf of society as a whole. It would be unfair and unrealistic to treat them as no more than a cynical attempt to manipulate public opinion in the interests of the companies concerned; as discussed in Chap. 3, a range of motivations is invariably at work.[73] Particularly where industry associations are involved, they can help to crystallise a sector-wide perspective on the interests of a sector as a whole which can to some extent dampen an individual firm's self-interest. Nonetheless, while initiatives such as these can be thought of as 'social' within the social contexts from which they emerge, they are also used to shape external perceptions, and any claim to be social by reference to society as a whole is necessarily qualified.[74]

Finally, there are the multiple groups commonly identified as being involved in giving an SLO for commercial projects outside the financial sector. These include, especially, local communities and NGOs.[75] Like those working in companies, the individuals in these groups are only part of society (and, like financial groups, large NGOs are often international). NGOs sometimes advance written codes for commercial activities which might be seen as an attempt to articulate some of the terms of a social licence. There is a substantial body of these codes, although only some are relevant to the financial sector.[76] However, NGOs and similar groups also produce commentary and lead campaigns, bringing them into debates about business activity as a result of which social expectations emerge.[77] Social media have transformed the potential impact of these groups, operating from within and outside a particular community, but this raises a legitimacy issue where it results in other voices being crowded out.[78] Add to these bodies a myriad of others, such as academic institutions, think-tanks, public relations firms and media who seek to understand, analyse and shape social attitudes, publishing a variety of papers, reports and opinion pieces in the process. In doing so, they too may at times give voice to and influence the terms of a social licence. Indeed, responsible public media have a particularly important role to play.[79] And yet, the net result of these dialogues can be very challenging for those who need to interpret them; company directors can sometimes inevitably feel as if they are being presented with a complex list of irreconcilable expectations.[80]

Given this multitude of sources, it might be tempting to conclude that it is not possible to identify with confidence the precise terms of a social licence, and that the recognition of a social licence for financial markets is therefore of limited practical use. However, the prime significance of recognising a social licence for financial markets lies elsewhere: in the account it provides of aspirations that lie behind financial market activity, and in highlighting the networks of relationships on which financial markets rest which can either be nourished or damaged to the extent that aspiration is or is not realised.

The fora identified above are all places where it is possible to look in seeking to establish what pursuing that aspiration might involve. However, what the social licence for financial markets means for financial activity day-by-day also needs to be worked out in the multiple relationships that comprise financial markets, at the coal face of market practice. Just as that cannot be exhaustively legislated for, nor can any group or body provide a complete statement of what it might mean in practice for every relationship within the ecosystem of financial markets, let alone every relationship affected by financial markets, even if doing that were desirable or meaningful. Commentary on the SLO leads in a similar direction. It does not generally attempt to describe the precise terms of licences. Rather, it concentrates on the steps needed to obtain and maintain a licence. Doing so is generally presented as a relational process: a dialogue, where the company concerned (through its staff) needs to identify those with an interest in a given project, to understand the terms on which they will accept it and to engage with them in establishing support. In practice, community support depends as much, if not more, on building multiple relationships of trust, and the fairness of the process followed, as it does stipulating a set of prescribed licence terms.[81] But in the case of the social licence for financial markets, trust about what?

4.6.2   The Social Licence for Financial Markets— Aspirations and Desired Ends

Ultimately, references to a social licence for financial markets reach beyond precise licensing terms to address a relationship, or rather multiple relationships. Relationships do not proceed by way of rules, not at least the sort of rules that might attach to something like a legal licence.[82] Indeed, detailed prescription can sap the life from them. Rather, they are animated by the desired ends the parties bring to them which can powerfully shape behaviour and the way a relationship develops. Part I looked at the power of desired ends to drive behaviour when applied to the world as it is believed to be, and at the sort of desires or motivations involved in financial market activity. The social licence for financial markets seems to address valued ends; to express an aspiration for the relationship between financial markets and society (and the multitude of relationships involved) at which the licensed activity should be directed. This question of ultimate ends sometimes peeps through in discussion of the SLO, for example, in references to the need for 'trust', implying recognition of a desire for a valued end to be realised in a trustworthy manner.[83] However, it has not featured prominently.[84] What of the social licence for financial markets?

Defining the substance of the social licence is, as noted, challenging. However, it is reasonable to suppose that it would incorporate an aspiration for financial activity to be conducted in a way that accords with broadly accepted social values and that it should produce outcomes consistent with those; not values in the sense of the preferences the members of a society happen to display at any given time,[85] but what is held to be valuable. 'We do expect people to come to work and follow good values without needing to make a rule to require it…' says the head of the UK's Financial Conduct Authority.[86] A desire can, in part, be thought of as the experience of wanting something that is valued.[87] What valued ends might be involved in a social licence for financial markets? Part I, distinguished between two sorts of desires: intrinsic (or ultimate) desires, which are ends in themselves, and instrumental or intermediate desires, which are things a person desires because they will help to realise an ultimate desire. In each case, what is desired is valued: in the case of the first, intrinsically, and in the case of the second, instrumentally. The main focus here is on the first.

The most notable references to a social licence have been those of the Governor of the Bank of England. While it is beyond any one person to provide a comprehensive definition, there is reason to think that what he has said resonates with a broader constituency, not least because his comments were based on Bank of England work with the public (in the aftermath of the LIBOR and other market manipulation scandals) and, as noted, they have not proved controversial. So, this is a good place to start in assessing what desired ends might be involved in talk of a social licence. The way the Governor talked about it suggests that he saw the licence as extending both to the outcomes of financial activity and the processes by which those are achieved. For him, the licence is the 'consent of society' that is needed by markets if they are to function: that consent can be called into question by repeated misconduct but, in the words at the start of this chapter, markets that are resilient, fair and effective retain their social licence.[88] This might appear to suggest that the social licence solely concerns good conduct in financial markets; the way that the *process* of market activity takes place. However, Carney's use of the concept has gone beyond that, linking it to the *outcomes* of financial activity: 'Markets are not ends in themselves, but powerful means for prosperity and security for all. As such they need to retain the consent of society – a social licence – to be allowed to operate, innovate and grow.'[89]

This situates financial market activity in the context of the need to realise social goods; prosperity and security for all, an aspiration echoed by Christine Lagarde while head of the IMF.[90] The reference to 'all' seems to distance it from purely utilitarian models ('the greatest good for the greatest number'), locating it more closely to the ultimate desire for human dignity for every person discussed in Chap. 3. In his view, the goods will be lost if financial activity is conducted as if it were an end in itself, detached from its social context. This echoes the discussion in Chap. 3 of financial self-interest as compared with the desire for human wellbeing or dignity. The goods of prosperity and security for all can be seen as 'social' goods in at least two senses: first, because the outcomes benefit society as a whole ('security for all', for example, cannot be individually realised but speaks of a state of social relations) and, secondly, because they can only be realised in a way that relies upon a social framework. Put differently, these are relational goods that rely upon a process of positive reciprocity and broad-based mutuality.

Logically, this association between social licence, social goods and the realisation of the human dignity of members of society makes sense. Communities cannot prevent everything they do not like. However, a community could not be expected to facilitate activities anticipating that the result would be social damage by extending permission for them. Yet it is implicit in the notion of a licence that the activities concerned are, nonetheless, capable of causing damage if not conducted as contemplated by the licence; they need to be pursued within parameters consistent with the relevant goods. Consequently, while talk of a social licence may incorporate hard regulatory structures such as licensing regimes, it is also profoundly aspirational. It recognises the opportunity for private and social goods, but also the possibility for business to be conducted in a way that means that these are not achieved, and it expresses an aspiration for former without the latter.

This idea of a reciprocal balance between realising private goods (the wellbeing of those directly involved in the activity) and social goods (the wellbeing of all) echoes the discussion in Chap. 3 of motivation and the ultimate desires pursued in financial markets. Extremes of self-interest or altruism can be destructive, either entirely denying the other or the self, neither of which provides a sound basis for the wellbeing for those in denial. Another way of thinking about this sort of balance is in terms of what is just (substantive justice, in the sense of what is right, not just formal justice, in the sense of the proper administration of law): in the words of philosopher, Michael Sandel, 'A just society distributes … goods in the right way; it gives each person his or her due.'[91] Indeed, if the idea of a social licence can be regarded as extending both to the ends and means (or processes) of financial activity, one way to view it might be as a permission to those who engage in financial market activity *to pursue just ends in a just manner in financial markets.*[92] Consistent with this, discussion of emotions and, in particular, the emotion of anger in Chap. 2 (Sect. 2.1.2) also highlighted the way in which anger, such as the public anger displayed towards some parts of the financial sector, can be the result of perceived injustice.

The nature of what is just is, of course, highly contested and it is not possible to do more here than draw attention to its apparently foundational presence in talk of a social licence for financial markets. Working it out is an 'inescapably discursive' exercise.[93] However, making the link is critical because it connects talk of a social licence directly with some of the most powerful sources of human reflection on what just relationships look like and how they come about. It suggests that references to a social licence are not rhetorical colour or expressions of transient preference, but are grounded in the sort of outcomes that people have cared deeply about for millennia. Further, while there is no consensus on the nature of what is just, we should not lose sight of the common ground. Debate on different theories of justice can tend to emphasise divergences between them. However:

… concern about goodness, rightness and justness … has a powerful presence – manifest or latent – in our minds. Distinct theories of justice may compete in finding the right use of that concern, but they share the significant feature of being involved in the same pursuit.[94]

The recognition of a social licence for financial markets seems to involve a re-rooting of financial market activity in just these concerns.

Taking this a step further, Chap. 3 highlighted an association between the ultimate desires brought to bear on financial market activity and human dignity for self and other. In view of that, one broad way of conceiving of justice in this context is as *a state of affairs where, to the extent they are affected by financial activity, the relationships between and within the different groups in society is such that the human dignity of each individual in those groups is fully realised.*[95] Justice, '… is drawn from dignity and aims at dignity.'[96] Among other things, dignity is connected with the goal of social and environmental sustainability.

Importantly, the individuals whose dignity is to be respected include those to whom a licence is given (who are also involved in granting the licence in the first place). Seeing the social licence in terms of human dignity would mean that the goods distributed (going back to Michael Sandel's description of a just society) are not limited to financial and material goods. They also include others, such as the relational goods discussed in Chap. 3 and prosperity and security in their broadest sense, which can be severely undermined when financial markets do not work well.

It was suggested above that law and regulation can be seen as part of a social licence. If it is correct to think of a social licence for financial markets as a permission to pursue just ends in a just manner in financial markets, the challenge of fully articulating in advance what this aspiration might mean in every circumstance also dovetails with the limits of positive law.[97] Chapter 5 comes back to this. The creation and application of laws and regulations can be understood by reference to justice but can never be a full articulation of it.[98]

Is there any other support for the idea that justice based on a realisation of human dignity may lie behind talk of a social licence for financial markets? Chapter 3 looked at the likely presence of other-regarding aspirations in financial markets (be they self-interested, altruistic or reciprocal in a way that seems to involve both). If aspirations of that sort exist within financial markets, it seems reasonable to suppose that they also exist in the communities in which market activity takes place and are likely to be applied to that activity. Further, as mentioned above, substantive values can sometimes show through in talk of a social licence to operate. For example, in the politicised debate on the social licence to operate and resource extraction in Canada, one critic asserts that environmentalists would never grant a 'social licence' 'because their standard of value is not human flourishing', so identifying human flourishing (similar to the experience of human dignity) as the end upon which permission for these activities should be given.[99]

Work on the nature and operation of human values appears to provide further support.[100] Perhaps that is why a number of regulators have intuitively called for behaviour in the financial sector to move beyond being 'rules-based' to become 'values-based'.[101] As noted, the word 'value' can sometimes be used loosely to describe what is little more than a personal preference or shifting social attitude. However, in substance, it concerns the worth that something holds for a person or group and is therefore intimately connected with desired ends. Indeed, Shalom Schwartz, one of the leading experts on human values across multiple cultures, suggests that values have six features, one being that they reference desirable goals that motivate action, such as a desire for justice; it is the identity of the goal that is key in distinguishing one value from another. He also suggests: that values transcend specific situations not stipulating precisely how to act, so that they could be equally relevant in, for example, social or work settings (much like ultimate desires or aspirations); that they guide behaviour in any given set of circumstances based on consistency with the relevant value (or, we could say desired end); and that people do not hold all values with equal strength, so that behaviour involves a trade-off between values (or, we could say balancing of desires) based on their relative dominance for a particular person, which means that they are more likely to influence action when they are seen to be relevant in a particular situation and are important to the person concerned.[102]

Consistent with common sense and experience, Schwartz's research on values held by different societies, has consistently identified a similar hierarchy of prioritisation between different values, on average within those societies, across most of those societies.[103] This suggests a consistency in what humans value most. Schwartz identifies ten of these universal values, all of which are either related to individual or group needs (the needs of others) or both. Classifying different values and seeking to measure their strength and prioritisation is not an exact science. However, by way of contrast with what we might expect from *The Wolf of Wall Street* genre of narratives about financial life, at the top of Schwartz's hierarchy are other-regarding values that can be described as 'benevolence' (preserving and enhancing the welfare of those with whom one is in frequent personal contact), and 'universalism' (understanding and regard for the welfare of all people and for nature). These are closely followed by what he calls 'self-direction' (a desire for individual autonomy). This should not come as a surprise in the light of the discussion of other-regarding behaviour and motivation in Chap. 3. Individuals and groups within a society can differ substantially in the relative importance they attribute to those values; they may prioritise values differently from the societies in which they operate. This helps in understanding the potential for mismatches between the attitudes of participants in financial markets and those of the communities in which market activity takes place. Further, the notion of 'benevolence' clearly does not need to be understood by reference to the same community as the one associated with talk of a social licence; going back to market rigging (see Chap. 3), it could, for example, operate by reference to a trading team within a bank.

Schwartz's hierarchy of values does not specifically address the extent to which people value or display justice, reciprocity or fairness (involving a balancing of interests and needs). Instead he focuses on the potential conflicts between values, especially those that are self- and other-regarding. However, other studies have looked at justice, reciprocity and fairness and they confirm that these are also commonly observed or valued across different cultures as a feature of human relationships.[104]

Taken together, this work appears to support the expectation that a set of other-regarding values, or a recognition of the need for positive reciprocity or fairness, is likely to be an important feature of any social licence for financial markets, both in terms of behaviour across the market ecosystem and the relationship between market participants and members of society more widely. Apparently consistent with this, much academic research in the field of ethical behaviour in organisations begins with the premise that ethical (broadly, other-regarding) behaviour is good and unethical behaviour bad, with the objective of helping organisations produce more of the former and less of the latter.[105] A balancing of personal interests with other-regarding values has long been associated with justice. While it may have a self-regarding dimension, 'justice, alone of the virtues, is thought to be 'another's good', because it is related to another; for it does what is advantageous to another.'[106] Justice is not about me and it is not exclusively about you. It is about us. It concerns the realisation of relational goods that depend upon broad-based mutuality, which can be undermined if market relationships do not operate in a way that is positively reciprocal. Talk of a social licence for financial markets seems to be rooted in this.

4.7   How Do We Know if a Social Licence Has Been Given?

Against this backdrop, what does it mean for a social licence to be given? Discussion of the social licence to operate often highlights the importance of earning the trust of those giving the licence.[107] A similar link is consistently made in talk about a social licence for financial markets: 'If you like, it is the trust of society which gives finance licence to operate.'[108] It is the loss of this trust that has provoked talk of a social licence for financial markets:

> … lack of trust is the mirror-image of the perception gap between the financial sector and wider society, the Great Divide. The Great Divide matters because it signals a pronounced and protracted erosion of social capital. It puts finance on notice for losing its social licence.[109]

The 2008 financial crisis grew out of a 'credit crunch' in the narrow financial sense, but has led to a loss of credit more broadly.[110] Trust is derived from the reality of relationships and is implicit in the idea of a licence; licensing involves giving a freedom, and freedom can be abused. There is risk for the licensors, who nonetheless display optimism that their trust will generally not turn out to have been misplaced. In other words, there is an element of reciprocity in trusting.[111] Trust has been described in the context of organisational management as, 'the willingness of a party to be vulnerable to the actions of another party based on the expectation that the other party will perform a particular action important to the trustor, irrespective of the ability to monitor or control that other party.'[112] The extent of the trust involved in talk of the social licence for financial markets is reflected in the limits of law and regulation as a way of articulating the licence. Applying legally sanctioned force or the threat of force to achieve behavioural goals is an alternative to trusting people to behave consistently with those outcomes. However, as noted, law and regulation can only ever be incomplete. Expressly or not, they assume and depend upon an extensive body of other-regarding behaviour and motivation.

The nature and origins of trust are multi-faceted. However, it involves the person giving trust perceiving as trustworthy the individual or institution they are being asked to trust and the person trusted proving trustworthy in the long-term (so that trust is not disappointed). It also involves a propensity to trust on the part of the person giving their trust, which may be affected by factors external to their relationship with the person or institution they are being asked to trust. For example, mistrust generated in other contexts could affect the propensity to trust participants in financial markets, and mistrust arising from behaviour in financial markets could undermine the solidarity of other relationships, especially with political institutions.[113] Enhancing the propensity to give well-placed trust could be thought of as a relational good on which many other social goods depend (a form of 'social capital'[114]), and damaging it socially corrosive.[115]

For a person to be trustworthy (rather than just reliable) they generally need to be other-regarding towards the person giving trust.[116] On that basis, trust can be expected to emerge as people come to believe that the activity concerned is carried on in a manner consistent with realising their own dignity and that of their group[117]—what has been described as trust based on benevolence (a desire to do good to the trustor, aside from an egocentric profit motive) and integrity (underlying principles the trustor finds acceptable, such as a sense of justice).[118] Much as with the description of the social licence, above, the emergence of trust therefore depends on how a particular activity is conducted (is it procedurally fair, in the sense of attending to the dignity of those involved), and its outcomes. Where outcomes confirm that trust has been well-placed, trust strengthens. Equally, trust (and hence a licence) given on the basis of false perceptions would ultimately be unsustainable. For there to be a sustainable social licence, the trust would need to be based on trustworthy behaviour by market participants.

However, it seems that the likelihood of trust being given also increases when those involved perceive themselves as being members of the same salient social group, perhaps because of their knowledge of the shared standards operating within the group. This has been observed experimentally and in situations of geopolitical conflict, such as Northern Ireland.[119] That is another reason why the recognition of a social licence for financial markets (highlighting the membership of those being licensed in the same community that is giving the licence, based on shared end goals, and thereby increasing its salience) is potentially so significant.

So, the consent involved in giving the licence involves an act of trust that the person to whom it is given will use their freedom in accordance with the aspired ends of the licence. A person to whom the licence has been given could be taken to have complied with it to the extent that, within the scope of their financial activity, they have been trustworthy in pursuing financial market activity in a manner consistent with that aspiration. The word 'aspiration' is important since justice cannot be perfectly realised in practice. However, clearly this in no way detracts from the importance of reaching towards it, as Part III will go on to discuss. Notably, assessing the level of trust within a society has been identified as one of the most promising components in measuring its civic capital (a form of social capital), which is, in turn, linked with positive financial development.[120]

To what extent do people need to understand the finance sector to be able to give their trust in this way? Clearly, few people understand all of the intricate workings of the finance sector, even those within it, and many know little at all. Trust can only, therefore, be based on what people experience of it and hear about it. That is, after all, also how trust can be lost, and it is one reason why the untrustworthy activities of one firm can be harmful for all. It is also why the financial narratives of Chap. 1 are potentially so corrosive; why would you trust people or firms if you are constantly told that they are self-seeking and only want to make money out of you? People 'get' narratives. That is one reason why the jury system works. Chapter 6 will discuss how the social licence can be seen as a form of narrative, very different from the narratives of Chap. 1, describing a relationship between finance and society that is consistent with justified trust. Even if people do not understand the inner workings of finance, they should be able to measure their own experience of it, and what they see and hear, in assessing consistency with that.[121]

4.8   What Does It Mean?

Recognition of a social licence for financial markets advances an account not only of the ends of market activity but also its nature—what we take it to mean. Chapter 1 looked at the potential power of financial narratives in defining beliefs about the meaning of the world and, as noted, Chap. 6 will return to the power of narratives more generally. This question of meaning is important because it sets a framework within which people pursue desired ends (see Chap. 2); assume one thing and the resulting action to realise a goal is likely to be different from assuming another. Accounts, such as the economic models and associated narratives discussed in Chap. 1, have tended to cast markets as the key organising force in human affairs, and individuals and companies in an isolated, conflictual pursuit of financial self-interest. As already discussed, they pose the question why anyone would ever trust those in the finance sector. However, they can also lead to a dualism between markets and the state, with government intervention increasingly seen as the only way left to control supposedly self-serving individuals and firms when their activities become harmful.[122] By contrast, the social solidarity on which the health of both markets and government (and its laws and regulations) depend has tended to get written out of the script. The account advanced by the social licence for financial markets challenges that by putting it back at the centre of the story. Drawing a number of threads together from earlier in this chapter, how does it do that?

4.8.1   Markets and Society

Recognition of a social licence makes it possible to see the relationship between markets, market participants and the communities within which they operate in a different light. First, as already noted, it suggests a hierarchy. Society and markets are not equal, since it is for society to give a permission to markets by extending a licence to those who participate in them. Secondly, and closely related, ultimately, markets depend upon social coherence—upon pre-existing social solidarity. That solidarity is based on something more than the invisible hand of markets. However, market activity can strengthen social solidarity when it works well, and destroy it when it does not. Thirdly, and also closely related to the first two, recognising the existence of a social licence makes clear that expectations are placed on financial market participants which are not fully within their control (in contrast with other concepts such as corporate citizenship, corporate social responsibility and stakeholder theory which are more amenable to use by firms in seeking to establish their legitimacy).[123] Fourthly, although there is a hierarchy, in many cases, the individuals to whom the licence is given are also part of the community granting it. This establishes a level of common identity between those within and outside the markets; market participants are not simply those who participate in markets, but at some level participants in the community that licences the markets. Fifthly, the permission provided by the social licence is not restrictive, but a form of freedom. However, the connection between the social licence and desired ends suggests that the freedom is not 'freedom from', but 'freedom for': it is freedom with an end goal in view. Sixthly, the freedom is given. It involves an element of gift, potentially opening the prospect of reciprocal giving of the sort discussed in Chap. 3, not simply narrowly self-interested economic exchange. Seventhly, the freedom being given is supposed to benefit both those wishing to be licensed (otherwise they would not want the licence), but also the society providing the licence; again, the arrangement involves mutuality. Where that ceases, the licence is potentially called into question. Eighthly, these reciprocal benefits cannot be measured in terms of financial value alone. That is because the social licence seems to be connected with the intrinsic value of all human beings and the need to realise social goods through financial activity, including, but going beyond, financial goods, if the dignity of all is to be experienced in practice.

4.8.2 Conflict and Consensus

A community is constituted by shared concerns and ambitions (see Sect. 4.4). The idea that the social licence for financial markets is 'social' therefore suggests that it is not for any individual or single group within a society to determine whether the licence has been given or to define its terms. While the possibility of tension between private financial interests and the needs of a wider community is inherent in the idea of a social licence, the social licence is nonetheless fundamentally about shared concerns and ambitions, and these require some level of consensus. This distinguishes talk of a social licence for financial markets from some approaches to the SLO, which treat it as an exercise in managing competing stakeholder interests:[124] conflict more than consensus.[125] While the language of shareholder and stakeholder value can provide valuable insights, it risks turning companies into a battleground of conflicting interests, as if a company is a pie to be divided between competing groups and consumed.[126] Talk of a social licence for financial markets, however, has grown out of a recognition of the interdependency between communities and the financial markets that operate within them.

Clearly, financial market activity is a focus for many different interests. Yet assuming a conflictual relationship between finance and the communities within which it operates, rather than highlighting the common ground risks embedding division and suspicion rather than building positive reciprocity and broad-based mutuality.[127] Some of the commentary in the Australian and Canadian debates on the social licence to operate conveys just this sense of a struggle for social perceptions between companies and campaigning organisations. In the words of one former CEO of a Canadian energy company, 'As the social-licence snowball gained momentum, it accumulated anti-fossil fuel zealots, multi-national environmental groups, aboriginal bands claiming control over huge tracts of "traditional lands," and scores of others opposing projects for whatever reason.'[128]

By contrast, the social licence for financial markets seems to point towards a cooperative, potentially mutually sustaining, relationship between finance and the communities in which it operates. It has not so far become a forum for conflict. That makes it all the more important to understand the common values that lie behind it on the basis of which positive reciprocity can be strengthened, so that it operates as a framework for cooperation.[129]

4.8.3   Is the Social Licence for Financial Markets a Form of Social Contract?

The embeddedness of the social licence for financial markets in the realities of financial and social life suggests that it should not be viewed in the same way as a social contract of the sort advanced by theorists such as Thomas Hobbes, John Locke, Jean-Jacques Rousseau or, perhaps most influentially today, John Rawls.[130] This has important implications for our understanding of the activities to which it is applied.

There are various streams in social contract theory and it is not necessary to pursue each of them here. However, essentially, most of them involve the idea that political authority is derived from some sort of consent given by those who are subject to it, with consent being given in the form of a, usually hypothetical, contract between those involved. These theories tend to begin with a form of pre-contractual 'state of nature' or 'original positon' of humanity theorising forwards to a notional contract based on concepts such as self-interest, or fairness, reasonableness and bounded rationality.

Recognition of a social licence does not advance a theory of political authority, distinguishing it straight away from these accounts. But, in any event, it seems to take a different approach. With the social licence, there is a sense in which we start with a reality in which some level of consensus can be seen operating in practice, and work backwards to understand the nature of the licence. It concerns circumstances as they exist, rather than a hypothetical original position, detached from the situation in which justice is to be realised and the social frameworks available for securing change. It does not depend upon the idea of a contract that was never entered, but is based on an observation of humans in practice, the substantive ends to which they aspire and the role of mutuality in realising those ends.

Whereas social contract theory originally concerned the basis for the state, talk of a social licence for financial markets addresses the relationship between a society and those conducting financial activities that could affect it. There have nonetheless been various attempts in recent years to extend social contract theory to business organisations based on, among others, John Rawls' *Theory of Justice*. Some of that work may be helpful in understanding the nature of any social licence.[131] Indeed, discussion of the concept of an SLO sometimes treats the SLO as a form of 'social contract'.[132] However, there is an obvious response: if we are really talking about a social 'contract', why describe it as a social 'licence'? The two are not the same and, if anything, using the expression social 'licence' instead of 'contract' serves to distance the social licence for financial markets from social contract theory. It highlights important distinctions between the two.

In particular, as noted, contract-based theories tend, in various ways, to involve an assumption of self-interested, rational individuals (much like those in the financial narratives discussed in Chap. 1). Because each person pursues their self-interest, especially material self-interest, they are driven by self-interest to find a way of protecting themselves from each other. Their interests need to be balanced or even held in check.[133] The state emerges as the main way of doing that (contrasting with the myth of the invisible hand where it is the market). Particularly for Hobbes, there are no commonly desired ends, only the potential for conflict between individuals pursuing their preferences. However, the same self-interest leads them to find a means of self-preservation, in particular through the state.[134] Relational coherence, then, arises through the mediation of the state, more than directly between individuals and groups within society. The social licence for financial markets is altogether different. While this chapter has taken the state as one way of defining which societies might grant social licences, the licence is nonetheless based on a set of relationships that *transcend the state* (the machinery of which is represented, e.g., by statutory licensing regimes) just as they do markets. Recognition of a social licence draws attention to the way in which markets rest on a form of pre-existing consensus; on social solidarity, not conflict. That consensus is not ultimately derived from the state, although the state supports and mediates it. Rather, it depends on a broad-based mutuality on which the state and the effectiveness of its machinery also rest. It is a mutuality that markets can destroy, thereby undermining both themselves and the state.

Further, as noted, licences are given. This tends to distinguish the idea of a social licence for financial markets from a process of contractual engagement and negotiation. The framework of commercial contracts does not exclude the role of gift between the parties (see Chap. 3). However, applying the metaphor of a contract to the relationship between businesses and the societies in which they carry on their activities could be understood as reducing that relationship to a simple commercial (financialised) exchange between two parties: you (society) get X, I (the finance house) get Y and I will pay you damages (or a regulatory fine) if I fail to deliver, and you owe me duties too.[135] This reduction of business relationships to a series of self-interested financial and material transactions is reflected in some areas of economic theory, for example, the theory of the firm.[136] However, talk of a social licence seems to differ from this by placing commercial exchange within a broader social framework that involves the gift of social trust. And rather than the ongoing mutual obligation implied by the metaphor of a contract, talk of a social licence seems to emphasise how responsibility for responding appropriately to that gift of social trust lies principally with the licensee.

4.8.4   Is Social Licence the Same as 'Legitimacy'?

The answer depends upon what is meant by 'legitimacy'. The SLO is frequently associated with attempts by companies to establish the legitimacy of a commercial project with interested parties.[137] However, legitimacy is a slippery concept.[138] In the context of the SLO, it tends to be used to describe a *perception* of acceptability of a company and its project by reference to shared community understandings of standards and values.[139] So, in the context of the SLO, the main focus of attention is the extent to which, in practice, a community gives its active consent to the activities of a company rather than being forced into acquiescence or simply acting out of habit; it is something more than mere compliance with the wishes of the company, but there is nonetheless an emphasis on what is needed to obtain consent.

However, this 'social legitimacy' can be contrasted with 'normative legitimacy', which concerns the underlying standards or values that need to be satisfied for an organisation or its activities to be considered acceptable.[140] This comes closer to the discussion of the social licence for financial markets, above. Justice can be seen as one of the main bases on which normative legitimacy could be established.[141] Where perception is not aligned with reality or underlying normative standards, social legitimacy will be undermined if and when the perception turns out to have been inaccurate.

4.9   Conclusion

The social licence for financial markets is more than a metaphor. It is embedded in the realities of social and market *practice*. It is an observation about things as they are and an expression of aspiration for what they could be. It is a sign of trust. It provides an account of the meaning of financial activity. The end to which it reaches seems intimately connected with realising the dignity of all—an outcome that could be described as justice.

Part III goes into the practical implications of this and, in particular, how it might help in addressing the challenges identified in Chap. 1, by influencing behaviour *in practice*. However, before that, Chap. 5 looks more closely at one of the main ways in which communities seek to change behaviour so as to realise justice—the use of various sorts of written rules in the form of law, regulation and other codes of behaviour. What is the relationship between these and the social licence for financial markets?

Notes

1. Caroline Binham and Martin Arnold, 'Bank of England governor Mark Carney to extend market abuse rules', *Financial Times*, London, 11 June 2015.

2. The idea of a 'social licence to operate' has been around in the mining sector since the late 1990s, but talk of a 'social licence for financial markets' is largely novel. It was not mentioned in the final report on the UK Fair and Effective Markets Review published in June 2015 by the Bank of England, HM Treasury and the Financial Conduct Authority, following an extensive assessment of how to re-establish confidence in the fixed income, currency and commodities markets. However, it subsequently became a key topic at the Bank of England's Open Forum in November 2015, held as a result of the Review.

3. For example both ABN Amro and HSBC noted it in their 2018 reporting: *ABN AMRO Value Creating Topics*, ABN AMRO 2018; *Environmental, Social and Governance (ESG) Update: Supporting Sustainable Growth*, HSBC Holdings plc, April 2018. See also the *Salz Review* of Barclays, which also assumes that a bank's 'licence to operate' is based upon social trust: *Salz Review: An Independent Review of Barclays' Business Practices*, April 2013 at paragraph 2.4, available at https://online.wsj.com/public/resources/documents/SalzReview04032013.pdf (accessed 8 November 2019).

4. *The Asset Owner of Tomorrow: Business Model Changes for the Great Acceleration*, Thinking Ahead Institute, Willis Towers Watson 2017, available at https://www.thinkingaheadinstitute.org/en/Library/Public/Research-and-Ideas/2017/11/The-asset-owners-of-tomorrow (accessed 9 April 2019).

5. A word search of the *Financial Times* on 20 March 2019 discloses almost no discussion of the topic in the context of the financial sector and nor does it seem to have occasioned much debate among the main financial industry associations.

6. Justin O'Brien, et al., *Professional Standards and the Social Licence to Operate: A Panacea for Finance or an Exercise in Symbolism?* Law and Financial Markets Review, 2015, Vol. 9(4), 283–292, 284.

7. A further question concerns how the licence is enforced. However, the processes by which the recognition of a social licence for financial markets can change behaviour will be covered in the following chapters.

8. Very broadly, the law regulating the relationship between the state and individuals (but also the state's power to run a country).

9. https://www.gov.uk/licence-finder/sectors

10. *Russell v Ministry of Commerce for Northern Ireland* [1945] NI 184 per Black J.

11. This is not to suggest that governments perfectly represent the aspirations of the governed. For example, the machinery of state is susceptible to 'capture' by interest groups including large businesses and single-issue campaigning organisations (in the context of the SLO, see, for example, Shane Gunster and Robert Neubauer, *From Public Relations to Mob Rule: Media Framing of Social Licence in Canada*, Canadian Journal of Communication, 2018, Vol. 43(1), 11–32). However, if the government concerned has a basic level of legitimacy, there should be some correlation.

12. Those writing about the SLO have tended to treat legal licences as distinct from the 'social licence' (see, for example, Kieren Moffat, et al., *The Social Licence to Operate: A Critical Review*, Forestry, 2016, Vol. 89(5), 477–488, 481–482; John Morrison, *The Social License: How to Keep Your Organization Legitimate* (Palgrave Macmillan 2014), 21). However, since in many countries the grant of a legal licence is also the expression of a social process, it seems more appropriate to regard statutory licensing as part of the exercise of obtaining a social licence. The close connection between the two and the way in which statutory licensing strengthens the operation of a wider social licence is highlighted in Neil Gunningham, Robert A. Kagan and Dorothy Thornton, *Social License and Environmental Protection: Why Businesses Go Beyond Compliance*, Law and Social Enquiry, 2004, Vol. 29(2), 307–341.

13. L.C.B. Gower, *The English Private Company*, Law and Contemporary Problems, 1953, Vol. 18, 535–545. See also David Ciepley, *Beyond Public and Private: Toward a Political Theory of the Corporation*, American Political Science Review, 2013, Vol. 107(1), 139–158.

14. Mark Granovetter, *Economic Action and Social Structure: The Problem of Embeddedness*, American Journal of Sociology, 1985, Vol. 91(3), 481–510; Alejandro Portes, *Economic Sociology: A Systematic Inquiry* (Princeton University Press 2010).

15. Martin Brueckner and Marian Eabrasu, *Pinning Down the Social License to Operate (SLO): The Problem of Normative Complexity*, Resources Policy, 2018, Vol. 59, 217–226; Gunster and Neubauer, *From Public Relations to Mob Rule: Media Framing of Social Licence in Canada*; Joel Gehman, Lianne M. Lefsrud and Stewart Fast, *Social License to Operate: Legitimacy by Another Name?* Canadian Public Administration, 2017, Vol. 60(2), 293–317; John R. Owen and Deanna Kemp, *Social Licence and Mining: A Critical Perspective*, Resources Policy, 2013, Vol. 38(1), 29–35.

16. Robert G. Boutilier, *Frequently Asked Questions About the Social Licence to Operate*, Impact Assessment and Project Appraisal, 2014, Vol. 32(4), 263–272; Kieren Moffat and Airong Zhang, *The Paths to Social Licence to Operate: An Integrative Model Explaining Community Acceptance of Mining*, Resources Policy, 2014, Vol. 39(1), 61–70, 61; Charles Mather and Lucia Fanning, *Social Licence and Aquaculture: Towards a Research Agenda*, Marine Policy, 2019, Vol. 99, 275–282; Peter Edwards, et al., *Social Licence to*

Operate and Forestry – An Introduction, Forestry, 2016, Vol. 89(5), 473–476; Gunningham, Kagan and Thornton, *Social License and Environmental Protection: Why Businesses Go Beyond Compliance.*

17. Moffat and Zhang, *The Paths to Social Licence to Operate: An Integrative Model Explaining Community Acceptance of Mining*, 61.

18. Brueckner and Eabrasu, *Pinning Down the Social License to Operate (SLO): The Problem of Normative Complexity*, 223; Owen and Kemp, *Social Licence and Mining: A Critical Perspective.*

19. Gunster and Neubauer, *From Public Relations to Mob Rule: Media Framing of Social Licence in Canada*; Brueckner and Eabrasu, *Pinning Down the Social License to Operate (SLO): The Problem of Normative Complexity*, 218; Owen and Kemp, *Social Licence and Mining: A Critical Perspective*; Morrison, *The Social License: How to Keep Your Organization Legitimate.*

20. Moffat, et al., *The Social Licence to Operate: A Critical Review*, 481; Morrison, *The Social License: How to Keep Your Organization Legitimate*; Leeora Black, *The Social Licence to Operate: Your Management Framework for Complex Times* (Dō Sustainability, 2013).

21. Public responses are available at https://www.asx.com.au/regulation/corporate-governance-council/review-and-submissions.htm (accessed 13 March 2019).

22. Comments from the Law Council of Australia (which was not acting on behalf of the directors) came closest to it (paragraph 47), but even they raised the question 'exactly what does it mean?'

23. Chapter 7 returns to the need for legal certainty (Sect. 7.1.2).

24. *Corporate Governance Principles and Recommendations*, 4th Edn, ASX Corporate Governance Council, February 2019. The final drafting of the Principle retains the original reference to acting 'lawfully, ethically and responsibly', which clearly extends beyond simple compliance with legal obligations. The associated guidance now references the legal duties of directors by linking them to the need to 'build long-term sustainable value for security holders'. However, the guidance talks about the need for a company to have 'values' in a manner that contemplates those values not being purely financial. A new recommendation (Sect. 3.1) then states that 'A listed entity should articulate and disclose its values.'

25. It emerged in the Canadian press in 2014 and has been ongoing. The press seem to have broadly accepted the idea of an SLO until then. However, a group of journalists and others have since published a series of articles calling into question whether there is such a thing, stimulated, in part, by the way campaigning groups and some political figures had used the idea in advancing their agenda. However, as with the Australian debate, even some of those raising concerns seem to acknowledge that business does indeed need some sort of social consent (see, e.g., Brian Lee Crowley, *When Demands for "Social Licence" Become an Attack on Democracy* (Macdonald-Laurier

Institute November 2014); Dwight Newman, *Be Careful What You Wish for: Why Some Versions of the "Social Licence" are Unlicensed and May Be Anti-social* (Macdonald-Laurier Institute November 2014)). However, the tone of the press commentary risks turning the idea of an SLO into a battleground rather than a context within which reciprocally beneficial practice can emerge: Ross McKitrick, 'Let's stop pretending 'social licence' is an actual thing', *Financial Post*, 20 April 2016; Goldy Hyder, 'The 'social licence' myth', *National Post*, 4 October 2016; Jaana Woiceshyn, 'Snub the 'social licence' scam', *National Post*, 23 August 2016; Jaana Woiceshyn, 'Business Needs Freedom and Not a "Social License" to Operate', *Capitalism Magazine*, 28 January 2019. See generally Gunster and Neubauer, *From Public Relations to Mob Rule: Media Framing of Social Licence in Canada*.

26. Pierre Bourdieu, *The Force of Law: Toward a Sociology of the Juridical Field*, translated by Richard Terdiman, Hastings Law Journal, 1987, Vol. 38(5), 805–853.

27. *The Financial Crisis Inquiry Report: Final Report of the National Commission on the Causes of the Financial and Economic Crisis in the United States*, The Financial Crisis Inquiry Commission, January 2011.

28. Adam Tooze, *Crashed: How a Decade of Financial Crises Changed the World* (Allen Lane 2018).

29. The Act establishes the UK authorisation regime for firms wishing to engage in investment or financial business.

30. Timothy Macklem, *Law and Life in Common* (Oxford University Press 2015). In the context of the SLO, for example, Brueckner and Eabrasu, *Pinning Down the Social License to Operate (SLO): The Problem of Normative Complexity*, identify a gap between statutory licensing regimes and legitimacy for a commercial project (giving the example of the Adani Group Carmichael mining project in Australia).

31. Investment research has begun to pick up on the damage that can be done to a mining business (and potentially those investing in it) if it fails to obtain and maintain a social licence. See for example, *Social License to Operate: The Relevance of Social License to Operate for Mining Companies*, Schroders Research Paper, July 2012, https://www.schroders.com/staticfiles/schroders/sites/americas/us%20institutional%202011/pdfs/social-licence-to-operate.pdf (accessed 1 April 2019).

32. See, for example, the Code of Hammurabi, a collection of rules compiled towards the end of the forty-two year reign of Hammurabi, sixth ruler of the first Dynasty of Babylon (1792–1750 BC): Martha T. Roth, *Law Collections from Mesopotamia and Asia Minor* (Scholars Press, Atlanta, 1995) 71. See also William Blair, 'Reconceptualising the Role of Standards in Supporting Financial Regulation', in *Reconceptualising Global Finance and Its Regulation*, eds. Ross P. Buckley, Emilios Avgouleas and Douglas W. Arner (Cambridge University Press 2016), 442.

33. *What is banking for?*, remarks by Baroness Onora O'Neill, Federal Reserve Bank of New York, 20 October 2016.

34. In the same interview for Women's Own, she also referred to a tapestry of human relationships in a way that bears a resemblance to aspects of the definition of 'society', provided below.

35. Anthony Giddens and Philip W. Sutton, *Essential Concepts in Sociology* (Polity Press 2017), 20, 117.

36. Macklem, *Law and Life in Common*, 194.

37. For most of the twentieth century, sociologists primarily associated the idea of society with the community connected with a nation sate. However, with the advance of globalisation, that picture has become more nuanced.

38. International law is a system of international rules, distinct from the law of any individual state. It does not have direct effect in individual states. From an individual state perspective, the application of international law is subject to the law of that state. However, from the perspective of international law, a state should comply with its international legal obligations, even if that involves the state concerned amending its law to bring that about. Particularly in the case of the financial services sector, these 'hard' law standards are often accompanied by 'softer' international standards in the form of memoranda and statements of principles promulgated by international bodies that are not legally binding, but are nonetheless highly authoritative.

39. *Protect, Respect and Remedy: a Framework for Business and Human Rights*, UN Human Rights Council A/HRC/8/5 7 April 2008, paragraph 54; Karin Buhmann, *Public Regulators and CSR: The 'Social Licence to Operate' in Recent United Nations Instruments on Business and Human Rights and the Juridification of CSR*, Journal of Business Ethics, 2016, Vol. 136(4), 699–714; Sally Wheeler, *Global Production, CSR and Human Rights: The Courts of Public Opinion and the Social License to Operate*, International Journal of Human Rights, 2015, Vol. 19(6), 757–778.

40. *Bear Creek Mining Corporation v Republic of Peru*, International Centre for Settlement of Investment Disputes Case No ARB/14/21, Award (30 November 2017), paragraph 406. The ICSID was established by the 1966 Convention on the Settlement of Investment Disputes between States and Nationals of Other States, a multilateral treaty formulated by the executive directors of the World Bank.

41. I am grateful to Elise Ruggeri Abonnat for this observation. See also, Mihaela-Maria Barnes, *The 'Social License to Operate': An Emerging Concept in the Practice of International Investment Tribunals*, Journal of International Dispute Settlement, 2019, Vol. 10, 328–360.

42. David Vogel, *Private Global Business Regulation*, Annual Review of Political Science, 2008, Vol. 11(1), 261–282, 266.

43. Discussion of the concept of a 'social licence to operate' often seems to proceed on the basis that those licensed are not part of the group giving the licence, leading to a sense of 'them' and 'us'.

44. Andrew Crane, Dirk Matten and Jeremy Moon, *Corporations and Citizenship* (Cambridge University Press 2008), 17 et seq.

45. Giddens and Sutton, *Essential Concepts in Sociology*, 194.

46. Michael E. Bratman, 'The Intentions of a Group', in *The Moral Responsibility of Firms*, eds. Eric Orts and Craig Smith (Oxford University Press 2017).

47. For example, Melanie (Lian) Dare, Jacki Schirmer and Frank Vanclay, *Community Engagement and Social Licence to Operate*, Impact Assessment and Project Appraisal, 2014, Vol. 32(3), 188–197.

48. Geert Demuijnck and Björn Fasterling, *The Social Licence to Operate*, Journal of Business Ethics, 2016, Vol. 136(4), 675–685; Mather and Fanning, *Social Licence and Aquaculture: Towards a Research Agenda*.

49. *Transforming culture in financial services*, speech by Andrew Bailey while Chief Executive of the Financial Conduct Authority, 19 March 2018.

50. As noted above at note 12, commentary on the SLO concept often seems to distinguish between a 'social licence' and a 'legal licence'. This may partly result from the origins of the SLO in local project management. However, it is not clear why one would not treat the rules and regulations a society applies to a business as part of the permission being given.

51. Again, this puts to one side for the present the question of how far regulators are pursuing the public interest and the extent to which power structures can be dominated by particular interest groups; see, for example, Mike Feintuck, 'Regulatory Rationales Beyond the Economic: In Search of the Public Interest', in *The Oxford Handbook of Regulation*, eds. Robert Baldwin, Martin Cave and Martin Lodge (Oxford University Press 2011).

52. The polarisation of politics in many western jurisdictions in particular may raise a question about whether the communities in those jurisdictions are capable of shared ends. However, the fact that there is disagreement seems to suggest that, lying somewhere behind these debates, there is something worth disagreeing about; some ultimate end.

53. In the case of the idea of an SLO see Moffat, et al., *The Social Licence to Operate: A Critical Review*, 480, 481.

54. Richard Parsons and Kieren Moffat, *Integrating Impact and Relational Dimensions of Social Licence and Social Impact Assessment*, Impact Assessment and Project Appraisal, 2014, Vol. 32(4), 273–282, 274 (talking of the social licence to operate in mining).

55. A risk which seems to have materialised in some of the debates on the 'social licence to operate' in Australia and Canada, mentioned above.

56. David George, *Preference Pollution: How Markets Create the Desires We Dislike* (University of Michigan Press 2004).

57. Hans Bernhard Schmid, 'The Feeling of Being in a Group: Corporate Emotions and Collective Consciousness', in *Collective Emotions*, eds. Christian von Scheve and Mikko Salmela (Oxford University Press 2014).

58. Gunster and Neubauer, *From Public Relations to Mob Rule: Media Framing of Social Licence in Canada*.

59. Moffat, et al., *The Social Licence to Operate: A Critical Review*; Sara Bice, *What Gives You a Social Licence? An Exploration of the Social Licence to Operate in the Australian Mining Industry*, Resources, 2014, Vol. 3(1), 62–80.

60. Gunningham, Kagan and Thornton, *Social License and Environmental Protection: Why Businesses Go Beyond Compliance*, 309.

61. Subject to various caveats, including those in note 13 above.

62. Capital that a firm is required to hold which exceeds a statutory minimum. The amount is based on the firm's own assessment of the risks in its business, but is agreed with its regulator. See in particular Article 73 of Directive 2013/36/EU of the European Parliament and of the Council on access to the activity of credit institutions and the prudential supervision of credit institutions and investment firms.

63. As to how far the resulting standards can be thought of as 'social', this again puts to one side the possibility of regulators developing their own agendas or being unduly influenced by interest groupings, or simply not understanding their own rules or the activities they are seeking to regulate.

64. https://ec.europa.eu/info/system/files/161028-press-release_en.pdf (accessed 13 August 2019).

65. In the case of corporate codes, see Lorenzo Sacconi, *The Social Contract of the Firm: Economics, Ethics and Organisation* (English edition, Springer 2000), 3–4. The content of industry and corporate codes may also be influenced by shareholders and other commercial interests through discussions with professional advisors, the expectations of auditors, analysts and customers, the standards applied by ratings agencies, dialogues with NGOs and broader social commentary. See, for example, Vogel, *Private Global Business Regulation*.

66. For example, in relation to professional codes, see Donald Nicholson, *Making Lawyers Moral? Ethical Codes and Moral Character*, Legal Studies, 2005, Vol. 25(4), 601–626, 604.

67. To be credible, they will need to set standards sufficiently close to those that might otherwise be introduced. Vogel, *Private Global Business Regulation*, 265.

68. Julia Black, *Mapping the Contours of Contemporary Financial Services Regulation*, Journal of Comparative Law Studies, 2002, Vol. 2(2), 253–287. The Financial Conduct Authority takes account of market codes in considering whether staff in financial firms have complied with the principle that they should observe proper standards of market conduct, and has a regime for recognising market codes for this purpose: https://www.fca.org.uk/about/recognised-industry-codes (accessed 13 August 2019). At the time of

writing, it has so far recognised the Global FX Code and the UK Money Markets Code. Similarly, the Financial Conduct Authority maintains a list of privately originated guidance; where a firm has acted consistently with the guidance, the FCA will treat that as helping to establish compliance with related FCA regulations: https://www.fca.org.uk/about/rules-and-guidance/confirmed-industry-guidance (accessed 13 August 2019). See also the ABI Code of Good Practice for Unit Linked Funds (2014), which it describes as having been revised by an ABI working group in consultation with the FCA and a wide range of stakeholders and which addresses an area where the FCA has not made detailed rules:, https://www.abi.org.uk/news/news-articles/2014/05/abi-publishes-guide-to-good-practice-for-unit-linked-funds/ (accessed 13 August 2019).

69. For example, the UK Money Markets Code, the Global FX Code and the Global Precious Metals Code, *The Basel Committee on Banking Supervision Principles for the Sound Management of Operational Risk*, June 2011 and *The Model Code of Ethics*, a report of the SRO consultative committee of IOSCO, June 2006.

70. *In codes we trust – Redefining the social licence for financial markets*, speech by Sarah John, Head of the Sterling Markets Division of the Bank of England, 13 June 2017.

71. Vogel, *Private Global Business Regulation*.

72. In the context of the social licence to operate for mining see, for example, Sara Bice, *What Gives You a Social Licence? An Exploration of the Social Licence to Operate in the Australian Mining Industry*.

73. In the case of CSR, see Tareq Emtairah and Oksana Mont, *Gaining Legitimacy in Contemporary World: Environmental and Social Activities of Organisations*, International Journal of Sustainable Society, 2008, Vol. 1(2), 134–148.

74. Frances Bowen, *Marking Their Own Homework: The Pragmatic and Moral Legitimacy of Industry Self-Regulation*, Journal of Business Ethics, 2019, Vol. 156(1), 257–272; Richard Parsons and Kieren Moffat, *Constructing the Meaning of the Social Licence*, Social Epistemology, 2014, Vol. 28(3–4), 340–363, 344.

75. Vogel, *Private Global Business Regulation*, 266.

76. For example, the database maintained by the International Trade Centre, a multilateral aid agency operating under the umbrella of the United Nations contains over 250 of them, https://sustainabilitymap.org/standards?q=eyJzZWxlY3RlZENNsaWVudCI6Ik5PIEFGRklMSUFUSU9OIn0%3D (accessed 26 October 2019).

77. The Global Reporting Initiative, for example, responded to the Australian corporate governance proposals discussed above, https://www.asx.com.au/documents/regulation/GRI.pdf

78. In the context of the SLO, Gehman, Lefsrud and Fast, *Social License to Operate: Legitimacy by Another Name?*; Vogel, *Private Global Business Regulation*, 267, 276.

79. Amartya Sen, *The Idea of Justice* (Allen Lane 2009), 335 et seq.

80. See, for example, the response of the Australian Institute of Directors to the Australian corporate governance proposals above which provides a hypothetical example at Sect. 4.3: https://www.asx.com.au/documents/regulation/Australian-Institute-of-Company-Directors.pdf

81. For example, Moffat and Zhang, *The Paths to Social Licence to Operate: An Integrative Model Explaining Community Acceptance of Mining*; Airong Zhang, Thomas G. Measham and Kieren Moffat, *Preconditions for Social Licence: The Importance of Information in Initial Engagement*, Journal of Cleaner Production, 2018, Vol. 172, 1559–1566. See further at Sect. 4.7, below.

82. 'Rules' of behaviour are, however, involved. See Chap. 5 and Sect. 6.6.2.

83. Peter Edwards, et al., *Trust, Engagement, Information and Social Licence – Insights from New Zealand*, Environmental Research Letters, 2019, Vol. 14(2), 024010.

84. Brueckner and Eabrasu, *Pinning Down the Social Licence to Operate (SLO): The Problem of Normative Complexity*. But see Demuijnck and Fasterling, *The Social Licence to Operate*, who seek to establish its normative content based on contractarian principles, and Justine Lacey, Peter Edwards and Julian Lamont, *Social Licence as Contract: Procedural Fairness and Agreement-Making in Australia*, Forestry, 2016, Vol. 89(5), 489–499 based on procedural justice.

85. Corresponding with the sort of approach taken by revealed preference theory.

86. *Transforming culture in financial services*, Bailey.

87. Graham Oddie, 'Desire and the Good: In Search of the Right Fit', in *The Nature of Desire*, eds. Federico Lauria and Julien A. Deonna (Oxford University Press 2017); Simon Blackburn, *Ruling Passions* (Oxford University Press 1998), 66.

88. See *Building real markets for the good of the people*, Carney.

89. Ibid.

90. *Ethics and finance – aligning financial incentives with societal objectives*, speech by Christine Lagarde, Managing Director of the International Monetary Fund, 6 May 2015.

91. Michael J. Sandel, *Justice* (Farrar, Straus and Giroux 2009), 19.

92. The concept of 'legitimacy' may also help to make sense of the idea of a social licence. However, in the context of the SLO, it is often used in ways that tend to treat it as being about whether a company's activities are socially perceived as acceptable. By contrast, justice concerns the right ordering of relations: it sets a normative standard by reference to which acceptability may be measured. Connecting the licence with justice therefore seems more

consistent with the apparently aspirational dimension of the licence. The aspiration behind talk of a social licence is not primarily that markets should be socially perceived as acceptable, but that they should realise certain desired ends, the result of which should be greater social trust. See further the brief discussion at Sect. 4.8.3 below.

93. Amartya Sen, *The Idea of Justice*, 337. The work is under way. See, for example Lisa Herzog ed. *Just Financial Markets? Finance in a Just Society* (Oxford University Press 2017).

94. Amartya Sen, *The Idea of Justice*, 414.

95. This connection seems evident from attempts to embed the Universal Declaration of Human Rights (the over-arching principle of which is human dignity and equal and inalienable rights, as noted in Chap. 3) in everyday business practice (see Sect. 3.2.4). These have drawn on the idea of a 'social licence' granted in the 'courts of public opinion' which could be lost if dignity is not upheld. See also Rosa M. Lastra and Alan H. Brener, 'Justice, Financial Markets, and Human Rights', in *Just Financial Markets? Finance in a Just Society*, ed. Lisa Herzog (Oxford University Press 2017), 48 et seq. However, highlighting the connection here is not intended to suggest that the social licence is essentially a matter of human rights. Adam Smith also made a connection between the value of the human person and justice (see Sect. 3.2.4).

96. Ronald Dworkin, *Justice for Hedgehogs* (Belknap Press of Harvard University Press 2011), 423, writing of justice provided by government as beginning with equal treatment and respect. See also Michael S. Pritchard, *Human Dignity and Justice*, Ethics, 1972, Vol. 82(4), 299–313.

97. Law that has been formally articulated.

98. The nature of the relationship between law and justice, and morality more generally, has been a subject of prolonged debate, most famously in the exchanges between H.L.A. Hart, (see especially *The Concept of Law* (Clarendon Press Oxford 1963)), Lon Fuller (see especially *The Morality of Law* (Yale University Press 1964)) and Ronald Dworkin (see especially *Law's Empire* (Belknap Press of Harvard University Press 1986)). There is not the scope to explore those discussions here.

99. Woiceshyn, 'Snub the 'social licence' scam'.

100. Work on human values is a field in its own right and a detailed discussion lies beyond the scope of the current exercise. The following draws particularly on the influential work of Shalom Schwartz and his collaborators. However, he is by no means the only person to have highlighted a consistency between different cultures in what humans value. See, for example, Oliver Scott Curry, Daniel Austin Mullins and Harvey Winehouse, *Is It Good to Cooperate? Testing the Theory of Morality-as-Cooperation in 60 Societies*, Current Anthropology, 2019, Vol. 60(1), 47–69; Jesse Graham, et al., *Mapping the Moral Domain*, Journal of Personality and Social

Psychology, 2011, Vol. 101(2), 366–385; Katherine Dahlsgaard, Christopher Peterson and Martin E. P. Seligman, *Shared Virtue: The Convergence of Valued Human Strengths Across Culture and History*, Review of General Psychology, 2005, Vol. 9(3), 203–213. The authors of these studies advance various explanations for the patterns they observe, with evolutionary processes as a common theme. The aim here is to draw attention to the patterns themselves as evidence of what humans consider important in the way they relate to each other rather than their origins. As discussed in Chap. 3, it is reasonable to suppose that underlying motivations could be self-regarding and altruistic, and that there could be a reciprocal point at which the two become largely indistinguishable. These studies are generally descriptive rather than attempting to advance theories of what is observed is 'good' or 'bad', 'right' or 'wrong'. However, they are nonetheless suggestive of what people might think of as the normative content of a social licence.

101. For example, see *Ethics and Finance – Aligning Financial Incentives with Societal Objectives*, Lagarde.
102. Based on the description of values developed by Shalom Schwartz for the purposes of his theory of basic values: Shalom H. Schwartz, *Les Valeurs de Base de la Personne: Théorie, Mesures et Applications*, Revue Française de Sociologie, 2006, Vol. 47(4), 929–969, 931.
103. Shalom H. Schwartz and Anat Bardi, *Value Hierarchies Across Cultures: Taking a Similarities Perspective*, Journal of Cross-Cultural Psychology, 2001, Vol. 32(3), 268–290.
104. Curry, Mullins and Winehouse, *Is it Good to Cooperate? Testing the Theory of Morality-as-Cooperation in 60 Societies* (reciprocity features more strongly in cross-cultural comparisons than fairness); Jesse Graham, et al., *Mapping the Moral Domain*; Dahlsgaard, Peterson and Seligman, *Shared Virtue: The Convergence of Valued Human Strengths Across Culture and History*.
105. Linda Klebe Treviño, Niki A. den Niewenboer and Jennifer J. Kish-Gephart, *(Un)Ethical Behavior in Organizations*, Annual Review of Psychology, 2014, Vol. 65, 635–660, 637.
106. Aristotle, W. D. Ross and Lesley Brown, *The Nicomachean Ethics* (Oxford University Press 2009), Book V.1, 1130a.
107. For example, Moffat and Zang, *The Paths to Social Licence to Operate: An Integrative Model Explaining Community Acceptance of Mining*; Sara Bice and Kieren Moffat, *Social Licence to Operate and Impact Assessment*, Impact Assessment and Project Appraisal, 2014, Vol. 32(4), 257–262, 261; Boutilier, *Frequently Asked Questions About the Social Licence to Operate*, 264; Edwards, et al., *Trust, Engagement, Information and Social Licence – Insights from New Zealand*; Cindy Gallois, et al., *The Language of Science and Social Licence to Operate*, Journal of Language and Social Psychology, 2017, Vol. 36(1), 45–60; Dare and Vanclay, *Community Engagement and Social Licence*

to Operate; Morrison, *The Social License: How to Keep Your Organization Legitimate*, 62 et seq.

108. Andrew Haldane, 'Book Review: Other People's Money by John Kay', *Prospect*, 17 September 2015. *The Salz Review of Barclays Business Practices*, April 2013, states that a bank's licence to operate is built on the trust of its customers.

109. *The Great Divide*, speech by Andrew Haldane, Executive Director and Chief Economist of the Bank of England, 18 May 2016. See also, *Turning back the tide*, speech by Mark Carney, Governor of the Bank of England, 29 November 2017; *In codes we trust – Redefining the social licence for financial markets*, John; *Challenges for financial markets*, speech by John Cunliffe, Deputy Governor Financial Stability, 3 November 2016; *What is banking for?*, O'Neill; *The future of financial reform*, speech by Mark Carney, Governor of the Bank of England, Singapore 17 November 2014.

110. The word 'credit' is derived from *credere*, the verb for 'to trust' in Latin.

111. Martin Tanis and Tom Postmes, *A Social Identity Approach to Trust: Interpersonal Perception, Group Membership and Trusting Behaviour*, European Journal of Social Psychology, 2005, Vol. 35(3), 413–424.

112. Roger C, Mayer, James H. Davis and F. David Shoorman, *An Integrative Model of Organizational Trust*, Academy of Management Review, 1995, Vol. 20(3), 709–734, 712.

113. Bret Crane, *Revisiting Who, When and Why Stakeholders Matter: Trust and Stakeholder Connectedness*, Business & Society, February 2018, https://doi.org/10.1177/0007650318756983; Heikki Ervasti, Antti Kouvo and Takis Venetoklis, *Social and Institutional Trust in Times of Crisis: Greece 2002–2011*, Social Indicators Research, 2019, Vol. 141(3), 1207–1231; Ginés Navarro-Carrillo, et al., *Do Economic Crises Always Undermine Trust in Others? The Case of Generalized, Interpersonal, and In-group Trust*, Frontiers in Psychology, October 2018, Vol. 9, Article 1955; Chase Foster and Jeffry Frieden, *Crisis of Trust: Socio-Economic Determinants of Europeans' Confidence in Government*, European Union Politics, 2017, Vol. 18(4), 511–535; Carin van der Cruijsen, Jakob de Haan and David-Jan Jansen, *Trust and Financial Crisis Experiences*, Social Indicators Research, 2016, Vol. 127(2), 577–600.

114. This expression is used in various ways, but here it is intended as a reference to broad-based social benefit (rather than, for example, the more technical sense in which it has been used by Pierre Bourdieu).

115. Francis Fukuyama, *Trust: The Social Virtues and the Creation of Prosperity* (Simon and Schuster 1995), 27 et seq.; Karen Jones, 'Distrusting the Trustworthy', in *Reading Onora O'Neill*, eds. David Archard, et al., (Routledge 2013); Stephanie Chaly, et al., *Misconduct Risk, Culture, and Supervision*, Federal Reserve Bank of New York, December 2017, 11.

116. Natalie Gold, 'Trustworthiness and Motivations', in *Capital Failure*, eds. Nicholas Morris and David Vines (Oxford University Press 2014). There is

an alternative view, which sees trustworthiness as being self-interested. On the basis of Chap. 3, it seems more realistic to expect that a mixture of self-interested and other-regarding motivations is involved to the extent that the two may become largely inseparable in the context of relationships of reciprocity. However, relationships may fall along a spectrum from 'thick' or 'strong' trust (where other-regardingness is a strong element) through to 'thin' or 'weak' trust based on an experience of the self-interest of the person trusted reliably causing them to meet needs of the person relying upon them. The problem with the latter is that if the demands of self-interest change, it cannot be relied upon.

117. Moffat and Zhang, *The Paths to Social Licence to Operate: An Integrative Model Explaining Community Acceptance of Mining*, 63.

118. Mayer, Davis and Shoorman, *An Integrative Model of Organizational Trust*. The authors were at pains to point out that their work addresses an organisational context and not, for example, broader social systems. However, there is no obvious reason why their insights should not be of broader application.

119. Martin Tanis and Tom Postmes, *A Social Identity Approach to Trust: Interpersonal Perception, Group Membership and Trusting Behaviour*, 414; Ananthi Al Ramiah and Miles Hewstone, *Intergroup Contact as a Tool for Reducing, Resolving and Preventing Intergroup Conflict: Evidence, Limitations and Potential*, American Psychologist, 2013, Vol. 68(7), 527–542.

120. Luigi Guiso, Paola Sapienza and Luigi Zingales, 'Civic Capital as the Missing Link', in *Handbook of Social Economics Vol. 1A*, eds. Jess Benhabib, Alberto Bisin and Matthew O. Jackson (North-Holland 2011).

121. This does raise the question of why more people have not done that with the financial narratives of Chap. 1 and realised that their account is distorted, as discussed in Chap. 3. It is a sign of how deeply embedded the worldview advanced by those narratives has become.

122. See, for example, Paul de Grauwe, *The Limits of the Market: The Pendulum Between Government and Market* (Oxford University Press 2017).

123. Richard Parsons, Justine Lacey and Kieren Moffat, *Maintaining Legitimacy of a Contested Practice: How the Minerals Industry Understands Its Own 'Licence to Operate'*, Resources Policy, 2014, Vol. 41, 83–90, 85.

124. For example, Boutilier, *Frequently Asked Questions About the Social Licence to Operate*, 269–270.

125. Parsons and Moffat, *Constructing the Meaning of the Social Licence*.

126. See for example Marc Orlitzky, *The Politics of Corporate Social Responsibility or: Why Milton Friedman Has Been Right All Along*, Annals in Social Responsibility, 2015, Vol. 1(1), 5–29.

127. Owen and Kemp, *Social Licence and Mining: A Critical Perspective*, 35, highlight corporate fear in the context of the social licence to operate that expectations could spiral out of control.

128. Gwyn Morgan, former CEO of EnCana quoted in Gunster and Neubauer, *From Public Relations to Mob Rule: Media Framing of Social Licence in Canada*, 12.

129. This danger, and the potential for the SLO to provide a framework for fruitful dialogue has also been recognised: Moffat, et al., *The Social Licence to Operate: A Critical Review*, 481.

130. John Rawls, *A Theory of Justice* (original edn, Harvard University Press 1971) in which he first advanced a theory of justice based on the concept of fairness. He subsequently refined it considerably.

131. For one of the most well-known theories, see Thomas W. Dunfee and Thomas Donaldson, *Ties That Bind: A Social Contracts Approach to Business Ethics* (Harvard Business School Press 1999).

132. Morrison, *The Social License: How to Keep Your Organization Legitimate*; Demuijnck and Fasterling, *The Social Licence to Operate, Journal of Business Ethics*; Lacey, Edwards and Lamont, *Social Licence as Contract: Procedural Fairness and Agreement-Making in Australia*; Dare, Schirmer and Vanclay, *Community Engagement and Social Licence to Operate*.

133. There is a divergence between 'contractarian' approaches that emphasise self-interest and 'contractual' approaches that emphasise what is necessary to secure human dignity.

134. Rawls is different in that he places individuals behind a 'veil of ignorance', where they know nothing of their social identity, to provide a context in which self-interest would lead them to commit to 'fairness for all' on the basis that, without knowing their social identity, it is the logical thing to do.

135. John Hasnas, *The Normative Theories of Business Ethics: A Guide for the Perplexed*, Business Ethics Quarterly, 1998, Vol. 8(1), 19–42.

136. For example, Lorenzo Sacconi, *The Social Contract of the Firm: Economics, Ethics and Organisation*. Revealingly, it also featured in an early attempt by one UK regulator in the aftermath of the financial crisis to explain what had gone wrong and the steps needed to 'redraw' the social contract for banking, which was presented as largely a matter for regulators (thereby also restating market-state dualism in the form of what was effectively a 'regulatory contract'): see *Macro and microprudential supervision*, speech by Paul Tucker, Deputy Governor for Financial Stability at the Bank of England, 29 June 2011.

137. Gehman, Fast and Lefsrud, *Social License to Operate: Legitimacy by Another Name?*

138. While the concept of legitimacy is applied to business organisations, it grew out of attempts to understand the relationship between political authority and the governed. It is often taken to have originated with Max Weber who used the idea to understand the circumstances in which political power would be perpetuated, based on people's beliefs about why they should obey, legitimacy being distinguished from coercion and self-interest. This is dis-

tinct from the question of the standards by which the legitimacy of an authority ought to be assessed (for example, whether a regime is 'just'). However, others have approached it from this 'normative' perspective rather than using Weber's 'descriptive' approach. Some, such as David Beetham, have taken a course between the two. He highlights the fact that beliefs about legitimacy are likely to be based on an assessment of a regime by reference to underlying beliefs: 'A given power relationship is not legitimate because people believe in its legitimacy, but because it can be *justified in terms of* their beliefs... We are making an assessment of the degree of congruence ... between a given system of power and the beliefs, values and expectations that provide its justification.' David Beetham, *The Legitimation of Power* (2nd edn, Palgrave Macmillan 2013), 11.

139. Mark C. Suchman, *Managing Legitimacy: Strategic and Institutional Approaches*, Academy of Management Review, 1995, Vol. 20(3), 571–610, 574; Gehman, Lefsrud and Fast, *Social License to Operate: Legitimacy by Another Name?* Suchman's definition of organisational legitimacy echoes Beetham's. However, it seems to leave untested the soundness of the underlying beliefs, values and expectations on the basis of which an assessment of legitimacy is made; for example, the extent to which they might have been manipulated or rest on unstable assumptions. The populations of at least some of the great powers prior to the First World War might have considered the activities of their respective governments legitimate even though they were to result in slaughter on a previously inconceivable scale. See also Morrison, *The Social License: How to Keep Your Organization Legitimate*, especially Chap. 5.

140. In other words, the emphasis in discussion of the SLO is often empirical (assessing whether people treat a business as legitimate) more than normative (assessing whether that perception is indeed justified), a distinction usefully teased out in the context of the social licence to operate by Demuijnck and Fasterling, *The Social Licence to Operate*.

141. Christopher A. Thomas, *The Uses and Abuses of Legitimacy in International Law*, Oxford Journal of Legal Studies, 2014, Vol. 34(4), 729–758.

5

Realising Justice: the Role of Written Standards

Fast Track

Speed Read

Behaviour in financial markets emerges from a multitude of relationships in practice. Ultimately, it turns not on written rules, but on how those relationships are lived and felt.

Yet one of the most common ways of regulating behaviour is to set out behavioural expectations in writing in the form of **written standards** and enforce them: laws, regulations, contracts, codes of best practice, codes of ethics and so on. Indeed, the response to the 2008 crisis and its aftermath involved rule-making on a massive scale. That has transformed many areas of finance, but it has not healed the fracture between finance and society, nor has it been sufficient to mobilise the level of response that is needed to tackle humanity's increasingly urgent sustainability challenges.

Recognition of a social licence for financial markets goes beyond written standards to the desires and beliefs that animate relationships. Nonetheless, it connects with written standards in various ways. Firstly, if it is correct to see the social licence as a freedom given to market participants to pursue just ends by just means in financial markets, then this corresponds with the aspired ends of law and regulation: justice. Secondly, both the social licence and written standards concern the meaning of the financial world: the social licence because it advances an account of it, and written standards because of the considerable extent to which financial business is legally defined, indeed legally defined much

(continued)

This chapter builds on David Rouch, 'The Social Licence for Financial Markets, Written Standards and Aspiration', in *Edward Elgar Handbook on Law and Ethics in Banking and Finance*, eds. Costanza Russo, Rosa M. Lastra and William Blair (Edward Elgar 2019).

© The Author(s) 2020
D. Rouch, *The Social Licence for Financial Markets*,
https://doi.org/10.1007/978-3-030-40220-4_5

(continued)

more than perhaps any other commercial activity. Thirdly, Chap. 4 suggested that at least some written standards can be thought of as expressing the terms of a social licence.

Distinguishing between different sorts of standards throws further light on these connections:

- Firstly, there is a key difference between the behavioural regularities seen in financial markets (**behavioural norms**) and the written standards advanced in the hope of maintaining those that are desirable or changing those that are not. Just as relationships do not generally operate according to written rules, most day-to-day finance activity appears to follow behavioural norms, with little conscious regard to written standards.
- Secondly, written standards in financial markets **originate** from a variety of sources. Law and regulation largely comes from the state and some from international governmental or regulatory bodies. However, financial firms, industry and professional associations and NGOs and other civil society groups also generate written codes and statements of expectation. The social origin of written standards has a bearing on the extent to which they can be viewed as part of a social licence.
- Thirdly, written standards can be roughly grouped into (1) those that set the structures within or by which financial market activity can be carried on (**structural written standards**) and (2) those that concern the way it is carried on (**behavioural written standards**). Examples of the first include the rules establishing the regime for limited liability companies and rules that define money and financial instruments, such as shares. Examples of the second include obligations such as the regulatory duty on financial services firms to 'treat their customers fairly'. The distinction should not be pressed too far, not least because behavioural standards are sometimes used to uphold legal structures. The recognition of a social licence for financial markets is relevant to both sorts of standard. However, structural written standards have a particular role in defining the meaning of the financial world and what is possible within it; like the road network for those holding driving licences, they tend to shape the context in which the benefit of a social licence can be enjoyed. Meanwhile, behavioural written standards are more closely concerned with the terms under which that can happen—the terms of the social licence. They are more directly concerned with desired behaviour and its outcomes.
- Finally, there are differences in how written standards are used to influence behaviour. Some are more closely connected with the aspirations apparently involved in recognition of a social licence than others.

  - Written standards influence behaviour in a range of ways. Because they express group expectations, they can exert an influence through the desire to be part of the group, through social pressure or because of the way they define the meaning of a person's world. Some, especially structural standards, do it by answering a coordination problem (like which side of the road to drive on), so that once the solution has been provided the standard becomes almost self-enforcing.
  - However, written standards can also be used to influence behaviour more directly. Most commonly, they do that through positive and negative incentives: punishments and rewards connected with the relevant stan-

(continued)

(continued)

dard, to encourage compliance. But written standards can also make an appeal to people's other-regarding values, such as their sense of fairness, seeking to draw directly on those to motivate the desired behaviour. These standards could be thought of as *aspirational*. In a sense, all written standards involve a behavioural aspiration; otherwise, why bother? But some more than others. Aspirational standards operate in essentially two ways. Some reference other-regarding values explicitly (e.g. 'fairness' in the 'treating customers fairly' rule, just mentioned). Others rely upon other-regarding values of those to whom they are addressed to generate behaviour consistent with the standard more than using positive or negative incentives. Standards of this sort can be seen as an aspirational meeting point between the use of written standards to influence behaviour and the sort of aspirations that seem to lie behind talk of a social licence. Yet evidence of the use of aspirational standards gives some reason to question how effective they have been to date.

So What?

The challenges and opportunities identified in Chap. 1 have revealed the limits of the usual regulatory toolkit. Yet written standards are one of the main ways of trying to regulate behaviour. They are a particularly prominent feature of financial life. That is not going to change, so it is essential to ensure that they work as effectively as possible.

The idea of a social licence seems to incorporate some forms of written standards and reach beyond all of them. It provides an account of the context within which written standards are used and complied with. In doing so, can it also affect their use and how they are followed in ways that can help in addressing the challenges and opportunities identified in Chap. 1? Part III will suggest that it has the potential to do precisely that, so strengthening the social solidarity on which wellbeing and financial markets themselves depend.

> The soundness of the country's financial system ultimately depends on having a sensible framework of well-enforced rules as well as institutions that are capitalised sufficiently to withstand … periodic shocks.[1]

Views like this are not uncommon in discussions about how to change behaviour in financial markets. They display considerable faith in the power of regulatory rules and, judging from the deluge of new regulations following the 2008 financial crisis, the faith is widely shared. But ask most people how many legal rules they complied with yesterday and they may struggle to identify any. They may have been in environments shaped by law and regulation, such as the checkout at a supermarket, but much of what went on there was probably not directly subject to legal rules at all (unless you count not engaging in various prohibited behaviours, from assault to theft, the thought of which rarely occurs). Something similar happens in financial markets too. Further, as noted in Chap. 1, while the post-2008 wave of new law and regulation has certainly affected behaviour, the usual regulatory toolkit has not so far worked to heal the fracture between finance and society. Regulators are looking for different ways of influencing behaviour,

> and have developed new … practices for identifying low cultural capital and finding ways to influence its build-up. This is critical because … there are limits to the deterrence and enforcement approach to addressing these challenges … due to the types of market failures.[2]

Yet the most obvious way in which groups of people try to align the behaviour of group members with the group's aspirations is nonetheless by using written rules. Laws and regulations are particularly prominent in financial life (see Sect. 2.2.3) and are likely to remain so.[3] It is therefore essential that they work well, and recognition of a social licence has the potential to help with this (see Sect. 6.6). But written rules in financial markets are not restricted to these alone.[4] They also include things like behavioural codes and other written statements of standards and expectations published by private bodies.[5] What follows refers to rules and standards of this sort, legal or otherwise, generically as 'written standards'.[6]

Not only are written standards common in financial markets, but there is often a correlation between them and the behaviour of market participants. That can give the impression that the behaviour results from the written standards, and sometimes it does. But the power of rules should not be overstated. You cannot get every inhabitant of France to paint their front door red simply by making a law requiring it. Does the soundness of a financial system really ultimately depend on written standards, or does it rest on something on which effective rules also depend? What if written standards express (as much as attempting to change) behavioural standards that many, if not most, people already adhere to most of the time, and reflect aspirations that are widely shared? And where rules essentially define social reality (e.g. rules about what counts as money), what if those rules rely upon (as much as attempting to define) the meaning already given by those in that society to their environment in seeking to achieve their desired ends (see Sect. 6.6.2)?[7] After all, as noted in previous chapters, language itself relies on a consensus about meaning, and law is a form of language, unique among other things because of the social processes involved in its creation and application. And what of rules that essentially solve a coordination problem (such as driving on the left or the right); the rule settles the behaviour, but largely because it is a consensual solution to pursuing a greater commonly held desire (travelling safely). What if both financial markets and the effectiveness of law and regulations and other written standards rely upon an underlying social solidarity and consensus about what is desirable: what is valued; what people aspire to?

In each case, if the aim is to influence behaviour, perhaps more investment is needed in what lies behind written standards rather than trying to craft a perfect set of them. That entails assessing the underlying desires of those to whom the rules apply and seeking to ensure the salience of those that are consistent with commonly desired ends for financial markets. It involves understanding the assumed meaning of the financial world on the basis of which individuals and firms pursue their goals and asking whether it makes sense in the light of those ultimate ends. These factors are important, not just because they affect the content of written standards and how they are applied by regulators. Written standards are incomplete (see Sect. 4.6). It is not possible to create a comprehensive written statement of how everyone should behave in every situation they encounter. Background understandings and desires are likely to affect what goes on in the considerable space that is left.

Chapter 6 will return to these themes. For now, however, the important point is that recognition of a social licence seems to concern both the desires brought to financial market activity and the meaning it holds, and it incorporates some written standards, but also reaches beyond them (see Chap. 4). This leads to two questions. Firstly, what written standards apply in financial markets and what is their connection with the recognition of a social licence and, secondly, how might greater recognition of a social licence affect the way written standards are followed and used and, in particular, could it help to strengthen their role in addressing the challenges identified in Chap. 1? The second of these questions is covered in Part III. This chapter addresses the first.

Chapter 4 suggested that some types of written standards can be seen as part of a social licence, but only some. So, taking the written standards that apply in the UK financial markets as a case study, this chapter looks more closely at which standards these might be. For those standards that cannot be regarded as part of a social licence, it highlights how they nonetheless shape the environment in which the ends of the social licence can be pursued—the framework of meaning within which and the goals at which activity is channelled. Because of that, recognition of a social licence is still relevant to the formulation and operation of written standards of this sort. For those written standards that can be seen as part of a social licence, the chapter goes on to consider how they might express its substance. It looks particularly at the role of written standards that expressly require or depend on behaviour by reference to other-regarding values: written standards which could be called 'aspirational standards' because they are closely aligned with an aspiration for those values to be realised in practice; standards that reach beyond, 'the deterrence and enforcement approach'. The chapter identifies common ground between the idea of a social licence and written standards that apply in financial markets, and especially these aspirational standards. Both seem to concern the pursuit of just ends by just means in financial markets. If there is a need to break away from, or to supplement, the 'deterrence and enforcement approach', these aspirational standards may have a particularly important role to play.

In view of the vast expansion in regulatory rules in the finance sector in the thirty years since the UK's 'Big Bang' of 1986 and similar 'deregulation' processes elsewhere,[8] there has unsurprisingly been considerable attention to the forms, types and uses of regulatory rules in financial markets and their relationship with other regulatory methods.[9] The literature is now extensive. What follows draws on, but is not intended to rehash, that. Rather, it places regulatory rules in the context of the full range of written standards that apply in the UK financial markets, so clarifying how different sorts of written standards might be related to the idea of a social licence for financial markets.

5.1   Norms, Behavioural Norms, Written Standards, the Social Licence and Justice

But before looking at written standards, it is important to draw out a fundamental distinction between the regular behavioural patterns of firms and individuals in financial markets ('behavioural norms') and written standards that are deliberately advanced to influence that behaviour towards what is desired by the originators of the standards. There is also a third broad category of norms at work in financial markets: those that are neither written down nor fully reflected in market practice, but which nonetheless influence behaviour, ranging from a sense of moral obligation through to matters of etiquette that are part of a 'background understanding' of what is appropriate. Chapter 6 picks up on the interaction of these with behavioural norms and the way written standards are followed (see Sects. 6.5 and 6.6).

Chapter 2 touched on the emergence of behavioural norms in groups (see Sect. 2.4.1). Behavioural norms are the regularities of behaviour that can be seen in the day-to-day operation of financial life *in practice*: how people relate, the objects of their transactions and how they are struck, the way staff are employed and promoted and interact with colleagues and staff at other firms, how conflicts emerge and get resolved and so on. Most of these behavioural regularities are not *formally* enforced by any external body. They are simply 'the way things are'. They emerge and are shaped by a range of factors, including the cultural environment and, within that, 'market forces'.

Written standards are, in part, intended to sustain or influence behavioural norms, but they do not single-handedly generate the norms. The recognition of a social licence for financial markets is neither a behavioural norm nor a written standard. However, Chap. 4 suggested that it does express an aspiration about what behavioural norms should be and the outcomes they should produce: just ends pursued in a just manner. Written standards are also social. Social behavioural aspiration lies behind them too. They emerge from social processes and are advanced to influence behavioural norms in the groups at which they are directed. Because of that, it is unsurprising to find an apparent alignment between them and the social licence: as with the social licence, an aspiration towards justice is also the stuff of law and regulation, if not written standards more widely. Both written standards and the social licence recognise things as they are, but reach towards an aspired end.

Consistent with this, the highest duty of English and Welsh lawyers when working with their clients in the financial markets or otherwise is not simply to apply law and regulation, but to uphold '… the rule of law and the proper administration of justice'.[10] Likewise, the United Nations Basic Principles on the Role of Lawyers talks of lawyers as 'essential agents of the administration of justice' and 'promoting the cause of justice', stating that, in doing so, lawyers should 'seek to uphold human rights and fundamental freedoms' under national and international law.[11] As noted in Chap. 3, the international human rights regime is founded on an understanding of intrinsic human dignity, the realisation of which was connected with justice in Chap. 4 and is increasingly influential in business contexts. Meanwhile, the International Bar Association International Principles on Conduct for the Legal Profession states that lawyers are to treat the interests of clients as paramount, 'subject always to … the interests of justice'.[12] Whether lawyers in the financial markets are used to thinking of their role in these terms in practice is another matter.

5.2 Types of Written Standard and Their Relationship with a Social Licence

The written standards that apply in the UK financial markets can be categorised in various ways.[13] None of the available categorisations offers a single authoritative basis for looking at them. Even where categories of written standards have been identified, they are rarely rigid, but overlap and display inter-dependencies.[14] Some sort of categorisation is nonetheless needed in seeking to understand the relationship between written standards in financial markets and the recognition of a social licence.

The Appendix to this chapter therefore provides an overview of the various types of written standards at work in the UK financial markets (the 'Written Standards Map'). Together with what follows, it highlights a number of features that cast light on how they relate to the idea of a social licence: firstly, by distinguishing between the originators of those standards (i.e. those who promulgate them) and those to whom the standards are addressed, and secondly, by providing an indication of how far each category of written standards seems deliberately to draw on aspirations based on other-regarding values and could therefore be thought of as 'aspirational'. It does the second in three ways: it applies a rating based on the extent to which standards in the relevant category expressly reference other-regarding values (an 'aspirational rating'); it rates standards based on the extent to which they rely upon enforcement administered by a public body to secure compliance (a 'legal hardness rating'); and it indicates the way in which public and private enforcement mechanisms are available to enforce the relevant standard. The basis for these ratings is described further below.

Because the Written Standards Map is only an overview, it comes with any number of health warnings and qualifications. However, none should be material for current purposes. In particular, it will be clear that the aspirational and legal hardness ratings do not depend upon an especially scientific process. It is challenging to apply a single rating to some categories of written standards covered in the map, for example, because some are comprised of a mixture of written standards that fall at various points along each spectrum. The ratings are therefore no more than an indication of how far a given category of written standards has characteristics of the sort concerned. It would certainly be possible to debate the ratings assigned to each; indeed, there might be merit in doing so to develop a better understanding of the role and operation of each. However, for current purposes this looser guide must suffice.

5.2.1   The Originators of Written Standards

The source of written standards affects the extent to which they can be regarded as part of a social licence (see Chap. 4, Sect. 4.6). Those with the closest connection to public authorities arguably have the strongest claim.[15] The Written Standards Map helps to show how the promulgation of written standards for financial markets is 'polycentric'. A multitude of what can loosely be described as 'public' and 'private' actors is involved, the first being more dominant in its output. Distinguishing between the different originators of written standards is important. The involvement of public bodies is not only relevant in assessing how far each sort of written standard can be regarded as part of the social licence. It also affects how formal legal enforcement powers attach to them and, in consequence, the nature of their relationship with the idea of a social licence. In particular, the mode of enforcement has a bearing on their power to inspire behaviour by appealing to desires based on other-regarding values.

Public Originators of Written Standards

Governments and public authorities advance written standards (laws and regulations) principally through the legislature, the courts (subject to judicial independence) or regulators. These standards can broadly be divided into two groups:

(1) Public law standards: very loosely, these are legal standards created by public bodies such as governments and regulators (including regional governmental and regulatory bodies, such as the European Union), usually in the form of statutes and regulations, which concern the relationship between individuals and the state, or relationships between private individuals which are of wider public interest.
(2) Private law standards (i.e. those arising at common law and which rely upon the courts): returning to underlying social consensuses, these have grown through a process of legal dialogue with the community and are carried in a set of authoritative stories in the form of case law; they include the law of contract (from which flows a host of private contractual standards, from standard form documentation created by industry associations such as ISDA to entirely private arrangements between two or more parties), tortious standards (e.g. negligence, negligent misstatement) and equitable standards, especially fiduciary duties (the duty of loyalty to a principal).[16]

The role of the first group is mainly to ensure that the activities of private actors are aligned with the aspirations of society at large. The role of the second is to protect individuals and other entities and allow them to regulate their relationships bilaterally, but this also serves socially desirable ends such as the need for people to be able to engage in economic activity and for relational certainty and social stability.

International governmental and regulatory organisations also generate 'public' standards. Very broadly, these fall into two categories. Firstly, there are those promulgated by the United Nations and associated agencies. These do not generally apply directly to businesses, but take the form of international instruments and treaties between member states of the United Nations who seek to reflect them in varying degrees in national law and policy. Some of the more important for the financial sector include the United Nations Declaration of Human Rights, the Sustainable Development Goals and the Paris Climate Agreement.[17] Where these standards are enforceable against individual firms, it is usually because they have been incorporated into local law. However, there have been numerous initiatives by United Nations agencies and business working groups facilitated by them to supplement some of these standards with statements of good practice for business organisations. Examples include the United Nations Global Compact, a grouping of firms in the global business community that seeks to develop and share good practice in advancing UN goals and values, and the United Nations Environment Programme Finance Initiative, a partnership between the UNEP and the finance sector intended to promote sustainable finance. While good practice standards are voluntary, firms that publicly commit to them are likely to be under some level of obligation to comply, if only reputational, and standards of this sort can acquire a harder legal edge, for example, if they come to define legal duties of care. The United Nations Guiding Principles on Human Rights are particularly notable.[18] They are principles for states and businesses on the prevention of human rights abuse, accompanied by guidance on how to put them into practice, reflecting the United Nations human rights 'Protect, Respect and Remedy' Framework. They seek to enlist state and non-state actors in remedying abuses. As noted in Chap. 4, the 'Protect, Respect and Remedy' Framework references the idea of a social licence to operate.[19]

Secondly, a range of other international regulatory bodies and committees (comprised of representatives from participant countries) also issue sets of written standards, for example, the Financial Stability Board, the Organisation for Economic Co-operation and Development, the Basel Committee on Banking Supervision and the International Organization of Securities Commissions. Their standards are principally a way of coordinating the activities of national regulators, rather than directly regulating market participants. Nonetheless, since the standards are ultimately directed at financial market activity and are sometimes taken into account by market participants in deciding how to act, they are included in the Written Standards Map. Their inclusion is for completeness. They are not considered further in what follows.

Private Originators of Written Standards

Chapter 4 highlighted various fora in which expectations are expressed that might help in understanding the terms of a social licence for financial markets, including a number of private bodies. These expectations sometimes take the form of written standards. As noted in Chap. 4, in spite of their private origins, written standards of this sort could nonetheless be seen as potentially articulating the terms of a social licence, in particular, where they are an attempt by the originator to operate in accordance with wider social values, are part of an attempt to avoid public sector regulation, where they have been specifically required or adopted by public sector bodies or where they have otherwise been 'enlisted' in the regulatory project. Elements of these can be seen in the standard generating activities of a number of the categories of private bodies considered below.

Firstly, industry bodies comprised of financial services firms issue written standards. Industry associations generally act in the interests of their members, for example, lobbying on regulatory reform and maintaining a sector's good standing with its client base. However, other sorts of industry body are closer to public-private initiatives, so that their standards have a stronger claim to be part of a social licence; for example, the UK's FICC Markets Standards Board was established with regulatory encouragement as a private standard setting body in the fixed income, currency and commodities markets.[20] Written norms issued by industry bodies include, in particular, codes of conduct and statements of good practice (particularly in areas of regulation that involve a significant element of judgement or where the rules are uncertain) and, in some cases, industry standard contractual documentation such as ISDA's standard form derivatives documentation, mentioned earlier; contracts that can be enforced in the courts, highlighting the blurred boundary between public and private standard setting. Industry-driven conduct codes are less common where an industry sector is heavily regulated, as compared with unregulated or lightly regulated markets. The FX Global Code is an example of the latter. It is a set of global principles of good practice in the largely unregulated foreign exchange markets and was the product of a joint project between regulators, central banks and market participants.[21]

Secondly, there are professional bodies for individuals working in financial markets. Essentially, they help members to achieve standards of professional competence and seek to maintain professional conduct standards. They do this largely by offering professional training and qualifications programmes. Their activities are therefore based on commonly agreed standards of professional competence and behaviour, the latter usually articulated in codes of ethics or conduct. Professional bodies currently have a relatively low profile in the finance sector. It is therefore questionable how far they have influenced behaviour in recent years, even in those parts of the sector they cover.[22] However, their role might develop in future given heightened regulatory attention to the individual accountability of staff of financial firms for regulatory compliance. For example, the UK has introduced a 'Senior Managers and Certification Regime', which places higher expectations on individual staff carrying on management activities and requires firms to certify the fitness of staff carrying on core activities (see Sect. 2.4.3).

A third group of standard-promulgating private bodies is financial firms. These make extensive and varied use of written standards, for example, (1) as a compliance and risk management tool; (2) to comply with specific regulatory requirements to maintain policies in areas such as conflict management[23] or statements of ethics;[24] (3) to establish their credentials with their potential customer base and other third parties, such as regulators and (4) to define their relationship with those with whom they deal (i.e. the contractual terms on which firms transact whether with counterparties, clients, suppliers or staff, again, enforceable in the courts). Written standards in categories (1)–(3) can take many different forms including codes of behaviour, codes of ethics, statements of good practice and internal policies of various sorts (e.g. remuneration schemes, appraisal standards and policies on matters like risk management, which clients to take on and mandates to accept, conflict management, trade execution and allocation, product development and staff discipline).

Fourthly, investment exchanges and trading platforms, and market infrastructures such as payment systems, depositaries and clearing houses also generate written standards in the form of membership agreements, rules and operating manuals governing access to, operation of, and conduct within the relevant market or infrastructure. In many cases, the platforms are directly or indirectly required to maintain these by law, as a condition of being permitted to operate. For example, EU-regulated exchanges are required under the EU Markets in Financial Instruments Directive to maintain 'transparent and non-discriminatory rules and procedures that provide for fair and orderly trading and establish objective criteria for the efficient execution of orders'.[25] Likewise, there are rules for the operation of 'multilateral trading facilities' and 'organised trading facilities', which are essentially investment markets operated by financial firms and market operators; use of these will be subject to agreeing to comply with a range of platform-specific written standards.[26] Again this highlights the close relationship between publicly and privately originated written standards, and so their proximity to the idea of a social licence.

Finally, there is a loose category of private bodies that could be described as public interest groupings and NGOs. These would include organisations such as Tomorrow's Company[27] or Transparency International[28] (which are seeking to encourage changes in market behaviour, among other things, by promoting codes, statements of good practice, 'score cards' and other forms of ratings), the Global Reporting Initiative (which maintains widely used sustainability reporting standards) and the International Integrated Reporting Council (which seeks to foster integrated company reporting and maintains a set of standards in support of that). Their criteria are a form of written standards. Some of these bodies and groupings fall somewhere between being NGOs and industry associations. In particular, as noted above, United Nations agencies facilitate or have helped to establish various fora in which business and other groups can interact to generate statements of principles and good practice standards, such as the United Nations Global Compact and the United Nations Environment Programme Finance Initiative.

In spite of the distinction, above, between 'public' and 'private' originators of standards, it is clear from this brief overview that the threshold between the two is porous. In particular, private actors may rely on private law, enforced in the courts, in setting standards (e.g. contract law) and in setting their own internal standards (e.g. conduct codes). However, the latter are partly intended to secure compliance with public law standards. Conversely, private standards may also affect the application of public standards (e.g. in determining whether a duty has been properly discharged) or be enlisted in public law regimes (e.g. the UK's Corporate Governance Code, promulgated by the UK Financial Reporting Council but used as part of the UK's listing regime).[29] There are also standard setting bodies such as the UK's Takeover Panel that started life as essentially private sector initiatives, but which have progressively become incorporated into the public sector regulatory structure.[30] As noted, the degree of proximity to public sector standard setting bodies is one factor in assessing the extent to which the standards originated by private bodies can be viewed as, in some way, articulating a social licence. However, it is also relevant in understanding the behavioural force of their standards, considered further below; in particular, the extent to which it relies on negative incentives (especially sanctions) or draws on other-regarding aspirations by referencing values.

5.2.2 The Subjects of Written Standards

To whom are these standards addressed? Not 'markets'. As discussed in Chap. 4, the social licence can best be regarded as granted to market participants and those who operate the markets. Consistent with that, market participants and operators are the principal subjects of written standards. However, there is an important distinction between written standards that apply to firms (including market operators) and those that apply to individuals working for firms.

Written standards that are specifically addressed to individuals are shown in the Written Standards Map in italics. From this, it is clear that most categories of standards in the map apply to firms rather than individuals. Professional codes and written standards promulgated by firms usually apply to individuals (the latter, in part, designed to help the firm to comply with its own legal and regulatory obligations by applying a form of 'private' regulation). Where legal rules and regulations apply to companies rather than the individuals within them, a company's incorporation can operate not just to limit liability for shareholders but also create a sense of limited responsibility among staff for ensuring the firm's compliance (see Sect. 2.4.3). In this context, written standards that apply to individuals can be especially important in seeking to realise aspired behaviours since the activities of the legal vehicles used to carry on financial business are largely determined by the individuals and groups of individuals brought together using them (see Sect. 2.5). The UK's Senior Managers and Certification Regime is designed to address this dissipation of responsibility (as is current regulatory emphasis on the need for finance firms to maintain a robust culture, see Sect. 1.2.4). It does so, among other things, by clarifying the 'individual accountability' of specific staff for their firm's compliance with the regulatory regime in the areas of the business for which those staff are responsible. However, its full impact remains to be seen, since its emphasis upon accountability and control does not seem to operate within a broader concept of character formation (see Chap. 6).

5.2.3 Written Structural and Behavioural Standards

Not all written standards can be seen as articulating a social licence. Some set the context within which licensed activities can take place or define their subject matter. Very broadly, written standards tend to affect or seek to affect behaviour in one of two ways: firstly, by establishing or formalising structures within or by reference to which behaviour takes place ('written structural standards')[31] and, secondly, by prescribing or proscribing behaviours ('written behavioural standards').

Written structural standards typically take the form of law or regulation, or contract-based arrangements, and establish structures that affect behaviour, intentionally or otherwise. They do so both by determining what is legally possible and by defining how people think about financial markets and understand the meaning of their social world.[32] Essentially, they do this in two ways. Firstly, they can set the framework within which behaviour takes place; examples in financial markets would include arrangements such as ring-fenced banks,[33] clearing houses,[34] the limited liability company and recognised investment exchanges. Secondly, structural standards can be used to establish or formalise structures by reference to which behaviour takes place. Financial market examples include the notion of private property, money, shares, and debt and security interests. These structures are defined, supported and operated in accordance with a network of legal and regulatory rules. Because they concern the structures within or by reference to which financial activity can take place, standards of this sort should not principally be thought of as articulating a social licence. Rather, they *set the context* for what it is possible to do with a licence because they define the raw material of financial activity and establish the channels through which it can be pursued. By analogy, a driving licence permits a person to drive a car, but different laws and regulations define what a car is and support the infrastructure necessary to enjoy the licence.[35] So it is with an authorisation to engage in financial activity. For example, on one view, '…a property right is a guarantee allowing actions to occur within the opportunities and constraints defined by the right.'[36] Or take money. Money grew out of the behavioural norms of social exchange, but now also rests on an underpinning of structural law and regulation; almost all finance sector activity is organised around it and takes it as a given (see Sect. 2.2.2).

However, it would be wrong to draw too hard a line between structural and behavioural written standards. Sometimes, the latter are needed to uphold structures: examples include some aspects of banking regulation which constrain the activities of banks, among other things, thereby maintaining the value of money; rules stipulating the operating standards for those proposing to operate investment exchanges as a condition of being permitted to do so; and regimes such as the European Union regulation on indices used as benchmarks in financial instruments which uses a combination of structural and behavioural rules in seeking to ensure the robustness of benchmarks that are used in valuing financial instruments.[37] Here, written standards that could be regarded as expressing the terms of a social licence for financial markets (i.e. the terms of participation in the markets) also support structures on which financial markets themselves and wider social solidarity depend. So, while it may be more appropriate to see the social licence for financial markets as a licence to those who operate and participate in the markets, it is nonetheless a licence 'for' financial markets in the sense that behaviours consistent with the licence should help to sustain structures that are vital to markets and more broadly, potentially, social solidarity.

Conversely, structural standards can also be used to pursue specific behavioural outcomes aligned with the aspirations that seem to lie behind recognition of a social licence. For example, the structural metaphor of 'Chinese walls' is used to describe measures that firms are required to take to prevent conflicts of interest from adversely affecting their client and market-facing relationships.[38] Meanwhile, in the words of one regulator talking about regulatory rules on banks' employee remuneration regimes, 'The objective here is to align structures with incentives, and create the culture that people have skin in the game...,'[39] so that they do not behave in a reckless manner.

As with the relationship between public and private standard setting, the distinction between structural and behavioural written standards is, then, porous and there is a close relationship between the two. Although written structural standards principally uphold structures, by doing so they nonetheless have behavioural impacts beyond marshalling behaviour in support of the structure. That is because they define what is possible and create and underpin structures which are also stores of cultural significance, such as money, so setting the parameters for, or establishing the objects of, behaviour. The behavioural effect of conducting business out of a limited liability entity is not the same as conducting it out of a partnership with unlimited liability (see Sect. 2.4.3); activity based on money subject to the gold standard is different from using fiat money; and the behavioural impact of a debt relationship (with creditor controls on the debtor through security interests) is entirely different from a transaction between two people financed by cash. Structures of this sort carry meaning, which drives behaviour when it becomes the subject of desire (see Chap. 2).

So, while structural written standards may have a limited claim to be articulating a social licence for financial markets, they can nonetheless have a significant impact on realising the aspirations that seem to lie behind it. Because of that, recognition of a social licence is relevant in creating standards of this sort. Structures that structural written standards help to sustain and, more importantly perhaps, the meaning tied up in those structures can either support or undermine the sort of aspirations that seem to lie behind talk of a social licence. An example is the UK Financial Conduct Authority's ('FCA') duty to promote effective competition in the interests of consumers in the markets it regulates.[40] It can involve, among other things, taking steps to alter the structure of those markets.[41] But perhaps the most striking example is the 1986 'Big Bang'. This was a major structural change to the UK financial markets that involved, among other things, the abolition of fixed commissions and the distinction between client-facing stock brokers and market-dealing stock jobbers. At least in part, it lay behind the need for, and the subsequent vast expansion of, written behavioural standards to ensure that the UK's financial markets remained fair and effective.

5.2.4   Written Behavioural Standards and the Role of Aspiration

Written behavioural standards articulate accepted or desired behaviours or behavioural outcomes. It is therefore easier to see a relationship between these and the sort of aspirations that Chap. 4 identified as lying behind talk of a social licence. To clarify the nature of that relationship, it is helpful, firstly, to distinguish between the different sorts of written behavioural standards that apply in the UK financial markets and, secondly, to look at the nature of any aspirational overlap with the idea of a social licence.

Written behavioural standards are often grouped into those that are *pre-scriptive* (stipulating precise behaviours leaving little discretion with those to whom they are addressed) and those in the form of *principles* (leaving those to whom they are addressed with discretion about how to achieve the standard or outcome they set). However, it is also possible to rate them by reference to their *aspirational* force based on the extent to which they rely for their impact on other-regarding values.[42] All written behavioural standards are advanced with the aspiration of shaping behaviour in some way. Even a simple requirement to provide a notice to a client (e.g. setting out a firm's contact details) involves an aspiration for firms to behave in one way rather than another. However, the 'aspirational standards' considered below are notable for the way they draw on other-regarding values: the sort of values that that are likely to be relevant in addressing the challenges and opportunities identified in Chap. 1. They do this in essentially two ways: firstly, in the *content* of the relevant standards (by explicitly referencing other-regarding values), and secondly how they are expected to influence people (the extent to which this depends upon the other-regarding values of those to whom the standard is addressed). Standards relying on other-regarding values are often drafted as principles, but not necessarily the second category.

Aspirational standards are particularly significant for the relationship between written standards and the idea of a social licence. If it is right that recognition of a social licence involves aspiration towards just ends pursued justly in financial markets, standards of this sort most clearly reflect similar aspirations because of their relationship with other-regarding values. As with the recognition of a social licence, aspirational standards reach beyond individually prescribed behaviours to values that transcend them. There is therefore a sense in which aspirational standards could be regarded as the greatest aspirational meeting point between recognition of a social licence and the use of written standards in financial markets.

Content-Based Aspirational Standards

Turning first to standards with aspirational *content*, most written behavioural standards are prescriptive. In other words, they describe or reflect specific behavioural standards and either (1) guide, require or incentivise those to whom they are addressed to attain them or (2) ban behaviours that fall short. An example would be regulatory rules on the prevention and detection of money laundering. Although these allow a significant degree of discretion on how to comply, they nonetheless apply precise requirements on, among other things, systems and controls to verify customer identity and detect and report money laundering.[43] Standards of this sort have two broad functions: they help coordinate activity where there is a consensus about a particular desired end but social organisation is needed to achieve it (driving on the right or left) and they get people to behave in a way consistent with commonly accepted standards (not speeding).

However, the category of written behavioural standards also includes a smaller group of written standards formulated as foundational principles. Principles are less specific about the action they require, but tend to operate by reference to (1) values that should be applied or (2) broad outcomes that should be achieved (e.g. that a bank is adequately capitalised[44]).[45] Principles in the first category often reference the kind of other-regarding values that would commonly be regarded as integral to just behaviour, such as a duty to 'act fairly', recalling the discussion of values in Chap. 4, Sect. 4.6.2. They involve a balancing of self-interest and the needs of others. This seems to suggest a connection with the aspirational dimension of talk of a social licence for financial markets. It is this quality that Ronald Dworkin may have had in mind in describing legal principles as '…a standard that is to be observed … because it is a requirement of justice or fairness…'.[46] For current purposes, principles (whether legal or non-legal) that reference values of this sort are treated as aspirational standards because they invite or require behaviour by reference to over-arching values that express how people themselves generally desire to be treated. The standards they reference are understood to transcend any specific set of circumstances. What follows refers to them as 'content-based aspirational standards' because the aspiration is expressed in their content.

The Written Standards Map in the Appendix provides an indication of the distribution of content-based aspirational standards among the various categories of written standards in UK financial markets. It does that by including an 'aspirational' rating (in column 4) for each category of written standards in the map. The rating is based on the extent to which standards in each category involve content-based aspirational standards. The map treats a standard as a content-based aspirational standard where it references an other-regarding value used in the FCA Principles for Businesses: integrity, due care, proper standards of conduct and fairness. Fairness is particularly prominent in the FCA Principles. It appears in three of them and is arguably implicit in others. The standard of 'fairness' is especially significant in the current context because of its common association with justice.[47] Indeed, some theories of justice are largely based on it.[48] The FCA Principles are over-arching standards that apply to all firms in the UK financial markets. They are taken as a baseline here because, in the context of talk of a social licence, public regulatory standards probably have the strongest claim to be part of the licence, as compared with written standards produced by private bodies. In addition to these four expressions, a written standard has also been deemed aspirational if it references 'honesty' or 'ethics'. The first is included because it appears in another over-arching FCA rule, which the FCA refers to as the 'client's best interests rule'.[49] The second is included on the basis that references to 'ethics' in written standards generally seem intended to encourage other-regarding behaviour based on commonly understood values.[50] The Written Standards Map uses a rating of A1–A3: categories of written standards that, on their face, make material use of content-based aspirational standards have a rating of A1, whereas those that tend to be based on prescriptive standards receive a rating of A3.

Aspirational Influence-Based Standards

The second basis on which written behavioural standards could be regarded as aspirational turns not on their content, but on how they are expected to influence people in practice. The issue here is how far that influence relies on the other-regarding values of those subject to the standard, or whether it depends on incentives: punishment or reward.

It should by now be clear that written behavioural standards can affect behaviour in various ways: among other things, because they express the expectations of a group to which people want to belong (see Sect. 2.4), because they key into a human tendency to imitate or follow the standards of a group (see Sect. 2.4) or because they alter the perceived meaning of the social world on the basis of which people decide how to pursue their desires (see Sect. 2.2 and Chap. 6).[51] However, written standards also rely more directly on people's self-interested and other-regarding desires to influence behaviour. Broadly, that can happen in one of three ways: (1) deterrence (relying on negative self-interest, especially sanctions for those in breach), (2) positive incentive (relying up positive self-interest, for example, enhanced remuneration for those who comply) and (3) inspiration to comply with the standard by appealing to an aspiration on the part of the subject about the way others deserve to be treated.[52] The first and second are familiar. An example of the third is the Lord George Principles for Good Business Conduct of the Worshipful Company of International Bankers of the City of London, which rely largely on the desire to be part of the Company and their strongly values-based content for their impact.[53]

It is important to avoid an either/or approach here; as noted, an element of other-regarding aspiration is involved in most written standards, and the same written standard can influence people in different ways. However, the more that adherence to a written standard is secured using incentives, the more likely it is that adherence will be treated as a compliance exercise rather realising an other-regarding value. That is because incentive-based enforcement relies on appealing to an instrumental desire to avoid or secure something that will serve the subject's self-interest. It tends to rehearse self-interested desires more than those that are other-regarding, whether self-interested or otherwise. The risk of this is that narrow self-interest is strengthened, and once satisfied, the motivation for the particular behaviour is gone. Self-interest is an important and necessary feature of financial markets (see Sect. 3.2.2), as in life more broadly. Because of that, incentives have a key role in realising the sort of aspirations that seem to lie behind talk of a social licence. However, it is also important to recognise that incentivised compliance involves the subject of the standard in a very different deliberative and motivational exercise.[54] If the aim is a balancing of self-interest and other-regardingness, then it may also be necessary to reflect this balance in the way written behavioural standards are designed.

It is challenging to provide a simple snapshot of how every category of written standards in the Written Standards Map gets enforced. However, as a proxy, column 5 of the map applies a 'legal hardness' rating. This is intended to indicate the extent to which formal legal enforcement tools are available to incentivise compliance with each category of written standards, or whether they rely on something else for their force, in particular, positive self-interest (such as remuneration or career progression) or their inspirational power to motivate behaviour.

Clearly, this rating only provides a partial perspective on the relationship between reliance on incentives and other-regarding aspirations in getting people to follow written standards. Among other things, how standards are enforced in practice does not just depend on what formal enforcement powers are available but also the style and approach of the originating body to enforcement. Having enforcement powers does not necessarily mean that they will be used or that regulators will ignore the power of other-regarding aspirations among the regulated to change behaviour.[55] The hardness ratings take no account of regulatory style and activism, for example, the widely publicised move towards 'credible deterrence' by the FCA in the aftermath of the financial crisis, heralding a period of more intense enforcement activity. Regulators can use a range of methods to seek to secure compliance, and, most of the time, their activities involve softer tools such as supervisory dialogue, advice and persuasion, not sanctions. However, the effectiveness of these tends to rely at some level on the underlying power to sanction.[56] Separately, the hardness ratings do not cover the use of positive incentives (rather than legal sanctions) used privately by firms in seeking to shape staff behaviour, such as career progression and remuneration. These principally rely upon an appeal to positive self-interest, and, even though firms' incentive frameworks are generally constructed using private law rights and obligations, they do not have the same characteristics as a regulatory enforcement regime; it is rarely the possibility of legal enforcement action that makes these incentive frameworks effective. It is beyond the scope of the map to seek to cover all of the different public and private enforcement mechanisms associated with written standards or the sometimes complex interplay between them. However, in addition to the legal hardness rating in column 5 of the Written Standards Map, some indication of this variety of enforcement methods is provided in column 3.

The legal hardness ratings in column 5 distinguish between H1 (written standards enforced using legal powers given to public authorities), H2 (written standards which can be enforced using private law remedies available to the parties affected by a breach where restitution may be at least as important as the enforcement of a particular standard) and H3 (those that do not seem heavily reliant upon any legal or regulatory enforcement mechanism or are not reliant at all). A rating of H2 has also been given to official guidance on the meaning and application of standards rated H1 since the guidance itself is generally not enforceable, but may have a bearing on the outcome of enforcement of the underlying standard. H1 represents standards with the highest legal hardness rating and H3 the lowest. Category H1 is further split into H1.1 and H1.2, the former being applied to standards that can be enforced using criminal sanctions and the latter to standards that are subject to civil enforcement tools. However, as noted, we should not assume that a high legal hardness rating means that other-regarding aspirations are not also at work to secure conformity with a particular standard. Other-regarding aspiration can still operate at H1.1 (e.g. because someone recognises that the standard reflects what is just), and positive and negative enforcement can still operate within H3 (e.g. expulsion from membership of an association or 'cold shouldering'). Further, different firms and different individuals will respond differently to the same standard. For many, the fact that a standard describes a sort of behaviour that accords with commonly held values will be sufficient for them to act accordingly regardless of the possibility of sanctions. Consequently, just because a category of standards has been given a particular rating does not mean that behaviour that is consistent with it relies exclusively upon only one of the three factors mentioned above.

Aspirational Standards—Observations Based on Aspirational and Legal Hardness Ratings

What becomes clear from these ratings is that content-based aspirational standards (i.e. expressly referencing other-regarding values) are ubiquitous. This ubiquity seems consistent with what one might expect from the values prioritisation work of Schwartz discussed in Chap. 4. Content-based aspirational standards are promulgated by most types of originator, public or private, and apply to both to firms and individuals. What the Written Standards Map does not show, but is nonetheless relevant in thinking about aspirational overlap between aspirational standards and talk of a social licence, is that content-based aspirational standards issued by the FCA in the form of its Principles for Businesses tend to be referenced to the interests of customers and market users (associating them closely with firms' transactional activities), whereas the drafting of some of the more private aspirational standards (ironically, with perhaps less of a claim to be articulating a social licence) appears to acknowledge a broader, reciprocal social remit, closer to the apparent scope of the social licence. For example, the CEO's introduction to Barclays Bank's code suggests that following it will realise the essence of the bank's purpose,

'… that customers, clients, shareholders, colleagues, *and broader society* can have a sustainable and prosperous future' (emphasis added).[57] Others hold themselves out by reference to high other-regarding standards, such as Morgan Stanley which states that it strives to adhere to 'the highest standards of ethical conduct' and JPMorgan Chase which describes itself as being committed to 'the highest level of integrity and ethical conduct'.[58] While these do not expressly reference social responsibilities, in view of the embeddedness of financial activity in and its impact on networks of wider social relations (see Chaps. 2, 3 and 4), it is not obvious how such a standard could be satisfied without substantial reference to the firm's impact on those networks.

The legal hardness ratings provide an additional insight into the operation of content-based aspirational standards. There are content-based aspirational standards in all categories of legal hardness, except for H1.1 (since, in view of the broad drafting, it would be inappropriate to criminalise breach). Content-based aspirational standards originated by public regulatory bodies are, inevitably, associated with harder enforcement powers (but noting comments above concerning the range of regulatory enforcement approaches and regulators' possible reliance on the power of other-regarding values). By contrast, the content-based aspirational standards of private bodies, especially professional associations, are usually subject to softer legal enforcement powers.

This raises a question. If a content-based aspirational standard associated with 'hard enforcement' mechanisms appears in one context, and a similar standard placing more reliance on its intrinsic inspirational force appears in another, could the former crowd out the aspirational dimension of the latter?[59] Apparently consistent with that, as noted above, it is less common for industry associations to issue broad codes of conduct, including content-based aspirational standards, where the part of the industry they cover is heavily regulated.[60] This may suggest that the role of industry associations in the regulated sector in aspirational standard setting has been largely crowded out by regulatory intervention.[61] Nonetheless it raises a question as to whether industry codes, or at least content-based aspirational standards less closely associated with hard enforcement powers, could play a more important role in future in the regulated sector, much as is hoped for in the unregulated sector (e.g. in the case of the Global FX Code), particularly in the area of aspiration that talk of a social licence seems to address.[62]

What else can be learnt from the legal hardness ratings? Unsurprisingly, little use is made of aspirational standards that are not content-based by public bodies, since laws and regulations tend to be associated with legal enforcement powers. Conversely, they are more prevalent among the written standards of non-public originators. However, where written behavioural standards are advanced by firms, they are likely to be associated to some degree with contractual private law enforcement mechanisms which use remuneration and disciplinary processes to incentivise compliant behaviour. As noted above, they are often also associated with a system of positive incentives in the form of remuneration structures and similar, hence the H2 rating, rather than H3, in the Written Standards Map. As with the use of sanctions by regulators, the precise impact of positive and negative incentive mechanisms on the way staff relate to the standards is likely to depend materially upon how the firms concerned deploy them. It will also vary between different staff members. However, the use of remuneration structures to manage the risk of negative behaviours and incentivise behaviours thought desirable by firms or regulators is widespread, receiving heightened attention in the aftermath of the financial crisis. How far this has taken account of the possible 'crowding out' effect of incentivising compliance on the power of other-regarding values to motivate behaviour and the potential impact on character formation is less clear (see Sects. 6.4, 6.5 and 7.2.5).

Aspirational Standards—Observations Based on Experience

There is a further question which cannot be addressed in the Written Standards Map: to what extent have aspirational standards helped in practice to support the kind of behaviours which seem to be involved in talk of a social licence? Further, has there been any difference in effect between aspirational standards that are associated with hard enforcement tools (i.e. H1) as compared with those which are associated with softer forms of enforcement? Clearly, it is impossible to know what would have happened had the relevant standards not been there, but on the available evidence the picture seems mixed. One of the most significant examples, discussed below, of content-based aspirational standards having a material impact is the UK's 'treating customers fairly' initiative. However, this has involved public sector regulatory standards, combined with the possibility of regulatory sanction, in other words, compliance, at some level incentivised by the possibility of enforcement (i.e. H1). Yet using enforcement to procure 'compliance' potentially undermines the inspirational dimension of standards to motivate particular behaviours. This returns to the possible tension, highlighted above. At the point at which written standards might be regarded as most closely aligned with aspirations apparently involved in the recognition of a social licence, negative self-interest (the desire to avoid sanctions) has been relied upon at some level to secure compliance, with the risk of undermining the same aspirations. The following considers briefly the available evidence on the use and operation of aspirational standards: firstly, those originated by public bodies and, secondly, those promulgated by private bodies.

Aspirational standards emanating from the public sector and addressed to financial firms have been a feature of the UK regulatory regime since 1990 when the UK's Securities and Investments Board published the precursor to the current FCA Principles for Businesses.[63] There have been numerous behavioural failures over that period; some aspirations have not been met, but we cannot know whether the shortfall would have been more marked without the presence of those standards. There are certainly examples of aspirational standards originated and enforced by public bodies being associated with changed market behaviour during this period. In particular, there is little doubt that the UK regulatory initiative known as 'treating customers fairly' or 'TCF', based on the aspirational standard in Principle 6 of the FCA's Standards for Businesses that firms should 'treat their customers fairly', has materially influenced behaviour in parts of the UK financial services sector.[64] That said, the part of the TCF initiative concerning the manufacture and distribution of investment products has now been converted from regulatory guidance on Principle 6 into a rule-based regime as a result of MiFID II.[65] This suggests that, in spite of the considerable industry work in generating good practice standards, for example, within ISDA among structured product providers, regulators were still not satisfied that reliance upon the Principle combined with guidance was sufficient to generate behaviours consistent with their aspirations.

The record of public sector aspirational standards directed at individuals is even less promising. The UK's Parliamentary Commission on Banking Standards in its final report in 2013 concluded that the UK's regulatory regime for finance professionals that had applied until then, known as the 'Approved Persons Regime' (including its aspirational Code of Conduct), had been materially defective.[66] The response has been a new set of rules and content-based aspirational standards—the Senior Managers and Certification Regime including new conduct codes, mentioned earlier.[67] This requires greater accountability from key individuals within a business ('senior managers') for their own conduct and for the activities of the part of a firm's business for which they are responsible. As a result, there is heightened regulatory enforcement risk for senior managers where they fail to discharge their responsibilities: the regime makes greater use of negative incentives. The content-based aspirational standards that had applied to staff under the Approved Persons Regime have been largely replicated in a new Conduct Code. In addition to the Code being directly enforceable by the regulator,[68] senior managers are responsible for ensuring that it is adhered to, strengthening the likelihood of the Code's private enforcement. The new regime does not prescribe how firms and their senior managers should seek to align behaviour with the Code. They are free to decide how far to rely upon positive and negative incentives, reward and sanction (as inevitably they must to some degree) and how much upon steps to strengthen the aspirational force of the Code. The extent to which firms appreciate the potential significance of these choices is unclear. However, the default position is that incentives are likely to have a dominant role:

> …you can look at how you compensate people, how you promote people… And by having an appropriate set of incentives, you're probably going to get the behaviors that are more consistent with what you desire. And if you get that, over time, that will actually establish the culture of the organization.[69]

It is also challenging to assess the impact of aspirational standards issued by private bodies. As noted above, it is not common for industry associations covering regulated markets to publish codes of conduct, except on matters of technical compliance. However, the effectiveness of those for the unregulated fixed income, foreign exchange and commodities markets was heavily criticised by the UK's Fair and Effective Markets Review following its review of behavioural and operational failures in those markets.[70] Notably, one of the criticisms was that the mechanisms for ensuring that code signatories complied with the codes were insufficient; apparently, vague aspiration combined with market forces was not enough.[71]

Aspirational standards are more common in the codes of professional bodies such as the Chartered Banker Code of Professional Conduct[72] and firms operating in the financial markets. However, there is a material question as to the impact of written standards promulgated by the former, at least in the banking sector.[73] Indeed, the striking finding of one survey for the Banking Standards Board ('BSB') was that fewer than 25% of respondents thought that 'to improve their ethical standards' was an advantage of membership of a professional body, and fewer than 40% saw 'to earn the trust of the public' as an advantage, most viewing the main benefit of professional associations as technical training.[74]

Turning to aspirational standards in corporate codes of conduct, studies on the quality and effectiveness of these codes generally suggest at best a mixed picture.[75] However, caution is needed since the studies have been undertaken in a variety of contexts by different individuals and have not used the same methodology.[76] In the case of financial services firms specifically, in practice there rarely seems to be much reference to their codes of conduct in taking legal advice; discussions can tend to proceed on the assumption that legal and regulatory standards are determinative. This may partly reflect the fact that one function of corporate codes is to reinforce messages about the need to comply with law and regulation.[77] If so, it lends weight to the idea that legally enforceable regulatory rules that overlap with aspirational standards may diminish the force of the latter. But content-based aspirational standards in private codes often express an aspiration for standards of behaviour that are higher than the legal and regulatory baseline, among other things, because they sometimes reference social purpose or responsibilities to groups beyond shareholders, markets and customers (the second and third commonly being the focus of regulatory rules). If they did not do that, there would be little obvious point to them, since firms could simply replay existing legal standards or give guidance to staff on how to comply with law and regulation.

The apparent absence of reference to corporate codes in daily practice does not necessarily mean that they have no role in setting the corporate 'mood music' in some way. However, the BSB 2016 assessment of culture in twenty-two of its members seemed to hint at tensions between what employees feel under pressure to do and firms' espoused values.[78] It found that only 65% of employees responding to the BSB assessment agreed that there is no conflict between their firm's stated values and the way the firm does business and 14% claimed that they did see such a conflict.[79] Further, 12% of employees had seen instances where unethical behaviour was rewarded, and 13% considered it difficult to get ahead in their careers without 'flexing' their ethical standards.[80] The survey has been repeated each year since 2016, and there has been some limited improvement. However, the BSB has concluded from its most recent survey that 'making continuing significant changes to the method of operation of large and/or long-established businesses is a long hard slog, and that many firms are in the hard yards of achieving progress in improving their culture'.[81]

Aspirational standards may be aligned with the sort of aspirations that seem to underlie talk of a social licence and may support their realisation. However, whether originated by public or private bodies, the indications to date do not seem entirely encouraging for those who favour their use as a way of bringing behaviour in the financial markets into line with those aspirations. This is particularly the case where the aspirational standards are not directly backed by the power of formal public sector enforcement. Yet, as noted, the introduction of legal enforcement powers risks undermining their aspirational force by reducing the exercise of responding to them to one of incentivised compliance more than following what aspiration might demand.

5.3   Conclusion

Achieving the sort of behaviour change contemplated by talk of a social licence for financial markets relies in part on written standards, and written behavioural written standards in particular have a claim to be setting out some of the terms of the licence. Within the class of behavioural written standards, aspirational standards appear to represent the point of greatest overlap between written standards and the kind of aspirations apparently involved in the recognition of a social licence. They also reach beyond the 'deterrence and enforcement approach' which has been reaching its limits as a way of addressing the challenges identified in Chap. 1. In view of that, they deserve greater attention, not just aspirational standards originated by public bodies but also those published by private bodies which have so far tended to operate in the shadow of the former and may to some extent have been crowded out by them. It is not clear how effective these aspirational standards have been in practice hitherto, and there is a challenge with seeking to increase their impact: evidence to date suggests that they are taken most seriously when combined with legal enforcement, whereas reliance on enforcement may weaken their inspirational force.

A particular area for attention is where publicly originated aspirational standards cover (or could be perceived as covering) the same ground as privately originated aspirational standards. As noted above, FCA work on industry codes of conduct suggests that it recognises a crowding out risk here although it does not articulate it in quite that way.[82] Instead of making compliance with industry codes for unregulated sectors directly enforceable, the FCA adopts a lighter touch approach of treating compliance with FCA 'recognised' industry codes as indicating compliance with its rules on proper standards of market conduct.

Market participants are ranged across a broad behavioural and aspirational spectrum. Legal enforcement will always be necessary. However, the idea of a social licence for financial markets may itself be one of the most important means of strengthening the operation of aspirational standards, by clarifying the ends of aspiration, and this is considered further in Chap. 6 (Sect. 6.6).

Appendix

The Written Standards Map[83]

Standards that apply to individuals rather than firms are shown in italics.

1. Category of written standard	2. Application to UK market participants	3. Extent to which reliant upon public or private legal enforcement mechanisms	4. Aspirational rating	5. Hardness rating
International				
United Nations: various standards relevant to finance sector including Sustainable Development Goals, Paris Climate Agreement, Declaration of Human Rights Numerous initiatives to encourage business to align their activities with these standards such as the Principles of the UN Global Compact, United Nations Guiding Principles on Business and Human Rights and the United Nations Environment Programme Finance Initiative	Not legally binding, except to the extent enshrined in national law, but businesses can voluntarily adhere to or seek to align their business with all or some standards. Otherwise, operate as a framework for national and international legislative initiatives (e.g. the European Union sustainable finance initiative which is intended to orientate EU finance law and policy behind the Paris Agreement and Sustainable Development Goals) and may be referenced in international investment treaties Initiatives such as the Global Compact and UNEPFI generate good practice standards which companies can adhere to, and as a way for society to monitor companies' sustainability and human rights impact	Public: not enforceable except where enshrined in national law (see further below) or investment treaties Private: no private law enforcement (unless incorporated in some way by the parties into their relationship). However, the Guiding Principles are sufficiently specific to facilitate monitoring (e.g. by NGOs) so encouraging compliance	A1	H3

(continued)

(continued)

1. Category of written standard	2. Application to UK market participants	3. Extent to which reliant upon public or private legal enforcement mechanisms	4. Aspirational rating	5. Hardness rating
International standards for regulators set by bodies such as the Financial Stability Board, Basel Committee on Banking Supervision, the OECD, the International Organisation of Securities Commissions, International Association of Insurance Supervisors and the Financial Action Task Force to coordinate legal and regulatory standards globally	Not directly applicable to market participants, but assumed to be relevant to: • The way other directly applicable regulatory standards may be interpreted or applied • The future shape of the regulatory regime Hence, larger firms pay attention to emerging policy and statements at this level	Public: not enforced against market participants since they generally define standards for regulators, but may influence practice through a belief that they could influence the enforcement of rules identified below that are directly applicable Private: no private law enforcement (unless incorporated in some way by the parties into their relationship)	A2	H3
International private law coordination: in particular the Hague Convention, UNIDROIT and UNCITRAL—principally focused on harmonisation of standards relating to property, contract and insolvency rights and the elimination of legal uncertainty	Only applicable to the extent incorporated in national law or contractually adopted by the parties	Public: no direct enforcement against market participants Private: no private law enforcement (unless incorporated in some way by the parties into their relationship)	A3	H2

Other international standard setting bodies: these are a mixture of (a) public-private bodies (such as the Task Force on Climate Related Financial Disclosure, established by the FSB but with industry members), (b) private bodies (such as Transparency International, the Global Reporting Initiative and the International Organization for Standardization) and (c) industry associations (such as ICMA and ISDA). As to the last, see further below	Only applicable to the extent incorporated in national law or voluntarily adopted by the parties. Strong UK regulatory encouragement to adhere to TCFD and moves to incorporate into some areas of regulation[84]	Public: no direct enforcement against market participants. However, compliance with the TCFD in particular is likely to be relevant to regulatory assessments of compliance with UK regulation, where relevant Private: limited, but could be referenced as a guide to good practice in private law actions, and enforceable between parties if incorporated in some way by the parties into their relationship	A2–3	H3
European Union[85] EU Regulations (Level I/Level II)	Apply directly to businesses. Must be enforced by relevant UK authorities and applied by English courts, subject ultimately to the Court of Justice of the European Union (CJEU)	Public: generally enforced at UK level using public enforcement tools. EU trend to stipulate minimum requirements Private: limited, but could be taken into account in private law actions. May rely upon market forces to secure desired result. Breach could affect attitudes of counterparties and clients and therefore firm's commercial position	A2–3	H1.2

(continued)

(continued)

1. Category of written standard	2. Application to UK market participants	3. Extent to which reliant upon public or private legal enforcement mechanisms	4. Aspirational rating	5. Hardness rating
EU Directives (Level I/Level II)	Implemented by UK authorities in rules that apply to businesses. Enforced by relevant UK authorities and applied by English courts, subject ultimately to the CJEU	Public: generally enforced at UK level using public enforcement tools. EU trend to stipulate minimum requirements Private: limited, but could be taken into account in private law actions. May rely upon market forces to secure desired result. Breach could affect attitudes of counterparties and clients and therefore firm's commercial position	A2–3	H1.2
Regulatory Technical Standards and Implementing Technical Standards	Detailed implementing rules made under Regulations or Directives. Enforced by relevant UK authorities and applied by English courts, subject ultimately to the CJEU	Public: as for framework legislation Private: limited, but could be taken into account in private law actions	A3	H1.2
EU Commission guidance	Relevant principally because it expresses the EU Commission's view on the meaning and application of EU legislation	Public: no direct sanction, but may influence the enforcement of EU Regulations or rules implementing EU Directives Private: limited, but could be taken into account in private law actions	A2–3	H2

EBA/ESMA/EIOPA[86] (ESAs) guidance and recommendations	To promote supervisory convergence, the ESAs have the power to issue guidelines that are addressed to individual member state regulatory authorities or, less frequently, to market participants. ESAs may also address an individual decision to a market participant where a member state authority has failed to act. Need not be specifically related to the application of Regulations and Directives, but often will be	Public: in most cases ESAs do not currently have direct enforcement rights, but should influence member state enforcement of EU rules or those implementing relevant EU legislation Private: limited, but could be taken into account in private law actions	A2–3	H2
EU Commission Q&A/EBA/ESMA/ EIOPA Q&A	Provides the views of the EU Commission/ESAs on the meaning and application of EU legislation, but is not legally binding	Public: not directly enforceable against market participants, but could be used by member state courts and regulators in assisting in the interpretation and enforcement of EU legislation Private: limited, but could be taken into account in private law actions	A2–3	H2
Commission and ESA consultations, feedback documents and other commentary	No direct legal effect, but is sometimes referenced by industry participants in seeking to understand the purpose and effect of the resulting provisions in Regulations and Directives	Public: not directly enforceable against market participants, but could be taken into account in assisting in member state and judicial interpretation and enforcement of EU legislation Private: limited, but could be taken into account in private law actions	A3	H3

(continued)

(continued)

1. Category of written standard	2. Application to UK market participants	3. Extent to which reliant upon public or private legal enforcement mechanisms	4. Aspirational rating	5. Hardness rating
UK				
Private law, especially contract law and fiduciary duties	Directly applicable, as a minimum, to those located and conducting activities in the UK. Contractual rights are a particularly important feature of the financial markets, especially under industry standard documentation such as the master documentation maintained by the International Capital Market Association or ICMA (bond market documentation and repurchase agreements), ISDA (derivatives), the International Securities Lending Association or ISLA (securities lending) and the Loan Market Association or LMA (lending)	Public: enforced by the courts using the full range of private law remedies and sanctions Private: may be used as a basis for enforcing written norms promulgated by private bodies	A1–2	H2
UK Statute/Statutory Instruments	Directly applicable to all persons within their jurisdictional reach—that is, very broadly, those carrying on activity with a UK connection. (Also implement EU regulatory standards—see above)	Public: will depend upon the relevant statute, but generally apply criminal sanctions for breach of the primary legislation. See regulatory regimes below for sanctions upon breach of rules made by regulators under the legislation Private: not generally applicable save to the extent the legislation makes use of private enforcement mechanisms or market forces	A2–3	H1.1–1.2

Prudential Regulatory Authority ('PRA')—prudential regulation of UK incorporated banks and insurers

PRA Fundamental Rules—technically PRA 'General Rules' (see below), but in the form of high-level principles rather than precise targeted requirements	Directly applicable to all PRA authorised firms. (Also implement EU regulatory standards—see above)	Public: full range of PRA sanctions applies if breached. Could also have other consequences such as increased capital requirements Private: limited, but could be taken into account in private law actions Breach could affect attitudes of counterparties and clients and therefore firm's commercial position	A1	H1.2
PRA General Rules (under s137G of the Financial Services and Markets Act 2000 ('FSMA')), specialised rules and various other rules made under other powers	Directly applicable to all PRA authorised firms. (Also implement EU regulatory standards—see above)	Public: full range of PRA sanctions applies if breached. Could also have other consequences such as increased capital requirements Private: limited, but could be taken into account in private law actions May rely upon market forces to secure a given result. Breach could affect attitudes of counterparties and clients and therefore firm's commercial position	A2–3	H1.2

(continued)

(continued)

1. Category of written standard	2. Application to UK market participants	3. Extent to which reliant upon public or private legal enforcement mechanisms	4. Aspirational rating	5. Hardness rating
PRA Evidential Rules (s138C FSMA)	Apply to all PRA authorised firms except inward business under an EU cross-border passport. However, indicative only. Compliance with these will tend to establish compliance with another specified rule and breach will tend to establish specified non-compliance	Public: no sanction for breach, but may be relevant to whether a binding rule breached—see above Private: limited, but could be taken into account in private law actions	A2–3	H2
PRA Guidance including guidance statements in the PRA Handbook **PRA Supervisory Statements** **Other materials such as PRA letters**[87]	Guidance on the operation of specified parts of FSMA and on the PRA rules and the PRA's functions, therefore, relevant to authorised firms in complying with the above	Public: may be taken into account by the PRA in considering whether a standard has been breached Private: limited, but could be taken into account in private law actions	A2–3	H2
PRA Directions/Requirements given under various Acts (including s138A FSMA) and statutory instruments	Binding on the persons or categories of persons to whom they are addressed. Relevant to the way particular rules apply to those persons	Public: as for the rules to which the direction relates Private: as for the rules to which the direction relates	A3	H1.2

PRA Senior Managers Regime[88]	Requirement for PRA individual approval for those managing aspects of the firm's affairs relevant to regulated activities which could involve a risk of serious consequences for the firm or business or other interests in the UK	Public: a range of PRA sanctions can be applied under the PRA Conduct Rules to an individual who fails to discharge responsibilities Private: limited, but could be taken into account in private law actions, including between an individual and their employer. Could also be taken into account in the context of membership of professional bodies and by future potential employers	A2	H1.2
PRA Conduct Rules	Apply to all PRA senior managers and PRA certified persons and others involved in the business of the firm	Public: a range of PRA sanctions can be applied to an individual who is in breach Private: limited, but could be taken into account in private law actions. Could also be taken into account in the context of membership of professional bodies and by future potential employers	A1	H1.2

(continued)

(continued)

1. Category of written standard	2. Application to UK market participants	3. Extent to which reliant upon public or private legal enforcement mechanisms	4. Aspirational rating	5. Hardness rating
FCA—conduct of business regulation for all firms in the UK market, prudential regulation of non-PRA UK firms, listing authority				
FCA Principles for Businesses—technically FCA 'General Rules' (see below), but in the form of high-level principles rather than precise targeted requirements	Increasing use made of these. Directly applicable to all authorised firms except inward business under an EU cross-border passport. (Also implement EU regulatory standards—see above)	Public: full range of FCA sanctions applies if breached. Could also have other consequences such as increased capital requirements Private: limited, but could be taken into account in private law actions Breach could affect attitudes of counterparties and clients and therefore firm's commercial position	A1	H1.2

FCA General Rules (under s137A-F, H, O-R and T FSMA), specialised rules (under s140-7 FSMA), listing rules under s73A and various other rules	Directly applicable to all authorised firms except inward business under an EU cross-border passport. (Also implement EU regulatory standards—see above)	Public: full range of public enforcement mechanisms used. FCA sanctions apply if breached. In some circumstances, can also lead to an action for damages from those who suffer loss as a result of the breach. Could also have other consequences such as increased capital requirements Interplay with Financial Ombudsman complaints process for firms dealing with private individuals Private: limited, but could be taken into account in private law actions May rely upon market forces to secure a given result. Breach could affect attitudes of counterparties and clients and therefore firm's commercial position	A2-3	H1.2
FCA Evidential Rules (s138C FSMA)—applicable to firms	Apply to all authorised firms except inward business under an EU cross-border passport. However, indicative only. Compliance with these will tend to establish compliance with another specified rule and breach will tend to establish non-compliance	Public: no sanction for breach, but may be relevant to whether a binding rule breached—see above Private: limited, but could be taken into account in private law actions	A2-3	H2

(continued)

(continued)

1. Category of written standard	2. Application to UK market participants	3. Extent to which reliant upon public or private legal enforcement mechanisms	4. Aspirational rating	5. Hardness rating
FCA General Guidance (s139A FSMA) Generally set out in the FCA Handbook or in a separate 'Regulatory Guide' or, in an emergency, in a Guidance Note	Guidance on the operation of specified parts of FSMA and on the FCA rules and the FCA's functions, therefore, relevant to authorised firms in complying with the above. Must generally be consulted upon in the same way as rules Not binding on the courts	Public: not binding and does not have evidential effect. Enforcement action would turn on breach of a binding rule to which the guidance relates However, FCA has indicated that where a person acts in accordance with general guidance, FCA will proceed as if the person has complied with the requirement to which the rule relates Private: limited, but could be taken into account in private law actions	A2–3	H2
Other FCA material: informal guidance/expressions of view—in consultation papers, feedback statements, discussion papers, speeches	Potentially relevant to all authorised firms except inward business under and EU cross-border passport to the UK	Public: not binding and does not have evidential effect, but taken by the industry as providing a further gloss on the way the FCA is likely to enforce particular Principles or Rules Private: limited, but could be taken into account in private law actions	A2–3	H2

FCA Senior Managers Regime[89]	Requirement for FCA individual approval for those managing aspects of the firm's affairs relevant to regulated activities which could involve a risk of serious consequences for the firm or business or other interests in the UK	Public: a range of FCA sanctions can be applied under the FCA Code of Conduct to an individual who fails to discharge responsibilities Private: limited, but could be taken into account in private law actions, including between an individual and their employer. Could also be taken into account in the context of membership of professional bodies and by future potential employers	A2–3	H1.2
FCA Code of Conduct	Applies to all employees in a firm other than those performing a role not specific to the financial services business of the firm, such as drivers	Public: full range of FCA sanctions applies if breached. Could also have other consequences such as increased capital requirements Private: limited, but could be taken into account in private law actions including between an individual and their employer. Could also be taken into account in the context of membership of professional bodies and by future potential employers	A1	H1.2

(continued)

(continued)

1. Category of written standard	2. Application to UK market participants	3. Extent to which reliant upon public or private legal enforcement mechanisms	4. Aspirational rating	5. Hardness rating
Regulated markets				
Membership rules, etc. of UK regulated markets (IPSX, London Metal Exchange, ICE Futures Europe, London Stock Exchange, Euronext London, NEX Exchange, Cboe Europe Equities)[90]	Apply to market participants that need membership of the relevant markets to carry on business, and may have an impact on the terms on which those participants can transact in the market. Concern the operation of and conduct within the relevant markets	Public: regulated markets are required to maintain these as condition of being permitted to operate. Breaches by market participants could affect the exercise of regulatory discretion or even involve a breach of regulatory rules. Private: generally enforceable against members as a private law matter under the terms of membership; may also involve rights between members. Breach could affect market perception	A2–3	H2

Multilateral trading facilities/ organised trading facilities				
Effectively a form of investment market operated by financial firms or market operators.[91] Access will generally depend upon entering into a user agreement and agreeing to comply with various operating standards setting out the terms on which the operator is willing to allow access, and also reflecting regulatory requirements	Apply to market participants that need access to the relevant platforms to carry on business, and may have an impact on the terms on which those participants can transact in the market	Public: operators are required to maintain these as a condition of being permitted to operate. Breaches of user terms and standards by market participants could affect the exercise of regulatory discretion or even involve a breach of regulatory rules. Private: user terms generally enforceable against users by operator as a private law matter under the terms of membership; may also involve rights between users	A3	H2
Infrastructure providers				
Membership and operating rules of market infrastructure providers (e.g. payment systems such as CHAPS, central securities depositaries such as Euroclear UK & Ireland and central counterparties such as LCH Limited)[92]	Apply to market participants that need membership of the relevant organisations to carry on business (i.e. effect payments, clear transactions and hold UK securities), and may have an impact on the terms on which those participants can transact with third parties	Public: the relevant infrastructures are required to maintain these as a condition of being permitted to operate. Breaches by market participants could affect the exercise of regulatory discretion or even involve a breach of regulatory rules Private: generally enforceable against members as a private law matter under the terms of membership; may also involve rights between members	A3	H2

(continued)

(continued)

1. Category of written standard	2. Application to UK market participants	3. Extent to which reliant upon public or private legal enforcement mechanisms	4. Aspirational rating	5. Hardness rating
Other UK Codes with a legal footing				
The Corporate Governance Code (FRC)	Sets out standards of good practice in relation to board leadership and effectiveness, remuneration, accountability and relations with shareholders. All companies with a Premium Listing of equity shares in the UK are required under the Listing Rules to report in their annual report and accounts on how they have applied the Code. Tends to be regarded as relevant by other authorised firms because it is believed that the PRA and FCA refer to it in setting governance standards	Public: 'comply or explain' for UK-listed firms. Otherwise, no direct sanction. Private: relevant to assessment of company by potential investors/clients. Could be taken into account in private law actions	A1–2	H2–3
The Stewardship Code (FRC)	A statement of good practice to which the FRC believes institutional investors should aspire. It also describes steps asset owners can take to protect and enhance the value that accrues to the ultimate beneficiary	Public: all UK-authorised Asset Managers are required under the FCA's Rules to produce a statement of commitment to the Stewardship Code or explain why it is not appropriate to their business model. Private: 'comply or explain'. Could be taken into account in private law actions and by potential clients	A1–2	H2–3

The Takeover Code (Takeover Panel)

Intended to reflect collective opinion of those professionally involved in takeovers as to appropriate business standards, fairness to offeree company shareholders and an orderly framework for takeovers. While the Takeover Panel was originally a private body, it has since been designated as the authority to carry out certain regulatory functions set out in Chapter 1 of Part 28 of the Companies Act 2006. As a result, the rules set out in the Code now have a statutory basis

Public: may issue a private or public censure, suspend or withdraw any exemption, approval or other special status which the Panel has granted

May report conduct to a regulatory authority particularly the FCA to decide whether to take action (including fines), for example, where a firm fails to observe proper standards of market conduct

May publish a Panel Statement indicating that the offender is someone who is not likely to comply with the Code. FCA rules and certain professional bodies oblige their members, in certain circumstances, not to act for the person in question in a Code transaction (cold shouldering)

May issue directions (enforceable through the courts) and order the payment of compensation

Certain breaches of bid documentation rules constitute a criminal offence

Private: Panel grew from the private not public sector but now placed on a statutory footing

Regime is intended to reduce scope for recourse to the courts in matters covered by the Code

(continued)

(continued)

1. Category of written standard	2. Application to UK market participants	3. Extent to which reliant upon public or private legal enforcement mechanisms	4. Aspirational rating	5. Hardness rating
The Joint Money Laundering Steering Group Guidance Notes	The JMLSG is comprised of the leading UK financial services trade associations. Its aim is to promulgate good practice in countering money laundering and to give practical assistance in interpreting the UK Money Laundering Regulations, principally by publishing guidance	Public: no sanction for not complying with the guidance, but potentially relevant to whether the primary money laundering prohibitions, the Money Laundering Regulations or other regulatory rules have been breached. Courts required to take account of behaviour in accordance with the guidance in certain circumstances. FCA has regard to whether conduct complied with the guidance in determining whether requirements breached[93] Private: limited	A2–3	H2

Private UK codes 'confirmed' by the FCA[94]

Libor Code of Conduct, Investment Association guidance on electronic instructions	The first was adopted by ICE Benchmark Administration Limited for benchmark submitters to ICE LIBOR. Intended to provide a framework within which contributing banks can operate and to assist users of LIBOR rates when deciding whether LIBOR is an appropriate rate to use in contracts	Public: the FCA will regard firms following the guidance as complying with the relevant FCA Handbook rule. But failure to comply with the guidance does not indicate failure to comply with the rule.[95] (Knowingly or deliberately making false or misleading statements in relation to benchmark-setting is a criminal offence under the Financial Services Act 2012 and the FCA's rules on benchmark submission are in Chapter 8 of its Market Conduct Sourcebook) Private: limited, but could be taken into account in private law actions and impact market perception	A2–3	H2

(continued)

(continued)

1. Category of written standard	2. Application to UK market participants	3. Extent to which reliant upon public or private legal enforcement mechanisms	4. Aspirational rating	5. Hardness rating
Other private UK/international industry codes for financial services firms				
Codes produced with the active involvement of regulators, especially the Bank of England and other central banks: (a) the UK Money Markets Code (a voluntary code of good practice for the money and securities financing markets facilitated by the Money Markets Committee which is chaired by the Bank of England), (b) the FX Global Code (a voluntary code of good practice in the global FX markets developed by the FX Global Committee comprised of central banks and FX market participants) and (c) the London Bullion Markets Global Precious Metals Code (standards and best practice expected of participants in the global wholesale precious metals markets)	Voluntary, but regulators take a keen interest in adherence. Central banks (through the FX Working Group) have published a 'blueprint' on adherence to the FX Global Code.[96] The Bank of England is involved in key oversight committees *The FCA has formally 'recognised' the FX Global Code and the UK Money Markets Code. As a result, behaviour consistent with these codes will tend to indicate a person subject to the Senior Managers and Certification Regime is meeting their obligation to observe 'proper standards of market conduct' in relation to unregulated activities*[97]	Public: not directly enforceable, but levels of compliance could influence the exercise of regulators' supervisory powers and could be relevant to whether other rules have been complied with, whether by firms or individuals Private: limited, but could be taken into account in private law actions and impact market perception	A1–2	H2–3

Industry association conduct standards produced by, for example, the Alternative Investment Management Association, the Asset Backed Finance Association, the Association of British Insurers, the British Private Equity and Venture Capital Association, the International Capital Markets Association, the Investment Association, the International Forum of Sovereign Wealth Funds, the International Swaps and Derivatives Association, the Lending Standards Board, the Standards Board for Alternative Investments, the Wolfsburg Group	Generally voluntary in that firms usually have a decision as to whether or not to join the relevant body or on the extent to which they will adhere to the relevant written norms. Codes issued by industry bodies in areas of the financial markets that are heavily regulated generally concern matters of technical compliance with regulatory rules, whereas codes concerning conduct in more lightly regulated parts of the market are more likely to be in the form of over-arching conduct codes	Public: no direct sanction, but in some cases, these standards could be referenced by regulators in deciding whether standards under their rules have been met Private: in some cases, private bodies may rely to some degree upon Court-enforced contracts (such as membership agreements) to secure compliance. Otherwise, generally rely upon a mixture of private enforcement mechanisms. Could affect market perception if not followed	Lightly regulated market sectors: A1–2 More heavily regulated market sectors: A1–3	H3

Other private UK codes for individuals working in the financial services sector

Codes produced by the Chartered Banker Institute, the Chartered Financial Analysts Institute, the Chartered Institute for Securities & Investment, the Chartered Insurance Institute, The London Institute of Banking & Finance, The Worshipful Company of International Bankers	*UK professional and other membership bodies. Codes voluntary, but could affect continued membership*	*Public: no direct sanction.* *Private: generally rely upon a mixture of private enforcement mechanisms. Breach could be relevant to whether employment contracts breached and employment decisions by employers and potential employers*	A1[98]	H3

(continued)

(continued)

1. Category of written standard	2. Application to UK market participants	3. Extent to which reliant upon public or private legal enforcement mechanisms	4. Aspirational rating	5. Hardness rating
Firms' own codes of conduct				
Firm-specific	*Frequently apply group-wide within international financial services groups, including UK staff who are expected to comply as part of the terms of their employment*	*Public: no direct sanction, but the extent to which a firm has complied with its own standards could be relevant to the exercise of regulatory discretion* *Private: privately enforced within the firm, including under the terms of employment contracts, but also using career progression and remuneration decisions. Could be relevant to private law action, for example, in assessing the nature of a firm's duties to third parties*	A1–2	H2–3

Notes

1. 'Culture is a matter for banks not UK regulators', editorial, *Financial Times*, London, 12 January 2016.
2. Stephanie Chaly et al., *Misconduct Risk, Culture, and Supervision*, Federal Reserve Bank of New York, December 2017.
3. This book uses the word 'regulations' to distinguish regulatory rules from the process of regulation by regulators which does not rely upon rules alone.
4. The prolonged jurisprudential debate over what distinguishes law from other sorts of expectations, associated with names like Jeremy Bentham, John Austin and H. L. A. Hart, lies beyond the scope of the current exercise.
5. Where these standards are in the form of law, the main focus of this chapter is on what can be described as 'primary rules' that require people to do or refrain from doing something (or have a similar effect by defining the context for action) rather than 'secondary rules' which concern the making, administration and enforcement of the primary rules (see H. L. A. Hart, *The Concept of Law* (3rd edn, Oxford University Press 2012), 79 et seq.).
6. Written standards are by no means the only way of seeking to change behaviour, but they are the principal focus of this chapter. In particular, the activities of regulators can be a hybrid affair with written standards often advanced to support the use of other regulatory techniques. However, even these frequently involve articulating standards in writing in one form or another.
7. As with Chap. 4, putting to one side for the present the question of control over rule-making within a group which can result in rules that reflect the wishes of a minority rather than a consensus.
8. It now seems ironic that this was ever referred to as 'deregulation', although it did involve a form of structural deregulation of the financial markets.
9. Starting with Julia Black, *Rules and Regulators* (Clarendon Press Oxford 1997).
10. *Solicitors Regulation Authority Principles 2018*, contained in the SRA Handbook.
11. *Basic Principles on the Role of Lawyers*, adopted by the Eighth United Nations Congress on the Prevention of Crime and the Treatment of Offenders, Havana, Cuba, 27 August to 7 September 1990, Principles 12 and 14.
12. *IBA International Principles on Conduct for the Legal Profession*, approved on 25 May 2019 by the Council of the International Bar Association, Principle 5.
13. This chapter has already made use of one of them. As noted above, it does not address 'secondary rules' concerning the creation, administration and enforcement of rules with more primary behavioural intent.
14. See, for example, Bronwen Morgan and Karen Yeung, *An Introduction to Law and Regulation: Text and Materials* (Cambridge University Press 2007), 79 et seq. While they discuss a broader range of regulatory instruments and techniques than just written standards, many involve written standards and the issues are similar.

15. Subject to the qualifications in Chap. 4.
16. Although the distinction between public and private law originates from civil law jurisdictions, it has increasingly been made in common law jurisdictions such as England and is helpful for current purposes.
17. There have been attempts by the United Nations to establish binding international rules for multinational corporations, the main one being the UN Intergovernmental Working Group on a Code of Conduct for Transnational Corporations, the work of which ground to a halt in the early 1990s. More recently, the United Nations Human Rights Council established an intergovernmental working group on transnational corporations and other business enterprises on human rights tasked with developing an international legally binding instrument to regulate their activities in relation to human rights (14 July 2014, A/HRC/RES/26/9). A preliminary draft treaty has been published. If eventually adopted, as currently drafted it would still rely upon enforcement by individual states rather than in an international court.
18. *The United Nations Guiding Principles on Human Rights: Implementing the United Nations 'Protect, Respect and Remedy' Framework*, 2 March 2011, A/HC/17/31, Annex.
19. Sally Wheeler, *Global Production, CSR and Human Rights: The Courts of Public Opinion and the Social Licence to Operate*, International Journal of Human Rights, 2015, Vol. 19(6), 757–778.
20. https://fmsb.com/what-we-do/#1 (accessed 25 October 2019).
21. https://www.globalfxc.org/docs/fx_global.pdf (accessed 25 October 2019).
22. Jim Baxter and Chris Megone, *Exploring the Role of Professional Bodies and Professional Qualifications in the UK Banking Sector*, a report prepared for the Banking Standards Board, October 2016.
23. See, for example, SYSC 10.1, FCA Handbook.
24. See, for example, section 406 of the US Sarbanes-Oxley Act of 2002, made in the aftermath of the Enron scandal.
25. Art. 47(1)(d) of Directive 2014/65/EU of the European Parliament and of the Council on markets in financial instruments.
26. Directive 2014/65/EU of the European Parliament and of the Council on markets in financial instruments, especially Articles 18–20 and 30–31.
27. Tomorrow's Company describes itself as an independent non-profit think tank that inspires and enables businesses to be a force for good in society.
28. The international anti-bribery and corruption organisation.
29. LR 9.8.6R, FCA Handbook. At the time of going to press, the FRC remains a private body. However, following a review by Sir John Kingman during 2018, a decision has been taken to put it on a statutory footing; see *Independent Review of the Financial Reporting Council*, December 2018 (HMSO 2018).
30. Part 28, Companies Act 2006.

31. John C. Coates, *The Volcker Rule as Structural Law: Implications for Cost–Benefit Analysis and Administrative Law*, Capital Markets Law Journal, 2015, Vol. 10(4), 447–468.
32. Jeff Hass, *Economic Sociology: An Introduction* (Routledge 2007), 14–15.
33. Bank ring-fencing refers to the requirement for banking groups to separate their retail banking activities from their wholesale banking and investment activities, so that the former will be less affected by a failure in the latter. Among other things, this involves the ring-fenced retail banking activities being run out of a separate legal entity with its own board of directors, subject to discrete liquidity and capital requirements.
34. Once two parties have entered into an investment transaction, clearing houses provide a standardised means for settling it, including making the necessary payments and delivering the relevant financial instruments. In addition, central counterparty clearing, which is now common in the derivatives markets, involves the clearing house being interposed between two parties to a trade, thereby assuming an obligation to each of them to perform the other's obligations under the contract. The central counterparty is independently capitalised and operated and must be provided with collateral to cover the exposures it assumes under cleared trades. The aim of this is to manage counterparty risk more effectively within the financial system, with the possibility of mutualisation should it crystallise. However, questions remain over the extent to which central counterparty clearing could be a source of new risks.
35. Speed limits, by contrast, concern the behaviour of a person when making use of the licence and are therefore more similar to behavioural standards, considered below.
36. Vernon L. Smith, *Human Nature: An Economic Perspective*, Dædalus, 2004, Vol. 133(4), 67–76, 71.
37. Regulation (EU) 2016/1011 of the European Parliament and of the Council of 8 June 2016 on indices used as benchmarks in financial instruments and financial contracts or to measure the performance of investment funds.
38. SYSC 10.2, FCA Handbook.
39. *Culture in financial institutions: it's everywhere and nowhere*, speech by Andrew Bailey while Chief Executive of the Financial Conduct Authority, 16 May 2017.
40. Section 1E, Financial Services and Markets Act 2000. The Prudential Regulation Authority also has a competition objective (section 2H, Financial Services and Markets Act 2000).
41. An example would be the rules implementing the FCA's 'Retail Distribution Review' which prohibited financial advisors being remunerated directly or indirectly by firms that produce the financial products they sell, thereby exposing both advisory and product charges to greater transparency and competitive pressure. See COBS 6.1A-F, FCA Handbook.

42. A distinction between prescriptive standards and aspirational standards is reasonably well established. See, for example, Mark S. Frankel, *Professional Codes: Why, How, and with What Impact*, Journal of Business Ethics, 1989, Vol. 8(2), 109–115; Judith Lichtenberg, 'What Are Codes of Ethics for?', in *Codes of Ethics and the Professions*, eds. Margaret Coady and Sidney Block (Melbourne University Press 1996); Brian Farrell, Deirdre Cobbin and Helen Farrell, *Codes of Ethics—Their Evolution, Development and Other Controversies*, Journal of Management Development, 2002, Vol. 21(2), 152–163, 159; Geoffrey C. Hazard, *Legal Ethics: Legal Rules and Professional Aspirations*, Cleveland State Law Review, 1981, 571–576; Donald Nicholson, *Making Lawyers Moral? Ethical Codes and Moral Character*, Legal Studies, 2015, Vol. 25(4), 601–626, 619; Constantine Boussalis, Yuval Feldman and Henry E. Smith, *An Experimental Analysis of the Effect of Standards on Compliance Performance*, Regulation and Governance, 2018, Vol. 12(2), 277–298.

43. Money Laundering, Terrorist Financing and Transfer of Funds (Information on the Payer) Regulations 2017, SI 2017/692, Part 3.

44. PRIN 2.1.1R, Principle 4, FCA Handbook.

45. Robert Baldwin, Martin Cave and Martin Lodge, *Understanding Regulation: Theory, Strategy and Practice* (2nd edn, Oxford University Press 2012), 302; Julia Black, 'The Rise, Fall and Fate of Principles Based Regulation', in *Law Reform and Financial Markets*, eds. Kern Alexander and Niamh Moloney (Edward Elgar 2011).

46. Ronald Dworkin, *The Model of Rules*, University of Chicago Law Review, 1967, Vol. 35(1), 14–46, 23.

47. PRIN 2.1, FCA Handbook.

48. Most notably, John Rawls: John Rawls and Kelly Erin, *Justice as Fairness: A Restatement* (Harvard University Press 2001).

49. COBS 2.1.1, FCA Handbook which requires firms to act 'honestly, fairly and professionally in accordance with the best interests of their clients'.

50. However, written standards requiring a person to behave 'ethically' are somewhat empty without an understanding of which ethic is involved, and cynics might suggest that this is precisely the reason the word is used. Indeed, it would be possible for an ethic to be far from other-regarding.

51. Cass R. Sunstein, *On the Expressive Function of Law*, University of Pennsylvania Law Review, 1995, Vol. 144(5), 2021–2053.

52. Tom R. Tyler, *Reducing Corporate Criminality: The Role of Values*, American Criminal Law Review, 2014, Vol. 51(1), 267–291.

53. Available at https://internationalbankers.org.uk/thecompany (accessed 31 October 2019).

54. Iris Bohnet, Bruno Frey and Steffen Huck, *More Order with Less Law: On Contract Enforcement, Trust, and Crowding*, American Political Science Review, 2002, Vol. 95(1), 131–144.

55. Neil Gunningham and Peter Grabosky, *Smart Regulation: Designing Environmental Policy* (Clarendon Press Oxford 1998).
56. See, for example, the enforcement pyramid in Ian Ayres and John Braithwaite, *Responsive Regulation* (Oxford University Press 1992), 35.
57. *The Barclays Way: How we do business*, July 2019, 4, https://home.barclays/content/dam/home-barclays/documents/citizenship/our-reporting-and-policy-positions/policy-positions/CS1924559%20V04%20The%20Barclays%20Way%202019_Online.pdf (accessed 24 October 2019).
58. *Morgan Stanley 2019 Code of Conduct* (https://www.morganstanley.com/about-us-governance/code-of-conduct); *JPMorgan Chase & Co Code of Conduct 2019* (https://www.jpmorganchase.com/corporate/About-JPMC/document/code-of-conduct.pdf), both accessed 24 October 2019. However, see comments at note 50 about use of the word 'ethics'.
59. For example, both the FCA's Conduct Code for staff in regulated firms in its Handbook of Rules and Guidance and the Lord George Principles for Good Business Conduct state that those to whom they are addressed should act honestly, fairly and with integrity.
60. The possibility of this crowding out effect is recognised by the FCA. See, for example, *Industry Codes of Conduct and Feedback on Principle 5*, Policy Statement PS18/18, Financial Conduct Authority, July 2018, paragraph 1.19.
61. Industry associations covering more heavily regulated sectors of the financial services markets do issue various pieces of guidance and codes of good practice. However, these often concern how to comply with technical legal and regulatory rules and can therefore be thought of as related to the enforcement regimes attached to those rules.
62. *Industry Codes of Conduct and Feedback on Principle 5*, Financial Conduct Authority.
63. Julia Black, *Forms and Paradoxes of Principles-Based Regulation*, Capital Markets Law Journal, 2008, Vol. 3(4), 425–457, 433.
64. Dan Awrey, William Blair and David Kershaw, *Between Law and Markets: Is There a Role for Culture and Ethics in Financial Regulation?* Delaware Journal of Corporate Law, 2013, Vol. 38(1), 191–245.
65. Articles 16 and 24 of Directive 2014/65/EU of the European Parliament and of the Council on markets in financial instruments and Articles 9 and 10 of Commission Delegated Directive (EU) 2017/593.
66. *Changing Banking for Good*, Report of the Parliamentary Commission on Banking Standards, First Report of Session 2013–2014, Volume II: Chapters 1 to 11 and Annexes, together with formal minutes, HL Paper 27-II HC 175-II, June 2013, paragraph 283.
67. See Sect. 5.2.2.
68. Section 66, Financial Services and Markets Act 2000.

69. Remarks by William C. Dudley, President and CEO of the Federal Reserve Bank of New York, 7 February 2018: https://www.newyorkfed.org/newsevents/speeches/2018/dud180209 (accessed 25 October 2019).
70. *Fair and Effective Markets Review*, Final Report, HM Treasury, Bank of England and Financial Conduct Authority, June 2015.
71. Nonetheless, regulators have sought to avoid recourse to 'hard law' enforcement mechanisms in seeking to secure compliance with the replacement codes: *Report on Adherence to the Global FX Code*, Foreign Exchange Working Group, May 2017.
72. https://www.charteredbanker.com/uploads/assets/uploaded/5e917c8b-7bc6-45ed-a43287ee7466612b.pdf (accessed 30 November 2019).
73. '...all professional bodies have a code of ethics, but it was not always clear whether members engaged seriously with the code, or whether there were serious consequences for those who breached the code...,' Baxter and Megone, *Exploring the Role of Professional Bodies*, paragraph 76.
74. Ibid., paragraph 32.
75. For an industry view, see *Codes of Conduct: A Barrier or a Breakthrough for Corporate Behaviour?* PWC 2013.
76. Muel Kaptein and Mark S. Schwartz, *The Effectiveness of Business Codes: A Critical Examination of Existing Studies and the Development of an Integrated Research Model*, Journal of Business Ethics, 2008, Vol. 77(2), 111–127.
77. However, it is important to distinguish between corporate codes of conduct and the various compliance policies that firms maintain specifically to comply with aspects of the regulatory regime, such as policies on customer verification, trade execution and allocation and managing conflicts of interest.
78. *Annual Review 2016/17*, Banking Standards Board, 2017.
79. The percentage was higher in systemically important institutions.
80. One 2013 report put the figure rather higher: 'While respondents admit that an improvement in employees' ethical conduct would improve their firm's resilience to unexpected and dramatic risk, 53% think that career progression at their firm would be difficult without being flexible on ethical standards.' *A Crisis of Culture—valuing ethics and knowledge in financial services*, Economist Intelligence Unit, 2013, 4. However, it is not clear whether the difference in numbers reflects an improvement or simply a different sample of firms and set of questions. For example, the BSB states that some of the percentages noted above were higher in larger financial institutions.
81. *Annual Review 2018/19*, Banking Standards Board, 2019, 7.
82. See note 61.
83. As of 30 November 2019. See note 86 concerning the impact of the UK's anticipated departure from the European Union.

84. See, for example, *Climate Change and Green Finance: Summary of Responses and Next Steps, Feedback to DP 18/8*, Feedback Statement FS 19/6, Financial Conduct Authority, October 2019.

85. When the UK leaves the European Union, there will be a transition period during which EU law will continue to apply as it did before exit. When that period ends, it is expected that, initially at least, the bulk of European Union financial services regulation will be incorporated into UK law (to the extent not already reflected in UK law), with some amendment to address the fact that the UK is no longer a European Union member state. The European Union (Withdrawal) Act 2018 (the 'Withdrawal Act') set the framework under which incorporation would happen in the event of a 'hard Brexit', with no withdrawal agreement in place. However, the UK's departure will now be governed by the terms of a withdrawal agreement with the EU; that agreement provides for the transition period during which EU law continues to apply, pending the negotiation of the UK's long-term relationship with the EU. At the end of the transition period, it seems likely that EU financial services law will be incorporated much as contemplated by the Withdrawal Act. Incorporated law may then develop in ways that diverge from European Union law in future. Broadly, English courts will continue to follow European Union jurisprudence as it applies to pre-exit matters and are permitted to have regard to it in other cases when construing incorporated European Union law. Similarly, UK regulators are likely to continue to have regard to some EU Commission and European Supervisory Authority guidance on European Union law where it is reflected or incorporated in UK law.

86. European Banking Authority, European Securities and Markets Authority and the European Insurance and Occupational Pensions Authority.

87. Mainly relevant to firms, but potentially also relevant to individuals in relation to the Conduct Rules.

88. Strictly, the regime applies to *firms* rather than individuals. However, the effect of the Conduct Rules is that senior managers have heightened responsibility for that part of the firm for which they are allocated responsibility as a result of the Senior Managers Regime, which therefore defines their duties under the Code.

89. Ibid.

90. Financial Services Register: https://register.fca.org.uk/shpo_searchresultspage ?preDefined=RM&TOKEN=3wq1nht7eg7tr (accessed 26 October 2019).

91. A list of UK MTFs and OTFs is available at https://register.fca.org.uk (accessed 26 October 2019).

92. For an overview, see https://www.bankofengland.co.uk/financial-stability/ financial-market-infrastructure-supervision (accessed 26 October 2019).

93. DEPP 6.2.3G, EG 12.1.2 and EG 19.14, FCA Handbook.

94. See https://www.fca.org.uk/about/rules-and-guidance/confirmed-industry-guidance (accessed 26 October 2019). The FCA lists four pieces of guidance, but only two have a confirmation expiry date of later than 31 December 2019.
95. DEPP 6.2.1(4)G, FCA Handbook.
96. *Report on Adherence to the Global FX Code*, Foreign Exchange Working Group, May 2017.
97. DEPP 6.2.4(A), FCA Handbook.
98. The disciplinary powers of the professional associations are currently limited, and there seems to be confusion even within some of the associations themselves as to the extent of their disciplinary powers and the basis upon which they can be exercised (see *Exploring the Role of Professional Bodies*, note 23, in Sect. 4.3.4.1).

Part III

In the End, a Beginning

Fast Track

Parts I and II looked at what drives behaviour generally and in financial markets, and the substance of the social licence for financial markets.

Part III now connects the two by exploring the potential for greater recognition of the social licence to make a difference in practice.

- Chapter 6 looks at how the account of financial markets advanced by greater recognition of a social licence could be expected to influence the character of market relationships, and the way written standards are used and followed, in practice.
- Chapter 7 considers the policy implications.

6

Behaviour—Change in Practice

Fast Track

Speed Read

The social licence for financial markets expresses a narrative. It concerns the relationship between market participants and the societies in which they operate. It is not a fiction. It is based on the way the relationship can be seen operating in practice. It is radically different from financial narratives of the sort considered in Chap. 1. These present financial markets as a relentless pursuit of money as an end in itself. It is underpinned by a deeper, long-term understanding of the relationship between economic activity and social life: one that involves interdependency between the two, and broad-based mutuality. It is an understanding those narratives have obscured.

Narratives are powerful. They can appeal to hearts and minds. They can change behaviour. This one speaks to all levels of the financial market ecosystem. It advances a framework for navigating through the current re-evaluation of finance in society and a language to use in doing so. It has the potential to help heal the relationship between the two, strengthening positive reciprocity and injecting greater urgency in tackling humanity's many challenges.

How? By influencing behaviour in broadly three ways: firstly, by making the wider desired ends of financial activity more salient, increasing the likelihood that they will become a behavioural **focus**; secondly, by providing a **frame** of reference for market decisions; and, thirdly, in **forming** market participants. Returning to the key drivers of human behaviour discussed in Chap. 2, the first corresponds with the power of **desire** to motivate, the second with the way beliefs about the **meaning** of the world impact behavioural decisions and the third with how **habit** develops and shapes behaviour:

- **Focus**. Chapter 4 argued that the recognition of a social licence reaches towards a desired end: a reciprocal balancing of desires for human dignity, for the self and for others, in a way that is just. The existence of aspirations of

(continued)

© The Author(s) 2020
D. Rouch, *The Social Licence for Financial Markets*,
https://doi.org/10.1007/978-3-030-40220-4_6

(continued)

this sort in financial markets often gets lost (see Chap. 3). Recognising it explicitly has the potential to give it greater coherence and space for it to find a clearer voice, strengthening something already present, not creating it ground-up. Recognition of a social licence also throws light on the wider relationships involved in any financial transaction, proximity of relationship being a precondition for altruism, which is integral to positive reciprocity.

- **Framing**. The framing of a situation—its perceived meaning—influences behaviour. The first day in a new job is different to a funeral, a business meeting differs from a beach party. The account of financial markets advanced by the social licence does not ignore the power of financial self-interest, but emphasises the inter-dependency of self-interest and regard for others held in a reciprocal balance in realising intrinsic human value. In doing so, it brings a different framework of meaning to bear on market relationships. A succession of studies suggests that economic and financial frameworks can dampen other-regarding behaviour and that using self-interest, especially financial self-interest, to incentivise other-regarding behaviour, can sometimes backfire and produce the opposite result. In reaching beyond the framework of self-interest, recognition of a social licence begins to take financial markets out of the 'Wall Street game' (or perhaps *The Wolf of Wall Street* game) and into one more closely connected with the rest of humanity in which its dependence on broad-based mutuality is clear: a 'Community Game'.
- **Formation**. There are also potential implications for the evolution of individual character and group culture—the way people and institutions, and their relationships, *are*. Much, if not most, market behaviour is driven by habit. It follows a set of **behavioural norms** largely controlled by processes that are non-conscious and sometimes so embedded as to become part of an individual's or institution's identity. These get absorbed and understood in a similar way to language. Greater recognition of the social licence offers the possibility of influencing how these behavioural norms are followed and change over time in at least two ways. Firstly, repeated behaviours based on the aspirations and frames of reference just discussed can become habits and, consequently, take on a life of their own. Secondly, following behavioural norms in the course of day-to-day practice, even at the level of the non-conscious, involves a process in which the meaning given to a relationship and the values applied not only influence the immediate behaviours of those involved but also *who they become*. For example, there is evidence to suggest that repeatedly rehearsing narratives that assume that individuals and markets are inherently financially self-interested forms people (specifically, economics students) in a manner consistent with that. More importantly, financial narratives of the sort discussed in Chap. 1 seem to have formed financial markets and the firms and people within them, their culture and character, and lay behind the policy, regulatory and commercial mistakes that preceded the 2008 financial crisis and what followed. The account advanced by the social licence for financial markets also has the potential to form, but by reference to very different values.

Previous chapters emphasised the continuing importance of law, regulation and other types of written standards in financial markets. The aspirations and meanings embedded in talk of a social licence have a bearing on the making and following of these as well. Chapter 7 looks at the use of new law and regulation.

(*continued*)

(continued)

However, the account of financial markets advanced by the social licence also has the potential to influence the way written standards are applied, among other things, helping to re-purpose the highly abstracted mass of regulation now confronting market participants, increasing the likelihood that it is applied in accordance with its spirit, not just its letter. It could also help to underpin the more effective operation of aspirational written standards—those which seem to have the closest connection with the aspirations apparently involved in talk of a social licence (see Chap. 5)—including corporate codes.

Discussion of framing and formation, in particular, can raise concerns about undermining individual choice. Do they involve a kind of manipulation? However, both processes are ongoing the whole time in financial markets, whether explicitly acknowledged or not. Better to be transparent and develop a consensus on what outcomes are desirable.

So What?

There is good reason to expect that greater attention to the social licence can impact behaviour in ways that can both help to heal the fracture between finance and society and galvanise market participants in addressing some of humanity's most pressing challenges.

On that basis it is important to find ways of ensuring that it receives just that: greater attention at all levels, whether in the course of market or regulatory practice, or in policy and rule-making. That is the conviction that lies behind the writing of this book. The next chapter looks at how policy can support it.

Fourscore and seven years ago our fathers brought forth ... a new nation, conceived in liberty, and dedicated to the proposition that all men are created equal. Now we are engaged in a great civil war, testing whether ... any nation so conceived ... can long endure. ... We are met on a great battle-field of that war ... to dedicate a portion of that field, as a final resting-place for those who here gave their lives, that that nation might live. ... But, in a larger sense, we cannot dedicate ... this ground. The brave men, ... who struggled here, have consecrated it ... It is rather for us to be here dedicated to the great task remaining before us ... that this nation, under God, shall have a new birth of freedom, and that government of the people, by the people, for the people, shall not perish from the earth.[1]

Narratives can engage hearts and minds, so influencing behaviour.[2] Abraham Lincoln understood that in November 1863 as he gave his Gettysburg Address. Confronted with profound social fracture, he told a story. Indeed he wove together multiple stories: stories of individual self-sacrifice, the stories of those who were listening and an over-arching national story. The result was not a fiction, but it was a story nonetheless, with characters, a conflict and a desired end.[3] The conflict partly concerned the relationship between markets and society—the markets in humans and cotton. Although he did not use the words, the end goal concerned human dignity.

The social licence for financial markets is also a form of narrative. That is not the only way to approach it, but doing so (as this chapter will) can help in teasing out some of its potential to change market practice. It too is not a fiction. It concerns the relationship between market participants and the societies in which they operate. It does not have a conclusion, but it does have an end, based on a recognition of how commercial and financial activity relies upon, but can also affect social solidarity positively or negatively. That reality has been obscured by narratives of a different sort. These narratives emphasise money and material wealth as the goal of finance, often pursued through conflict: popular narratives of *The Wolf of Wall Street* genre, key economic models such as economic man, shareholder value and the invisible hand, and evolutionary narratives of nature red in tooth and claw. They do not accurately represent reality, but they can shape it. However, the embeddedness of finance in social relations is being rediscovered, as are the limits of financial self-interest, through a process of re-evaluation (see Chaps. 1 and 3).

Recognition of a social licence for financial markets provides a framework and language for working through that re-evaluation *in practice*. Can it impact market practice in a way that helps to heal the current fracture and galvanise the financial sector in tackling the challenges identified in Chap. 1? Can it help to strengthen positive reciprocity within financial market relationships, providing a basis for justified trust in the people and firms that comprise those markets, and greater social solidarity?

As discussed in previous chapters, as the expression is used here, positive reciprocity involves an orientation of market relationships beyond the immediate goals of individual transactions, in a way that benefits those in the wider networks affected by them. To foster that in practice, greater recognition of the social licence would need to heighten other-regarding aspirations within market relationships towards those wider chains of relationships. It would also need to make it more likely that the aspirations are realised. It would need to do so throughout the financial ecosystem because of the way group dynamics influence individual behaviours and vice versa (see Chap. 2); it would need to have a coordinating effect that supports systemic change.[4]

Change of this sort cannot be imposed by legal rules. It is a relational good that emerges where people are reliably mutually regarding of the needs and interests of each other (see Sect. 3.3). Rules have a role, but enforced compliance leaves little room for trust. Rather, positive reciprocity, and broad-based mutuality, grow out of the substance of relationships *in practice*. Like relationships, narratives are experienced and felt. Indeed, the sort of narratives discussed in this chapter are, in a sense, constitutive of relationships and the identity of those in them. Is the account of financial markets advanced by the social licence the kind of narrative that can reach into the substance of relationships throughout the financial market ecosystem so as to result in this sort of reorientation—so that the parties to them live, feel and understand them in a different way? There is reason to think that it is. But how?

What follows is not an exhaustive answer to that. Rather it highlights three ways in which greater recognition of the social licence could be expected to foster a change in practice: its potential to strengthen other-regarding desires, the way it frames market decisions and its possible role in forming individual character and group culture. These loosely correspond with the drivers of human behaviour outlined in Chap. 2: the power of desire to motivate, the way beliefs about the meaning of the world impact behavioural decisions and how habit develops and shapes behaviour. While the three strands are approached separately here, they are closely interwoven.

The chapter goes on to consider the significance of this for the use and operation of written standards. That is important given extensive reliance on written standards in seeking to change behaviour, especially in financial markets, and the close connection between written standards and the social licence for financial markets (see Chap. 5). In closing, the chapter also briefly considers the wider implications for individual choice of deliberately attempting to influence market behaviour. But first, what is it about narratives that gives them the potential to influence behaviour and why might the account of financial markets advanced by the social licence have that kind of potential?

6.1   The Power of Narratives—Minds and Hearts

To a significant degree, 'narrative organizes the structure of human experience'.[5] Narratives are a way of ordering events and circumstances into a whole, giving them meaning.[6] People develop self-narratives to understand themselves.[7] Indeed, it has been suggested this is the primary way in which humans '… construct the dimension of their life's meaningfulness …'[8]

Something similar happens with group identity and purpose. Nations develop narratives about themselves and what they stand for: histories, overarching stories, 'master narratives'.[9] Likewise companies and the groups within them.[10] A group's narrative influences the way it acts. It '… renders concerted action possible … it is literally *constitutive* of the group'.[11] Lincoln advanced an over-arching narrative at Gettysburg. The social licence for financial markets could be seen as another, as could the narratives discussed in Chap. 1.

Groups carry multiple narratives.[12] Individuals tend to understand their own story by reference to group narratives. The group narratives which become dominant therefore influence both what a group does and the behaviour of individuals within it.[13] Is it, for example, the social licence or the 'invisible hand'? The development of group narratives is, in turn, influenced by those of individuals in the group. Group and individual narratives are connected.[14]

But narratives do more than carry meaning. They also engage emotion. Reason is important in deciding how to act. But the impact of narratives on behaviour goes beyond conscious reasoning. Firstly, their force is derived more from their *verisimilitude* (broadly, whether they seem to provide a realistic account) than scientific verification or logic.[15] Secondly, they often involve *emotional engagement*, so that, at some level, people feel and experience the story: the story *becomes part of them* and they part of the story.[16] Far from being rational utility maximisers, humans may be more governed by narrative processes.

Identifying with a narrative involves a 'felt-belief' based on 'an immediate emotional, intuitive response'.[17] Emotions help people register whether circumstances are consistent with a desired end and can galvanise them into action (see Sect. 2.1.2), be it the survival of a nation or commercial success.

> Narrative allows us to communicate the emotional content of our values. Narrative is not talking "about" values; rather narrative embodies and communicates those values. It is through the shared experience of our values that we can … motivate one another to act…[18]

This motivating power of narratives is well-recognised, for example, among politicians,[19] those campaigning for social change,[20] those wanting the best from employees[21] and those wanting people to buy their products.[22] Television soaps that appeal to aspirations can materially influence behaviour.[23]

Importantly for the social licence, narrative motivates in financial and commercial practice too. For example, a corporate mission statement is a type of narrative designed to establish emotional engagement with the company's goals and strategy[24] and 'brand narrative' with its business.[25] Growing attention to corporate purpose has been connected precisely with the object of achieving valued or desired ends.[26] A company's accounts provide an *account* and its report a narrative of its progress in achieving its end goals on the basis of which shareholders may act.[27] Likewise, prospectuses for securities offerings are sometimes described as telling the 'story' behind the offering—essentially, what will inspire people to invest.[28]

Narratives affect economic behaviour. They '... may be seen as ... *scripts*. ... [that] partially govern our activities, including our economic actions'.[29] The spread of popular narratives can help to explain economic fluctuations.[30] Conversely, *economic* narratives affect behaviour more widely. Chapters 1 and 3 looked at their influence on financial markets. But, beyond that, economic narratives have had 'huge implications for the world – in particular, in the way we craft policy, think about globalisation, and dismiss dissent'.[31] The practical significance of narratives about financial markets reaches far beyond those markets.

Narratives, then, can affect behaviour because they reach hearts and minds. However, their precise impact depends, in turn, upon which narratives come to define individuals and groups. 'I can only answer the question 'What am I to do?' if I can answer the prior question 'Of what stories do I find myself a part?'.'[32]

6.2   The Resonance of the Social Licence

So, whether the account of financial markets expressed by recognition of a social licence can counter financial narratives of the sort discussed in Chap. 1 partly depends on whether people are likely to identify with it. Ultimately, the only way of finding out if they will do that is to try it and see (see Chap. 7). However, one way of assessing its potential is to apply two tests based on a distinction developed by communications theorist Walter Fisher between 'narrative probability' and 'narrative fidelity'.[33] According to Fisher, where a narrative has both, people are more likely to identify with it.

Narrative probability concerns 'what constitutes a coherent story':[34] does the narrative 'hang together'? Narrative fidelity is a more complex (and controversial) concept. However, essentially it concerns a listener's assessment of 'whether or not the stories they experience ring true with the stories they know to be true in their lives':[35] does the story 'represent accurate assertions about social reality and thereby constitute good reasons for belief or action'?[36] For example, when bankers are branded greedy and self-interested, does this chime with experience? It is not necessary to go into Fisher's more detailed test for narrative fidelity here, except to highlight that, among other things, it involves an assessment of the *values* reflected in the narrative against those of the listener: it partly concerns *desired ends*.[37] The basic idea that some implicit or explicit assessment of values is involved when a person identifies with a story seems plausible (see Sect. 6.1). It also seems correct that 'Stories' persuasive power lies in their ability to call up other compelling stories.'[38]

How does the social licence fare against these tests? Reasonably well against the narrative probability test. Discussion of a social licence for financial markets does indeed seem to make sense (Chap. 4). What of the basic narrative fidelity test? Firstly, it is reasonable to think that references to the social licence in official speeches have not occasioned more discussion precisely because they do indeed, intuitively, 'ring true' (see Sect. 4.1). Secondly, in terms of values, Chap. 3 looked at what seem to be the intrinsically desired ends of financial market participants; ends reflected in financial practice once you peer behind default narratives of financial self-interest. It identified the presence of desires to realise dignity for self and others as ends that are intrinsically valued. Likewise, the discussion in Chap. 4 of the social licence sought to draw out commonly desired ends that seem to lie behind it and, in particular, justice understood in terms of human dignity. It is based on valued ends which seem to be echoed at some level in financial life, even if they are not always *realised* in practice. Like the narratives of Chap. 1, it recognises the powerful role of financial self-interest. However, it goes further, placing financial self-interest in the context of an aspiration for a just balancing of self-interest with regard for the interests of others. While the narratives discussed in Chap. 1 reflect something of reality, viewed as an account of both market practice and aspiration, the social licence nonetheless seems to display greater fidelity to what is encountered in practice.

But in terms of the challenges identified in Chap. 1, being a narrative that people may identify with is only the first step. To make a difference, greater recognition of a social licence would also need to help to orient financial market relationships in a way that creates positive reciprocity systemically between the financial world and the societies it affects as a basis for broad-based mutuality. The remainder of this chapter therefore considers its potential to change hearts and minds *in practice*.

6.3   Focusing Motivation

The intensity of desires can change.[39] People can be motivated to do things and become demotivated. Economists have looked at these variations through the lens of preferences.[40] What they mean by preferences is not quite the same as desires. However, talk of preferences often recognises that motivations lie behind them,[41] that preferences can change based on variations in motivation and that they are influenced by cultural context.[42]

As discussed, common narratives exert an important cultural influence. Narratives can engage with desires, and desires motivate action. Chapter 4 suggested that recognition of a social licence identifies an aspiration for finance that involves a just balancing of desires for self-dignity and that of others. Realising that end would be consistent with the kind of positively reciprocal outcomes described above. What follows considers how greater recognition of the social licence has the potential to strengthen these aspirations: by making them more salient; by creating social space in which they can be voiced and pursued; and by heightening awareness of the relational proximity between those in markets and in the societies they affect, providing a basis for shared identity and empathy. In each case, this involves nurturing something already present, not creating it ground-up.

6.3.1 Direct Appeal to Other-Regarding Desires—Salience

Greater recognition of the social licence could reasonably be expected to strengthen the salience of the valued ends it seems to reach towards, so influencing behaviour.[43] The desire for justice is a powerful motivator. In countless cases, from the abolition of slavery to the defeat of totalitarian regimes, action has been motivated by an 'indignation with injustice... our values, moral traditions, and sense of personal dignity function as critical sources of motivation to act'.[44]

Chapter 3 has already suggested that concerns of this sort carry over into financial markets looking particularly at public service motivation, the 'justice motive' and people's desire for work to be 'meaningful' (Sect. 3.2.3). Chapter 4 touched on the Schwartz hierarchy of values with benevolence and universalism at the top, and noted the prevalence of justice concerns across cultures (Sect. 4.6.2). Work on 'organisational justice' confirms that the just operation of business organisations is important to their success and staff wellbeing.[45] But there is no obvious reason why at least some, and perhaps many, of those in financial markets would not hold broader aspirations for the positive impact of finance. Indeed, there is reason to think that they do.[46] Other-regarding aspirations in work contexts are under-explored.[47] Clearly, not everyone has them to the same degree. For example, studies on employees' sense of calling[48] suggest that some have stronger justice aspirations than others.[49] The self-selection that takes place when people seek to join groups (see Sect. 2.4) may also affect who ends up in jobs perceived as having more or less social purpose.[50] Nonetheless, people with a sense of calling are found across different sorts of jobs, not just those considered 'vocational'.[51] More widely, staff often care about making a positive difference in other people's lives.[52]

Indeed, Chap. 3 noted how firms devote significant resources to community volunteering. This involves an element of gift, both to staff and to communities.[53] There is some suggestion that it responds to a feeling that other-regarding aspirations cannot be fully expressed through work.[54] For example, reasons given by the British business organisation Business in the Community for why community engagement enhances employee relations include '… build[ing] satisfaction and motivation through doing *something worthwhile*, such as helping disadvantaged individuals or community groups…' (emphasis added).[55]

But what if it were to turn out that business activity *is worthwhile* because of its power to advance human dignity in ways that include but also transcend financial value? Putting it like that reveals the absurdity of the question and returns us to the irony identified in Chap. 3. The issue is not whether finance can be 'worthwhile', but how to make the connection more salient, so that motivations are strengthened and positive impact increased. And that is precisely where the account of financial markets advanced by talk of a social licence seems to point. Throwing a different set of aspirations for finance into starker relief—rehearsing an account that appeals to them—has the potential to strengthen them by comparison with others:

> An effective story – a story that mobilizes – probably heightens feelings that people already have about particular issues, or reinterprets the sources of those feelings, or attaches them to new issues or lines of action.[56]

This chimes with work of business writer, Stephen Denning, on the use of narratives in business. He lists a number of principles for business leaders who want staff 'to *want* to act differently'.[57] The goal must, he says, be *worthwhile* for its own sake and for the particular audience.[58] It echoes studies of people's desire for meaningfulness in work; one of the sources they identify is congruence between individual values and company mission.[59] In view of the widespread desire for justice, it is reasonable to think that realising just ends by just means in financial markets is a goal that people might feel is worthwhile. But even for those who do not, greater emphasis on the social licence may nonetheless motivate other-regarding behaviour. For example, in a context defined more clearly by reference to the social licence, a self-interested desire for esteem or acceptance could also cause behaviour to align.[60] It may also influence the role of self-selection in determining who ends up in finance jobs, facilitating greater motivational diversity.

6.3.2 Making Social Space

Social context influences people's willingness to express and pursue aspirations *in practice* (see Sects. 2.4 and 2.5). Market participants may be more likely to pursue aspirations consistent with the social licence if they believe, firstly, that they are not alone and, secondly, that this is acceptable in a work context. The account of financial markets advanced by recognition of a social licence is relevant to both.

Firstly, it seems to highlight a broad-based, but often unobserved, aspiration towards justice in financial market activity; in other words, it can help to tackle the apparent misapprehension about what motivates people in financial markets (Chap. 3). This is related to the influence of framing (see Sect. 6.4). A person's beliefs about others' behaviour and beliefs can influence their own; making other-regardingness more visible offers some prospect of inducing more of the same. For example, one recent study identifies an apparent correlation between the extent to which British and American people perceive that self-transcendence values (care for the welfare and interests of one's community and others) are strongly held by other citizens, and feeling less estranged and reporting being more civically engaged, and vice versa.[61]

Secondly, more explicit recognition of a social licence throughout the financial ecosystem should help to reassure market participants that the aspirations it embeds are institutionally acceptable and, indeed, essential for the wellbeing of the financial sector. Workplaces can be more or less conducive to people finding meaning, including where meaning is derived from socially orientated aspirations.[62] For example, the outworking of public service motivations can be strengthened by a person's organisational setting, including the clarity of its public service mission.[63] Situational pressure can lead people to conform with perceived group norms rather than following their own values.[64] Research on 'issue selling' in business organisations, for example, suggests that staff wishing to advance a social issue may default to narrowly economic arguments, or give up, because of their beliefs about what is valued by the organisation.[65] However, where a company has publicly espoused wider social values, referencing them in issue selling may be more effective than using economic justifications.[66] Individuals may therefore sometimes misread an employer's attitude to social issues. In view of that, firms that are not following a narrowly financially defined strategy (and most these days claim that they are not) may need to make their mission and values more salient to staff, so that they can advance them more effectively, in a sense, defining the public space in a way that makes it possible to do so.[67] Recognising explicitly the relevance of a social licence for financial markets to the business of a firm, as some firms are beginning to (see Sect. 4.1), is a way of doing that. It can help to provide 'permission' for the aspirations it apparently embeds to be expressed and pursued.[68] The common emphasis on 'tone from the top' to change the culture of financial firms reflects this.

A form of group dynamic is also at work between financial firms. Chapter 3 highlighted how many have already made public commitments to operate in a manner consistent with broader social goods. Viewing these from the perspective of the social licence potentially gives them greater coherence and, importantly, systemic salience; it can contextualise them within an account of the financial ecosystem as a whole. This could be expected to strengthen firms' commitments in various ways. In particular, it could have a coordinating effect (so that senior management in financial institutions that are sympathetic do not feel they are going out on a limb) or influence market pressure (as with the current reorientation of the asset management market towards ESG investing).[69]

At a more modest level, systemic space of this sort seemed to open up following a speech by then UK Prime Minister David Cameron in 2012 (in the aftermath of the Occupy phenomenon), in which he set out his vision for greater social responsibility within the capitalist system.[70] While it would be difficult to demonstrate a causal link, in the weeks after the speech, social responsibility and related concepts seemed to make their way more overtly into market discourse. This was paralleled in the pages of the *Financial Times*. A word search for the expression 'responsible capitalism' disclosed only eight references from 2004 until the end of 2011, but 40 during 2012.[71]

6.3.3   Empathy, Trust and Shared Identity

Recognition of a social licence may also help to strengthen other-regarding desires by drawing attention to collective identity and inter-dependency. It highlights, firstly, the fact that those licensed are frequently also members of the licensing community (it helps to 're-member' that relationship) and, secondly, the embeddedness of financial activity within multiple social relationships.

Chapter 4 suggested that the level of justified trust towards the financial sector is an indication of the extent to which a social licence has been given. The likelihood of trust being given seems to increase when those involved perceive themselves as members of the same salient social group, perhaps because of their knowledge of the shared standards operating within the group. As noted in Chap. 4, this has been observed experimentally and in situations of social fracture, such as Northern Ireland.[72]

Further, altruism and other cooperative behaviour can emerge from feelings of collective identity.[73] Relational proximity may help to strengthen feelings that can result in other-regarding behaviour.[74] These include empathy, which may be one source of altruistic desire (see Sect. 3.2.3).[75] Consistent with this, in a work setting, while transformational leadership may help staff rise above self-interest, evidence suggests it may be most effective when staff interact with the beneficiaries of their action so that they can see meaningful consequences.[76] On one view, in order to feel empathetic concern for another, it is necessary for a person (1) to perceive that the other is in need and (2) to value the other's welfare.[77] A pre-requisite for this is to recognise their presence and needs at all.[78] Recognition of a social licence throws light on the multiple relationships potentially affected by any market transaction. The clearer this becomes, the more difficult it is to approach transactions as little more than isolated economic exchanges, neutral but for their financial value.

6.4 Framing

As well as reaching towards an aspired end, the social licence advances an account of the *meaning* of financial activity (see Sect. 4.8). In doing so, it provides a framework for understanding financial markets quite different from the kind of narratives discussed in Chap. 1: one emphasising social embeddedness and reciprocal balance between self-interest and wider needs.

Chapter 2 looked at how people's beliefs about situations affect behaviour through 'bottom-up' and 'top-down' thought processes. Beliefs obviously influence more deliberative, bottom-up, reasoning about how to act. However, they also affect faster, top-down, processing, involving a less conscious categorisation of a situation, following which people are thought to apply habitual mental models (or 'schemas') to navigate through it. Resulting behaviour depends on which mental model is activated.[79] The potential for recognition of a social licence to influence the content of these models is addressed in Sect. 6.5. However, the meaning advanced by the social licence could also affect the initial categorisation stage and that is the focus here, in particular, research on 'framing', 'priming' and 'motivation crowding out', each considered, in turn.[80]

The findings of game-based experiments on these phenomena require caution. They may not reliably predict what would happen in real life, they can be affected by design flaws and undetected background factors, they are often based on small sample groups and they rarely involve those involved in financial markets.[81] However, a significant body of research suggests an association between people applying monetary, economic and financial market frameworks and more individualistic or less cooperative behaviour, as compared with frameworks that emphasise a community context or the needs of others. Since recognition of a social licence does the latter, this is potentially significant for the objective of strengthening positive reciprocity.

6.4.1   Wall Street, Community or Social Licence?

Framing concerns how a situation is presented to someone making a decision. The tendency of subjects to be more cooperative in a prisoner's dilemma game framed as 'community game' as compared with a 'Wall Street game' was first highlighted in research involving university students and Israeli Air Force pilots. Simply by changing the name of the game to 'community game', cooperation rates significantly improved.[82] More experiments using similar framing have been undertaken since, with mixed results. However, many have suggested an association between community or similar framing and higher levels of cooperation.[83] The reason for this is not entirely clear, but attention has focused on whether, broadly, the framing affects either the meaning a situation has for those involved or the preferences, or desires, that are engaged. Common sense suggests that it could be a mixture of both, not least because of their inter-dependency (see Chap. 2).[84]

As to beliefs, among other things, there is evidence suggesting that framing may influence not just subjects' first-order beliefs about what others in the relevant game will do but also second-order beliefs, that is, beliefs about the beliefs and motivations of others.[85] This is important because the willingness of many people to act in an other-regarding manner may be affected by whether they think others will too.[86] It may help to explain higher levels of cooperation in a 'community game' as compared with one described more 'neutrally' and seems potentially significant in terms of the possible impact of greater recognition of a social licence, emphasising the socially cooperative nature of financial markets.[87] The Wall Street label, on the other hand, may key into beliefs about others more akin to the sort of narratives discussed in Chap. 1, including those of *The Wolf of Wall Street* genre.

Turning to preferences, describing a repeated public goods game as a 'community game' has been found to result in the prosocial behaviour of those already expressing prosocial preferences being sustained more strongly throughout a series of rounds of the game, whereas it declined in parallel games described either neutrally, as the environment game or as the Wall Street game, especially so with the last. So, it may not just be that Wall Street framing is associated with a decline in cooperative behaviour, but also that community framing supports the other-regarding behaviour of those with prosocial preferences.[88] The authors conclude that 'Engaging individuals based on their endogenous social preferences, and using framing to emphasize these preferences ... may provide ... [an] avenue by which large-scale cooperation can be effectively ... encouraged.'[89]

The concept of a social licence for financial markets has not yet been tested in this way. However, these studies seem significant in assessing its potential. While the account it advances affirms the importance of financial return in financial markets, it nonetheless places it firmly in a social context, connecting it with desired ends very different from those in the kind of narratives considered in Chap. 1. It is therefore reasonable to suppose that greater recognition of a social licence could help to strengthen the sort of cooperative behaviours associated with the community game and reduce the negative impacts of the Wall Street game.[90]

6.4.2   Financial and Economic Priming

Priming involves introducing a cue into a decision-making situation that may prompt a person to characterise it one way rather than another. For example, referencing money may result in a task being approached through a financial frame. Financial framing affects behaviour. This is obvious, not least from the discussion in Chap. 2 of behaviour in relation to Warhol's 200 Dollars. However, experimental work on money priming seems to suggest that financial frames may weaken other-regarding behaviour. In particular, one widely reported set of experiments suggested a connection with less helpful, more individualistic behaviour.[91] As noted, caution is required.[92] However, other studies seem to identify similar associations.

Another set of experiments suggests a connection between triggering 'economic schemas' (emphasising rationality, efficiency and self-interest) and lower levels of compassion towards others. This may result from, among other things, dampened feelings of empathy towards those in need.[93] Activating economic schemas (described by the researchers as the 'homo economicus assumption') may also lead to lower levels of trust, potentially systemically.[94] However, it is important to remember that market activity can also help to strengthen trust;[95] indeed, this is central to the account advanced by recognition of a social licence.

Looking at the financial sector more specifically, another widely reported experiment seemed to suggest that bank employees became more inclined to cheat when their identity as bankers was primed. This was apparently specific to bankers; the pattern was not repeated in people from other professions. Interestingly, in the absence of this priming, bankers were less likely to cheat than other groups, primed or not. In other words, the research could also suggest that, as a social group, they displayed higher levels of honesty than the average.[96]

Again, caution is required in interpreting work like this.[97] The researchers suggested that the results reflected a tolerance of dishonesty in banking culture. An alternative proposes that the behaviour resulted from a social stereotype of how bankers behave to which bankers are more susceptible.[98] Either way, it seems as if finance framing correlated with less trustworthy behaviour. However, in terms of the account of financial markets advanced by the social licence, perhaps the most significant finding was the apparently higher than average level of trustworthiness among finance workers absent financial priming. It seems consistent with the mixture of market participant motivations discussed in Chap. 3. It challenges simplistic assumptions and is an encouragement to think that the reframing of financial market activity advanced by recognition of a social licence could produce more other-regarding results. Consistent with that, a further set of experiments has found that priming 'moral identity' (essentially, a person's mental model for their social responsiveness to the needs of others) seems to strengthen other-regardingness, whereas priming that emphasises self-interest (specifically, financial self-interest) tends to displace it.[99]

6.4.3   Crowding Out/Crowding In

'Crowding out' is essentially the idea that incentivising behaviour using rewards or penalties can undermine people's intrinsic motivation, their innate desire, to do what is being incentivised.[100] Incentives can also heighten innate desires, depending on how they are used ('motivation crowding in').[101] Crowding out is not limited to negatively affecting altruistic motivations. It extends, for example, to the desire to find satisfaction in a job well done. However, a common reason for incentivising behaviour is to ensure that it meets the needs of others.

The nature and extent of motivation crowding out is much debated.[102] Nonetheless, there is enough work to suggest that incentives, especially financial incentives, can crowd out behaviour motivated by innate desires. It is not feasible to survey all of that work here. However, one of the most widely quoted examples involved Israeli day-care centres where parents were late picking up their children.[103] A small but not insignificant fine was introduced to incentivise punctuality. However, punctuality deteriorated significantly. Importantly, the context was a wider commercial transaction. Each parent had a child care contract with their nursery. Like all contracts, it was incomplete (see Sect. 3.1.2). It did not specify what would happen if parents arrived late. The plausible explanation given by the researchers for what they observed was that the fine changed the meaning of the situation for the parents.

Exactly how the meaning changed is debateable. The researchers advance essentially two options. The fine may have removed contractual uncertainty about the consequences of being late. However, their alternative suggestion picks up on, perhaps, a more obvious change of meaning. Prior to the introduction of the fine, care of children until parents arrived could be seen as, essentially, a gift from the teachers since it was not specifically charged for. Thereafter, the interaction was more like a commercial exchange for the provision of a service. Being late was framed differently. Prior to introduction of the fine, parents may have felt an obligation to respect the generosity of the teacher. After the fine, it had a price.

So, the fine might not have had the result it did had the situation been presented differently. The study did not test this. However, the importance of context to the way monetary payments affect behaviour emerges from a separate study of cash payments, following cognitive behavioural therapy, to previously criminally engaged men. The payments were associated with a significant reduction in criminal activity as compared with the payment or the therapy on their own. The researchers suggest that this was, essentially, because the provision of the money was instrumental to the end of the therapy; it provided the subjects with the space and resources needed to put what they had learnt into practice.[104] Another study has identified a connection with significantly improved job performance when motivational talk (affirming the diligence of employees or the importance of their task) was combined with performance pay, but not when the two were separated; indeed, performance pay on its own reduced performance.[105] It seems that monetary payments do not necessarily crowd out intrinsic motivation; the wider framework of meaning within which they take place has an important role.

The account of financial markets advanced by recognition of a social licence provides a framework of meaning for the financial transactions that comprise financial markets. Financial incentives are a major feature of these, but are only a part (see Chap. 3). Chapter 4 suggested that recognition of a social licence frames financial ends by reference to intrinsic aspirations for human dignity and draws attention to a substantial element of gratuity in the relationship between the financial world and the societies in which it operates. Intrinsic aspirations such as these may be vulnerable to being crowded out. However, recognition of a social licence seems to define a role for money in the context of which they can be crowded in.

6.5   Formation—Character and Culture

To a considerable degree, behaviour in financial markets is habitual and this displays itself in the form of behavioural norms (see Chap. 5). Indeed, the framing effects, just discussed, rest on habitual ways of categorising the world and mental models that are applied in consequence.

Habits define people and institutions—their character and culture. They are the embedded memory of past experience, not just the memory of individuals but also that of the groups and societies they inhabit, communicated through a process of cultural interaction and practice,[106] including social narratives. That process 'shapes *who people are*'.[107] It moulds preferences 'as an accent or taste for national cuisine is acquired…'.[108] In the words of one UK regulator, 'Positive culture … goes right to *the heart of what firms and their staff are*, what values they represent …' (emphasis added).[109] It concerns the core of what they value and desire. Culture is an ongoing process that 'not only shapes its members, but is shaped by them'.[110] In the course of communication, culture is transformed, as are those within it.

No one was born into eighteenth-century Britain thinking that slavery was normal; it was a practice that was received and, seeming normal, went on to become the subject of people's desires and what they did to pursue them. In consequence, a society evolved in which it was integral, and it took enormous imagination, energy and financial resources to dismantle it. However, once an imaginative step of that sort is made, '… new ways of thinking and alternative understandings of the world can expand the available set of mental models and thus play an important role in development.'[111] Recognition of a social licence has the potential to be one such step.

Societies have long recognised the power of habit and the need to be intentional about how it develops or is 'formed'. Indeed, in French, Italian and Spanish, training is linked to the notion of formation,[112] while Germans talk not just of 'erziehung' (education) but also of 'bildung'—maturing into personhood with a sense of values and responsibility. Consistent with that intuition, attempts to change financial market practice are described as re*form* or trans*formation*; what is needed to change practice is so profound that it could almost be seen as physical:

> Good corporate governance … involves moving beyond … "rules-based" behaviour to "values-based" behaviour. … virtues are moulded from habit …[113]

> … in a regulated industry like financial services, the public interest is embodied in the objectives of the regulator. But … they have to be internalised by firms and their staff.[114]

Can greater recognition of a social licence influence this formative process and in ways that foster the sort of positive reciprocity described in the introduction? There is reason to think that it can. Firstly, activity repeatedly influenced in the ways described in Sects. 6.3 and 6.4 is more likely to become habituated.[115] Secondly, however, greater recognition of the social licence also has the potential to influence how behavioural norms evolve, in particular, because of its account of the ultimate value, or desired ends, of financial activity and its meaning.[116] This section looks more closely at how. It starts by considering how financial narratives and economic models may have formed financial market participants hitherto. It then explores what it is about this process of formation that makes it reasonable to think that greater recognition of a social licence could help to form beliefs and values consistent with greater positive reciprocity.

6.5.1   How Are Financial and Economic Narratives Formative?

Chapters 1 and 3 considered how financial and economic narratives and models, or at least the assumptions, values and meanings they carry, have influenced market practice. The comment from the British civil servant reported in Chap. 1 that the establishment had made a monumental, collective, intellectual error in the run up to the 2008 financial crisis suggests that this influence had been formative. In what way?

Experimental Evidence

Much as with framing, experimental evidence suggests that one way in which financial and economic models may form people is to predispose them towards the self-interested behaviour the narratives assume.[117] Again, this kind of experimental evidence needs to be handled with considerable caution. However, it may help to cast some light on financial market behaviour. The relationship between finance and economics is deep. Finance is fundamentally affected by the macroeconomic environment, and microeconomic theory frequently influences financial decisions. Unsurprisingly, therefore, economists and those with economics training (e.g. through finance and management courses) have a material role in the finance sector and its regulation. Their views influence not only market-facing decisions but also how firms are run and strategy develops and their cultural tone. Their values and beliefs really count in financial markets.

What do the studies tell us? There is evidence, at least at a student level, of an association between studying economics and being more self-interested,[118] being less cooperative,[119] displaying lower levels of generosity,[120] having a more positive view of greed in oneself and others[121] and displaying a tendency to be less honest.[122] Likewise, students on business courses (with significant economic content) have been found to display higher levels of instrumental behaviour[123] and to be more unethical in their behaviour and attitudes than non-business students.[124]

It is essential to avoid shallow dualisms. The behaviours in these studies were by no means entirely self-serving. There are also experiments that suggest no or limited impact. They nonetheless raise some obvious questions. One is especially pertinent in terms of formation: were these observed behaviours the result of nature or nurture. In other words, did they reflect self-selection (i.e. those opting to study economics come to it with these attitudes) or were they the result of studying economics (i.e. so that those concerned had been formed in some way)?[125] There is considerable debate over this, with evidence pointing both ways.[126] However, a recent assessment of studies to date concludes that more than half, some providing high-quality evidence, seem to suggest that economics training is involved in some way—some sort of formation is going on.[127] Precisely how is not especially clear. For example, is it to do with the assumptions underlying what is being studied, or membership of a group of economists? The studies have focused more on the former. However, the discussion in Chap. 2 would suggest that group membership as much as the inherent potency of the group's values and beliefs is also important. Something similar happens with legal culture. Either way, it seems that people may be formed by studying economics.

Formation in Professional Life?

Could something similar happen in professional financial life? Experimental evidence is limited. However, if those trained in economics have the value profile suggested by these experiments, they may gravitate towards jobs that are presently perceived as aligned with self-enhancement more than a calling to serve others, those offering wealth and power status, such as finance.[128] They may then also reflect these orientations in their work. That could have an impact on those around them, particularly in view of the importance of economics in financial life, strengthening self-interested behaviour in others or dampening the aspirations of those with a stronger sense of calling. Think of the induction programme reported at the start of Chap. 3.[129] As discussed in Chap. 3, there is little doubt that financial self-interest is a potent feature of financial markets, as debates on bankers' remuneration bear out.

Certainly, the values and meanings advanced by economic and financial narratives shape the environment in which market participants operate and hence the direction of their lives. That would suggest that they may also be formed in the process. As noted in Chap. 1, economic frameworks and models and the assumptions that lie behind them structure market activity. One major study of the impact of financial economics on financial markets, referred to in Chap. 1, concludes that it '… did more than analyze markets; it altered them. It was an … active force transforming its environment…'.[130] It '… has become incorporated into the infrastructures of financial markets … in at least three ways: technical, linguistic, and legitimatory … most evident in the case of financial derivatives …'.[131] Likewise, pursuit of shareholder value has affected corporate form and remuneration structures.[132] In turn, market structures affect how the lives of market participants develop, most obviously, because they spend their time carrying on and become defined by one activity rather than another. Market structures:

> … impose characteristic patterns of interaction … affecting who meets whom, on what terms, to perform which tasks, and with what expectation of rewards.
>
> One risks banality, not controversy, in suggesting that these allocation rules therefore influence the process of human development, affecting personality, habits, tastes, identities and values.[133]

Think of the massive change of desires and behaviours unleashed by the industrial revolution.[134]

Further, Chap. 2 discussed the structuring effect of money in financial markets. The power of money to form beliefs and desires is hinted at by the experiment described above involving latecomers at Israeli nurseries. Lateness did not fall back to its old level once the fines had been withdrawn. Introducing a monetary sanction seems to have had a longer-term behavioural impact, perhaps because it led to the relationship being seen as one of exchange. The authors conclude 'once a commodity, always a commodity'.[135] The experiment involving payments to criminals following cognitive behaviour therapy also led to a longer-term behaviour change (reduction in criminality, hence, greater other-regardingness), but in the context of a different purpose.[136]

Therapeutic use of 'token economies' to treat behavioural disorders also suggests that narratives emphasising the pursuit of financial self-interest may form desire in a manner consistent with themselves.[137] In psychology, a token economy is a technique used to change behaviour. It involves people being given tokens (such as poker chips) to 'reinforce' the performance of a desired behaviour. Tokens are given as the desired behaviour occurs and are convertible later into privileges, such as food or access to television. In the language of psychology, the privileges are 'primary' reinforcers and the tokens 'secondary' reinforcers. A reinforcement is a stimulus given shortly after a desirable behaviour designed to increase the likelihood of repetition. A stimulus is any event or influence that is capable of exciting the senses and of causing a response in a person. A primary reinforcer (or unconditioned stimulus) is one that naturally causes a response of this sort, such as food. A secondary reinforcer is some stimulus that has acquired its power to reinforce behaviour because it has come to be associated with an unconditioned stimulus. While currently out of vogue, when used therapeutically, token economies operate within self-contained environments by reference to a desired behavioural end, based on some over-arching understanding of healthy behaviour. There is good evidence that they work to condition, or form, a person to behave in the desired way in the future.[138]

Money is a kind of token.[139] Markets can be seen as arrangements for incentivising people to do things by earning these tokens. Financial and economic narratives tend to treat the thing that is incentivised in financial markets as obtaining and handling the same tokens. Consequently, in the absence of a broader narrative about the role of financial markets, there is a risk of circularity, with money operating as an incentive to behave so as to do little more than earn more of itself. As indicated, token economies usually operate in relatively closed institutional settings. However, the experience of using token economies would seem to suggest that monetary incentives in financial markets may, in turn, condition or form financial utility maximising behaviour. Greater recognition of a social licence introduces a potentially powerful counter-narrative, contextualising money as an instrument in pursuing broader intrinsic ends.

6.5.2   Habitus: How Greater Recognition of a Social Licence Can Influence Formation

How might greater recognition of a social licence influence processes of formation like these? It turns on its quite different account of the meaning of financial market activity and its valued ends. Sociologist Pierre Bourdieu's concept of *habitus* provides a way of thinking about it. Bourdieu uses this idea to address various dichotomies, especially how people can be formed by their social world, but also retain their autonomy.[140] *Habitus* is not another word for habits. Rather, it is a way of describing what generates practices described as habits. To Bourdieu, *habitus* is the disposition a person develops that influences the way they interact with their world. He describes *habitus* as personal systems of durable, 'structured structures predisposed to function as structuring structures, that is, as principles which generate and organize practices'.[141] It is the product of a person's history and drives, broadly, their behaviour in a way that '…ensures the active presence of past experiences, which deposited in each organism in the form of schemes of perception, thought and action, tend to guarantee the 'correctness' of practices … more reliably than all formal rules…'.[142] It is history internalised as 'second nature and so forgotten as history'.[143] Each behavioural step is, then, a 'regulated improvisation'—spontaneous, yet structured through *habitus*.[144]

Habitus is formed through a person's interaction with the social space they inhabit—their *field*. It is there that their unique set of experiences and knowledge accumulates. They develop aspirations consistent with living in the field[145] and a practical sense for how to live in it. Bourdieu calls this practical sense a 'feel for the game' (the field being where the game is in progress).[146] The reference to 'practical sense' emphasises the physicality of *habitus*. It is not simply intellectual adherence to a set of beliefs or rules, but a 'state of the body'. In other words, much of it exists in an unarticulated form, simply in ways of behaving. Yet there is a close relationship between *habitus* and *belief*. Bourdieu talks of *habitus* in terms of 'practical belief' (c.f. the reference in Sect. 6.1 to narratives as 'felt-belief'), and where a person's *habitus* is attuned to their social world, their field, it is displayed in a 'pre-verbal taking for granted of that world', not unlike the taken for grantedness of Mr Greenspan's pre-financial crisis world described in Chap. 1 or the world of behavioural norms described in Chap. 5.[147] But *habitus* involves embodied *values* as well as beliefs:

> One could endlessly enumerate the values given body, *made* body, by the hidden persuasion of an implicit pedagogy which can instil a whole cosmology, through injunctions as insignificant as 'sit up straight' … and inscribe the most fundamental principles … of a culture in seemingly innocuous details of bearing or physical and verbal manners, so putting them beyond the reach of consciousness and explicit statement.[148]

The physicality of the idea of *habitus* resonates with work on the self in the field of psychology,[149] and on embodied cognition,[150] and with neuroscientific work on neuroplasticity (the way the brain reshapes itself over the course of a person's life, even in adulthood, in response to changing circumstances).[151] Neuroplasticity has been connected with habit formation.[152] Significantly for the relationship between *habitus* and the narratives at work in a person's social field (narratives which, as discussed, can create a sense of the meaning of that world and embed its values), Bourdieu describes this physical state as 'political mythology realized, *em-bodied*, turned into a permanent disposition…'[153] Clearly, this is a profoundly different account of human behaviour from that assumed in economic man's rational utility maximisation. And yet, it recognises that narratives and models such as economic man can nonetheless become embodied so as to influence practice.

It is also inherent in the idea of *habitus* that it can change. Since *habitus* and a person's social field are deeply inter-related, change in one necessitates change in the other.[154] In stable conditions, changes in *habitus* are gradual.[155] However, changes can be more abrupt where there is some sort of crisis in a social field so that the 'game' is disrupted—where there is a re-evaluation (such as the re-evaluation discussed in Chap. 1), and a different set of meanings and values comes into play, such as those thrown into relief by recognition of a social licence. Then, since *habitus* involves developing a sense for the rules of the game, a person's *habitus* will need to change through practical experience in interaction with what has emerged. The crisis brings 'the undiscussed into discussion, the unformulated into formulation';[156] as noted in Chap. 4, recognition of a social licence does just that, throwing into a sharper relief a set of meanings and values in financial markets quite different from those assumed by the financial and economic narratives discussed in Chap. 1.[157] Yet there is inertia.[158] Since *habitus* is a set of 'durable dispositions', it can 'outlive the economic and social conditions' in which it was produced.[159] This resonates with the frequent observation that culture change in finance firms is a long-term process, and the idea that it rests not simply on consciously learning more rules, but something more physical, something that concerns the very substance of relationships and the way they are experienced and understood by the parties to them. The sort of behaviour change now needed requires this sort of re-formation.

6.6   Written Standards

Bourdieu did not especially have written standards in mind when he talked about the 'rules of the game'. Written standards are, nonetheless, part of those rules and, notwithstanding their limits, they clearly have an important role in changing behaviour. Chapter 4 suggested that they can be seen as part of a social licence for financial markets, and Chap. 5 noted that law, in particular, is commonly viewed as reaching towards a similar end: justice. How might the account of financial markets advanced by recognition of a social licence influence the use of written standards in meeting the challenges discussed in Chap. 1? What follows sketches a response to that.

Chapter 5 considered how negative and positive incentives attached to written standards are used to change behaviour. It also highlighted other ways in which written standards can influence behaviour. It particularly looked at 'aspirational standards': written standards that rely for their impact on engaging other-regarding aspiration. However, written standards can also influence behaviour in all of the ways discussed above: focusing people's attention on some motivating ends more than others;[160] framing the meaning of the social world people inhabit, and, particularly for law, actually defining what it means (see Sect. 2.2.3);[161] and influencing how people are formed.[162]

Because of that, the *content* of written standards, and *how they come to be followed* in practice, is important at many levels. However, both are influenced, in turn, by the wider framework of values and meanings that exist in the societies and groups that generate the standards, often carried in the form of social narratives. The account advanced by recognition of a social licence is one such framework. This section looks, firstly, at how these frameworks influence the content of written standards and, secondly, their impact on the way standards are followed.

It is well established that law and regulation is a storied process and that prevailing social narratives influence what laws and regulations are made, their substance and how they are applied and complied with:[163] 'No set of legal institutions or prescriptions exists apart from the narratives that locate it and give it meaning. For every constitution, there is an epic… law and narrative are inseparably related.'[164] Financial law and regulation is no exception.[165] There is also little reason why the same would not apply for written standards more widely. This narrative lens is not the only way of approaching written standards. However, again, it is useful in teasing out the potential impact of the recognition of a social licence.

6.6.1 The Social Licence and the Substance of Written Standards

Probably more than any other industry sector, the financial world, its meaning for people, is defined by law and regulations (see Sect. 2.2.3). They are used to structure markets, the instruments dealt through them and the legal entities that transact, and to regulate market behaviour (see Chap. 5). In addition to public law standards, market participants use private law arrangements such as contracts and trusts to structure their world;[166] lawyers helped to craft the financial world that collapsed in 2008.[167] As noted in Chap. 1, the toolbox of law and regulation has limitations; monumental regulatory reform has not secured the sort of behaviour change now needed. Nonetheless, laws and regulations and other sorts of written standard are clearly important in determining behaviour. Prevailing social narratives can affect the *substance* of these written standards in, broadly, two ways: firstly, by influencing what standards are created and what they say and, secondly, by affecting the way they are interpreted by courts, regulators and others who have originated them.

Express Content

Prevailing social narratives, economic narratives among them, affect the content of laws and regulations and private law structures. For example, the UK Financial Services and Markets Act 2000 reflects the kind of economic models discussed in Chap. 1 when it imposes a duty on UK regulators to promote competition in financial markets.[168] The preambles to legislative measures sometimes draw on these narratives, in telling the story of the purpose of the legislation.[169] The very process of legislation is storied. Just as case law can be thought of as a 'chain novel',[170] so can the emergence of legislation. For example, the mainstay of European Union financial market regulation, the Markets in Financial Instruments Directive[171] ('MiFID'), has been through various rounds of revision (including bifurcating into MiFID and the Markets in Financial Instruments Regulation ('MiFIR')[172]) and builds on the earlier Investment Services Directive.[173] This process has partly been driven by changing circumstances, but has also involved weighing up different accounts of the world; in the case of MiFID, visions for harmonised European markets, and the role of competition in particular.[174] Likewise, the economic models discussed in Chap. 1 lay behind legislation introduced at the time of the 1986 deregulation of the UK securities markets, known as the 'Big Bang'. They also led governments and regulators into sharing in Mr Greenspan's big mistake in the rules they created for financial firms (or chose not to) in the years preceding the financial crisis.

But prevailing narratives are not only relevant to public law standards. The multiple transactional relationships that comprise financial markets also carry stories. Much like the interaction between individual and group narratives (see Sect. 6.1), these develop in the context of and absorb aspects of broader prevailing narratives influencing both their substance and the ends at which they are directed. The relationships are generally enshrined in private law structures such as contracts and trusts, indeed snatches of their stories are sometimes explicitly stated in the 'recitals' at the start of some contracts.[175] Nor is the impact of narratives confined to written legal standards. For example, corporate codes of conduct and statements of purpose are often framed by introductions telling a story about what the company stands for, explaining the reason for the code and hence its content. Likewise codes issued by other bodies. As discussed in Chap. 4, these statements are influenced by what those inside and outside the relevant institution want to hear—prevailing social narratives.

Application

Social narratives also influence how courts and regulators apply law and regulation, and so the development of 'case law' and precedent. Like contracts, as noted in Chap. 4, all law is, in a sense, incomplete, and background values and understandings fill the gaps. Sometimes this is explicit. For example, the requirement on UK financial services regulators to act in a way that facilitates or promotes completion was noted above. It includes the way they apply their rules.[176] Particularly in construing statute, courts are subject to strict rules to ensure close adherence to meaning of the legislation. Nonetheless, judges and regulatory enforcement agencies unavoidably draw on background values and meanings in determining cases, a process which is itself fundamentally 'storied' as the parties to actions rehearse their competing narratives of events, potentially drawing on broader social narratives. Again, echoing the relationship between over-arching narratives and personal narratives (see Sect. 6.1), judicial and regulatory processes involve a weighing of these different stories by judges and regulators as a result of which a determination is reached; there is a 'complex interpenetration and cross-fertilization from the mainstream to the legal culture and vice versa'.[177]

There is a further interaction between law as developed by judges and market practice since courts sometimes draw on the latter in determining cases. However, market practices also often emerge as a result of a legal dialogue with practising lawyers who therefore indirectly shape the law. A well-known financial market example is the credit default swaps market in the UK, the development of which was substantially based on a 1997 legal opinion from Robin Potts QC to the effect that these instruments are not contracts of insurance.[178] However, much of the influence of private practice lawyers in the

development of practice is day to day, incremental and less dramatic in helping to design and document market structures and in navigating the boundar-
ies of law and regulation.[179] English contract law has been affected by these
processes and economic narratives in particular. Classical economic narratives
of the free market and perfect competition had a significant influence on
English lawyers and the judiciary in the nineteenth-century development of
the legal concept of freedom of contract.[180] From the same stable, a dominant
narrative in financial services contract law is that of arm's length dealings,
where the parties are treated as if they were strangers, acting in their own
interests, and owing no duties to each other, except the terms of their contract.[181] Elsewhere, research on the impact of US judges attending a particular
economics training programme between 1976 and 1999 has found that, following attendance, the judges used more economics language, rendered more
conservative verdicts in economics cases and imposed longer criminal sen-
tences.[182] It seems as if the experience may have formed them in a way that
affected how they applied the law. Likewise, a study of US case law between
1900 and 2016 has revealed how courts have come to embrace and apply the
principle that corporate managers should maximise shareholder wealth.[183]

6.6.2   The Social Licence and Following and Complying with Written Standards

But social narratives also materially influence how people *follow* and *comply*
with written standards. There are many examples, but two will suffice. Both
involve legal standards.

The first concerns the duties of those responsible for investing pension
funds and other pools of wealth ('institutional investors'), and whether they
should invest solely to achieve the best financial return, or whether they
should also take account of the environmental and social track record ('ESG')
of companies in which they invest. For example, an investment might look
financially attractive, but what if the company concerned destroys South
American rainforests? For many years, there has been confusion among institutional investors over whether they should invest solely to achieve the best
possible financial outcome and ignore factors such as these. As a legal matter,
the answer turns on the law in the jurisdiction in which they are located and
the precise terms of their appointment. However, the story of institutional
investors under English law is not dissimilar to that in other jurisdictions.

Noting confusion on the point, in 2004 the United Nations Environment
Programme Finance Initiative appointed law firm Freshfields Bruckhaus

Deringer to undertake an international survey to establish whether ESG integration into the investment process was legally permissible, legally required or hampered by law and regulation. Their report concluded, among other things, that integrating ESG considerations into investment analysis to predict financial performance more reliably is clearly permissible and is arguably required in all jurisdictions.[184] It also noted that, in some cases, it might be possible to go beyond that. In the UK at least, this seems to have come as something of a surprise. There, thinking was still dominated by the belief that investment should reference narrower financial considerations, echoing debates around shareholder value.

The Freshfields Report was reasonably clear, but apparently not clear enough for institutional investors. In 2011, the UK Government appointed economist John Kay to review the impact of UK equity market activity on the long-term performance and governance of UK quoted companies. In his report, he found it necessary to recommend that the English Law Commission should be asked 'to review the legal concept of fiduciary duty as applied to investment to address uncertainties and misunderstandings on the part of trustees and their advisers'.[185] The Law Commission was duly asked and also concluded, much as had Freshfields, that trustees should take account of factors that are 'financially material' to the performance of an investment, including ESG issues where trustees consider them 'financially material'.[186] It went on to confirm that while the pursuit of financial return should be the predominant concern of pension trustees, English law is sufficiently flexible to allow trustees to take other, subordinate, concerns into account subject to conditions. It put all this in a succinct guide for investors.[187]

That ought to have been it, but no. Another six years passed and following research by the UK Government Department of Work and Pensions, in February 2018 it concluded that pension fund trustees still did not understand the potential relevance of ESG factors in discharging their fiduciary duties: 'lack of attention and outright misunderstanding remain widespread …'[188] Thirteen years had passed since the Freshfields Report and apparently there was still investor nervousness on the point, even though it did not challenge the priority of financial return. What was going on was not so much based on the law, but prevailing social understandings.

The second example concerns the other side of the investment relationship: the duties of directors to their company. Until recently, these had come to be understood by reference to 'shareholder value', often in narrowly financial terms (see Sect. 1.1.2). Indeed, the relevant UK duty (in section 172 of the Companies Act 2006) is often described as taking an 'enlightened shareholder value' approach, apparently suggesting that the basic duty of directors is to pursue 'shareholder value'. However that is not what the relevant section says. It is a gloss provided by prevailing social narrative. A director of an English company is required to act in the way he or she considers, in good faith, would be most likely to promote the success of the company for the benefit of its members and in doing so have regard (amongst other matters) to various 'stakeholder' interests. The relevant section does not mention shareholder value. Nor does it stipulate how success is to be measured (although it is implicit in the notion of success that the company has a purpose against which it can be assessed) or how the benefit to members should be defined (whether financially or more widely). Indeed, government notes on section 172 emphasise this: 'The decision as to what will promote the success of the company, and what constitutes such success, is one for the director's good faith judgment.'[189] A similar interplay, between surrounding social norms and associated belief systems and legal standards, has been noted in the context of US corporate law.[190]

The idea of *habitus*, discussed above, can once again help in understanding what is going on here: how prevailing social understandings about values and meaning influence the way people follow rules and the formative impact that has on them.[191] Philosopher Charles Taylor looks at this in his essay, *To Follow a Rule*.[192] Taylor builds on Wittgenstein's discussion in *Philosophical Investigations* of what it means to 'understand' a rule. 'Understanding' a rule cannot involve each person going through a mental process every time they are presented with a decision to determine which out of the range of possible readings of the relevant rule is correct; identifying and assessing all of them, and the meanings and concepts needed to evaluate them, would be an enormous undertaking, in a sense stretching towards infinity, even for simple rules. Rather, Taylor suggests, adherence to a particular standard is based on an unarticulated background understanding that is 'taken for granted, just relied on' in deciding how to behave. This is the domain of a person's *habitus*.

What determines the person's response to a rule is their embedded sense for social situations: '… rules aren't self-interpreting; without a sense of what they're about, and an affinity to their spirit, they remain dead letters … This … can only exist … in our unformulated, embodied understanding … the domain of the habitus….'[193] Importantly, Taylor sees this process of rule following as being 'dialogical', or relational. It involves an integration of personal practice into common behavioural rhythms and the pursuit of common purposes, not a series of individual acts driven by an atomised, isolated deliberative process of weighing options. Two important changes take place as a result: firstly, a person's *habitus* is formed and re-formed (as to which, see above), but secondly, behavioural norms are transformed as well—there is a 'reciprocal relation between rule and action … the second doesn't just flow from the first but also transforms it'.[194] A person's action always carries the possibility of irreversible change, however, 'rule-guided' because a rule is not an unchanging formula, but exists 'in the practice it guides…'[195] Rules are subject to continual interpretation and reinterpretation in the course of practice so that 'If enough of us give a little "above" ourselves and our gesture is reciprocated, we will have altered the generally understood margins of tolerance for this kind of exchange…'[196]

From this perspective, greater recognition of a social licence has the potential to influence the dialogue by emphasising some meanings and values more than others and hence to impact behaviour. It also suggests that compliance with written standards should be seen as being as much about formation as enforcement. But what might greater recognition of a social licence mean for the operation of the various categories of written standards, identified in Chap. 5? The following draws out two broad areas of impact.

Re-purposing Written Standards

Firstly, the Written Standards Map in Chap. 5 gives a sense of the towering complexity of the financial services regulatory regime. The written standards that apply in financial markets are now so numerous and complex that they are becoming abstracted from any broader sense of purpose or context. Post-crisis regulatory reform has added another tranche of complexity.[197] This sort of abstraction can result in compliance developing into a self-contained exercise, increasing the likelihood of 'box ticking', or that a rule is intentionally or unintentionally 'gamed' by reference to a purpose different from what originally motivated its formulation. This has sometimes seemed to be the case, for example, in discussions with market participants over many years about whether receiving or making a given payment (such as a fee or commission) would breach MiFID rules restricting the provision or receipt of 'inducements' (payments or benefits from third parties) where these conflict with client interests.[198] Discussions of this sort start with a narrow focus on whether the relevant payment is within the precise terms of the rule, without recognising the wider context, including broader regulatory principles, for example, on the management of conflicts of interest and the fair treatment of customers and legal duties of loyalty to the client.

The UK financial regulatory regime does convey some limited sense of its purpose.[199] However, recognition of a social licence seems to reach beyond it. It offers the potential to 're-purpose' this multitude of written standards, placing them within a stronger framework of other-regarding outcomes, potentially increasing the likelihood that they are followed in accordance with their spirit. That may not come especially readily to those lawyers whose education has been influenced 'by legal formalism's banishment of all questions of … justice from the study and teaching of law'.[200] However, it is realistic. Observations like these can also cause lawyers to fret about the risk of legal uncertainty and the operation of the rule of law. Preserving both is enormously important, a point which is picked up in Chap. 7.

Aspirational Standards and Desired Ends

Secondly, for reasons discussed in Sect. 6.3.1, greater recognition of a social licence could also help to give greater aspirational force to the 'aspirational standards' identified in Chap. 5. These either explicitly reference other-regarding values or depend upon people's other-regarding values for their behavioural force, or both. Evidence for their impact on behaviour is mixed (see Sect. 5.2.4). However, they are arguably more dependent than other sorts of standards upon clarity about an over-arching aspired end, firstly, because they rely on the motivational force of aspiration and, secondly, because they leave more room for interpretation. Greater recognition of a social licence can potentially help with both.

In terms of the first, for example, corporate codes of behaviour are often seen as the Cinderella of written standards. Yet, paralleling the growth of regulatory rules, their use has increased substantially over the last thirty years, starting in the US but now extending into the UK, Europe and beyond.[201] Senior management attention to corporate codes in finance firms has sharpened in the aftermath of the financial crisis, along with work to strengthen governance and culture.[202] However, while these codes purport to articulate a firm's essential values, they tend to exist in a parallel universe. They rarely seem to be referenced in decision making 'on the ground', for example, where they clearly set a higher standard than the legal rules on which legal advice is being sought (although that does not necessarily mean that they have no subliminal impact). Since these codes are clearly not just about corporate window dressing, enhancing their effectiveness should be of interest to senior management, and the aspirational dimension of the social licence has a potential role to play. As noted in Chap. 4, codes could be viewed as partially articulating the basis on which the relevant firm understands its activities as being consistent with that licence. It may not be usual to see codes that way. However, it has been suggested that a reason that codes are not more effective is the lack of just this sort of 'social grammar', that 'the failure to acknowledge the crucial interdependency of business and society is instrumental in stripping codes of their potential significance and value'.[203] Greater recognition of a social licence for financial markets provides precisely that context.

Turning to the interpretation of aspirational standards, the UK Financial Conduct Authority recognises the merit of aspirational principles in encouraging market participants to exercise judgement about how they act, leaving them with greater responsibility for determining behaviour.[204] However, that makes the surrounding framework of meanings and values especially important for behavioural outcomes as compared with prescriptive standards. It follows from the discussion of rule following and *habitus*, above, that social meanings and values are always at work in the process of following rules, and forming those involved. No ground is neutral. However, the key question is which meanings and values. In financial markets, it might be tempting to assume that it is often those advanced by the sort of narratives considered in Chap. 1, but Chap. 3 made clear that the picture is much more complex. Within market participants' motivational mix, recognition of a social licence can help to emphasise meanings and values that reach towards justice.

6.7 Conclusion—'Social Control' and Individual Choice

Talk of influencing behaviour and individual and institutional formation raises questions of social control and individual choice. It is not feasible to address those in detail here. There are no simple answers. However, a few observations are appropriate.

Firstly, it follows from the above that people are always being influenced and formed by the groups they are in, including the written standards that apply to them. Most obviously, the advertising industry is devoted to manipulating behaviour in ways that suit its clients. The question is not whether people are being influenced and formed, but how and to what end. If it is right, for example, that the development of preferences is influenced by a person's social environment, we cannot duck the question of whether the formation of some preferences (such as the desire to help) is more desirable than others (such as the desire to murder). Chapter 4 argued that the formative end to which the social licence reaches is justice, involving a balanced mutuality in which the intrinsic value of each person is most fully realised in practice. There is plenty to suggest that this is consistent with common human aspirations, but it is fair to say that it is currently unclear whether there is a consensus that this should be the end of financial activity. This leads to the second point.

Much formation happens at a non-conscious level. However, recognition of a social licence makes something explicit, something that is inherently dialogic; greater recognition of a social licence means making relationships more visible, where they can be the subject of proper deliberation.[205] The next chapter discusses ways of doing that. Importantly, as discussed in Chap. 4, the idea that the social licence is 'social' means that market participants are a part of the societies that grant the licence; everyone can have a deliberative role. Discussion of 'deliberative democracy' sometimes has an air of unreality about it, especially when applied to something as complex as financial markets. Nonetheless, through deliberation, beliefs and valued ends can become clear and may change, potential conflicts can be resolved and consensuses can develop. That is important both as an end in itself and to inform the decisions of those (in a sense, everyone, but particularly senior management, policymakers and regulators) who must inevitably take decisions that affect others' freedom.

Thirdly, living in any group must involve some limit on negative freedom (i.e. freedom from any constraint). Discussion of individual freedom can sometimes assume that the implications of individual choice are confined to the individual, but that is clearly not so—witness the case of LIBOR manipulation discussed in Chap. 3. This is one reason why the end goal at which freedom is ultimately directed, the question of intrinsic desire, is so important. As discussed, the end to which the social licence seems to reach is justice, a balanced mutuality in which the human dignity of each person, to the extent dependent upon financial activity, is most fully realised in practice. Among other things, that is a situation in which freedom is realised in conditions in which it can be most fully enjoyed. It involves a recognition of the profound inter-dependency of market and non-market actors. In view of that end, the kind of framework advanced by discussion of a social licence should serve in many cases to increase, not reduce, individual and institutional freedoms, not least because of the way in which their enjoyment (such as having the confidence to try things that might fail, critical in risk-taking) relies on trust, generosity and reciprocity.[206]

Notes

1. Address delivered by President Abraham Lincoln at the dedication of the Soldiers' National Cemetery, Gettysburg, Pennsylvania, on 19 November 1863, from the version in Cornell University Library (http://rmc.library.cornell.edu/gettysburg/good_cause/transcript.htm).

2. Work in this area sometimes distinguishes between narratives and stories. Here, these expressions are used interchangeably.

3. Walter E. Fisher, *Narration as a Human Communication Paradigm: The Case of Public Moral Argument*, Communication Monographs, 1984, Vol. 51(1), 1–22, 2. There is no need to go as far as Fisher's 'narrative paradigm' to recognise the narrative in the speech.

4. Karla Hoff and Joseph E. Stiglitz, *Striving for Balance in Economics: Towards a Theory of Social Determination of Behavior*, Journal of Economic Behaviour and Organization, 2016, Vol. 126, 25–57, 28.

5. Jerome Bruner, *The Narrative Construction of Reality*, Critical Inquiry, 1991, Vol. 18(1), 1–21, 21. The following is not intended to advance a 'hard' constructionist approach, but does recognise the significant extent to which social reality is socially constructed.

6. Donald E. Polkinghorne, *Narrative Knowing and the Human Sciences* (State University of New York Press 1988), 18.

7. Marya Schechtman, 'The Narrative Self', in *The Oxford Handbook of the Self*, ed. Shaun Gallagher (Oxford University Press 2011).

8. Polkinghorne, *Narrative Knowing and the Human Sciences*, 155. Again, the following is not intended to advance a 'hard' constructionist approach to a person's identity.

9. Phillip L. Hammack, 'Mind, Story and Society: The Political Psychology of Narrative', in *Warring with Words: Narrative and Metaphor in Politics*, eds. Michael Hanne, William D. Crano and Jeffery Scott Mio (Psychology Press 2015).

10. David M. Boje, *Storytelling Organizations* (Sage Publications 2008); Yannis Gabriel, *Storytelling in Organizations: Facts, Fictions and Fantasies* (Oxford University Press 2000).

11. David Carr, *Narrative and the Real World: An Argument for Continuity*, History and Theory, 1986, Vol. 25(2), 117–131, 128.

12. Francesca Polletta, et al., *The Sociology of Storytelling*, Annual Review of Sociology, 2011, Vol. 37, 109–130, 114; David Boje, *Storytelling Organizations*; Gary Alan Fine, 'The Storied Group: Social Movements as "Bundles of Narratives"', in *Stories of Change: Narrative and Social Movements*, ed. Joseph E. Davis (State University of New York Press 2002).

13. Polkinghorne, *Narrative Knowing and the Human Sciences*, 150 et seq.; Molly Andrews, *Shaping History: Narratives of Political Change* (Cambridge

University Press 2007); Phillip L. Hammack, *Narrative and the Politics of Meaning*, Narrative Inquiry, 2011, Vol. 21(2), 311–318.

14. Carr, *Narrative and the Real World: An Argument for Continuity*, 130; Polletta, et al., *The Sociology of Storytelling*, 118.

15. Bruner, *The Narrative Construction of Reality*, 4.

16. Melanie C. Green and Timothy C. Brock, *The Role of Transportation in the Persuasiveness of Public Narrative*, Journal of Personality and Social Psychology, 2000, Vol. 79(5), 701–721; Rick Busselle and Helena Bilandzic, *Measuring Narrative Engagement*, Media Psychology, 2009, Vol. 12(4), 321–347.

17. Walter R. Fisher, *Human Communication as Narration: Toward a Philosophy of Reason, Value, and Action* (University of South Carolina Press 1987), 161.

18. Marshall Ganz, 'Public Narrative, Collective Action, and Power', in *Accountability Through Public Opinion: From Inertia to Public Action*, eds. Sina Odugbemi and Taeku Lee (World Bank 2011), 288.

19. See, for example, Phillip L. Hammack and Andrew Pilecki, *Narrative as a Root Metaphor for Political Psychology*, Political Psychology, 2012, Vol. 33(1), 75–103; Ralf Schmälzle, et al., *Engaged Listeners: Shared Neural Processing of Powerful Political Speeches*, Social Cognitive and Affective Neuroscience, 2015, Vol. 10(8), 1137–1143; Stefanie Hammer, *The Role of Narrative in Political Campaigning: An Analysis of Speeches by Barack Obama*, National Identities, 2010, Vol. 12(3), 269–290; Amy Skonieczny, *Emotions and Political Narratives: Populism, Trump and Trade*, Politics and Governance, 2018, Vol. 6(4), 62–72; Drew Westen, *The Political Brain: The Role of Emotion in Deciding the Fate of the Nation* (Public Affairs 2007).

20. Francesca Polletta, 'Plotting Protest', in *Stories of Social Change: Narrative and Social Movements*, ed. Joseph E. Davis (State University of New York Press 2002), 31; Ganz, *Public Narrative, Collective Action, and Power*.

21. Stephen Denning, *The Secret Language of Leadership: How Leaders Inspire Action Through Narrative* (Jossey-Bass 2007); John Marshall and Matthew Adamic, *The Story Is the Message: Shaping Corporate Culture*, Journal of Business Strategy, 2010, Vol. 31(2), 18–23; Michael S. Carriger, *Narrative Approach to Corporate Strategy: Empirical Foundations*, Journal of Strategy and Management, 2011, Vol. 4(4), 304–324.

22. For example, Jennifer Edson Escalas, *Narrative Processing: Building Consumer Connections to Brands*, Journal of Consumer Psychology, 2004, Vol. 14(1), 168–180; Chingching Chang, 'Narrative Advertisements and Narrative Processing', in *Advertising Theory*, eds. Shelly Rodgers and Esther Thorson (Routledge 2012).

23. Walter Hyll and Lutz Schneider, *The Causal Effect of Watching TV on Material Aspirations: Evidence from the "Valley of the Innocent"*, Journal of Economic Behavior and Organization, 2013, Vol. 86, 37–51; Peter Bönisch and Walter Hyll, *Television Role Models and Fertility – Evidence from a Natural*

Experiment, SOE Paper No. 752, 2015, available at https://ssrn.com/abstract=2611597

24. See, for example, Edgar Schein, *Organizational Culture and Leadership* (4th edn, Jossey-Bass 2010), 73 et seq.

25. See, for example, Michael Dahlén, Fredrik Lange and Terry Smith, *Marketing Communications: A Brand Narrative Approach* (John Wiley & Sons Ltd 2010); Stephen Denning, *The Leader's Guide to Storytelling: Mastering the Art and Discipline of Business Narrative* (revised edn, Jossey-Bass 2011), 109.

26. Colin Mayer, *Prosperity: Better Business Makes the Greater Good* (Oxford University Press 2018), 109–110.

27. See, for example, *The Future of Narrative Reporting: Consulting on a New Reporting Framework*, Department for Business, Innovation and Skills, September 2011.

28. See, for example, *Thinking of Floating? Considerations for Private and Family Owned Businesses*, PwC, https://www.pwc.co.uk/audit-assurance/assets/pdf/considerations-private-family-owned-businesses.pdf   (accessed   12 October, 2019).

29. Robert J. Shiller, *Narrative Economics: How Stories Go Viral & Drive Major Economic Events* (Princeton University Press 2019), 37.

30. Ibid.

31. Kaushik Basu, *Beyond the Invisible Hand: Groundwork for a New Economics* (Princeton University Press 2011), preface.

32. Alasdair MacIntyre, *After Virtue: A Study in Moral Theory* (3rd edn, Bloomsbury 2007), 216.

33. Reservations have been expressed about aspects of Fisher's 'narrative paradigm', including of 'narrative fidelity' (e.g. Barbara Warnick, *The Narrative Paradigm: Another Story*, Quarterly Journal of Speech, 1987, Vol. 73(2), 172–182). However, the basic distinction, used as a descriptive framework, provides a rough test for current purposes.

34. Fisher, *Human Communication as Narration*, 64.

35. Ibid., 64.

36. Ibid., 105.

37. Ibid., 109.

38. Francesca Polletta and Jessica Callahan, *Deep Stories, Nostalgia Narratives and Fake News: Storytelling in the Trump Era*, American Journal of Cultural Sociology, 2017, Vol. 5(3), 392–408, 394.

39. For example, Nomy Arpaly and Timothy Schroeder, *In Praise of Desire* (Oxford University Press 2014), 101–102, 126 et seq., 136; Peter Railton, 'Learning as an Inherent Dynamic of Belief and Desire', in *The Nature of Desire*, eds. Federico Lauria and Julien A. Deonna (Oxford University Press 2017), 249, 270.

40. See, for example, Samuel Bowles, *Endogenous Preferences: The Cultural Consequences of Markets and Other Economic Institutions*, Journal of

Economic Literature, 1998, Vol. 36(1), 75–111; Margit Osterloh and Bruno S. Frey, 'Motivation Governance', in *Handbook of Economic Organization: Integrating Economic and Organization Theory*, ed. Anna Grandori (Edward Elgar 2013); Franz Dietrich and Christian List, *Where Do Preferences Come from?* International Journal of Game Theory, 2013, Vol. 42(3), 613–637.

41. See, for example, Ellen Peters, 'The Functions of Affect in the Construction of Preferences', in *The Construction of Preference*, eds. Sarah Lichtenstein and Paul Slovic (Cambridge University Press 2006).

42. Bowles, *Endogenous Preferences*; Hoff and Stiglitz, *Striving for Balance in Economics*.

43. Shalom H. Schwartz, *Les Valeurs de Base de la Personne: Théorie, Mesures et Application*, Revue Française de Sociologie, 2006, Vol. 47(4), 929–968, 953.

44. Ganz, *Public Narrative, Collective Action, and Power*, 278; see also Jesse J. Prinz and Shaun Nichols, 'Moral Emotions', in *The Moral Psychology Handbook*, eds. John M. Doris, et al. (Oxford University Press 2010), 131–132.

45. See, generally, Russell S. Cropanzano and Maureen L. Ambrose, *The Oxford Handbook of Justice in the Workplace* (Oxford University Press 2015).

46. See, for example, *The Ethics of Pay in a Fair Society, What Do Executives Think?* (PwC 2017), available at https://www.pwc.com/gx/en/people-organisation/pdf/pwc-fair-pay.pdf (accessed 12 October 2019).

47. Ruth Yeoman, et al., eds. *Oxford Handbook of Meaningful Work* (Oxford University Press 2019), 6; Brent D. Russo, Kathryn H. Dekas and Amy Wrzesniewski, *On the Meaning of Work: A Theoretical Integration and Review*, Research in Organizational Behavior, 2010, Vol. 30, 91–127, 117.

48. Understood as a calling towards activities that are morally, socially and personally significant: Russo, Dekas and Wrzesniewski, *On the Meaning of Work*, 99.

49. Amy Wrzesniewski, 'Finding Positive Meaning in Work', in *Positive Organizational Scholarship: Foundations of a New Discipline*, eds. Kim S. Cameron, Jane E. Dutton and Robert E. Quinn (Berrett-Koehler 2003).

50. Rosso, Dekas and Wrzesniewski, *On the Meaning of Work*, 96; Mark C. Bolino and Adam M. Grant, *The Bright Side of Being Prosocial at Work, and the Dark Side, Too*, The Academy of Management Annals, 2016, Vol. 10(1), 599–670; Eugene Tartakovsky and Eti Cohen, *Values in the Bank: Value Preferences of Bank Frontline Workers and Branch Managers*, European Journal of Work and Organizational Psychology, 2014, Vol. 23(5), 769–782.

51. Amy Wrzesniewski, *Finding Positive Meaning in Work*.

52. Bolino and Grant, *The Bright Side of Being Prosocial at Work*; Adam M. Grant, *Relational Job Design and the Motivation to Make a Prosocial Difference*, Academy of Management Review, 2007, Vol. 32(2), 393–417.

53. Jonathan E. Booth, Kyoung Won Park and Theresa M. Glomb, *Employer-Supported Volunteering Benefits: Gift Exchange Among Employers, Employees, and Volunteer Organizations*, Human Resource Management, 2009, Vol. 48(2), 227–249.

54. Adam M. Grant, *Giving Time, Time After Time: Work Design and Sustained Employee Participation in Corporate Volunteering*, The Academy of Management Review, 2012, Vol. 37(4), 589–615; Jessica B. Rodell, *Finding Meaning Through Volunteering: Why Do Employees Volunteer and What Does It Mean for Their Jobs?* Academy of Management Journal, 2013, Vol. 56(5), 1274–1294. However, the number who regard their work as 'socially useless' may be relatively small: Robert Dur and Max van Lent, *Socially Useless Jobs*, Industrial Relations, 2019, Vol. 58(1), 3–16.

55. https://www.bitc.org.uk/programmes/engage/engage-toolkit/employee-community-engagement/what-are-benefits-employees (accessed 12 October 2019).

56. Polletta, *Plotting Protest*, 36.

57. Denning, *The Secret Language of Leadership*, xxii.

58. Denning, *The Secret Language of Leadership*, 168–169.

59. Russo, Dekas and Wrzesniewski, *On the Meaning of Work*; Adam M. Grant, *Leading with Meaning: Beneficiary Contact, Prosocial Impact, and the Performance Effects of Transformational Leadership*, Academy of Management Journal, 2012, Vol. 55(2), 458–476.

60. B. Douglas Bernheim, *A Theory of Conformity*, Journal of Political Economy, 1994, Vol. 102(5), 841–877; Robert Akerlof, *Value Formation: The Role of Esteem*, Games and Economic Behavior, 2017, Vol. 102, 1–19.

61. But not necessarily a causal link: Rebecca Sanderson et al., *Strangers in a Strange Land: Relations Between Perceptions of Others' Values and Both Civic Engagement and Cultural Estrangement*, Frontiers in Psychology, 2019, Vol. 10, Article 559.

62. Ryan D. Duffy, Jessica W. England and Bryan J. Dik, 'Callings', in *The Oxford Handbook of Meaningful Work*, eds. Ruth Yeoman, et al. (Oxford University Press 2019).

63. Bradley E. Wright, *Public Service and Motivation: Does Mission Matter?* Public Administration Review, 2007, Vol. 67(1), 54–64; Yousueng Han, *Is Public Service Motivation Changeable? Integrative Modeling with Goal-Setting Theory*, International Journal of Public Administration, 2018, Vol. 41(3), 216–225.

64. Anat Bardi and Shalom H. Schwartz, *Values and Behavior: Strength and Structure of Relations*, Personality and Social Psychology Bulletin, 2003, Vol. 29(10), 1207–1220.

65. Scott Sonenshein, *Crafting Social Issues at Work*, Academy of Management Journal, 2006, Vol. 49(6), 1158–1172.

66. David M. Mayer, et al., *The Money or the Morals? When Moral Language Is More Effective for Selling Social Issues*, Journal of Applied Psychology, 2019, Vol. 104(8), 1058–1076.

67. Russo, Dekas and Wrzesniewski, *On the Meaning of Work*, 104.

68. Arjun Appadurai, 'The Capacity to Aspire: Culture and the Terms of Recognition', in *Culture and Public Action*, eds. Vijayendra Rao and Michael Walton (Stanford University Press 2004).

69. Pamela Hanrahan, *Corporate Governance, Financial Institutions and the "Social Licence"*, Law and Financial Markets Review, 2016, Vol. 10(3), 123–126.

70. Speech by David Cameron, New Zealand House, London, 19 January 2012, https://www.newstatesman.com/uk-politics/2012/01/economy-capi-talism-market (accessed 12 October 2019). The leader of the Labour opposition swiftly followed with his own version.

71. Undertaken on 27 August 2019.

72. Martin Tanis and Tom Postmes, *A Social Identity Approach to Trust: Interpersonal Perception, Group Membership and Trusting Behaviour*, European Journal of Social Psychology, 2005, Vol. 35, 413–424, 414; Ananthi Al Ramiah and Miles Hewstone, *Intergroup Contact as a Tool for Reducing, Resolving and Preventing Intergroup Conflict: Evidence, Limitations and Potential*, American Psychologist, 2013, Vol. 68(7), 527–542.

73. Hoff and Stiglitz, *Striving for Balance in Economics*, 38.

74. Daniel C. Batson, *Altruism in Humans* (Oxford University Press 2011), 12 et seq.

75. Batson, *Altruism in Humans*; Grant, *Relational Job Design and the Motivation to Make a Prosocial Difference*; Iris Bohnet and Bruno S. Frey, *Social Distance and Other Regarding Behavior in Dictator Games: Comment*, American Economic Review, 1999, Vol. 89(1), 335–339.

76. Grant, *Leading with Meaning*.

77. Batson, *Altruism in Humans*, 33 et seq.

78. Jamil Zaki, Niall Bolger and Kevin Ochsner, *It Takes Two: The Interpersonal Nature of Empathic Accuracy*, Psychological Science, 2008, Vol. 19(4), 399–404, provides experimental support at an individual level.

79. Vern L. Glaser et al., 'Institutional Frame Switching: How Institutional Logics Shape Individual Action', in *How Institutions Matter!* Research in the Sociology of Organizations, eds. Joel Gehman, Michael Lounsbury and Royston Greenwood (Emerald Group Publishing Limited 2017), Vol. 48A, 35–69.

80. Paul DiMaggio, *Culture and Cognition*, Annual Review of Psychology, 1997, Vol. 23, 263–287, 274.

81. Matteo M. Galizzi and Daniel Navarro-Martínez, *On the External Validity of Social Preference Games: A Systematic Lab-Field Study*, Management Science, 2019, Vol. 65(3), 976–1002.

82. Varda Liberman, Steven M. Samuels and Lee Ross, *The Name of the Game: Predictive Power of Reputations* Versus *Situational Labels in Determining Prisoner's Dilemma Game Moves*, Personality and Social Psychology Bulletin, 2004, Vol. 30(9), 1175–1185.

83. Tore Ellingsen, et al., *Social Framing Effects: Preferences or Beliefs?* Games and Economic Behaviour, 2012, Vol. 76(1), 117–130; Elizabeth Bernold, et al., *Social Framing and Cooperation: The Roles and Interaction of Preferences and Beliefs*, (30 January 2015), available at SSRN: https://ssrn.com/abstract=2557927

84. Bernold, et al., *Social Framing and Cooperation: The Roles and Interaction of Preferences and Beliefs*.

85. Glaser, et al., *Institutional Frame Switching*, 37.

86. Urs Fischbacher, Simon Gächter and Ernst Fehr, *Are People Conditionally Cooperative? Evidence from a Public Goods Experiment*, Economics Letters, 2001, Vol. 71(3), 397–404.

87. Martin Dufwenberg, Simon Gächter and Heike Hennig-Schmidt, *The Framing of Games and the Psychology of Play*, Games and Economic Behavior, 2011, Vol. 73(2), 459–478. The first iteration of their experiment was in Germany where the use of the word 'community' had connotations of individualism. In that context, first- and second-order beliefs and contributions were less generous under the community frame than under the neutral frame. However, when the experiment was repeated in Switzerland (where 'community' did not have the same connotations), the effect was reversed.

88. Bernold, et al., *Social Framing and Cooperation: The Roles and Interaction of Preferences and Beliefs*.

89. Ibid., 22.

90. But there are likely to be limits. For example, positive framing alone may not solve so-called 'tragedy of the commons' situations: Elisabeth Thuestad Isaksen, Kjell Arne Brekke and Andries Richter, *Positive Framing Does Not Solve the Tragedy of the Commons*, Journal of Environmental Economics and Management, 2019, Vol. 95, 45–56.

91. Kathleen D. Vohs, Nicole L. Mead and Miranda R. Goode, *Merely Activating the Concept of Money Changes Personal and Interpersonal Behavior*, Current Directions in Psychological Science, 2008, Vol. 17(3), 208–212; Kathleen D. Vohs, *Money Priming Can Change People's Thoughts, Feelings, Motivations, and Behaviors: An Update on 10 Years of Experiments*, Journal of Experimental Psychology: General, 2015, Vol. 144(4), e86–e93.

92. Eugene M. Caruso, Oren Shapira and Justin F. Landy, *Show Me the Money: A Systematic Exploration of Manipulations, Moderators, and Mechanisms of Priming Effects*, Psychological Science, 2017, Vol. 28(8), 1148–1159; Paul Lodder et al., *A Comprehensive Meta-Analysis of Money Priming*, Journal of Experimental Psychology: General, 2019, Vol. 148(4), 688–712; Doug Rohrer, Harold Pashler and Christine R. Harris, *Discrepant Data and Improbable Results: An Examination of Vohs, Mead, and Goode* (2006), Basic and Applied Social Psychology, 2019, Vol. 41(4), 263–271.

93. Andrew L. Molinsky, Adam M. Grant and Joshua D. Margolis, *The Bedside Manner of Homo Economicus: How and Why Priming an Economic Schema Reduces Compassion*, Organizational Behavior and Human Decision Processes, 2012, Vol. 119(1), 27–37.

94. Xin Ziqiang and Liu Guofang, *Homo Economicus Belief Inhibits Trust*, PLoS ONE, 2013, Vol. 8(10), E76671.

95. Joseph Henrich et al., *In Search of Homo Economicus: Behavioral Experiments in 15 Small-Scale Societies*, American Economic Review, 2001, Vol. 91(2), 73–78.

96. Alain Cohn, Ernst Fehr and Michel André Maréchal, *Business Culture and Dishonesty in the Banking Industry*, Nature, 2014, Vol. 516, 86–89.

97. Jean-Michel Hupé, *Shortcomings of Experimental Economics to Study Human Behavior: A Reanalysis of Cohn et al. 2014, Nature 516, 86–89, 'Business Culture and Dishonesty in the Banking Industry'*, SocArXiv, 22 March 2018, https://doi.org/10.31235/osf.io/nt6xk

98. Marek A.Vranka and Petr Houdek, *Many Faces of Bankers' Identity: How (Not) to Study Dishonesty*, Frontiers in Psychology, 2015, Vol. 6, Article 302.

99. Karl Aquino, et al., *Testing a Social-Cognitive Model of Moral Behavior: The Interactive Influence of Situations and Moral Identity Centrality*, Journal of Personality and Social Psychology, 2009, Vol. 97(1), 123–141.

100. This book generally avoids the expressions 'extrinsic' and 'intrinsic' motivation. The distinction may be helpful analytically, but risks creating a false dichotomy; ultimately, motivation is the force that drives all goal-directed behaviour and may be influenced by a range of external factors.

101. Samuel Bowles and Sung-Ha Hwang, *Social Preferences and Public Economics: Mechanism Design When Social Preferences Depend upon Incentives*, Journal of Public Economics, 2008, Vol. 92(8–9), 1811–1820.

102. See, for example, Ernst Fehr and Armin Falk, *Psychological Foundations of Incentives*, Institute for Empirical Research in Economics, European Economic Review, 2002, Vol. 46(4), 687–724; Agnès Festré and Pierre Garrouste, *Theory and Evidence in Psychology and Economics About Motivation Crowding Out: A Possible Convergence?* Journal of Economic Surveys, 2015, Vol. 29(2), 339–356.

103. Uri Gneezy and Aldo Rustichini, *A Fine Is a Price*, Journal of Legal Studies, 2000, Vol. 29(1), 1–17.

104. Christopher Blattman, Julian C. Jamison and Margaret Sheridan, *Reducing Crime and Violence: Experimental Evidence from Cognitive Behavioral Therapy in Liberia*, American Economic Review, 2017, Vol. 107(4), 1165–1206.

105. Ola Kvaløy, Petra Nieken and Anja Schöttner, *Hidden Benefits of Reward: A Field Experiment on Motivation and Monetary Incentives*, European Economic Review, 2015, Vol. 76, 188–199.

106. Barbara Rogoff, *The Cultural Nature of Human Development* (Oxford University Press 2003).

107. Hoff and Stiglitz, *Striving for Balance in Economics*, 26, original emphasis.
108. Bowles, *Endogenous Preferences*, 80.
109. *Transforming culture in financial services*, speech by Andrew Bailey while Chief Executive of the Financial Conduct Authority, 19 March 2018 (emphasis added).
110. Mark Granovetter, *Economic Action and Social Structure: The Problem of Embeddedness*, American Journal of Sociology, 1985, Vol. 91(3), 481–510, 486.
111. *Mind, Society, and Behavior*, World Bank 2015, 13, talking of development activities, but the point has wider application.
112. Formation, formazione and formación respectively.
113. *Ethics and finance—aligning financial incentives with societal objectives*, speech by Christine Lagarde while Managing Director of the International Monetary Fund, 6 May 2015.
114. *Trust and ethics—a regulator's perspective*, speech by Andrew Bailey while Chief Executive of the Financial Conduct Authority, 16 October 2018.
115. Stephen Stich, John M. Doris and Erica Roedder, 'Altruism', in *The Moral Psychology Handbook*, eds. John M. Doris, et al. (Oxford University Press 2010), 195, seems to be describing something of this sort in relation to the habituation of instrumental desires.
116. Charles Taylor, 'To Follow a Rule', in *Philosophical Arguments* (Harvard University Press 1995).
117. Simon Niklas Hellmich, *Are People Trained in Economics "Different," and if so, Why? A Literature Review*, The American Economist, 2019, Vol. 64(2), 246–268.
118. Gerald Marwell and Ruth E. Ames, *Economists Free Ride, Does Anyone Else? Experiments on the Provision of Public Goods, IV*, Journal of Public Economics, 1981, Vol. 15(3), 295–310; John R. Carter and Michael D. Irons, *Are Economists Different, and if so, Why?* Journal of Economic Perspectives, 1991, Vol. 5(2), 171–177; Neil Gandal, et al., *Personal Value Priorities of Economists*, Human Relations, 2005, Vol. 58(10), 1227–1252.
119. Robert H. Frank, Thomas Gilovich and Dennis T. Regan, *Does Studying Economics Inhibit Cooperation?* The Journal of Economic Perspectives, 1993, Vol. 7(2), 159–171, but note Anthony M. Yezer, Robert S. Goldfarb and Paul J. Poppen, *Does Studying Economics Discourage Cooperation? Watch What We Do, Not What We Say or How We Play*, Journal of Economic Perspectives, 1996, Vol. 10(1), 177–186.
120. Long Wang, Deepak Malhotra and J. Keith Murnighan, *Economics Education and Greed*, Academy of Management Learning and Education, 2011, Vol. 10(4), 643–660.
121. Wang, Malhotra and Murnighan, *Economics Education and Greed*.
122. Frank, Gilovich and Regan, *Does Studying Economics Inhibit Cooperation?*; Björn Frank and Günther G. Schulze, *Does Economics Make Citizens*

Corrupt?, Journal of Economic Behavior and Organization, 2000, Vol. 43(1), 101–113; Tobias Lundquist, et al., *The Aversion to Lying*, Journal of Economic Behavior and Organization, 2009, Vol. 70(1–2), 81–92.

123. Matthias P. Hühen, *You Reap What You Sow: How MBA Programs Undermine Ethics*, Journal of Business Ethics, 2014, Vol. 121(4), 527–541.

124. M. Lynnette Smyth and James R. Davis, *Perceptions of Dishonesty Among Two-Year College Students: Academic Versus Business Situations*, Journal of Business Ethics, 2004, Vol. 51(1), 63–73.

125. It is not feasible to go into all of the possible alternative explanations here, for example, to do with how the studies were undertaken or the operation of social stereotypes.

126. Examples of studies that suggest nature over nurture include Yezer, Goldfarb and Poppen, *Does Studying Economics Discourage Cooperation?*; Frank and Schulze, *Does Economics Make Citizens Corrupt?*; Bruno S. Frey and Stephan Meier, *Are Political Economists Selfish and Indoctrinated? Evidence from a Natural Experiment*, Economic Inquiry, 2003, Vol. 41(3), 448–462; Gandal et al., *Personal Value Priorities of Economists*; Yoram Bauman and Elaina Rose, *Selection or Indoctrination: Why Do Economics Students Donate Less Than the Rest?* Journal of Economic Behavior and Organization, 2011, Vol. 79(3), 318–327.

127. Hellmich, *Are People Trained in Economics "Different," and if so, Why?*.

128. Gandal, et al., *Personal Value Priorities of Economists*; Amy Wrzesniewski, et al., *Jobs, Careers, and Callings: People's Relations to Their Work*, Journal of Research in Personality, 1997, Vol. 31(1), 21–33.

129. Gandal, et al., *Personal Value Priorities of Economists*.

130. Donald MacKenzie, *An Engine, Not a Camera: How Financial Models Shape Markets* (The MIT Press 2006), 12. See also Gerald Faulhaber and William Baumol, *Economists as Innovators: Practical Products of Theoretical Research*, Journal of Economic Literature, 1988, Vol. 26, 577–600.

131. MacKenzie, *An Engine, Not a Camera*, 250.

132. Gerald F. Davis, *Managed by the Markets: How Finance Re-shaped America* (Oxford University Press 2009).

133. Bowles, *Endogenous Preferences*.

134. Frank Trentmann, *The Empire of Things: How We Became a World of Consumers, from the Fifteenth Century to the Twenty-First* (Allen Lane 2016).

135. Gneezy and Rustichini, *A Fine Is a Price*, 16.

136. Blattman, Jamison and Sheridan, *Reducing Crime and Violence: Experimental Evidence from Cognitive Behavioral Therapy in Liberia*.

137. Arpaly and Schroeder, *In Praise of Desire*, 126 et seq. It is not intended to suggest here that formation is limited to reinforcement.

138. Timothy D. Hackenberg, *Token Reinforcement: Translational Research and Application*, Journal of Applied Behavior Analysis, 2018, Vol. 51(2), 393–435.

139. Indeed, crypto currencies are sometimes described in terms of tokens. See, for example, Sabrina T. Howell, Marina Niessner and David Yermack, *Initial Coin Offerings: Financing Growth with Cryptocurrency Token Sales*, ECGI Finance Working Paper No. 564/2018, July 2018.

140. The following is no more than a summary of features of Bourdieu's concept of *habitus* that are useful in the current context. It is based largely on how he approaches it in his book *The Logic of Practice*. A wider assessment of *habitus* and of Bourdieu's theory of practice more generally for the recognition of a social licence lies outside the current exercise.

141. Pierre Bourdieu, *Le Sens Pratique* (Les Éditions Minuit 1980). Quotations taken from the English language edition, *The Logic of Practice*, translated by Richard Nice (Polity Press 1990), 53.

142. Ibid., 54.

143. Ibid., 56.

144. Pierre Bourdieu, *Esquisse d'une Théorie de la Pratique: Précédé de Trois Études D'ethnologie Kabyle* (Librairie Droz 1972). Quotations taken from the English language edition, *Outline of a Theory of Practice*, translated by Richard Nice (Cambridge University Press 1977) 79.

145. Ibid., 77.

146. Bourdieu, *The Logic of Practice*, 66.

147. Ibid., 68.

148. Ibid., 69. Discussion of 'adaptive preferences' seems to pick up on something of this sort in highlighting how social context affects the goals it is possible for a person to conceive of, even where the goal concerns what is just: Jessica Begon, *What Are Adaptive Preferences? Exclusion and Disability in the Capability Approach*, Journal of Applied Philosophy, 2015, Vol. 32(3), 241–257; Dale Dorsey, *Adaptive Preferences Are a Red Herring*, Journal of the American Philosophical Association, 2017, Vol. 3(4), 465–484. See also Arjun Appadurai, *The Capacity to Aspire: Culture and the Terms of Recognition*. Schwartz, *Les Valeurs de Base de la Personne: Théorie, Mesures et Application*, 949–950, also highlights the way in which values may adapt to life circumstances.

149. See, for example, Hazel Rose Markus and Shinobu Katayama, *Cultures and Selves: A Cycle of Mutual Constitution*, Perspectives on Psychological Science, 2010, Vol. 5(4), 420–430.

150. Andrea Bender and Sieghard Beller, *Cognition is … Fundamentally Cultural*, Behavioural Sciences, 2013, Vol. 3(1), 42–54; Andrew D. Wilson and Sabrina Golonka, *Embodied Cognition Is Not What You Think It Is*, Frontiers in Psychology, 2013, Vol. 4, Article 58.

151. See, for example, Kyle S. Smith and Ann M. Graybiel, *Habit Formation*, Dialogues in Clinical Neuroscience, 2016, Vol. 18(1), 33–43. On the impact of culture on cognition, see Margaret Wilson, *The Re-tooled Mind:*

How Culture Re-engineers Cognition, Social Cognitive and Affective Neuroscience, 2010, Vol. 5(2–3), 180–187.

152. Clare Carlisle, *On Habit* (Routledge 2014), 21 et seq.

153. Ibid., 69–70. Jerome Bruner, *Life as Narrative*, Social Research, 2004, Vol. 71(3), 691–710, also makes a connection between narratives and the structuring of people's lives.

154. Cheryl Hardy, 'Hysteresis', in *Pierre Bourdieu: Key Concepts*, ed. Michael Grenfell (2nd edn, Routledge 2014).

155. Bourdieu, *The Logic of Practice*, 60.

156. Bourdieu, *Outline of a Theory of Practice*, 168.

157. The possibility of forming this sort of behavioural predisposition in financial markets is posited by Nava Ashraf and Oriana Bandiera, *Altruistic Capital*, American Economic Review, 2017, Vol. 107(5), 70–75. The possibility that large-scale cultural changes may be caused by large-scale, more or less simultaneous frame switches by many interdependent actors is recognised by Paul DiMaggio, *Culture and Cognition*, 280.

158. Again, this resonates with work in the fields of psychology and neurology. See Bruce E. Wexler, *Brain and Culture: Neurobiology, Ideology, and Social Change* (MIT Press 2006).

159. Bourdieu, *The Logic of Practice*, 62.

160. Samuel Bowles and Sandra Polanía-Reyes, *Economic Incentives and Social Preferences: Substitutes or Complements*, Journal of Economic Literature, 2012, Vol. 50(2), 368–425.

161. Cass R. Sunstein, *On the Expressive Function of Law*, University of Pennsylvania Law Review, 1996, Vol. 144(5), 2021–2053; Kaushik Basu, *The Republic of Beliefs: A New Approach to Law and Economics* (Princeton University Press 2018); Geoffrey Brennan, et al., *Explaining Norms* (Oxford University Press 2016), 156 et seq.

162. Oren Bar-Gill and Chaim Fershtman, *Law and Preferences*, The Journal of Law, Economics, and Organization, 2004, Vol. 20(2), 331–352.

163. Robert M. Cover, *Nomos and Narrative*, Harvard Law Review, 1983, Vol. 97(1), 4–68; Michael Hanne and Robert Weisberg, *Narrative and Metaphor in the Law* (Cambridge University Press 2018). See also Timothy Macklem, *Law and Life in Common* (Oxford University Press 2015). Written standards can also become part of and define a national, institutional or personal narrative (e.g. Magna Carta) so shaping a behaviour in the present, as to which, see below.

164. Cover, *Nomos and Narrative*, 4, 5.

165. Joanna Benjamin, *The Narratives of Financial Law*, Oxford Journal of Legal Studies, 2010, Vol. 30(4), 787–814.

166. These expressions are used loosely. See discussion of public and private law in Chap. 5.

167. David Howarth, *Law as Engineering: Thinking About What Lawyers Do* (Edward Elgar 2013); MacKenzie, *An Engine, Not a Camera*.

168. Sections 1B, 1E and 2H, Financial Services and Markets Act 2000.

169. See, for example, Recital 164 of Directive 2014/65/EU of the European Parliament and of the Council on markets in financial instruments ('MiFID') which states that the purpose of the directive is 'creating an integrated financial market in which investors are effectively protected and the efficiency and integrity of the overall market are safeguarded'.

170. Ronald Dworkin, *Law's Empire* (Belknap Press of Harvard University Press 1986), 229.

171. Directive 2014/65/EU of the European Parliament and of the Council on markets in financial instruments.

172. Regulation (EU) No 600/2014 of the European Parliament and of the Council on markets in financial instruments.

173. Council Directive 93/22/EEC on investment services in the securities field.

174. *Markets in Financial Instruments Directive (MiFID): Frequently Asked Questions*, EU Commission, 29 October 2007, MEMO/07/439.

175. MacKenzie, *An Engine, Not a Camera*.

176. Sections 1B, 1E and 2H, Financial Services and Markets Act 2000.

177. Richard K. Sherwin, *The Narrative Construction of Legal Reality*, Vermont Law Review, 1994, Vol. 18, 681–719.

178. John Kay, *Other People's Money: Masters of the Universe or Servants of the People* (Profile Books 2015) 119. The opinion was obtained by ISDA and is not available to the public.

179. Howarth, *Law as Engineering*; John C. Coffee, *Gatekeepers: The Professions and Corporate Governance* (Oxford University Press 2006).

180. Patrick S. Atiyah, *The Rise and Fall of Freedom of Contract* (Clarendon Press Oxford 1979).

181. Benjamin, *The Narratives of Financial Law*, 793.

182. Elliott Ash, Daniel L. Chen and Suresh Naidu, *Ideas Have Consequences*, ETH Zurich, Centre for Law and Economics, Working Paper Series No. 04/2019; see also Robert Cooter, *Do Good Laws Make Good Citizens? An Economic Analysis of Internalized Norms*, Virginia Law Review, 2000, Vol. 86(8), 1577–1601, 1599.

183. Robert J. Rhee, *A Legal Theory of Shareholder Primacy*, Minnesota Law Review, 2018, 1951–2017.

184. *A Legal Framework for the Integration of Environmental, Social and Governance Issues into Institutional Investment*, October 2005 (the 'Freshfields Report'), 13.

185. *The Kay Review of UK Equity Markets and Long-Term Decision Making*, Final Report, July 2012, 13.

186. *Fiduciary Duties of Intermediaries Report*, Law Commission of England and Wales, 1 July 2014.

187. *"Is it always about the money?" Pension trustees' duties when setting an investment strategy: Guidance from the Law Commission*, Law Commission of England and Wales, 1 July 2014.
188. Letter from Guy Opperman MP, Minister of Pensions to Mary Creagh MP, Chair, Environmental Audit Committee, House of Commons, 15 February 2018, available at https://www.parliament.uk/documents/commons-committees/environmental-audit/180215-Guy-Opperman-to-Chair-Green-Finance.pdf (accessed 30 September 2019).
189. https://www.legislation.gov.uk/ukpga/2006/46/notes/division/6/2 (accessed 30 September 2019).
190. Melvin A. Eisenberg, *Corporate Law and Social Norms*, Columbia Law Review, 1999, Vol. 99, 1253–1292, especially 1278 et seq.
191. On the impact of individual behaviours on that of groups, and legal vehicles such as companies, see Chap. 2. An assessment of Bourdieu's broader work on the force of law is beyond the scope of the current exercise. The following is not intended to address the debate on rule following, provoked by Ludwig Wittgenstein in his *Philosophical Investigations* and elaborated upon by Saul Kripke, *Wittgenstein on Rules and Private Language: An Elementary Exposition* (Harvard University Press 1982).
192. Taylor, *To Follow a Rule.*
193. Ibid., 179.
194. Ibid., 176.
195. Ibid., 178.
196. Ibid., 178.
197. Zahid Amadxarif, et al., *The Language of Rules: Textual Complexity in Banking Reforms*, Staff Working Paper No. 834, Bank of England 2019.
198. Currently Article 24 of Directive 2014/65/EU of the European Parliament and of the Council on markets in financial instruments.
199. See, in particular, the Financial Conduct Authority's statutory objectives in sections 1B to 1G and the Prudential Regulation Authority's statutory objectives in sections 2B and 2C of the Financial Services and Markets Act 2000, and the over-arching regulatory principles of each regulator.
200. Donald Nicholson, *Making Lawyers Moral? Ethical Codes and Moral Character*, Legal Studies, 2005, Vol. 25(4), 601–626. Legal formalism has been described as 'a theory of adjudication according to which (1) the law is rationally determinate, and (2) judging is mechanical. It follows from (1), that (3) legal reasoning is autonomous, since the class of legal reasons suffices to justify a unique outcome; no recourse to non-legal reasons is demanded or required' (Brian Leiter, *Positivism, Formalism, Realism: 'Legal Positivism in American Jurisprudence,' Anthony Sebok (book review)*, Columbia Law Review, 1999, Vol. 99(4), 1138–1164).
201. Brian Farrell, Deirdre Cobbin and Helen Farrell, *Codes of Ethics—Their Evolution, Development and Other Controversies*, Journal of Management

Development, 2002, Vol. 21(2), 152–163; Gael McDonald, *An Anthology of Codes of Ethics*, European Business Review, 2009, Vol. 21(4), 344–372.
202. *Stocktake of Efforts to Strengthen Governance Frameworks to Mitigate Misconduct Risks*, Financial Stability Board, May 2017.
203. Mollie Painter-Morland, *Triple Bottom-Line Reporting as Social Grammar: Integrating Corporate Social Responsibility and Corporate Codes of Conduct*, Business Ethics: A European Review, 2006, Vol. 15(4), 352–364.
204. EG 2.8, Financial Conduct Authority Handbook.
205. Christian F. Rostbøll, *Preferences and Paternalism: On Freedom and Deliberative Democracy*, Political Theory, 2005, Vol. 33, 370–396.
206. In relation to 'nudges', see Cass R. Sunstein, *The Ethics of Influence: Government in the Age of Behavioural Science* (Cambridge University Press 2016).

7

Policy Implications

Fast Track

Speed Read

The aspirations involved in recognition of a social licence, discussed in Chap. 4, reach towards an end that lies beyond not only markets but also governments and their policy tools. Achieving it requires greater positive reciprocity in the many relationships that comprise financial markets. Positive reciprocity cannot ultimately be legislated for, so there are limits to what policy can achieve. The aspirations and meanings applied to market relationships, among other things, in the way they are narrated, are more powerful in affecting how they function, and Chap. 6 suggested that the account of financial markets advanced by recognition of a social licence has the potential to operate in just that way.

This suggests that a key policy objective should be to strengthen the **salience** of the social licence or at least what it stands for. It also suggests that policy should be focused on creating environments in which positively reciprocal relationships can develop more than enforced compliance with precise standards of behaviour.

The following examples are an indication of what that could mean in policy terms. They fall into two categories: those that would help to increase the salience of the social licence in market practice, and those concerned with aligning the content of existing law and regulation with it. They are not policy proposals: cross-disciplinary work and consultation would be needed to formulate those. Nor are they intended as a comprehensive reform programme. For example, they only look at policy as it directly concerns market participants, whereas demands and expectations on the financial sector from society more widely can also impact market behaviour. The examples are a starting point for discussion.

(continued)

© The Author(s) 2020
D. Rouch, *The Social Licence for Financial Markets*,
https://doi.org/10.1007/978-3-030-40220-4_7

(continued)
Salience

- **Connecting policy and regulation with the social licence**: regulators could make greater reference to the licence in explaining their approach and policy measures. Among other things, a clearer link should be made between the social licence and the role of finance in helping humanity to address its sustainability challenges.
- **Cross-sector work to test and articulate the terms of the licence**: there could be further public-private sector work to articulate the substance of the social licence more fully and what it should mean in practice. This is also desirable to avoid legal or regulatory uncertainty. Possible models for an exercise of this sort include the United Nations Global Compact and the UK's FICC Market Standards Board.
- **Financial firm purpose and the social licence**: firms could be encouraged to publish a 'social licence statement' explaining how they seek to operate in a manner consistent with the licence and how their other internal codes fit in. Ideally, firms would prepare these statements on a voluntary basis. However, various options would be available if regulatory underpinning were needed.
- **Financial firm reporting**: firms could also be encouraged to report on the extent to which their activities have been consistent with the aspirations set out in their social licence statement. Doing so would connect reporting more clearly with an over-arching end beyond financial return, and that would suggest a move towards fully integrated reporting. Integrated reporting should help to make it clear that exclusively financial measures are subsidiary to the broader goals of the social licence.
- **Professional advice**: firms could require their professional advisers, when providing advice, also to opine on the consistency of the advice with the firm's social licence statement. This might not be feasible or relevant for every sort of advice rendered. However, it could provide a valuable way of assessing whether the firm risks complying with the letter more than the spirit of any rules or failing to meet any higher standard to which the firm aspires.

Consistent Alignment

- **Making the social licence explicit in statements of regulatory purpose**: legislation establishing financial services regulators could be revised to ensure that their objectives adequately reflect the need for business to be conducted in a manner consistent with the licence, for example, referencing not just competition and consumer outcomes for financial markets but also the broader public interest.
- **Policy decisions**: in addition to the usual 'cost-benefit' analysis, policy steps should also be assessed for consistency with the goal of the social licence. While economic costs and benefits are relevant to that, relational goods cannot be assessed in purely economic terms.
- **Legal assumptions concerning the aspirations of investors/shareholders**: it is tolerably clear that a significant body of investors (the underlying beneficiaries on whose behalf large pension funds and the like are invested) care about how companies in which they invest generate investment return, not just about the return itself. However, legal duties of intermediary investors and directors tend to assume that shareholders only want financial return. That makes life simple by boiling decisions down to a financial calculation, but edits out broader aspirations, such as those involved in talk of a social licence.

(continued)

(continued)

This issue could be addressed by introducing an assumption, much like the UK policy on organ donation which assumes willingness to donate at death subject to an opt out, that, subject to clear evidence to the contrary, (a) company directors should assume that holders of financial instruments issued by the company wish the company to earn a return in a manner consistent with the ends of the social licence and (b) those investing assets on behalf of others are to make a similar assumption about the desires of those for whom they invest.

- **Speculation and investment**: there is confusion between these two activities, so that investment often gets treated as if it is just a form of speculation, as the common use of gambling terminology in describing all market activity confirms. The discussion in Chap. 6 would suggest that both activities can be formative, and there are those who see the monetary frame involved in speculation, detached from any wider social purpose, as being corrosive of the attitudes that make for a just society. Some types of speculative activity are needed, for example, to enhance liquidity, and there is no sharp distinction between speculation that has a wider purpose and speculation that does not. However, work could be undertaken to identify ways of making a clearer regulatory distinction between investment and speculation with and without a wider purpose. Distinguishing more clearly could influence which activities people want to spend their time on and is potentially relevant to what firms need to do in seeking to shape their culture and to form the character of their staff.
- **Supplementing individual accountability and remuneration—culture and character formation**: regulatory rules and policy should be reviewed to ensure that they make an adequate appeal to market participants' other-regarding aspirations and take account of the way in which people's character is formed by the environment in which they work. For example, firms could be required to incorporate their remuneration policy *within* (the contextualisation is important) a broader culture and character formation policy. This would set how the firm goes about shaping its culture and the character of its staff, including the role of positive and negative incentives as compared with aspirations for human dignity. Linking this with the firm's codes of conduct should help to sharpen the impact of codes in practice.
- **Enforcement and restorative justice**: restorative justice techniques could be used more widely in regulatory enforcement situations. For example, individuals and firms facing regulatory enforcement could be offered, as an alternative, the opportunity to engage in community service programmes of appropriate materiality aimed at financial capacity building, whether educational programmes, debt counselling or otherwise. Benefits would include replacing negative incentives for outward compliance with activities more closely related to the aspirational ends of the social licence (with the hope of strengthening those aspirations) and increasing the proximity of relationship between financial market participants and end users (potentially strengthening altruism; see Chap. 3).

So What?

The recognition of a social licence has potentially significant policy implications. The main importance of the account of financial markets advanced by recognition of a social licence lies largely beyond policy, and there is little to stop market participants addressing some of the areas identified above right away. However, regulators may nonetheless have an important role in priming the pump and shepherding the process along. Further re-evaluation is therefore needed from policymakers to assess how best they can do that.

A major collective failure preceded the financial crisis of 2008, and another has followed. It is the failure to articulate a compelling vision for the role of finance in human wellbeing. A re-evaluation may be underway, but we nevertheless remain in thrall to financial narratives of the kind discussed in Chap. 1, and to the idea that when markets fail, it is the government that must reach into the regulatory toolbox to remedy the situation. If we are to address the urgent challenges we presently face, this needs to change.

The recognition that financial markets operate subject to a social licence can help. The significance of this recognition lies largely beyond policy, in the radically different account it advances of the relationship between finance and society. It is a narrative with potential to alter the very substance of market relationships—the way they are lived, felt and understood by the parties to them—so as to change the behaviour they produce.

The recognition of a social licence is based on what can be seen in practice, but it also involves an aspiration for what could be. It reaches out towards an end that lies not only beyond markets but also beyond governments and their policy tools, including law and regulation. Indeed, it reaches out towards something that both markets and governments can reinforce, but also something on which they both rely: a broad-based mutuality in social relations that entails a balancing of interests in way that can help realise the wellbeing of all. This is what we might call justice. Though market activity, financial or otherwise, can frustrate that ambition, positive reciprocity in market relationships can help to realise it. This orientation of relationships, so that immediate ends are pursued in a way that takes account of broader human needs, cannot ultimately be achieved through legislation: healthy communities are not built or sustained by memorising legal rules. Nor are successful businesses. The hopes, values and meanings that are active in the relationships within them are much more powerful.

Yet the social licence itself seems to suggest a role for policy. Chapter 4 suggested that the licence incorporates laws and regulations and identified other policy fora in which we could expect its terms to be fleshed out. Further, Chap. 5's discussion of 'structural written standards' is a reminder that the freedom granted by the licence is enjoyed in a world partly shaped by policy.

How, then, should recognition of a social licence affect policy? Chapter 6 suggests a new policy focus. Firstly, a narrative must be told if it is to capture hearts and minds. A key objective should therefore be to strengthen the salience in public and market discourse of the account of financial activity advanced by recognition of a social licence. Secondly, individual character and institutional culture are *formed* by the way prevailing frameworks of values and meaning influence market practice. Formation has not so far received sufficient attention. And, since the valued ends and meanings implied by recognition of a social licence have the potential to support positive reciprocity, there particularly needs to be greater policy focus on long-term formation from a social licence perspective. This must involve more than incentives or 'nudges' to influence behaviour at the moment of decision, although these have their place. Regulatory work on culture is a start, but only a start. It cannot be left to 'markets' to determine what constitutes a good outcome and a good culture: all of us, policymakers included, need to reach a view on what good looks like and pursue it for, 'if preferences are endogenous, politics cannot hide behind the liberal principle of non-interference, or preference neutrality.'[1] Indeed, political processes have a central role in developing a consensus about outcomes; questions regarding what ends are valued and why must be asked and answered, and the account of financial markets advanced by the social licence is highly pertinent to both.

The recognition of a social licence, then, has significant policy implications. This chapter provides some examples of what that might mean in practice. These are not policy proposals, not least because thorough cross-disciplinary work and consultation would be needed if that were the case. Nor do the examples constitute a comprehensive reform programme. For example, they only look at policy as it directly concerns market participants, whereas the mutuality involved in recognition of a social licence highlights the way demands and expectations placed on the financial sector by society more widely can also impact market behaviour. Further, they do not cover factors such as the long-term sustainability of a consumption-based, debt-funded economic and social model or the implications of technological advances. Rather, these examples represent a starting point for discussion and, importantly, a number of the examples connect with existing work in finance firms and beyond. This should come as no surprise. Chapter 1 compared the recognition of a social licence to discovering an archaeological crop pattern in an aerial photograph: it is there, shaping the financial ecosystem whether we are aware of it or not. Once spotted, however, we should expect to notice existing work consistent with the account the recognition of a social licence advances, even if that work was not previously seen as having any connection to it. Indeed, this joining of the dots may give existing work more substance because of the framework—the 'meta-narrative'—the social licence provides.

The examples are divided into two groups. Firstly, those that could help to make the account of financial markets advanced by recognition of a social licence more salient in financial markets and beyond. Secondly, there are those that concern how the values and meanings it implies are reflected in policy, law and regulation. However, like many of the other distinctions examined in this book, the boundary between the two is porous: all of the examples come back to the need to foster environments in which the values and meanings advanced by the recognition of the social licence can alter the substance of market relationships. Because that process is organic, and does not simply boil down to more rules, the underlying assumptions are these: (1) alternatives to regulation should be favoured where possible and, when regulation is introduced, its connection with the aspirations and meanings that lie behind the social licence should be made clear; (2) structural law, which tends to define the parameters of what is possible behaviourally (see Sect. 5.2.3), should be favoured over rules that seek to stipulate standards of behaviour; and (3) where they are used, behavioural rules should favour those that are aspirational (see Sect. 5.2.4), especially those related to intrinsic aspirations towards, essentially, justice (see Sects. 3.2.3 and 6.3.1) over detailed prescription. Where necessary, these aspirational standards could be supported using 'process regulation', involving a regulatory framework of steps that market participants should take in seeking to follow them.[2] Where greater specificity is needed, there should be a starting assumption that guidance is preferable to prescriptive rules.[3] Particularly where aspirational standards are used, it is vital that a good level of legal certainty is maintained (see Sect. 7.1.2).

Policymakers and business people tend to like clear objectives and measurable outcomes.[4] The concept of a social licence, however, is broad and its potential impact qualitative and longer term: it does not reduce easily to simple measures. Indeed, the desire to measure may be partly to blame for some of our current problems.[5] Nonetheless, practical, actionable connections are essential. People must be able to identify the steps they need to take to realise their objectives if their motivation is not to weaken over time. This needs to happen throughout the financial ecosystem for financial market behaviour to change. Micro-policy prescription is not feasible, and nor is micro-regulation. But some of the examples that follow would bring about environments in which actionable steps would emerge (such as those examples that concern corporate purpose, integrated reporting and policies on formation). Measuring progress is too big a topic to address in detail here, but the chapter concludes by touching on whether it is possible to measure the extent to which a social licence has been granted to institutions and markets. It also acknowledges a thread that runs through a number of the examples that follow: the challenge of operating by reference to at least two different and seemingly incommensurable kinds of value—in particular, monetary value and intrinsic human value.

7.1   The Salience of the Social Licence

The account of financial markets advanced by the recognition of a social licence has the potential to focus aspiration, frame market activity and form those within markets, in ways that can strengthen positive reciprocity (see Chap. 6), and galvanise the financial sector in addressing humanity's urgent sustainability needs. To do so, it needs greater salience within the myriad relationships that comprise financial markets. Ideally, part of that would involve novelists and film makers challenging *The Wolf of Wall Street* genre of narratives with counter-narratives based on the social licence. However, the following outlines five examples of what policymakers and regulators could do.

7.1.1   Publicly Connecting Policy and Regulation with the Social Licence

Policymakers and regulators have previously drawn heavily on financial models of the sort discussed in Chap. 1. They could now make greater reference to the account of markets advanced by the social licence in formulating and explaining their approach and policy measures. Among other things, this would raise its profile, and a clearer connection with regulatory rules would stimulate greater engagement from the regulated, also influencing the way the rules are followed (see Sect. 6.6.2).

Regulators could do this by building on existing regulatory themes. For example, Bank of England officials have already been referencing the social licence in speeches in a way that seems to have made intuitive sense to those they have addressed. However, they have not yet said much about its substance. As noted in Chap. 1, the UK's Financial Conduct Authority ('FCA') has also been situating its activities and those of market participants in the context of the 'public interest'.[6] However, again, it is unclear what they mean by that; for example, whether it is a utilitarian 'greatest good for the greatest number' or, rather, something that takes account of the needs of all. If the 'public interest' involves social solidarity (as common sense suggests it should), there are good reasons for equating it with the ends of the social licence.

As noted in Chap. 1, discussion of similar concepts by US regulators seems to have been more muted, but with signs of a move in a similar direction. Meanwhile, Chap. 4 looked at the debates in Australia and Canada concerning the 'social licence to operate' ('SLO') of businesses more broadly, including finance firms. Those debates have generally assumed that there is some form of SLO, but have highlighted uncertainty over its substance. In the case of finance firms, a more explicit link with the social licence for financial markets could help to resolve this (see further below, especially Sect. 7.1.2).

Among other things, policymaker discussion of the social licence should seek to maximise its aspirational strength, especially by making a more explicit connection with the need for finance to help in charting a course to a sustainable future (where the current emphasis tends, understandably, to be on risk mitigation). They could also make a clearer connection with work on culture in financial institutions. For example, at present the UK's Prudential Regulation Authority ('PRA') says that it expects firms to 'have a culture that supports prudent management' but 'does not have any 'right culture' in mind'.[7] Meanwhile, the FCA in describing its mission talks of firms having a culture of 'wanting to do the right thing' and of culture as a source of potential harm, but could be more explicit about the framework within which what is 'right' and what is 'harmful' fall to be addressed.[8] In the case of both sustainability and culture, greater connection with the account of financial markets advanced by the social licence has the potential to provide aspirational drive, a conceptual framework and a language for navigating some of the potential tensions identified in Chap. 1 (Sect. 1.2.4).

7.1.2   Cross-Sector Work to Test and Articulate the Terms of the Social Licence

Recognition of a social licence can provide a context for broad-based dialogue, within the financial sector and beyond, to establish a consensus on the ends of financial activity and how they should be pursued, including testing the framework developed in Chap. 4. Engagement of this sort could build on Bank of England work on the meaning of the social licence as part of its 2015 Open Forum and would need to involve the various constituencies identified in Chap. 4 as having a role in the process of definition.[9] Possible models include the United Nations Global Compact and the United Nations Environment Programme Finance Initiative. These are fora in which firms (and, in the case of the former, NGOs and other bodies) develop and share good practice in advancing UN goals and values. As discussed in Part II, some of the output from initiatives like these already has a claim to be articulating the terms of a social licence. The UK's FICC Market Standards Board provides another possible model. It is a regulator-encouraged, private sector response to misconduct in the fixed income, currency and commodities markets with the aim of helping to improve conduct and make those markets more fair and effective.

Work of this sort could also be accompanied and grounded by groups of firms coming together to develop joint projects designed to tackle some of the sustainability and other challenges discussed in Chap. 1, much as with the 73 Dutch pension funds seeking to maximise their work on sustainability mentioned in Chap. 3 (Sect. 3.1.2). There could be a facilitating role for industry associations here, with an opportunity for the finance sector, not just individual firms, to be clearly seen making a positive difference.

As well as making the social licence more salient and giving it greater definition, a dialogue of this sort would have three further objectives. Firstly, Chap. 6 suggested that individual character and institutional culture formation involves a kind of behavioural dialogue which is influenced by prevailing social values and meanings (see Sects. 6.5.2 and 6.6.2); simply engaging with the values and meaning advanced by recognition of a social licence could itself be a source of change. Secondly, this sort of dialogue is important in respecting individual choice; if policy measures will be used to influence the way people and firms behave, and even form who they become, it is essential that there should be transparency about it and a reasonable level of consensus as to the ends pursued (see Sect. 6.7). Thirdly, establishing a consensus is important in terms of legal and regulatory certainty if written standards increasingly come to be made or construed by reference to the values and meanings advanced by the recognition of a social licence (see Sect. 6.6).

On the last of these, as discussed in previous chapters, just as no contract is complete, nor are legal codes or other written standards. That can create uncertainty about what they require. Consequently, written standards depend, in part, on an underlying consensus about the framework of values and meanings that applies in construing them; as Pierre Bourdieu recognised, the rule of law presupposes commitment to common values (see Sect. 4.2). If the account of financial markets advanced by the social licence receives greater recognition, a process of clarification and consensus building about its substance would be important to allay concerns that it could create legal or regulatory uncertainty. This has been a theme in Australian and Canadian debates on the broader concept of the SLO (see Sect. 4.2).[10]

Clarification is particularly important for aspirational written standards (see Sect. 5.2.4), especially those in the form of principles, referencing values such as fairness or integrity. Because regulatory principles, aspirational standards among them, are not tightly prescriptive, they are often perceived as a particular source of uncertainty.[11] This can raise questions about the rule of law: will the goalposts move to suit the regulatory enforcement agenda of the day? The FCA Enforcement Guide recognises the issue.[12] Aspirational standards seem to represent a particular meeting point between written standards that apply in financial markets and the kind of aspirations involved in recognition of a social licence because of the way they reach beyond precisely prescribed behaviours to valued outcomes. Given this apparent alignment of aspiration, greater clarity about the substance of the social licence could also help to provide greater certainty about what aspirational standards require.

7.1.3   Financial Firm Purpose and the Social Licence

Financial firms could be encouraged to publish a statement of their understanding of the social licence and how it influences the way they do business (a 'social licence statement'). The social licence is not an exhaustive set of requirements that apply to financial firms (see Sect. 4.6). A statement of this sort would not, therefore, involve a detailed description of licence terms, and nor would it need to 'double-layer' existing corporate and financial services regulatory requirements (which, as noted in Chap. 4, could be regarded as part of the licence in any event). Rather, it would operate as a narrative glue, delivering an account of the meaning and value of a firm's activity. It could include a description of the firm's purpose, an explanation of how that purpose aligns with the social licence and how the firm ensures that its activities are consistent with that.[13] It could connect, among other things, to the firm's policies and behavioural and operating codes (providing the conceptual and aspirational underpinning for behavioural codes that they sometimes lack—see Sect. 6.6.2).[14]

An obvious area for a statement of this sort to address is a firm's approach to the targets set by the Paris Agreement on Climate Change to limit the damage caused by climate change, given the urgency of the issue and the critical role of finance firms in addressing it. Essentially, the statement would explain whether the firm is seeking to align its business and portfolios of assets owned or managed with the Paris targets, how and within what timetable. Similarly, it would also be important for the statement to cover remuneration policies given the widespread recognition, including in business circles, that business remuneration levels are a significant source of social fracture.[15] Indeed, PWC have linked this with the possible loss of companies' licence to operate and have suggested steps that companies can take to address it.[16] Meanwhile, those surveyed for the 2019 Edelman Trust Barometer identified income inequality as the most important issue for the financial sector to address.[17] As another example, the statement could reference the product governance policies that firms must maintain under UK and EU regulation. These rules require firms to maintain processes for the design, creation, documentation and distribution of financial products. The aim is to ensure that the right products end up in the right hands and perform as anticipated. Linking product governance policies with the social licence statement, to counter future charges of 'socially useless' products, it would be possible for a firm to include a 'socially useful' test in its product governance policies as a condition for launching a new product.[18] If firms wanted to avoid the risk of this becoming a 'tick box' exercise, they could explore the use of 'red teaming', essentially, by establishing an independent group with a mandate to challenge any assessment of social usefulness by deliberately taking an adversarial role. Equally, it would be important that a test of this sort did not operate in a way that deterred valuable innovation.

The process of drafting and maintaining a social licence statement could be expected to generate debate within firms and market sectors which could strengthen the salience of the social licence. As noted, it would operate as a kind of narrative. Chapter 6 touched on the importance of narrative in business, including in motivating staff, investors and customers. Among other things, clearly articulating a firm's approach to the social licence could help to open up space in which employees are more easily able to pursue aspirations that are not narrowly financially confined (see Sect. 6.3.2).

There is already significant raw material for a statement of this sort. In particular, previous chapters have discussed growing attention to corporate purpose.[19] In the US, this process reached a milestone in August 2019 in the form of the Business Roundtable Statement on the Purpose of a Corporation.[20] In the UK, the need for a company board to establish the company's purpose was included in the 2018 edition of the UK Corporate Governance Code.[21] Purpose made a new entry in Principle 1 of the Australian Corporate Governance Code in February 2019.[22] It is something the FCA also considers in the course of supervision.[23] However, these initiatives build on extensive work over many years, for example, by the B Corporation movement,[24] Blueprint for Better Business[25] and the British Academy Future of the Corporation project.[26] As noted in earlier chapters, parts of the investor community have also become increasingly focused on the social purpose of investee firms.[27] All of this work is ongoing, not least because it is partly related to the growing desire among customers and others to see companies stand for something beyond making money, evidenced in the emergence of the concept of 'brand purpose'.[28] Indeed, having the right sort of purpose can make good business sense.[29]

This work tends to assume that 'corporate purpose' involves some sort of positive social impact, not just financial return. However, it sometimes seems to lack an anchoring framework beyond that. For example, one recent survey defined purpose as 'an aspirational reason for being which inspires and provides a call to action for an organization and its partners and stakeholders and provides benefit to local and global society'.[30] For some advisers on corporate purpose, it is almost as if 'any purpose will do' as long as it somehow involves a positive social impact. Recognition of a social licence potentially provides the anchor in a financial market context, establishing an over-arching standard by reference to which purpose can be understood. This is important in terms of individual institutional purpose. However, more importantly still, because the social licence concerns the financial ecosystem as a whole, it can also help with the systemic coordination needed to address current challenges and opportunities.

Ideally, social licence statements would be voluntary. For example, it would be possible for different industry sectors through industry associations or otherwise to create something similar to the 'public interest commitment' that UK water companies entered into April 2019, following regulatory encouragement, in which they committed to 'enshrine what it means to operate in the public interest within their business purpose, in line with best practice among leading socially-responsible businesses'.[31] Initiatives like this would need to be accompanied by some sort of monitoring, or group self-assessment, to ensure that the firms concerned followed through on their commitments. Again, industry associations or bodies operating on a similar basis to the UK's FICC Market Standards Board or Banking Standards Board could have a role here. There is a separate question as to how progress could be measured, and this is discussed in Sect. 7.3.

However, regulatory underpinning could be provided in various ways, if needed. The following three examples are organised in ascending order of 'legal hardness'. Firstly, regulators could take account of whether a firm publishes such a statement, and the internal processes that support it, in setting individual regulatory capital requirements (i.e. the amount of regulatory capital a firm has to carry in addition to the statutory minimum). They could also require details to be published as part of a firm's 'Pillar 3 disclosure', a disclosure that many regulated firms must make providing information about a firm's capital and risk position which is intended to inform those dealing with the firm, so strengthening market discipline.[32] This would be on the basis that the quality of a firm's engagement with the social licence is likely to be relevant to its risk profile. Secondly, process regulation could be introduced concerning the steps companies should take to define, measure and monitor adherence to their licence-defined purpose. It could be linked to regulatory personal accountability regimes, such as the UK's Senior Managers Regime (see Sects. 2.4.3 and 5.2.4) so that, for example, an identified senior manager is responsible for it (much as with the PRA requirement to allocate responsibility for overseeing the firm's culture to a designated senior manager[33]). Thirdly, the hardest regulatory intervention would be a requirement for firms to maintain a social licence statement as a condition of obtaining and continuing authorisation.

7.1.4 Financial Firm Reporting

Firms could be encouraged to report annually on how far their activities have been consistent with their social licence statement or, for commercially sensitive areas of assessment, to review those with a trusted independent third party such as, in the UK, the Banking Standards Board.[34] The level of trust towards financial firms and financial markets more broadly could be seen as a measure of the extent to which a social licence has been given (see Sect. 4.7). Greater transparency of this sort could strengthen trust, including by helping the public make the link between finance and solving humanity's sustainability challenges. Not least because of that, it should also be financially valuable to companies and their shareholders. The preparation of a report of this sort, much like the preparation of a social licence statement, would provide an opportunity for an organisation-wide assessment of a firm's activities by reference to the social licence, so heightening its salience. Indeed, Chap. 6 touched on how company reports and accounts operate as narratives that influence behaviour.

Once again, reporting of this sort could build on existing statutory reporting regimes and a considerable body of work that attempts to enrich them. Since recognition of a social licence embraces the need for firms to generate a financial return, the report would cover financial performance. This is already addressed in existing company accounting regimes, although accounting policies might need revisiting in the light of the social licence framework. But Chap. 4 suggested that the social licence reaches beyond financial performance to whether the purposes of the firm are just and are being pursued justly (see Sect. 4.6.2). Reporting would therefore need to include two further elements: an assessment of the extent to which the company has been successful in pursuing its purpose as described in its social licence statement and some assessment of whether the way it has been pursued is consistent with the social licence framework—broadly, is the firm satisfied that it has been pursuing just ends in financial markets in a manner that is just, and on what basis. The legal liability position for statements of this sort would need to be addressed to facilitate transparency.

The recognition of a social licence incorporates financial return within a wider framework. That would tend to suggest that these three streams (financial performance, performance against licence-aligned purpose and standard of conduct) should be incorporated into a single view on the overall success of the company. Again, there is lots of existing work to build on, particularly with the concept of 'integrated reporting'. Indeed, some firms such as Lloyds Banking Group have already been moving towards an integrated reporting model.[35] In the UK, large and medium-sized companies now have to prepare a 'strategic report' on how far the directors have discharged their duty to promote the success of the company.[36] This necessarily involves identifying the purpose of the company, since success can only be assessed by reference to that. For listed companies, the report must, among other things, include, where necessary to understand the company's business, factors likely to affect its future performance and information about environmental matters (including its impact on the environment) and social, community and human rights issues, including information on related company policies and their effectiveness.[37] In other words, the report requires an assessment of the company's impact on the natural and social environment, and this is clearly relevant to the ends of the social licence suggested in Chap. 4. Further, guidance on the strategic report states that it should include information on 'sources of value' that have not been recognised in the financial statements and how they are managed, sustained and developed.[38] It goes on to state that:

> The success of a company is dependent on its ability to generate and preserve value over the longer term. Companies do not exist in isolation; they need to build and maintain relationships with a range of stakeholders … to generate and preserve value.[39]

The regime for strategic reports therefore seems broadly consistent with the framework of the social licence outlined in Chap. 4, and the social licence could provide a valuable context for it. Chapter 4 suggested that the social licence concerns value sources in the form of relational goods and realising human dignity which is, in turn, connected with the goal of social and environmental sustainability. Guidance on disclosure under the requirement above concerning 'social and community matters' suggests that boards should consider whether the business is 'dependent on relationships with certain communities…'.[40] Manifestly, from the preceding discussion of the social licence, most financial businesses are profoundly dependent upon chains of relationships stretching into the communities in which they operate—far beyond customers, counterparties and service providers—and ultimately on trust between the financial world and wider society. It is these communities that can be regarded as extending the licence.

However, the UK regime does not currently require fully integrated reporting.[41] The International Integrated Reporting Council ('IIRC') defines integrated reporting as 'a process founded on integrated thinking that results in a periodic integrated report by an organization about value creation over time and related communications regarding aspects of value creation'.[42] So, instead of having separate reports covering financial performance, strategy, non-financial information, corporate sustainability and the like, they are integrated into a single coherent account of what the company is attempting to do and how it seeks to create value.

Integrated reporting is challenging. It involves companies directly addressing the relationship between financial and non-financial values for which recognition of a social licence for financial markets seems to provide a framework. It does not just cover a company's commercial and financial performance but also its relationship with its social and environmental context, so providing a single account of its success. Much of its importance derives from the conceptual integration needed to do this. It involves companies asking, potentially at all levels of the organisation, what is valuable about what they do, looked at on an integrated basis, not simply applying financial measures, and how that value is created. It means, for example, that sustainability is not approached in isolation, but as an integral part of the business as a whole. In this way, integrated reporting can help to drive more rigorous and better informed decision making throughout an organisation, the more integrated it becomes. Significantly from the point of view of the social licence, the framework developed by the IIRC recognises that the value created by a company includes not just financial capital but also other capitals including 'social and relationship capital'. This is defined as, among other things, 'the relationships within and between communities … including shared norms, and common values and behaviours'.[43]

7.1.5 Professional Advice

Prevailing narratives and the social meaning and values they carry influence how the law is complied with and what legal advice is given (see Sect. 6.6). A similar point applies to advice provided by other professionals. Financial firms could stipulate as a condition of firms being admitted to their panel of advisors that when their advice is sought, they should also opine on the consistency of their advice with the financial firm's social licence statement, including the firm's code of conduct. This would help to ensure that advisers are familiar with what is important to their clients and that the finance firm's key values are made salient in all major business decisions. It could also provide a valuable way of assessing the extent to which the firm risks complying with the letter more than the spirit of any applicable rules, or failing to meet any higher standard to which it aspires.

A requirement of this sort would need to reflect the fact that professional advisors do not always know enough about the context for their advice to offer a clear view and that it may not be appropriate for every kind of advice, for example, where a lawyer is simply asked to provide an objective survey of the law on a particular regulatory point in a number of jurisdictions. However, matters such as this could be covered by describing the basis upon which any view has been provided. If legal or regulatory underpinning were required for such an arrangement, one approach might be to require a disclosure in the annual directors report on whether the firm adopts a policy of this sort and what it has learnt as a result.[44]

7.2   Consistent Alignment of Policy, Law and Regulation with the Social Licence

The examples outlined in the first part of this chapter all concern how to strengthen the salience of the social licence in market discourse and practice. However, the *substance* of policy, law and regulation also needs to be consistently aligned with the valued ends and meanings of financial activity apparently advanced by recognition of a social licence, and that is the focus of what follows.

Chapter 5 highlighted two broad ways in which written standards, including law and regulation, influence financial markets: firstly, by shaping the structures within which or by reference to which activities take place ('structural written standards') and, secondly, by setting expectations for behavioural standards specifically. It also noted that the distinction should not be pressed too far, for example, because behavioural standards are sometimes used to uphold structures. The following suggestions therefore fall along a spectrum between the two. The growing debate about the future of the corporation, and whether corporate law needs changing, for example, to strengthen the role of long-term shareholders, largely concerns structural written standards. Applied in a financial market context, some of that work is potentially congruent with the recognition of a social licence. It is touched on above in the discussion of corporate purpose. However, in view of the extensive treatment it is receiving elsewhere, it is not covered in detail here.

Laws and regulations are not the only way in which regulators can influence markets. In particular, regulators also maintain a supervisory dialogue with firms. In view of that, the first two areas discussed below concern how their mission is defined and the criteria they apply in their regulatory processes.

7.2.1 Regulatory Purpose

Chapter 4 suggested that, to some extent, regulators can be seen as articulating and administering the terms of a social licence. Legislation setting the objectives of financial services regulators, and hence the scope of their activities and their approach, could therefore be reviewed to ensure that it properly reflects this. For example, at present, the UK's FCA which regulates the conduct of all financial services firms and prudentially regulates all firms other than banks and insurers has a 'strategic' objective to ensure that, broadly, financial markets 'work well'. This is supplemented by three operational objectives. These are, essentially, to secure appropriate protection for consumers, to protect and enhance the integrity of the UK financial system and to promote effective competition in the markets for financial services. There is also a further requirement for the FCA to operate in a way that promotes effective competition in the interests of consumers.[45]

The legislation is silent on what it means for financial markets to 'work well'. The concept is potentially broad enough to be consistent with the discussion in Chap. 4 about the ends of the social licence. However, the tenor of the FCA's operational objectives might be taken to suggest that it is largely about consumer outcomes and whether markets consistently follow an orderly and fair process. Recognition of a social licence reaches beyond both of these; it concerns the wider relationship between finance and society and, among other things, the damage that the former can do to the latter. This could be made clear by way of an elaboration on what it means for markets to 'work well'.

Again, there is already relevant work on this. Such an amendment could, for example, build on the concept of the 'public interest' which, as discussed in Chap. 1 (Sect. 1.2.4), has been making a relatively recent appearance in statements from the FCA about its mission (subject to resolving the definitional question discussed in Sect. 7.1.1). For example, the FCA says of itself that 'The aim of our regulation is to serve the public interest by improving the way the UK financial system works and how firms conduct their business. By doing this, it benefits individuals, businesses, the economy and so the public as a whole.'[46] This aim could be made explicit in the legislation. Likewise, clarification could pick up on the definition of 'effective markets' developed by the Fair and Effective Markets Review, which also looked beyond the immediate outcomes of financial market activity to its impact on the non-financial economy (see Sect. 3.1.3), although, as discussed in Chap. 4, the social licence seems extend to non-financial impacts as well.

7.2.2   Policy Decisions and Cost-Benefit Analysis

Policy decision-making processes should be reviewed for consistency with both the substantive framework for financial activity advanced by recognition of a social licence and its potential to influence market activity, discussed in Chap. 6.

In particular, a mainstay of regulatory policy since before the 2008 crisis has been cost-benefit analysis ('CBA'). Indeed, in the UK, subject to exceptions, the FCA is required to undertake CBA before making new rules although it does not rely upon it alone.[47] Essentially CBA rests on the uncontroversial principle that the benefits of a proposed regulatory step should outweigh its costs. In order to make this comparison, it is normally necessary to reduce all of the positive and negative implications of a particular decision to a single scale of measurement, frequently monetary.

Properly applied, CBA can be an important regulatory technique, introducing discipline and transparency into decisions. However, it also suffers from a number of long-debated potential weaknesses.[48] To a significant degree, these concern the framework of values and meanings by reference to which it operates. This is most obvious in CBA's use outside the financial sector, in decisions involving a trade-off between human life and profit, such as Ford's decision in the 1970s not to fit safer petrol tanks on its Pinto cars based on the cost to the company as compared with the benefit in terms of reduced deaths and injuries if it did, valuing a life at $200,000 and injury at $67,000.[49]

In other words, CBA using monetary values does not cope well with apparently incommensurable values, such as the intrinsic value of human life and wellbeing. However, as suggested in Chap. 4, one of the key insights provided by recognition of a social licence is that financial life is intimately concerned with and dependent upon precisely that—the intrinsic value of human life, not simply of parties to transactions but also those in the sometimes long chains of relationships affected by them. No financial transaction or regulatory decision reduces to monetary terms alone. Indeed, applying monetary measures to human value can result in commodification, as those who undertook the experiment involving Israeli nurseries, reported in Chap. 6 (Sect. 6.4.3), seem to have confirmed.

Value judgements are made at all stages of the CBA process: for example, in identifying and articulating the problem that needs tackling; in identifying and determining which positive and negative factors need to be weighed in the assessment (it will rarely be feasible to capture all of them); in assessing the time period in which those positive and negative factors need to crystallise to be taken into account; in assumptions about how people will behave in future; and, as noted, in addressing apparently incommensurable values.[50] Much as with following legal rules (see Sect. 6.6), cost-benefit assessments are therefore influenced by the framework of values and meanings advanced by dominant social narratives, and the framework of CBA is strongly economic.[51] CBA may be particularly unsuited to realising the relational ends of the social licence, the relational impacts of which are indirect.[52] Where it seems just too difficult to reconcile incommensurable values, there is a risk that we end up, 'valuing the measurable, rather than measuring, and regulating for the valuable'.[53]

These issues are not restricted to CBA, and in the UK, the FCA shows some awareness of CBA's limitations, indicating that alternative approaches are taken where it is insufficient.[54] Nonetheless, particularly in view of the financial context, there is still a risk that the wider human ends involved in the social licence will not be adequately taken into account without conscious and determined effort (see the discussion of top-down and bottom-up reasoning in Sect. 2.3).

For example, the FCA's principal policy statement on CBA tends to focus on financial costs, such as the compliance cost of new rules and reduction in profits, higher prices for consumers or its own supervisory costs or, in the case of benefits, the economic benefits to firms and benefits to market users.[55] There is some reference to wider benefits, such as enhanced consumer psychological wellbeing and time saved.[56] However, it is largely silent about wider relational goods and social costs and benefits, such as levels of social trust: 'Most of the benefits from our policies fall on consumers, though some or all firms may be positively affected too....'[57] There is also no discussion of the impact of policy on the formation of individual character and firm culture.

The FCA might justifiably say that it addresses these at other parts of its decision-making process, which is carefully crafted and operates by reference to its interpretation of its statutory objectives.[58] However, it is unclear whether that is the case or how, and the FCA is unlikely to be alone in that. Steps to help ensure that the framework advanced by recognition of a social licence is adequately taken into account could include a decision by or a requirement on regulators to disclose how they do so.[59] This could, for example, explain how they apply it in identifying potential harms from financial activity, how it affects their assessment of a given issue, how it helps them to define costs and benefits and how they weight them, and how they assess whether their regulatory activities have helped to ensure that business is conducted in a manner consistent with the social licence. This sort of transparency seems desirable, not least in view of the potentially formative impact of any regulatory regime (see Sect. 6.5). Indeed, regulators could clarify to what extent they see their activities as formative, how and by reference to what frameworks of value and meaning.

7.2.3 Legal Assumptions Concerning the Aspirations of Investors/Shareholders

The social licence draws attention to the multiple motivations involved in any financial decision, some financially self-interested, some self-regarding more widely and some other-regarding (see Chaps. 3 and 4). There is growing reason to think that a significant body, possibly a majority, of investors (including the underlying beneficiaries on whose behalf large pension funds and the like are invested) care about the way in which companies in which funds are invested generate investment return, not just about the return itself (see Sect. 3.1.2). Some may even be prepared to accept a reduction in the return they receive in the interests of achieving positive environmental and social outcomes. By contrast, the way legal standards are applied tends to assume that shareholders simply desire financial return and that wider factors are only relevant if they could prejudice that. This makes life simple by boiling decisions down to a financial calculation: it sidesteps issues of incommensurable values and can provide a pragmatic way of managing potential conflicts of interest. However, it is unrealistic and disempowering because it edits out peoples' broader wellbeing, and their aspirations for what their money, or the money out of which their pension will be paid, should achieve. Further, it potentially limits the kind of broadly reciprocal transactional activity which is needed to meet the challenges identified in Chap. 1. By contrast, recognition of a social licence reaches out towards an end goal where financial value, while important, is instrumental in the realisation of human value.

The underlying reasons for the current situation are complex and do not boil down to legal rules alone. However, one way of helping to unlock it might be to introduce an 'investor assumption', similar to automatic enrolment for workplace pensions that exists in some jurisdictions, or rules for those who die in the UK to be considered for organ donation, unless they have opted out. It would, essentially, partially reverse the current financial self-interest assumption. Instead, it would provide that, subject to consultation with shareholders and beneficiaries revealing otherwise, (1) company directors should assume that holders of financial instruments issued by the company wish the company to earn a return in a manner consistent with the aspired ends of the social licence, so that this is relevant in assessing the success or otherwise of the company (echoing Milton Friedman's assumption that shareholders expect a company to be run in accordance with ethical custom, discussed in Chap. 1), and (2) those investing assets on behalf of others are to make a similar assumption about the wishes of those for whom they invest. In other words, this would cover both of self-interested desires to live in a world that is environmentally and socially sustainable and aspirations for the wellbeing of others to be realised as well. Appropriate legal protections would be needed all round: for beneficiaries and shareholders, to protect them from directors and institutional investors using these assumptions to pursue their own agenda, and for directors and institutional investors, a form of safe harbour to protect them from the potential for claims alleging reduced financial performance following good faith decisions exercising reasonable skill and care.

7.2.4 Finance and Investment Versus Speculation

The popular financial narratives of Chap. 1 reflect a common tendency to equate most financial activity with speculation or even gambling—witness the Bernie Sanders reference to 'casino capitalism' (see Sect. 1.1). Something similar happens in the financial press: betting on, taking punts on, making a play, jackpots and so on.[60] Experience suggests that it happens in the financial world too.

Very broadly, financial speculation involves using money to get money based on fluctuations in asset prices, with little or no wider purpose in mind. By contrast, the account of financial markets advanced by the social licence, suggested in Chap. 4, positions getting money in the context of the broader goal of realising intrinsic human value. The following considers the possibility of distinguishing more clearly between types of transactions that are most closely aligned with the social licence and those that are not. That is important for at least two reasons. Firstly, if it becomes clear that some speculative activities have limited or no benefit beyond lining the pockets of the transacting parties or their paymasters, it may encourage those involved to do something more useful with their time (whether out of a desire for social esteem or otherwise). Secondly, it ought to be relevant to firms in assessing what is needed to ensure that staff are not formed in ways that create a risk of behaviour inconsistent with the social licence (see Sect. 7.2.5), whether by engaging in speculation or because investment is framed as speculation.

Speculation occupies an ambiguous position in relation to the social licence framework. Not only is speculation associated with narratives that do not sit comfortably with the account of financial markets advanced by recognition of a social licence, but in some cases it has clearly been socially damaging. In recognition, the post-financial crisis reform programme saw measures to insulate parts of the banking sector from some forms of financial activity, including speculation (e.g. the UK's retail bank ring-fencing regime and the 'Volcker Rule' in the US[61]) and to curb more egregious forms of speculation, for example, rules allowing for restrictions on some kinds of 'short selling'[62] and to protect commodities such as foodstuffs and commercial raw materials from speculation-inflated prices by imposing position limits for derivatives transactions.[63] Some think more is needed, for example, to control some types of high-frequency trading.[64]

These steps tackle more obvious sources of potential damage. However, Chap. 6 discussed how the framework of values and meanings within which people operate influences their behaviour and forms their character and the culture of their institutions. In particular, it looked at the potential for monetary frames to dampen other-regarding behaviour. Frameworks of gambling and speculation tend to be largely monetary. Little surprise then that, in addition to its more immediate financial and social risks, some see speculation as also having a potentially negative formative impact:

> [rewarding] … speculative pursuits that are untethered from socially useful purposes is corrosive of character. It is corrosive not only of individual character but also of the virtues and attitudes that make for a just society.[65]

In some much quoted lines, John Maynard Keynes highlighted the economic dangers of excessive speculation:

> Speculators may do no harm as bubbles on a steady stream of enterprise. But the position is serious when enterprise becomes the bubble on a whirlpool of speculation. When the capital development of a country becomes a by-product of the activities of a casino, the job is likely to be ill-done.[66]

But looking at the power of speculation to form character and culture highlights an issue that goes beyond what Keynes had in mind: the behavioural impact where what he refers to as 'enterprise' (meaning, essentially, investment) is not only overshadowed by speculation, but actually becomes confused with it.

This issue has so far received little policymaker attention. The relationship between speculation and investment remains confused, and there has not been much scrutiny of the potential formative impact on culture and character of operating in an environment where speculation is a dominant framework of values and meaning.

One response might be more restrictions on speculative activity, for example, using the concept of an 'insurable interest'.[67] That was introduced in eighteenth-century England to deal with the social evil of people gambling on the occurrence of events adverse to others, but to which they themselves were not exposed, and from which they needed no protection—for example, someone else dying, with the temptation for one party to the wager to bring it about. Requiring an insurable interest meant that unless a contracting party actually needed financial protection from the adversity (i.e. insurance), the contract would be treated as a gaming contract and therefore not legally enforceable. The EU Short Selling Regulation uses the idea in setting the rules for controlling speculative short selling activity.[68] But attempts to restrict speculation are fraught with difficulty, among other things, because of the complexity and speed of markets, the need to maintain legal certainty of contractual enforceability and the risk of unintended adverse consequences, for example, inadvertently restricting activities that are beneficial, such as genuine market making and commercial hedging, or diverting potentially damaging activities elsewhere.[69]

However, there is a different way of approaching the issue: establishing a clearer broadly shared understanding of the difference between investment and different sorts of speculation, and indeed gambling. The aim would be to reduce the scope for confusion between investment and speculation and to distinguish between speculative activities that are more aligned with the social licence framework and those that are not: in other words, the aim would be to situate these different transaction types more clearly within the account of markets advanced by recognition of a social licence so that processes of the sort described in Chap. 6 can do their work.

The Distinction Between Speculation, Investment and Gambling

Before considering possible regulatory steps to support this, it is worth looking briefly at the distinction between investment, speculation and gambling. This is well dug ground, and there are few clear definitional lines.[70] Any regulatory approach would need to reflect this. However, if a distinction can be drawn anywhere, it is in terms of the *purpose* and possibly the *effect* of these transactions.

The purpose of a financial transaction can be looked at from various per-spectives, but two stand out: firstly, the purpose for which the money gener-ated by the transaction is sought (e.g. is it to boost a pension fund or to finance international terrorism) and, secondly, the purpose of the transaction itself, in other words, what is the money that is the subject of the transaction being *used for* (e.g. is it financing a water utility company or human traffick-ing). Separately, regardless of the purposes of a transaction, there is a question as to whether its *effect* is consistent with the ends of the social licence.

Boosting a pension fund by investing in a water company could well be consistent with the social licence, but not by financing human trafficking. Conversely, investing in a water company might be consistent with the social licence, but not if the purpose is to fund a terrorist network. In other words, there are some purposes on each side of the equation that can undermine the transaction as a whole.

The distinctive characteristic of gambling is essentially that it involves using money as a stake with a purpose of getting money, based on the outcome of an uncertain event. Speculation and gambling are not the same.[71] However, they have this in common. As with any financial transaction, the money gen-erated by speculation can be used for any purpose, and some may be more consistent with the social licence than others. The principal difference, there-fore, concerns the use of the money that is *the subject* of the transaction.

The purpose of finance and investment involves generating an income or capital growth through the longer-term funding of productive enterprise: its purpose goes beyond simply financial ends. It is successful when the investee company uses the capital invested to achieve its goal. By contrast, the main aim of speculation is generating money based on correctly judging likely asset price movements. This might seem to suggest that the use of money in specu-lation is somehow a 'neutral' activity (neither investment in water utilities nor people trafficking) so that, as long as the proceeds are put to good use, the activity is aligned with the social licence.

However, for reasons already covered, speculation is clearly not 'neutral'. On the one hand, it is associated with the kind of financial narratives in Chap. 1 that have come to define financial and investment activity more widely, it has sometimes been socially damaging, it is associated with remuneration levels that seem out of kilter with any wider benefit provided by the recipients and, without more, the way in which it applies a monetary framing to financial life may form character and culture in ways not aligned with the end goals of the social licence. On the other hand, some transactions with a speculative ele-ment do involve an important social purpose, such as the provision of com-mercial hedging and market making. Even where that is not the case, other forms of speculation may have *effects* that are more or less aligned with the social licence. For example, speculation can provide market liquidity, although how much liquidity does an economy need?[72] It can also assist with 'price discovery'. This happens where a speculative trade communicates a 'view' on the value of an asset to other market users who may be helped to a more realistic assessment of value as a result, although the view often seems more focused on the likely behaviour of other market participants than the fundamental value of the asset itself, as John Maynard Keynes recognised. It is important that any regulatory approach does not damage what is beneficial, but the lines are blurred.

Distinguishing Speculation from Investment in a Way that Influences Behaviour

Drawing sharp distinctions is, then, challenging.[73] The difference between investment and speculation is more like a spectrum, and definition would probably need to concentrate on establishing a set of indicia that could be used to test whether activity is closer to one end than the other. Further, for financial activities that are not investment, it would be necessary to distinguish between those with a purpose or effects that are more closely aligned with the aspired ends of the social licence and those that are not.

However, while challenging, categorisation of this sort is not alien to financial markets. Regulatory regimes involve extensive categorisation of market activities to establish a framework within which financial activity is conducted and rules can be applied. Examples include categorisations of instruments, activities and the different sorts of client or counterparty with whom those activities can be carried on (see Sect. 2.2). And not all legal concepts are sharp-edged, for example, the UK's 'collective investment scheme' (broadly, a fund)[74] or, more widely, the concept of negligence.

Indeed, some of the ground has already been covered. As noted above, there are already rules to control activities that have been identified as speculative, such as forms of financial trading in commodities and short selling. In the banking sector, post-financial crisis rules to protect bank deposits such as the Volcker Rule in the US and the UK's ring-fencing regime also turn on identifying financial activities that are more risky and should not be conducted in banks holding deposits repayment of which is backed by state protection. Further, the UK FCA's rules already go some way in distinguishing between financial instruments and activities that are speculative, and the rest. For example, a rolling spot forex contract is defined as a future or swap entered into 'for the purpose of speculation';[75] there are rules to restrict the selling of 'contracts for differences and similar speculative instruments' to private individuals, based on the notion of a 'restricted speculative investment' which includes various forms of derivative contract;[76] and guidance on the hedging of unit classes in mutual funds states that the hedging should not be allowed to become speculative.[77]

The language of existing financial services regulation would also need revision, not to make new rules, but to establish the distinction more clearly there too. For example, the key European Union legislation in this area uses the concept of 'investment services and activities' to cover, essentially, all activities in relation to financial instruments whether speculative or otherwise and defines an 'investment firm' as any firm carrying on those activities.[78] Meanwhile, as well as incorporating these concepts, the UK financial services regulatory regime operates by reference to 'regulated investments', a category that covers all forms of derivative, even though derivatives are frequently used for speculation rather than investment, and there has been a nagging question as to whether and when they fall with the English common law understanding of what is an 'investment'.[79] In other words, the legislation tends to treat all financial market activities as 'investment' regardless of whether they are in fact speculation. The US definition of 'security' in the Securities Exchange Act of 1934 is more neutral, but does something similar.[80]

However, more would be needed to establish the distinction in a way that can structure market activity. Assessing precisely how to do that would need careful work and consultation, but, in very broad terms, it could be approached from either end of the spectrum or both. It would be possible to define genuine finance and investment activity more clearly, so as to carve it out from potentially speculative activity and give it favoured regulatory status. The alternative would be to develop the existing regulatory usage to produce a definition of speculative activity. Financial firms, not just banks, could then be asked, firstly, to categorise their activities so that it is clear internally which staff are engaged in investment activities and which in speculation (whether using the firm's balance sheet or through an investment vehicle) and, secondly, to disclose the nature and extent of the speculative activity they conduct and of any social benefit or risk. The first of these is relevant to the operating framework for staff and hence also the question of formation (as to which, see Sect. 7.2.5). The second is more directly relevant to the challenge of re-establishing public trust and could be linked to the idea of a social licence statement, discussed above.

7.2.5 Supplementing Individual Accountability and Remuneration—Culture and Character Formation

Chapter 6 looked at how people are formed by the environments they inhabit, including the surrounding framework of values and meanings, often expressed through social narratives. Culture forms character, and the way staff in finance firms are formed influences their future behaviour. Whether that behaviour is consistent with the firm's objectives, or the aspired ends of the social licence, will partly depend on how they are formed. Senior management can have a significant influence on a firm's internal environment and hence what direction the process of formation takes. Consequently, like policymakers, they also '…cannot hide behind the liberal principle of non-interference, or preference neutrality'.[81]

So far, regulatory work on individual behaviour has tended to focus less on formation and more on incentivising staff compliance in two ways: firstly, through rules on the remuneration policies that firms must maintain[82] and, secondly, through the creation of 'individual accountability regimes', such as the UK's Senior Managers Regime discussed in Chaps. 2 and 5. The first uses financial self-interest to ensure that remuneration incentivises compliant behaviour (echoing the token economy discussed in Sect. 6.5.1). The second uses the threat of sanctions to incentivise senior management to maintain compliance in those parts of the business for which they are responsible.

Work on culture in financial institutions (see Sect. 1.2.4) recognises that a firm's internal operating environment drives its behaviour and that of its staff. However, as discussed, that work does not always break free from the language of incentivised behaviour. Only relatively recently have more aspirational goals emerged, such as the 'public interest' (see above and Sect. 1.2.4). Again, Chap. 1 suggested that the framework of a social licence could provide a way of bringing these two emphases together.

Positive and negative incentives are an essential part of the picture. But over-reliance risks missing the powerful role of other-regarding aspirations in motivating behaviour. If misdirected, these aspirations can be just as damaging as badly incentivised behaviour (see the discussion of LIBOR manipulation in Sect. 3.1.3). However, if well-directed they can be consistent with addressing the challenges and realising the opportunities discussed in Chap. 1—consistent, in other words, with positive reciprocity.[83] Further, over-reliance on incentives risks 'crowding out' those very aspirations (see Sect. 6.4.3); if not balanced by a strong framework of meaningful valued ends, it can carry the message that staff are assumed to be self-interested rational utility maximisers, much like economic man. If that assumption takes root, then they may be more prone to behave accordingly and assume that others will do likewise.[84] People need to be reminded of their own self-transcendence and that of others.[85] The social licence advances just such a countervailing framework. Finally, over-reliance on incentives can also mean losing sight of the powerful influence of formation in driving behaviour and the way the incentives may be forming people. Regulatory rules and policy should be reviewed to ensure that they take a more holistic approach to human formation and motivation and make an adequate appeal to individuals' other-regarding aspirations and desire for meaning.

Meanwhile, there is nothing to stop firms incorporating their remuneration policy *within* (the contextualisation is important) a broader culture and character formation policy. This would set out a firm's understanding of how its culture develops and forms its staff, and the steps it takes to shape the character of its staff, including the role of positive and negative incentives as compared with aspirations for human dignity. It would cover, among other things, the use of corporate codes (as discussed in Chap. 6, a 'Cinderella' among written behavioural standards in financial markets) and could help to sharpen their role in practice. Much of this would build on the work already done by firms on their culture and by their 'Human Resources' departments on employee development and retention, with some reorientation. If a regulatory framework was needed, it could be focused on the process for creating and maintaining the policy (rather than stipulating its content), much as with the idea of a social licence statement (Sect. 7.1.3). For example, one step might be to moderate the severity of disciplinary sanctions by reference to not just a firm's level of cooperation in any investigation and enforcement process but also the quality of its work on culture and character formation. A concept of this sort already exists in US sentencing guidelines for business organisations where the severity of a sentence can be reduced if a particular offence occurred even though the organisation had in place at the time of the offence an 'effective compliance and ethics program'.[86]

7.2.6   Enforcement and Restorative Justice

Greater use could be made of restorative justice techniques in regulatory enforcement and more broadly, rather than simply defaulting to sanctions. Why might that be important?

Restorative justice is a process whereby all the parties with a stake in a particular offence—that is, where an *injustice* has been done—come together to resolve collectively how to deal with the harm and its implications for the future.[87] Precisely how this takes place is flexible, and it can draw on a range of techniques. However, common to all is that the person who has done the harm is not simply put on trial and sanctioned, but rather takes part in an exercise designed to restore the damaged relationships. Measuring the effectiveness of restorative justice is not straightforward. However, there is encouraging evidence that it improves outcomes both for the offender and victim in a range of settings, although that does depend on selecting the right approach.[88] Indeed, the concept has been developed more widely in the form of 'relational practice' to deal with situations where there has been no harm, but the quality of relationships needs to be improved so as to make it less likely.[89]

Because restorative justice and practice approaches need to be tailored to the context, what it might look like in practice would depend on the circumstances. However, one recorded Australian case involved senior management from an insurance company that had mis-sold policies to Aboriginal customers, visiting their communities over some days to attend meetings with victims, the local Aboriginal council and regulatory officials. As a result, compensation was paid, regulatory reforms were put in place (including the establishment of a consumer education fund), and internal investigations were undertaken, the results of which were published, and staff responsible for the mis-selling were dismissed.[90]

It is not usual to think of financial services regulatory enforcement processes in these terms. However, in the UK at least, there is scope to use restorative justice as an alternative to regulatory enforcement, and in less contentious situations in the course of supervision. Indeed, some approaches already used in enforcement processes do go some way in that direction. For example, the UK FCA already lists among its options for tackling serious misconduct, using its powers to put in place remedial and restorative measures where appropriate and encouraging firms voluntarily to account for and redress misconduct by imposing lower sanctions where they do.[91] It notes that the latter 'builds trust and confidence'.[92] However, its approach does not generally go as far as independently facilitated relational justice.

The significance of approaches of this sort in the context of the social licence should be fairly obvious by now. First, restorative justice appeals to an aspiration to see justice done (see Sects. 3.2.3 and 6.3.1), so helping to break out of the framework of incentive induced compliance. However, crucially, it also brings greater relational proximity, with potentially two-way benefits. As discussed in Chap. 6 (Sect. 6.3.3), the prospect of trust between individuals and groups seems to increase when they see themselves as part of a single group. The account of financial markets advanced by the social licence draws attention to precisely this sort of commonality between the market participants and those in the societies in which they operate; they are part of the same community that is giving the licence, based on shared ends. The level of justified trust towards the financial sector was identified in Chap. 4 as perhaps the best way of understanding the extent to which the social licence has been given. In addition, by increasing proximity, restorative techniques also potentially strengthen altruism, so increasing the prospect of other-regarding behaviour orientated beyond the immediate ends of transactions towards the broader societies in which those transactions take place.

Some kinds of regulatory infringement may seem as if they are unsuited to a restorative justice approach, for example, where the breach has systemic implications, as with LIBOR manipulation, or where there has been a failure in a firm's internal systems and controls, creating a risk of damage to third parties which has not crystallised. In cases like these, it would not be possible to bring finance staff into direct contact with those they have damaged. However, alternatives may be available. For example, those facing regulatory enforcement could be offered the opportunity to engage in community service programmes of appropriate materiality aimed at financial capacity building, whether educational programmes, debt counselling or otherwise.[93] This would still have the relational benefits of bringing staff into closer contact with those outside who are most vulnerable to damage if the activities of the financial world are not conducted in a manner consistent with the social licence. If properly constructed, it would also be empowering for those at risk. In more serious cases, it would be possible to consider national or regional equivalents of South Africa's post-Apartheid Truth and Reconciliation Commission. The Bank of England went some way towards a concept of this sort following the Fair and Effective Markets Review, discussed in Chap. 3, in holding its Open Forum in 2015.[94] However, the approach could be developed further.

But restorative practices do not need to be confined to disciplinary situations. Firms could use them in the ordinary course of their business, for example, as part of the kind of formation exercise discussed above. The objective would be to ensure that staff, especially those in more senior roles, are closely connected with and properly understand the financial realities of those outside the financial world, in the societies affected by the activities of those within it.[95] Many firms already run community engagement programmes (see Chap. 3). However, the focus here would be more specifically on helping staff to understand the impact of the financial sector on the condition of individuals and small businesses.

7.3   Conclusion—Incommensurate Values and Measurement

The challenge of balancing a variety of valued ends has emerged in a number of the examples above, especially monetary value and intrinsic human value. Like weight, distance and time, these values are not commensurate, although they are related. Because of the complexity, it is tempting to try to reduce all of the elements in a decision to the single measure of money. That is understandable and, up to a point, necessary. However, go too far and you risk changing the meaning of what is being measured (like Warhol's '200 One Dollar Bills' in Chap. 2), implicitly confining it within a monetary framework. It can also carry the dangerous implication that getting money is the ultimate goal, consistent with narratives and models in Chap. 1.

But few really think that getting money is the ultimate goal, and nor is much of life lived that way. Challenging though it is, and unfamiliar though it may be, there is a need to grapple more explicitly with this: to recognise that the goal of realising intrinsic human value needs to be more fully reflected in decisions made throughout the financial ecosystem if the financial world is to address humanity's pressing sustainability needs and the other challenges outlined in Chap. 1. At the highest level, the account of financial markets advanced by the social licence provides a framework for pursuing both financial and human ends. It suggests that financial return, while important, should only ever be instrumental in seeking to realise just ends by just means in financial markets, justice being understood in terms of intrinsic human value. Achieving that requires balance, not just balance sheets. Balance is inherent in justice. What it means in practice needs to be worked out within the substance of market relationships and does not reduce to a matter of price.

If attempting to measure non-financial factors in monetary terms can be distorting, is there another way of measuring the progress of the financial world, and the firms within it, towards the aspired end of the social licence? Detailed discussion of this point lies beyond the scope of the current exercise. Essentially, there is no simple measure since the social licence concerns a quality of relationships: its end is qualitative rather than quantitative.[96] However, there are various ways of developing a sense of the relative health of the relationships involved, and one of the most useful may be measuring trust. Firstly, that is because Chap. 4 suggested that one way to assess the extent to which the social licence has been given is to ask how far the societies in which the financial world operates have given their *justified trust* to those operating in financial markets (see Sect. 4.7). Secondly, the measurement of trust is already widely relied upon, by sociologists in particular, in attempting to gauge levels of 'social capital'. Social capital is a slippery concept, and it is not necessary to get into it here.[97] The basic point is that it has some similarity with the kind of outcomes this book has suggested that greater recognition of the social licence has the potential to produce. It has, for example, been defined as 'social networks and the norms of reciprocity and trustworthiness that arise from them'.[98] Like the aspired end of the social licence, it is largely qualitative rather than quantitative.

Chapter 4 spoke of *justified* trust, not just trust. Trust that is justified is not misplaced; the behaviour of the person to whom it is given is worthy of it, and the trust will not evaporate because someone discovers otherwise. In broad terms, how could you measure and assess not just trust, but justified trust? A starting point would be to seek to measure the levels of trust, firstly, towards the financial sector and, secondly, towards individual institutions that make it up.[99] As discussed in Chap. 4, the general capacity to trust can be systemically affected by the migration of mistrust from other areas of social life, such as the press or political leaders. Similarly the untrustworthy behaviour of one institution in a sector can undermine trust in all. Because of that, these measures would need to be relative to other non-financial sectors of society or, in the case of individual firms, relative to other firms in the sector.[100] Over time, assessments of this sort should help in building up a picture of the extent to which the financial sector and individual firms within it are trusted. However, they would not necessarily tell us whether that trust is justified rather than being the product of a sophisticated public relations exercise. To do that, it would also be necessary to develop an understanding of the trustworthiness of firms within the relevant sector. This requires further attention. However, the work of the New York Federal Reserve on the concept of 'cultural capital' and of the UK's Banking Standards Board on bank culture suggests that a range of indicia are available to test the quality of an institution's relationships internally and with those outside it.[101] Assessments of this sort often rely heavily on internal staff surveys. However, work is also ongoing to develop reliable methods for assessing firm culture based on publicly available metrics.[102] This could provide a relatively objective and independent comparative view, creating a greater incentive for firms to make progress.

A combination of these measures should make it possible to develop a sense for whether the health of the relationship is improving. None provides the apparent objectivity of financial measures and market prices. But financial measures are potentially distorting and in some cases useless or even damaging; you cannot measure the health of a marriage by the size of the family balance sheet. What is needed here is relational knowledge: knowledge about the health of the relationship on which markets themselves depend. Ultimately that is a quality that is sensed and felt more than measured, as the populist rage discussed in Chap. 1 seems to be telling us.

Notes

1. Sabine Frerichs, *Bounded Sociality: Behavioural Economists' Truncated Understanding of the Social and Its Implications for Politics*, Journal of Economic Methodology, 2019, Vol. 26(3), 243–258.
2. Dan Awrey, William Blair and David Kershaw, *Between Law and Markets: Is There a Role of Culture and Ethics in Financial Regulation*, Delaware Journal of Corporate Law, 2013, Vol. 38(1), 191–245.
3. Constantine Boussalis, Yuval Feldman and Henry E. Smith, *An Experimental Analysis of the Effect of Standards on Compliance Performance*, Regulation and Governance, 2018, Vol. 12(2), 277–298.
4. UK Government guidance on policy proposals indicates that they should be specific, measurable, achievable, realistic and time-limited: *The Green Book: Central Government Guidance on Appraisal and Evaluation*, HM Treasury 2018, paragraphs 4.8 and 4.9.
5. Jerry Z. Muller, *The Tyranny of Metrics* (Princeton University Press 2018).
6. See, for example, *FCA Mission: Approach to Supervision*, Financial Conduct Authority, April 2019, 5.
7. *The Prudential Regulation Authority's Approach to Banking Supervision*, Prudential Regulation Authority, October 2018.
8. *FCA Mission: Approach to Supervision*, Financial Conduct Authority.
9. Recognising the challenges of generating robust public discourse of this sort: Michael X. Delli Carpini, Fay Lomax Cook and Lawrence R. Jacobs, *Public Deliberations, Discursive Participation and Citizen Engagement: A Review of the Empirical Literature*, Annual Review of Political Science, 2004, Vol. 7(1), 315–344.
10. See, for example, comments from the Australian Institute of Directors that 'the concept of "social licence" is highly subjective and will be interpreted differently by different stakeholders … [it] introduces concepts with broad, perhaps changing, interpretations…', available at https://www.asx.com.au/regulation/corporate-governance-council/reviews-and-submissions.htm (accessed 4 November 2019).
11. Julia Black, *Forms and Paradoxes of Principles-Based Regulation*, Capital Markets Law Journal, 2008, Vol. 3(4), 425–457.
12. EG 2.8, FCA Handbook.

13. Emma Borg, *The Thesis of 'Doux Commerce' and the Social License to Operate*, in press, Business Ethics: A European Review (https://doi.org/10.1111/beer.12279) advances a similar suggestion, but differs in that she seems to contemplate a more detailed statement and places it in the context of a social contract.

14. For example, *Codes of Conduct: A Barrier or a Breakthrough for Corporate Behaviour?*, PWC 2013 makes a link between code effectiveness and its relationship with the firm's sense of purpose.

15. *The Ethics of Pay in a Fair Society: What Do Executives Think?*, PWC 2017.

16. Ibid., 4.

17. *2019 Edelman Trust Barometer, Financial Services*, Edelman 2019. See also Patrick Jenkins, 'If investors don't overhaul banker pay, populism will', *Financial Times*, London, 21 January 2019.

18. Angela Monaghan, 'City is too big and socially useless, says Lord Turner', *The Telegraph*, London, 26 August 2009. Lord Turner was, at the time, the Chairman of the UK's financial services regulator.

19. See also the discussion of firm reporting in Sect. 7.1.4.

20. https://www.businessroundtable.org/business-roundtable-redefines-the-purpose-of-a-corporation-to-promote-an-economy-that-serves-all-americans

21. Principle 1B, UK Corporate Governance Code, Financial Reporting Council, July 2018.

22. Recommendation 1.1, Corporate Governance Principles and Recommendations, 4th edn, ASX Corporate Governance Council, February 2019.

23. *FCA Mission: Approach to Supervision*, Financial Conduct Authority.

24. See https://bcorporation.net (accessed 4 November 2019).

25. See http://www.blueprintforbusiness.org (accessed 4 November 2019).

26. See https://www.thebritishacademy.ac.uk/programmes/future-of-the-corporation (accessed 4 November 2019).

27. See, for example, BlackRock CEO Larry Fink's annual letters to CEOs of companies in which BlackRock invests client funds in both 2018 and 2019 which both concerned purpose: see *A Sense of Purpose* and *Purpose & Profit*, available at https://www.blackrock.com/corporate/investor-relations/larry-fink-ceo-letter (accessed 5 November 2019).

28. See, for example, *Just How Much do Sustainability and Brand Purpose Matter*, Ipsos Global Trends, https://www.ipsosglobaltrends.com/just-how-much-do-sustainability-and-brand-purpose-matter/ (accessed 5 November 2019).

29. See, for example, ibid.; *The Business Case for Purpose*, Harvard Business Review Analytic Services Report (Harvard Business School Publishing 2015); Karl V. Lins, Henri Servaes and Ane Tamayo, *Social Capital, Trust and Firm Performance: The Value of Corporate Social Responsibility During the Financial Crisis*, The Journal of Finance, 2017, Vol. 72(4), 1785–1824.

30. *The Business Case for Purpose*, Harvard Business Review Analytic Services Report.
31. Available at https://www.water.org.uk/publication/public-interest-commitment/ (accessed 4 November 2019).
32. For details of the international principles that apply, see *Pillar 3 Disclosure Requirements – Updated Framework*, Basel Committee on Banking Supervision, December 2018.
33. Allocation of Responsibilities, Rule 4.1(6) and (14), PRA Rulebook.
34. An exercise of this sort is already undertaken by the Banking Standards Board in relation to culture within financial institutions.
35. *Lloyds Banking Group 2018 Annual Report and Accounts*, available at https://www.lloydsbankinggroup.com/globalassets/documents/investors/2018/2018_lbg_annual_report_v2.pdf (accessed 7 November, 2019).
36. Sections 414A(1), 414C(1) and 172, Companies Act 2006.
37. Section 414C(1)(7). The contents requirements are supplemented for large banking and insurance companies, by rules implementing the EU Non-Financial Reporting Directive (Directive 2014/95/EU), which require the publication of a non-financial reporting statement covering similar ground (sections 414CA and 414CB, Companies Act 2006).
38. Para 4.5, *Guidance on the Strategic Report*, Financial Reporting Council, 2018.
39. Ibid., para 4.6.
40. Ibid., para 7A.42.
41. Companies listed on the Johannesburg Stock Exchange have been required to adopt integrated reporting on an 'apply or explain' basis since 2010.
42. The IIRC is an international coalition of regulators, investors, companies, members of the accounting profession, NGOs and others which aims to establish integrated reporting as the norm in business practice. Its framework for integrated reporting is probably the most influential.
43. *International <IR> Framework*, International Integrated Reporting Council, 2013, paragraph 2.15.
44. See, generally, John C. Coffee, *Gatekeepers: The Professions and Corporate Governance* (Oxford University Press 2006).
45. Sections 1B–1E, Financial Services and Markets Act 2000.
46. *FCA Mission: Approach to Supervision*, Financial Conduct Authority, 5.
47. Section 138I, Financial Services and Markets Act 2000; *Our Mission 2017*, Financial Conduct Authority.
48. See, for example, Alasdair MacIntyre, 'Utilitarianism and Cost-Benefit Analysis: An Essay on the Relevance of Moral Philosophy to Bureaucratic Theory', in *The Moral Dimensions of Public Policy Choice: Beyond the Market Paradigm*, eds. John M. Gilroy and Maurice Wade (University of Pittsburgh Press 1992); Sven Ove Hansson, *Philosophical Problems in Cost-Benefit Analysis*, Economics and Philosophy, 2007, Vol. 23, 163–183; Eric A. Posner and Matthew D. Adler, *Rethinking Cost-Benefit Analysis*, Yale Law Journal,

1999, Vol. 109, 165–247; John C. Coates, *Cost-Benefit Analysis of Financial Regulation: Case Studies and Implications*, Yale Law Journal, 2015, Vol. 124(4), 882–1011; Eric A. Posner and E. Glen Weyl, *Cost-Benefit Analysis of Financial Regulations: A Response to Criticisms*, Yale Law Journal Forum, 2015, Vol. 124, 246–262; Cass R. Sunstein, *Financial Regulation and Cost-Benefit Analysis*, Yale Law Journal Forum, 2015, Vol. 124, 263–279.

49. Michael J. Sandel, *Justice* (Farrar, Straus and Giroux 2009), 43.

50. Sven Ove Hansson, *Philosophical Problems in Cost-Benefit Analysis*.

51. *Economics for Effective Regulation*, Occasional Paper 13, Financial Conduct Authority, March 2016.

52. *How We Analyse the Costs and Benefits of Our Policies*, Financial Conduct Authority, July 2018, 26.

53. Mike Feintuck, 'Regulatory Rationales Beyond Economic Theory: Regulating in the Public Interest', in *The Oxford Handbook of Regulation*, eds. Robert Baldwin, Martin Cave and Martin Lodge (Oxford University Press 2010).

54. See, for example, *Our Mission 2017: How We Regulate Financial Services*, Financial Conduct Authority, 2017.

55. *How We Analyse the Costs and Benefits of Our Policies*, Financial Conduct Authority, 22 et seq.

56. Ibid., 28 et seq.

57. Ibid.

58. *FCA Mission 2017*, 10 et seq.

59. For example, the UK Financial Conduct Authority is already required to publish guidance on how it intends to advance its operational objectives in discharging its general functions: section 1K, Financial Services and Markets Act 2000.

60. See, for example, Laurence Fletcher, 'Hedge fund hits jackpot by shorting M&S, Ted Baker and Metro Bank', *Financial Times*, London, 28 February 2019.

61. Section 142D, Financial Services and Markets Act 2000 and Section 13, Bank Holding Company Act of 1956, respectively.

62. For example, in the European Union, Regulation (EU) No. 236/2012 of the European Parliament and of the Council on short selling and certain aspects of credit default swaps (the 'Short Selling Regulation').

63. See, for example, in the European Union, Articles 57 and 58, Directive 2014/65/EU of the European Parliament and of the Council of 15 May 2014 on markets in financial instruments.

64. Philip Stafford, 'Futures exchanges eye shift to 'Flash Boys' speed bumps', *Financial Times*, London, 30 May 2019.

65. Michael Sandel, *The Moral Economy of Speculation: Gambling, Finance and the Common Good*, The Tanner Lectures on Human Values, University of Utah, 2013, 336.

66. John Maynard Keynes, *The General Theory of Employment, Interest and Money* (Royal Economic Society/Macmillan Press 1976 reprint), 159.
67. Tax policy might be another way, using a variation of the 'Tobin tax' concept. However, in addition to the complexities, its reliance on financial incentives risks conforming to financial narratives rather than breaking from them. The idea has been much debated elsewhere and is not considered further here.
68. Recital 21, Short Selling Regulation.
69. See, for example, Michael Stothard, 'Naked CDS ban fuels bank funding fears', *Financial Times*, London, 17 April 2013.
70. Stuart Banner, *Speculation: A History of the Fine Line Between Gambling and Investment* (Oxford University Press 2017); Jennifer N. Arthur, Robert J. Williams and Paul H. Delfabbro, *The Conceptual and Empirical Relationship Between Gambling, Investing, and Speculation*, Journal of Behavioral Addictions, 2016, Vol. 5(4), 580–591.
71. Some forms of financial speculation, such as spread betting, are a form of gambling, and there has been a long process of legal and regulatory definition to distinguish activities at the margins for regulatory purposes. For example, it was decided to exclude from the operation of the UK Gambling Act 2005 all activities that are financial services activities regulated under the UK Financial Services and Markets Act 2000, presumably reflecting uncertainty over whether they might otherwise involve gambling within the Gambling Act 2005. In addition, until the UK Financial Services Act 1986, there were concerns that certain derivatives transactions might fall to be treated as gaming contracts.
72. John Kay, *Other People's Money: Masters of the Universe or Servants of the People* (Profile Books 2015), 93 et seq.
73. Witness US debates over the Volcker Rule. See also Darrell Duffie, *Challenges to a Policy Treatment of Speculative Trading Motivated by Differences in Beliefs*, Journal of Legal Studies, 2014, Vol. 43, 173–182.
74. Section 235 Financial Services and Markets Act 2000.
75. Glossary, FCA Handbook, available at https://www.handbook.fca.org.uk/handbook
76. COBS 22.5 and Glossary, FCA Handbook.
77. COLL 3.3.5B, FCA Handbook.
78. Article 4.1(1) and (2), Directive 2014/65/EU of the European Parliament and of the Council on markets in financial instruments.
79. See the definition of 'regulated investment' in Article 3 of the Financial Services and Markets Act 2000 (Regulated Activities) Order 2001.
80. Section 3(10).
81. Sabine Frerichs, *Bounded Sociality*.
82. See, for example, Remuneration, PRA Rulebook for CRR firms.

83. Adam M. Grant, *Relational Job Design and the Motivation to Make a Prosocial Difference*, Academy of Management Review, 2007, Vol. 32(2), 393–417.

84. Ann-Kathrin Koessler and Stefanie Engel, *Policies as Information Carriers: How Environmental Policies May Change Beliefs and Consequent Behaviour*, IDEAS Working Paper Series from RePEc, 2019, 13.

85. Rebecca Sanderson, et al., *Strangers in a Strange Land: Relations Between Perceptions of Others' Values and Both Civic Engagement and Cultural Estrangement*, Frontiers in Psychology, 2019, Vol. 10, Article 559, 15.

86. US Sentencing Guidelines Manual (2018) at §8C2.5(f) and §8B2.1.

87. John Braithwaite, *Restorative Justice and Responsive Regulation* (Oxford University Press 2002), 11; *Regulatory Justice: Making Sanctions Effective*, Final Report of the Macrory Review (Cabinet Office, November 2006), 70. See, generally, Daniel Van Ness and Karen Heetderks Strong, *Restoring Justice: An Introduction to Restorative Justice* (5th edn, Routledge 2014).

88. John Braithwaite, *Restorative Justice and Responsive Regulation: The Question of Evidence*, Australian National University, RegNet Research Papers, No. 51, 2016.

89. Van Ness and Strong, *Restoring Justice: An Introduction to Restorative Justice*; Ted Wachtel, *Defining Restorative*, International Institute of Restorative Practices, 2013.

90. John Braithwaite, *Restorative Justice and Responsive Regulation*, 22 et seq.

91. *FCA Mission: Approach to Enforcement*, Financial Conduct Authority, April 2019, 8.

92. Ibid., 10.

93. Emma Borg and Bradford Hooker, *Epistemic Virtues Versus Ethical Values in the Financial Services Sector*, Journal of Business Ethics, 2019, Vol. 155, 17–27.

94. See further at https://www.bankofengland.co.uk/events/2015/november/open-forum-2015, accessed 21 November 2019.

95. In relation to senior management, see Andrew Edgecliffe-Johnson, 'Bosses must leave their bubble', *Financial Times*, London, 6 May 2019.

96. Robert Putnam, *Bowling Alone: The Collapse and Revival of American Community* (Simon & Schuster 2000), 24 et seq., Appendix 1.

97. Joel Sobel, *Can We Trust Social Capital*, Journal of Economic Literature, 2002, Vol. 40, 139–154.

98. Robert Putnam, *Bowling Alone*, 19.

99. Luigi Guiso, Paola Sapienza and Luigi Zingales, 'Civic Capital as the Missing Link', in *Handbook of Social Economics*, Volume 1A, eds. Jess Benhabib, Alberto Bisin and Matthew O. Jackson (North-Holland 2011); Henri Servaes and Ane Tamayo, *The Role of Social Capital in Corporations: A Review*, Oxford Review of Economic Policy, 2017, Vol. 22(2), 201–220.

100. Lins, Servaes and Tamayo, *Social Capital, Trust, and Firm Performance: The Value of Corporate Social Responsibility During the Financial Crisis*. The Edelman Trust Barometer, covered in Chap. 1, is sector-specific. See research

by Edelman over many years at https://www.edelman.com/research/edelman-trust-barometer-archive (accessed 14 October 2019). However, Edelman is a public relations firm and it would be preferable for the methodology and process of an assessment of the sort discussed here to be subject to much broader scrutiny.

101. *Reform of culture in finance from multiple perspectives*, remarks by Kevin Stiroh, Executive Vice President of the Financial Institution Group of the Federal Reserve Bank of New York, 26 February 2019; Stephanie Chaly et al., *Misconduct Risk, Culture, and Supervision*, Federal Reserve Bank of New York, December 2017; *BSB Annual Review 2018/2019*, Banking Standards Board, 2019.

102. Alex Chesterfield, Alex Gillespie and Tom Reader, *Measuring Culture – Can It Be Done?*, FCA Insight, https://www.fca.org.uk/insight/measuring-culture-can-it-be-done, accessed 30 November 2019.

8

Conclusion—Not an End, but a Beginning

'Would you tell me, please, which way I ought to go from here?'
'That depends a good deal on where you want to get to,' said the Cat.
'I don't much care where–,' said Alice.
'Then it doesn't matter which way you go,' said the Cat.
'–so long as I get *somewhere*,' Alice added as an explanation.
'Oh, you're sure to do that,' said the Cat, 'if you only walk long enough.'[1]

It can sometimes seem as if we have been living in Wonderland, behaving as if we 'don't much care where'. We go on as if our destination can be decided, miraculously, by a multitude of atomised individuals rationally pursuing their financial self-interest. That will lead somewhere, but not where we really want to be. In reality, we care very deeply where we end up and do not really think it can be left to markets.

And the stakes are high.[2] The goal to which recognition of a social licence seems to direct us is of the greatest value, and we are more than capable of moving towards it: lives not stunted by their reduction to financial and material measures; lives more human because they are lived in ways that help to realise the intrinsic value of others; and an environmentally and socially sustainable future, for all of us, our children and beyond, and for the commercial and financial activities needed to support that. But if we continue to dwell in a Wonderland, imagining that we are insulated from social and environmental damage while markets keep on giving, we will fail because we and our markets are ultimately not insulated. The cost will be disastrous, not just for financial markets, but for all. The issues are bearing in on us. Indeed, as I finish writing this book in the closing weeks of 2019, it increasingly looks as if

© The Author(s) 2020
D. Rouch, *The Social Licence for Financial Markets*,
https://doi.org/10.1007/978-3-030-40220-4_8

the steps we take or fail to take to protect the natural environment, even within the next five years, could be critical. We talk of protecting our environment, but of course, these steps are needed to protect ourselves from it.

Markets are an awesome source of potential good: not just financial and material goods but, even more importantly, relational goods. Those relational goods, in turn, can help to support the social solidarity upon which markets depend. If financial market participants are to flourish in providing these goods, and not undermine the environment on which they depend, more attention is needed to the question of 'where' and the steps needed to get there. It is needed urgently.

Greater recognition that markets operate subject to a social licence provides a framework for just that. It reaches towards an end goal. It expresses an aspiration for what financial markets could be. It has the potential to alter the substance of financial market relationships, because it concerns the desires and meanings that animate them. And it can be a source of positive reciprocity: just ends pursued by just means in financial markets. No behavioural decision or habit is neutral. It either advances that end or detracts from it.

So, this is a call to action. The need to heal the fracture between finance and society, and to galvanise the financial sector in helping to address humanity's many needs, is pressing. Chapter 1 noted that a process of re-evaluation—of what ends we value or desire—is under way, gaining considerable momentum since the 2008 financial crisis. The recognition that financial markets operate subject to a social licence is an end of that beginning. Whether you run or work in a financial firm, advise or regulate them, are a politician or make policy, or have an academic interest in financial markets, it is now time to pursue the end goal.

By defining our goal more clearly, by making it seem more manageable and less remote, we can help all people to see it, to draw hope from it, and to move irresistibly towards it.[3]

Notes

1. Lewis Carroll, *Alice's Adventures in Wonderland* and *Through the Looking-Glass, and What Alice Found There* (Oxford World Classics 2009), 57.
2. Please forgive the gaming metaphor (see Sect. 7.2.4).
3. *Commencement Address at American University*, John F. Kennedy, Washington, D.C., 10 June 1963.

Postscript: The Social Licence in a Time of Pandemic

24 April 2020

The impact of the Covid-19 health crisis is already immense. The immediate focus has been on saving lives. However, the world is now facing a severe and deepening recession.[1] Its eventual duration and intensity can only be guessed at. The uncertainties are enormous, not least the question on which much else hangs, of how fast and in what sense it will be possible to contain the virus, and how disruptive the necessary steps will be. Nonetheless, it is clear that the longer-term social, psychological and political consequences will be profound. Disruption may bring opportunities. However, the journey ahead will be arduous and fraught with risk.

In that context, the message of this book is more important, not less. Current events do not call any of what has already been said into question. Quite the opposite: they underscore the observation that financial markets operate subject to a social licence as well as its practical significance. This postscript highlights six of the more striking ways in which that is the case. It is organised so as to correspond with Parts I–III of the book.

In summary:

- Big questions are being asked. The crisis has significantly accelerated the re-evaluation, discussed in Chap. 1, of what end goals we really value. At the same time, experience is confirming key aspects of the discussion of behaviour in Part I, especially the strength of aspirations towards wellbeing,

D. Rouch, *The Social Licence for Financial Markets*,
https://doi.org/10.1007/978-3-030-40220-4

both for self and for others, incorporating but reaching far beyond financial goals—the intrinsic value of human life, experienced in practice.

- There has been much to validate the observation that financial markets operate subject to a form of social licence along the lines discussed in Part II, particularly its end goal.
- Part III considered the practical impact of greater recognition of a social licence. The relationship between private enterprise and the state, and their relationship with the societies in which they exist, has been shaken and is suddenly under scrutiny. Tensions could easily grow. From a financial market perspective, these relationships are the stuff of the social licence. This is a context in which the recognition that financial markets operate subject to a social licence can be even more valuable in providing coordinates for navigating the way ahead, shaping the expectations we have of each other and keeping the focus on long-term goals. More importantly still, it can help to form the sort of individuals and institutions that are up to making the journey since, as we are seeing, so much turns on how they decide to act in practice and cannot be legislated for.

Financial markets did not cause this crisis. However, as with the sustainability challenges noted in Chap. 1, which are even more serious and remain pressing, market participants can clearly help in getting us through. In doing so, they (like many in the wider business world) have an opportunity to address negative public perceptions and restore trust more rapidly than they might otherwise have done. Yet, their role as 'financial switchmen', controlling the provision and withdrawal of financial support at the micro level to businesses and individuals, will make this a very challenging path to tread, difficult, and unpopular, decisions will sometimes be needed to preserve their own commercial viability. Nonetheless, recognition that financial markets operate subject to a social licence provides a powerful and positive framework within which all of us, not just market participants, can approach it.

The Great Re-evaluation Accelerated and Valued Ends

Re-evaluation Accelerated

The re-evaluation discussed in Chap. 1 has now gained even greater momentum. Some of this reflects the determination of critics of market fundamentalism not to let a crisis go to waste. But it is also clear that after a decade of periodic panic attacks and endless rounds of nervous discussion in places such as the World Economic Forum, a significant threshold has now been crossed.

Markets have not done what societies needed most: preventing and managing the pandemic. Indeed, financial and economic life has needed protection. These tasks have largely fallen to the state, with government intervention on a massive scale. The significance of this swing in the state-market pendulum should not be over-egged. Although the state has decisively re-entered markets, doing so reflects its critical future role. Where else will respirators and groceries come from?

Nonetheless, the kind of economic orthodoxies discussed in Chap. 1, which assume the priority of financial and material goals, giving markets the lead role in delivering them, are being shredded. The invisible hand of the market may be a source of much good, but left to its own devices it does not, it seems, leave humanity best prepared for pandemics.[2] And, if not pandemics, what else? Indeed, unrestrained market forces could make things worse, while the austerity that followed the earlier market crisis of 2008 has undermined the social and health systems needed to cope. Doctrinaire adherence to narrow shareholder value does not deliver what shareholders really want, let alone wider society.[3] Something more is needed. What is it?

Valued Ends

At the same time as exposing the shortcomings of dominant market narratives, the pandemic has also focused attention, as crises often do, on what we really value: what end goals are intrinsically desired. Consistent with the discussion in Chap. 3, it turns out that what is valued is human life more than markets, wellbeing and the experience of human dignity over financial return.

Clearly, material wellbeing is part of that, as this book has been at pains to acknowledge. For that reason, the policy response will require a wrenchingly difficult balancing act between life preservation and the risk of extreme economic and social dislocation. Developing an acceptable approach will involve the sort of judgements discussed in Chap. 7, applying apparently incommensurable values. The debate over how to marry up economic and intrinsic human value in market and policy practice is long overdue and now seems to be gathering pace.[4] However, thus far, one of the most striking features of the pandemic response, at a national level at least, is an apparent commitment to the intrinsic value of human life over financial and material ends. A succession of nations, whose governments occupy a vast range of positions across the political-philosophical spectrum, has been willing to self-inflict massive economic pain to save life. Financial and material goals remain crucial to wellbeing; to suggest otherwise would be obscene with unemployment soaring and growing desperation among some of the world's most vulnerable.[5] However, it is increasingly clear that financial goals are instrumental in achieving some greater good; what is intrinsically valuable lies beyond them.

Taking this a step further, the pandemic has also generated abundant evidence in business contexts and beyond that, for many people, the desire for wellbeing does not stop at self-preservation but also involves a concern for others. Some of those in businesses do indeed display public service motivation (see Sect. 6.3.1).[6] Again, this is consistent with the assessment in Chap. 3. Naturally, there are countervailing examples (the scramble for medical resources, for one), and there will certainly be more in future. But that is not the dominant response. In the UK, one of the most visible examples of this other-regarding aspiration has been the recruitment of 750,000 volunteers in a matter of hours to support the National Health Service:[7] it seems that there is more of the courageous Guy's Hospital nurse, Kirsty Bowden, in us than we might have imagined (see the beginning of Chap. 3).

Further still, and again consistent with the discussion of realising human dignity in practice in Chap. 3, the pandemic is making clear just how far the wellbeing of the self, and of business enterprise, depends on the wellbeing of others. At a personal level this manifests itself, for example, in the emotional experience of social distancing or in the heightened infection risks where the economic and personal circumstances of others make it difficult for them to self-isolate, such as the homeless or those working in the 'gig economy'. It is similar at the level of business enterprises, where the extent of their reliance upon social wellbeing is now painfully clear; the physical separation of social distancing severely impedes commercial enterprise but is also a powerful metaphor for the business consequences of strained social relations and degraded trust. At an international level, where leadership and cooperation have so far fallen woefully short, there is a sense in which all countries can only be as safe as the country with the weakest economic and social security infrastructure.[8]

The Social Licence Validated

Part II looked at the existence and substance of the social licence and the relationship between it and written standards, like regulations. Again, the experience of the crisis tends to validate what was said. Two themes stand out particularly.

Permission

Chapter 4 considered the sense in which financial markets can be seen as operating subject to a form of social permission—a freedom given to market participants to pursue just ends by just means in financial markets. Evidence for this permission has been plentiful.

As discussed in Part II, although the recognition of a licence reaches far beyond the laws and regulations that apply to market participants, these are nonetheless one of its clearest manifestations. So, it is unsurprising that this element of permission is one of the most obvious in responses to the pandemic. For example, it can be seen in the form of government and regulatory intervention to ensure that business is conducted in accordance with societal objectives, although much of this has relied upon regulatory 'suasion' using the existing regulatory framework, rather than making new rules. Steps by regulators in some jurisdictions to get financial firms to preserve their capital and lending capacity, by not paying dividends to shareholders or bonuses to staff, are a case in point. However, financial firms' decisions have taken place within a broader framework of social expectations, concerning the social acceptability of distributions when businesses and individuals may be struggling to obtain funding from the financial sector or suffering wider hardship.[9]

A sense of social permission also comes through in discussion of whether financial businesses should exercise commercial discretion in a way that reflects broader social expectations and ends. It seems implicit, for example, in the debate over how insurers should approach construing their policies in the context of Covid-19 related claims where the wording of the policies does not obviously exclude coverage or is ambiguous.[10] Likewise, there has been considerable attention to banks' lending policies, especially where the finance being sought has essentially been provided by the government.[11]

More explicitly, the presence of an underlying social permission has also been picked up in talk of a renewed 'social contract' between business, and the state and society.[12] In the words of the chief executive of Schroders, in burnishing the firm's own social profile, '… companies receiving [government] support must demonstrate the strength of their social contract with stakeholders.'[13] It is easy to see why discussion of a contract has developed; the provision of extensive government financial support to businesses will ultimately need to be repaid from taxes and will inevitably come with strings attached, if nothing else, through government influence in its subsequent role as a long-term funding provider. In the case of banks, specifically, the changed relationship can also be seen in their role as, effectively, an agent of the state distributing state funding to stressed industry sectors—funding which is likely to be important in due course in preventing their own loan books from deteriorating.

However, for the reasons discussed in Sect. 4.8, recognition of a social licence for financial markets seems a more accurate reflection of reality than the idea that there is a 'social contract' or that it would be possible to impose such a thing. Indeed, some of the current discussion of social contracts seems to recognise this. As one commentator advancing a social contract framework puts it:

> ... it is in the vital interests of business to renew and retain its social licence to operate ... in the age of coronavirus. Unless they demonstrably reciprocate the extraordinary support they have received during the crisis, British businesses will be exposed to the significant risk of public – and thus political – backlash that will curtail their scope to operate and, in due course, harm the UK economy.[14]

Nonetheless, talk of a social contract can lead in a very different direction from the kind of licence discussed in Part II, shrouding regulatory agendas and giving the misleading impression of two parties locked in self-interested commercial negotiation, each paying damages to the other if the contract is breached, with the risk that 'a fine becomes a price' (again, see Sect. 4.8).[15] As discussed in Chap. 1, regulation has achieved much, not least, in helping to ensure that banks did not collapse in the early stages of the pandemic: so far, this has been a health and economic crisis, not a banking crisis.[16] However, law and regulation has fallen short in addressing some of our most pressing challenges. For similar reasons, it is unlikely to be the most potent solution for those ahead and could even stifle the very energy and initiative that will be needed. The observation that markets operate subject to a social licence recognises a role for laws and regulations but is not fundamentally about them; it reaches beyond them.

Aspiration and Justice: The End Goal of the Licence

The crisis also casts light on the purpose for which this permission is given. It does so in a way that chimes with the discussion in Part II of the end goal of the social licence. Chapter 4 suggested that recognition of a licence expresses an aspiration for market participants to pursue just ends by just means in financial markets, where justice is understood as a situation in which the dignity of all (the intrinsic human value of each person, including market participants) is most fully realised.

The crisis response has affirmed the value of human life and made other-regardingness more visible (see Valued Ends, above). However, it has also highlighted the extent to which business, including finance, is integral to realising intrinsic human value and is relied upon to do that. Supermarket chains are suddenly no longer faceless money machines, but turn out to be providing a critical human function—their staff treated as key workers, like medical staff.[17] It is similar with other industry sectors, such as transport, with transport workers on the front line of the pandemic response.[18] Finance is part of this. It is now clear, as perhaps never before, how far the wellbeing of businesses and individuals across the world depends upon the quality of their relationship with institutions in the finance sector.[19]

In the months ahead, financial markets will have a key role in a huge business recapitalisation process. Further, financial institutions will be faced with a multitude of decisions in running their client and counterparty relationships on which the wellbeing of millions, if not billions, of people will rest, not just economically but in sustaining the fabric of their lives and those of others. Yet their wellbeing also underpins the social fabric on which the health of the same institutions depends. The process of balancing these needs and interests in a way that secures mutual wellbeing can be thought of as the pursuit of justice, and the significance of financial activity in that exercise should now be clear.

Practical Implications

A way of looking at the world is being shattered (see Re-evaluation Accelerated, above). The unimagined has materialised. The world, it is said, will never be the same again. In the context of financial markets, the recognition of a social licence provides a compelling framework for navigating the emerging landscape.

Part III considered the practical impact of greater recognition of a social licence from two perspectives. First, Chap. 6 looked at it as a narrative, with power to influence behaviour by helping people see something different about their world (its meaning or framing), affecting the end goals that get pursued (the things on which desire is focused) and by forming people and institutions—its potential to re-form market relationships from the inside out, in a way that can strengthen social solidarity. Chapter 7 then looked at how it can inform and influence policy, accordingly.

The current crisis calls none of that into question. Rather, it makes greater recognition of the social licence even more important in charting the way ahead. At a time when old certainties have been disintegrating, the framework of the social licence has the potential positively to impact behaviour and guide policy through a new set of economic, social and political challenges. The following picks up on two areas in which this may be especially important.

State Versus Markets

The crisis has breathed new life into the hoary debate over whether states or markets are best at creating 'welfare' or whether it needs a mixture of the two and, if so, what that should look like.[20] In the early stages of the crisis, the pendulum has swung decisively towards the state, with intervention at levels not seen in the West since World War II. More will come. Meanwhile, the tax increases that seem almost certain to follow may heighten expectations further still.

But how far should the process go, what form should it take and how long should it last? These are vital questions, and a robust framework is needed within which to answer them. As discussed in Chap. 1, the shortcomings of existing economic frameworks are clear, and the process of their re-evaluation has now accelerated (see Re-evaluation Accelerated, above). In the context of financial markets at least, the recognition that there is a social licence provides a potentially powerful alternative: one that draws on important truths in the existing frameworks, but reaches beyond them.

As noted, much state intervention reflects an understanding that markets remain critical in the long term. The fast freeze applied to huge tracts of the economy will soon need to be eased in the interests of welfare. Intervention therefore reveals the importance of both markets and state in underpinning social cohesion. However, as the economic downturn creates widespread social distress, and in an environment where attitudes towards business are already inflamed, there is a growing risk of the relationship between the two becoming more conflictual, with desirable market dynamism being dampened by inappropriate regulation. From a financial markets perspective, how might greater recognition of a social licence help? Essentially, by emphasising the presence of a third element in the markets-state relationship—society—and the need for just relationships if the social solidarity on which the effectiveness of both markets and governments ultimately depends is to be maintained. Importantly, as discussed in Parts II and III, talk of a social licence involves recognising something about the way in which financial markets already work and relate to wider society, and existing aspirations about what they could be at their best, making it a realistic and valuable policy guide. How?

First, recognition of a social licence breaks away from the simple duality of state versus market. Success in tackling the virus and the resulting fallout ultimately needs to emerge from the multiple relationships that comprise whole societies; getting stuck on the creaking markets/state seesaw risks missing the extent to which this is the case, even down to the effectiveness of social distancing which has become, ironically, an exercise in social solidarity. Both financial markets and government contribute to this solidarity, but they also depend on it. The licence is a 'social' licence, not ultimately a state licence. It places society front and centre and applies a standard to which both market participants and states can be held to account and the role of each calibrated.

Second, that standard does not simply concern economic 'welfare' (which tends to dominate the state vs. markets debate), but wellbeing—the realisation of intrinsic human value in practice, reliant on broad-based mutuality, not the greatest good for the greatest number. Economic welfare is an essential element in this, but no more than that. The crisis has highlighted how it is wellbeing that really counts, and the limits, of economic welfare as a goal of both business activity and policy.[21]

Third, the licence recognises that realising intrinsic human value in practice depends to a significant degree on the quality of social relationships and, importantly, that these include commercial and financial relationships. In other words, it recognises the limits of what state intervention can achieve. Like a good marriage, healthy relationships cannot be created by legal rules and can be stifled by heavy-handed control. Greater recognition of a social licence advances an environment which reflects the need for them to flourish and in a way that has the potential to strengthen positive reciprocity.

Fourth, the licence is just that: a freedom. It is not about societal or state control, or about two parties locked in negotiation seeking to define their relationship contractually, but a release. Equally, however, it is 'freedom for', not 'freedom from'; it is a release subject to responsibilities, based on commonly held aspirations. The aspirations concern an intrinsically desired end which recognises the needs of those to whom the licence is given and those giving the licence (among them, the licensees): an end that is just. Like common economic models, it does not ignore the possibility of differing interests. However, unlike them, it offers a consensual common ground upon which to approach their reconciliation rather than treating it as an exercise in controlled conflict.

Social Division Versus Solidarity

The risk of strain is not restricted to the market-state relationship. In spite of the other-regarding aspirations revealed by the crisis, social solidarity is likely, once again, to be sorely tested in the time ahead.

Up to a point, Covid-19 is a leveller and has heightened awareness of social proximity, which can help to strengthen other-regarding motivation (see Sect. 6.3.3). However, it also isolates and divides: richer nations with infrastructure from those without; the well-off who can socially distance in comfort from the less well-off living in confined accommodation with limited resources and the prospect of unemployment; professionals able to work online, from those who need to be present in person; and so on. The loss of vital social infrastructure, as charities and similar institutions face a plunge in income and in some cases extinction, will only sharpen these differences. There is a risk of widespread disillusionment and anger towards systems that are perceived to have let people down, or that allowed only some to escape, frustration that is likely to find political expression, reopening old wounds and inflicting new ones, as recent European Union (EU) discussion of aid to member states struggling with the consequences of the pandemic serves to highlight.[22]

Meanwhile, the discontent discussed in Chap. 1 towards the finance sector, and business more generally, has not gone away. Deep suspicions of greed remain.[23] The increasingly dire social and economic damage caused by the pandemic could seriously inflame these discontents and result in a wider social fragmentation.[24] Ways are needed to strengthen the common bonds on which all rely to see us through.

Financial markets alone certainly cannot resolve all of this. The challenge is systemic. However, now more than ever, market participants need to address their part of the challenge, by displaying the sort of positive reciprocity that can be a source of broad-based mutuality rather than undermining it. Much depends on this, including their own ability to flourish. And work has already started, with spectacular speed, to facilitate it, for example, in keeping financial markets functioning and in streamlining the process of recapitalising cash-starved, but otherwise healthy, enterprises.[25] The work by some organisations to convert what were essentially 'bricks and mortar' operations involving thousands of individuals into a virtual network operating from spare rooms and kitchen tables has been astonishing.

However, as this book has repeatedly made clear, you cannot force people to be positively reciprocal. Positive reciprocity, and the kind of broad-based mutuality that can help hold people together, grows out of the way relationships are lived and felt *in practice*, not as they are legislated for. It emerges from what people and institutions *are* and what they *become*. And, for the reasons discussed in Chap. 6, the frameworks and narratives within which those relationships are understood and conducted are critical to that because of the way they focus desire, frame understanding and form those involved.

As also discussed in Chap. 6, old frameworks of rational financial self-interest pursued in a state of conflict and, more popularly, those of *The Wolf of Wall Street* genre are not a promising starting point from this perspective—whether at the level of individual, business or policy practice. A different narrative is still needed which is more closely connected with reality and which can focus, frame and form financial activity in ways that support broad-based mutuality and social solidarity. This book has argued that the recognition that financial markets operate subject to a social licence provides just such a framework. The Covid-19 crisis changes none of that. It makes the need to embrace it even more pressing.

Notes

1. *World Economic Outlook, Chapter 1*, The Great Lockdown, International Monetary Fund, April 2020.
2. Izabella Kaminska, 'Why the real economy needs a prudential authority too', *Financial Times*, London, 2 April 2020.
3. Jonathan Guthrie, Get ready for the $4.5tn takeover, *Financial Times*, London, 25 March 2020.
4. See, for example, Leader, 'Covid-19 presents stark choices between life, death and the economy', *The Economist*, London, 2 April 2020.
5. David Blanchflower and David Bell, 'Forget recession, this is a depression', *The Guardian*, London, 3 April 2020; Eric Morath and Sarah Chaney, U.S. Employers Cut 701,000 Jobs in March, *Wall Street Journal*, New York, 3 April 2020; *Shared Responsibility, Global Solidarity: Responding to the Socio-Economic Impacts of COVID 19*, United Nations, March 2020.
6. See, for example, Angie Brown, 'Coronavirus: I never thought I would be so proud to sell bread and butter', BBC News, 24 April 2020 (accessed 24 April 2020).
7. https://www.england.nhs.uk/participation/get-involved/volunteering/nhs-volunteer-responders/ (accessed 2 April 2020).
8. Abiy Ahmed, 'If Covid-19 is not beaten in Africa it will return to haunt us all', *Financial Times*, London, 25 March 2020; Raghuram Rajan, 'Rich countries cannot win the war against coronavirus alone', *Financial Times*, London, 20 March 2020.

9. Editorial, 'Bank dividend payments should be suspended', *Financial Times*, London, 30 March 2020; Martin Arnold, 'ECB financial supervisor urges banks to cut back on bonuses', *Financial Times*, London, 30 March 2020. The issue is sensitive and not clear-cut, not least because some of the main shareholders are pension funds who have their own social obligations.

10. Editorial, 'A solvent insurance industry is vital for all', *Financial Times*, London, 1 April 2020.

11. 'Denying coronavirus loans "completely unacceptable" banks told', *BBC News*, 2 April 2020, https://www.bbc.co.uk/news/business-52126658 (accessed 3 April 2020).

12. See, for example, Janan Ganesh, 'Dickens and Orwell – the choice for capitalism', *Financial Times*, London, 27 March 2020; Sean Healy, 'This crisis shows we need a social contract to protect all our people', *Independent*, Dublin, 29 March 2020; Editorial, 'Virus puts responsible capitalism to the test', *Financial Times*, London, 29 March 2020.

13. Peter Harrison, *How the investment industry can help during the Covid crisis*, Schroders, 24 March 2020 (available at https://www.schroders.com/bg/insights/economics/peter-harrison-how-the-investment-industry-can-help-during-the-covid-crisis/ accessed 3 April 2020).

14. James Kirkup, *Returning the Favour: A New Social Contract for Business*, Social Market Foundation, March 2020, 5.

15. Uri Gneezy and Aldo Rustichini, *A Fine Is a Price*, Journal of Legal Studies, 2000, Vol. 29(1), 1–17.

16. Relative stability to date is not just the product of regulation. The sector has also been helped by unprecedented state support to the real economy, without which there could have been a greater risk of a vicious circle of insolvencies and impaired bank balance sheets. Jon Danielsson, et al., 'We shouldn't be comparing the Coronavirus Crisis to 2008 – this is why', World Economic Forum, 2020, http://www3.weforum.org/docs/WEF_Stakeholder_Principles_COVID_Era.pdf (accessed 1 April 2020).

17. For the UK list, see https://www.gov.uk/government/publications/coronavirus-covid-19-maintaining-educational-provision/guidance-for-schools-colleges-and-local-authorities-on-maintaining-educational-provision (accessed 7 April 2020).

18. Harriet Brewis, '"Heartbroken" Sadiq Khan confirms 21 London Transport workers have now died from Covid 19', *Evening Standard*, London, 13 April 2020.

19. See, for example, Andy Verity, 'Coronavirus: A Fifth of Smaller UK Firms Will Run Out of Cash', BBC News, 1 April 2020, https://www.bbc.co.uk/news/business-52114414 (accessed 1 April 2020).

20. Paul de Grauwe, *The Limits of the Market: The Pendulum Between Government and Market* (Oxford University Press 2017). For example, contrast the approach in the following two articles: Leader, 'Bail-outs are inevitable – and toxic', *The Economist*, London, 4 April 2020; Mariana Mazzucato, 'The Covid-19 crisis is a chance to do capitalism differently', *The Guardian*, 18 March 2020.

21. For example, see Christopher Pissarides, 'Treat the self-employed fairly to aid the battle against Covid-19', *Financial Times*, London, 24 March 2020.

22. See, for example, Victor Mallet and Roula Khalef, 'Macron warns of EU unravelling unless it embraces financial solidarity', *Financial Times*, London, April 2020; 'Coronavirus: EU could fail over outbreak, warns Italy's Giuseppe Conte', *BBC News*, 9 April 2020 (accessed 9 April 2020).

23. See, for example, Banks under fire for coronavirus loan tactics, *BBC News*, 30 March 2020, https://www.bbc.co.uk/news/business-52043896 (accessed 30 March 2020).

24. See, for example, Angela Giuffrida and Lorenzo Tondo, 'Singing stops in Italy as fear and social unrest mount', *The Guardian*, London, 1 April 2020.

25. See, for example, *Statement of Policy: Listed Companies and Recapitalisation Issuances During the Coronavirus Crisis*, Financial Conduct Authority, 4 April 2020, developed in dialogue with issuers and their advisers.

Bibliography

Akerlof, G. A. and Kranton, R. E., *Identity Economics: How Our Identities Shape Our Work, Wages, and Well-being* (Princeton University Press 2010)

Akerlof, R., *Value Formation: The Role of Esteem*, Games and Economic Behavior, 2017, Vol. 102, 1–19

Al Ramiah, A. and Hewstone, M., *Intergroup Contact as a Tool for Reducing, Resolving and Preventing Intergroup Conflict: Evidence, Limitations and Potential*, American Psychologist, 2013, Vol. 68(7), 527–542

Algan, Y. and Cahuc, P., *Inherited Trust and Growth*, American Economic Review, 2010, Vol. 100(5), 2060–2092

Allen, J. G. and Lastra, R. M., *Border Problems II: Mapping the Third Border*, 1 January 2018, UNSW Law Research Paper No. 18–88

Amadxarif, Z., et al., *The Language of Rules: Textual Complexity in Banking Reforms*, Staff Working Paper No. 834, Bank of England 2019

Anderson, S. M. and Chen, S., *The Relational Self: An Interpersonal Social-cognitive Theory*, Psychological Review, 2002, Vol. 109(4), 619–645

André, K., et al., *Beyond the Opposition Between Altruism and Self-interest: Reciprocal Giving in Reward-based Crowdfunding*, Journal of Business Ethics, 2017, Vol. 146(2), 313–332

Andrews, M., *Shaping History: Narratives of Political Change* (Cambridge University Press 2007)

Appadurai, A., 'The Capacity to Aspire: Culture and the Terms of Recognition', in *Culture and Public Action*, eds. Rao, V. and Walton, M. (Stanford University Press 2004)

Aquino, K., et al., *Testing a Social-Cognitive Model of Moral Behavior: The Interactive Influence of Situations and Moral Identity Centrality*, Journal of Personality and Social Psychology, 2009, Vol. 97(1), 123–141

Aristotle, Ross, W. D. and Brown, L., *The Nicomachean Ethics* (Oxford University Press 2009)

Arpaly, N. and Schroeder, T., *In Praise of Desire* (Oxford University Press 2014)

© The Author(s) 2020
D. Rouch, *The Social Licence for Financial Markets*,
https://doi.org/10.1007/978-3-030-40220-4

Arrow, K. J., *Gifts and Exchanges*, Philosophy and Public Affairs, 1972, Vol. 1(4), 343–362

Arthur, J. N., Williams, R. J. and Delfabbro, P. H., *The Conceptual and Empirical Relationship Between Gambling, Investing, and Speculation*, Journal of Behavioral Addictions, 2016, Vol. 5(4), 580–591

Asch, S. E., *Opinions and Social Pressure*, Scientific American, 1955, Vol. 193(5), 31–35

Ash, E., Chen, D. L. and Naidu, S., *Ideas Have Consequences*, ETH Zurich, Centre for Law and Economics, Working Paper Series No. 04/2019

Ashraf, N. and Bandiera, O., *Altruistic Capital*, American Economic Review, 2017, Vol. 107(5), 70–75

ASX Corporate Governance Council, *Corporate Governance Principles and Recommendations*, 4th edn, February 2019

Atiyah, P. S., *The Rise and Fall of Freedom of Contract* (Clarendon Press Oxford 1979)

Awrey, D., Blair, W. and Kershaw, D., *Between Law and Markets: Is There a Role for Culture and Ethics in Financial Regulation?* Delaware Journal of Corporate Law, 2013, Vol. 38(1), 191–245

Axelrod, R. and Hamilton, W. D., *The Evolution of Cooperation*, Science, 1981, Vol. 211(4489), 1390–1396

Ayres, I. and Braithwaite, J., *Responsive Regulation* (Oxford University Press 1992)

Badré, B., *Can Finance Save the World* (Berrett-Koehler Publishers, Inc. 2018)

Bailey, A., *Culture in financial institutions: it's everywhere and nowhere*, speech at the HKMA Annual Conference for Independent Non-Executive Directors, Hong Kong, 16 May 2017

Bailey, A., *Transforming culture in financial services*, speech at the Transforming Culture in Financial Services Conference, London, 19 March 2018

Bailey, A., *Trust and ethics – a regulator's perspective*, speech at the launch of the St Mary's University School of Business and Society, London, 16 October 2018

Bailey, A., *The future of financial conduct regulation*, speech delivered at Bloomberg, London, 23 April 2019

Baldwin, R., Cave, M. and Lodge, M., *Understanding Regulation: Theory, Strategy, and Practice* (2nd edn, Oxford University Press 2012)

Banking Standards Board, *Annual Review 2016/17*

Banking Standards Board, *Annual Review 2018/19*

Banner, S., *Speculation: A History of the Fine Line Between Gambling and Investment* (Oxford University Press 2017)

Bar-Gill, O. and Fershtman, C., *Law and Preferences*, The Journal of Law, Economics, and Organization, 2004, Vol. 20(2), 331–352

Bardi, A. and Schwartz, S. H., *Values and Behavior: Strength and Structure of Relations*, Personality and Social Psychology Bulletin, 2003, Vol. 29(10), 1207–1220

Bargh, J., Lombardi, W. and Higgins, E. T., *Automaticity of Chronically Accessible Constructs in Person X Situation Effects on Person Perception: It's Just a Matter of Time*, Journal of Personality and Social Psychology, 1988, Vol. 55(4), 599–605

Barnes, M., *The 'Social License to Operate': An Emerging Concept in the Practice of International Investment Tribunals*, Journal of International Dispute Settlement, 2019, Vol. 10, 328–360

Basel Committee on Banking Supervision, *Pillar 3 Disclosure Requirements – Updated Framework*, December 2018

Basu, K., *Beyond the Invisible Hand: Groundwork for a New Economics* (Princeton University Press 2011)

Basu, K., *The Republic of Beliefs: A New Approach to Law and Economics* (Princeton University Press 2018)

Batson, D. C., *Altruism in Humans* (Oxford University Press 2010)

Bauer, R., Ruof, T. and Smeets, P., *Get Real! Individuals Prefer More Sustainable Investments*, February, 2019, available at: https://ssrn.com/abstract=3287430 (accessed 1 December 2019)

Bauman, Y. and Rose, E., *Selection or Indoctrination: Why Do Economics Students Donate Less Than the Rest?* Journal of Economic Behavior and Organization, 2011, Vol. 79(3), 318–327

Baxter, J. and Megone, C., *Exploring the Role of Professional Bodies and Professional Qualifications in the UK Banking Sector*, a report prepared for the Banking Standards Board, October 2016

Beetham, D., *The Legitimation of Power* (2nd edn, Palgrave Macmillan 2013)

Begon, J., *What Are Adaptive Preferences? Exclusion and Disability in the Capability Approach*, Journal of Applied Philosophy, 2015, Vol. 32(3), 241–257

Bender, A. and Beller, S., *Cognition is … Fundamentally Cultural*, Behavioural Sciences, 2013, Vol. 3(1), 42–54

Benjamin, J., *The Narratives of Financial Law*, Oxford Journal of Legal Studies, 2010, Vol. 30(4), 787–814

Benkler, Y., *The Wealth of Networks: How Social Production Transforms Markets and Freedom* (Yale University Press 2006)

Benkler, Y., *The Penguin and the Leviathan: How Cooperation Triumphs Over Self-interest* (Crown Business 2011)

Bernheim, B. D., *A Theory of Conformity*, Journal of Political Economy, 1994, Vol. 102(5), 841–877

Bernold, E., et al., *Social Framing and Cooperation: The Roles and Interaction of Preferences and Beliefs*, (30 January 2015), available at https://ssrn.com/abstract=2557927

Bicchieri, C., *The Grammar of Society: The Nature and Dynamics of Social Norms* (Cambridge University Press 2006)

Bice, S., *What Gives You a Social Licence? An Exploration of the Social Licence to Operate in the Australian Mining Industry*, Resources, 2014, Vol. 3(1), 62–80

Bice, S. and Moffat, K., *Social Licence to Operate and Impact Assessment*, Impact Assessment and Project Appraisal, 2014, Vol. 32(4), 257–262

Black, J., *Rules and Regulators* (Clarendon Press Oxford 1997)

Black, J., *Mapping the Contours of Contemporary Financial Services Regulation*, Journal of Comparative Law Studies, 2002, Vol. 2(2), 253–287

Black, J., *Forms and Paradoxes of Principles-Based Regulation*, Capital Markets Law Journal, 2008, Vol. 3(4), 425–457

Black, J., 'The Rise, Fall and Fate of Principles Based Regulation' in, *Law Reform and Financial Markets* eds. Alexander, K. and Moloney, N (Edward Elgar 2011)

Black, L., *The Social Licence to Operate: Your Management Framework for Complex Times* (Dō Sustainability, 2013)

Blackburn, S., *Ruling Passions* (Oxford University Press 1998)

Blair, W., 'Reconceptualising the Role of Standards in Supporting Financial Regulation', in *Reconceptualising Global Finance and its Regulation*, eds. Buckley, R. P., Avgouleas, E. and Douglas D. W. (Cambridge University Press 2016)

Blass, T., *The Milgram Paradigm After 35 Years: Some Things We Now Know About Obedience to Authority*, Journal of Applied Social Psychology, 1999, Vol. 29(5), 955–978

Blattman, C., Jamison, J. C. and Sheridan, M., *Reducing Crime and Violence: Experimental Evidence From Cognitive Behavioral Therapy in Liberia*, American Economic Review, 2017, Vol. 107(4), 1165–1206

Bohnet, I. and Frey, B. S., *Social Distance and Other Regarding Behavior in Dictator Games: Comment*, American Economic Review, 1999, Vol. 89(1), 335–339

Bohnet, I., Frey, B. S. and Huck, S., *More Order with Less Law: On Contract Enforcement, Trust, and Crowding*, American Political Science Review, 2002, Vol. 95(1), 131–144

Boje, D. M., *Storytelling Organizations* (Sage Publications 2008)

Bolino, M. C. and Grant, A. M., *The Bright Side of Being Prosocial at Work, and the Dark Side, Too: A Review and Agenda for Research on Other-oriented Motives, Behavior, and Impact in Organizations*, The Academy of Management Annals, 2016, Vol. 10(1), 599–670

Bönisch, P. and Hyll, W., *Television Role Models and Fertility – Evidence from a Natural Experiment*, SOE Paper No. 752, 2015, available at https://ssrn.com/abstract=2611597

Booth, J. E., Park, K. W. and Glomb, T. M., *Employer-Supported Volunteering Benefits: Gift Exchange Among Employers, Employees, and Volunteer Organizations*, Human Resource Management, 2009, Vol. 48(2), 227–249

Borg, E., *The Thesis of 'Doux Commerce' and the Social License to Operate*, in press, Business Ethics: A European Review (https://doi.org/10.1111/beer.12279)

Borg, E. and Hooker, B., *Epistemic Virtues Versus Ethical Values in the Financial Services Sector*, Journal of Business Ethics, 2019, Vol. 155, 17–27

Bourdieu, P., *Esquisse d'une Théorie de la Pratique: Précédé de Trois Études D'ethnologie Kabyle* (Librairie Droz 1972); quotations in this book taken from the English language edition, *Outline of a Theory of Practice*, translated by Nice, R. (Cambridge University Press 1977)

Bourdieu, P., *Le Sens Pratique* (Les Éditions Minuit 1980); quotations in this book taken from the English language edition, *The Logic of Practice*, translated by Nice, R. (Polity Press 1990)

Bourdieu, P., *The Force of Law: Toward a Sociology of the Juridical Field*, translated by Terdiman, R., Hastings Law Journal, 1987, Vol. 38(5), 805–853

Boussalis, C., Feldman, Y. and Smith, H. E., *An Experimental Analysis of the Effect of Standards on Compliance Performance*, Regulation and Governance, 2018, Vol. 12(2), 277–298

Boutilier, R. G., *Frequently Asked Questions About the Social Licence to Operate*, Impact Assessment and Project Appraisal, 2014, Vol. 32(4), 263–272

Bowen, F., *Marking Their Own Homework: The Pragmatic and Moral Legitimacy of Industry Self-Regulation*, Journal of Business Ethics, 2019, Vol. 156(1), 257–272

Bowles, S., *Endogenous Preferences: The Cultural Consequences of Markets and Other Economic Institutions*, Journal of Economic Literature, 1998, Vol. 36(1), 75–111

Bowles, S., *The Moral Economy: Why Good Incentives Are No Substitute for Good Citizens* (Yale University Press 2016)

Bowles, S. and Hwang, S., *Social Preferences and Public Economics: Mechanism Design When Social Preferences Depend Upon Incentives*, Journal of Public Economics, 2008, Vol. 92(8–9), 1811–1820

Bowles, S. and Polanía-Reyes, S., *Economic Incentives and Social Preferences: Substitutes or Complements?* Journal of Economic Literature, 2012, Vol. 50(2), 368–425

Bozeman, B. and Su, X., *Public Service Motivation Concepts and Theory: A Critique*, Public Administration Review, 2015, Vol. 75(5), 700–710

Braithwaite, J., *Restorative Justice and Responsive Regulation* (Oxford University Press 2002)

Braithwaite, J., *Restorative Justice and Responsive Regulation: The Question of Evidence*, Australian National University, RegNet Research Papers, No. 51, 2016

Bratman, M. E., 'The Intentions of a Group', in *The Moral Responsibility of Firms*, eds. Orts, E. W. and Smith, N. C. (Oxford University Press 2017)

Brennan, G. and Pettit, P., *The Economy of Esteem* (Oxford University Press 2004)

Brennan, G., et al., *Explaining Norms* (Oxford University Press 2013)

British Academy, *Principles for Purposeful Business: How to Deliver the Framework for the Purpose of the Corporation* (British Academy 2019)

Brueckner, M. and Eabrasu, M., *Pinning Down the Social License to Operate (SLO): The Problem of Normative Complexity*, Resources Policy, 2018, Vol. 59, 217–226

Bruner, J., *The Narrative Construction of Reality*, Critical Inquiry, 1991, Vol. 18(1), 1–21

Bruner, J., *Life as Narrative*, Social Research, 2004, Vol. 71(3), 691–710

Bruni, L., *Reciprocity, Altruism and the Civil Society: In Praise of Heterogeneity* (Routledge 2008)

Bryson, A. and Freeman, R. B., *The Role of Employee Stock Purchase Plans – Gift and Incentive? Evidence From a Multinational Corporation*, British Journal of Industrial Relations, 2019, Vol. 57(1), 86–106

Buelens, M. and van den Broeck, H., *An Analysis of Differences in Work Motivation Between Public and Private Sector Organizations*, Public Administration Review, January/February 2007, Vol. 67(1), 65–74

Buhmann, K., *Public Regulators and CSR: The 'Social Licence to Operate' in Recent United Nations Instruments on Business and Human Rights and the Juridification of CSR*, Journal of Business Ethics, 2016, Vol. 136(4), 699–714

Business Roundtable, Statement on the Purpose of the Corporation, available at https://opportunity.businessroundtable.org/ourcommitment/ (accessed 14 October 2019)

Busselle, R. and Bilandzic, H., *Measuring Narrative Engagement*, Media Psychology, 2009, Vol. 12(4), 321–347

Caillou, P., et al., 'A Simple-to-use BDI Architecture for Agent-based Modeling and Simulation', in *Advances in Social Simulation 2015*, eds. Wander Jager, et al. (Singer 2017)

Carlisle, C., *On Habit* (Routledge 2014)

Carney, M., *The future of financial reform*, the 2014 Monetary Authority of Singapore Lecture, Singapore 17 November 2014

Carney, M., *Building real markets for the good of the people*, speech at the Lord Mayor's Banquet for Bankers and Merchants of the City of London, London 10 June 2015

Carney, M., *Turning back the tide*, speech at a FICC Market Standard Board event, 'Two years on from the Fair and Effective Markets Review', Bloomberg, London, 29 November 2017

Carney, M., *Enable, empower, ensure: a new finance for the new economy*, speech Lord Mayor's Banquet for Bankers and Merchants of the City of London, London, 20 June 2019

Carney, M., *Remarks given during the UN Secretary General's Climate Action Summit 2019*, 23 September 2019

Carr, D., *Narrative and the Real World: An Argument for Continuity*, History and Theory, 1986, Vol. 25(2), 117–131

Carriger, M. S., *Narrative Approach to Corporate Strategy: Empirical Foundations*, Journal of Strategy and Management, 2011, Vol. 4(4), 304–324

Carter, J. R. and Irons, M. D., *Are Economists Different, and If So, Why?* Journal of Economic Perspectives, 1991, Vol. 5(2), 171–177

Caruso, E. M., Shapira, O. and Landy, J. F., *Show Me the Money: A Systematic Exploration of Manipulations, Moderators, and Mechanisms of Priming Effects*, Psychological Science, 2017, Vol. 28(8), 1148–1159

Cassar, L. and Meier, S., *Nonmonetary Incentives and the Implications of Work as a Source of Meaning*, Journal of Economic Perspectives, 2018, Vol. 32(3), 215–238

Chaly, S., et al., *Misconduct Risk, Culture, and Supervision*, Federal Reserve Bank of New York, December 2017

Chang, C., 'Narrative Advertisements and Narrative Processing', in *Advertising Theory*, eds. Rodgers, S. and Thorson, E. (Routledge 2012)

Chesterfield, A., Gillespie, A. and Reader, T., *Measuring Culture – Can It Be Done?*, FCA Insight, https://www.fca.org.uk/insight/measuring-culture-can-it-be-done, accessed 30 November 2019

Ciepley, D., *Beyond Public and Private: Toward a Political Theory of the Corporation*, American Political Science Review, 2013, Vol. 107(1), 139–158

Clayton, J., *Observations on culture at financial institutions and the SEC*, New York, 18 June 2018

Coates, J. C., *Cost-Benefit Analysis of Financial Regulation: Case Studies and Implications*, Yale Law Journal, 2015, Vol. 124(4), 882–1011

Coates, J. C., *The Volcker Rule as Structural Law: Implications for Cost-Benefit Analysis and Administrative Law*, Capital Markets Law Journal, 2015, Vol. 10(4), 447–468

Coch, L. and French, J. R. P., *Overcoming Resistance to Change*, Human Relations, 1948, Vol. 1(4), 512–532

Coffee, J. C., *Gatekeepers: The Professions and Corporate Governance* (Oxford University Press 2006)

Cohn, A., Fehr, E. and Maréchal, M. A., *Business Culture and Dishonesty in the Banking Industry*, Nature, 2014, Vol. 516, 86–89

Cooper, R., Shallice, T. and Farringdon, J., 'Symbolic and Continuous Processes in the Automatic Selection of Actions', in *Hybrid Problems, Hybrid Solutions*, ed. Hallam, J. (IOS Press 1995)

Cooter, R., *Do Good Laws Make Good Citizens? An Economic Analysis of Internalized Norms*, Virginia Law Review, 2000, Vol. 86(8), 1577–1601

Cover, R. M., *Nomos and Narrative*, Harvard Law Review, 1983, Vol. 97(1), 4–68

Crane, A., Matten, D. and Moon, J., *Corporations and Citizenship* (Cambridge University Press 2008)

Crane, B., *Revisiting Who, When and Why Stakeholders Matter: Trust and Stakeholder Connectedness*, Business & Society, February 2018, https://doi.org/10.1177/0007650318756983

Cropanzano, R. S. and Ambrose, M. L., *The Oxford Handbook of Justice in the Workplace* (Oxford University Press 2015)

Cunliffe, J., *Challenges for financial markets*, speech given at the Association for Financial Markets in Europe's annual dinner, London, 3 November 2016

Curry, O. S., Mullins, D. A. and Winehouse, H., *Is It Good to Cooperate? Testing the Theory of Morality-as-Cooperation in 60 Societies*, Current Anthropology, 2019, Vol. 60(1), 47–69

d'Adda, G., et al., *Do Leaders Affect Ethical Conduct*, Journal of the European Economic Association, 2017, Vol. 15(6), 1177–1213

Dahlén, M., Lange, F. and Smith, T., *Marketing Communications: A Brand Narrative Approach* (John Wiley & Sons Ltd 2010)

Dahlsgaard, K., Peterson, C. and Seligman, M. E. P., *Shared Virtue: The Convergence of Valued Human Strengths Across Culture and History*, Review of General Psychology, 2005, Vol. 9(3), 203–213

Dalbert, C. and Umlauft, S., *The Role of the Justice Motive in Economic Decision Making*, Journal of Economic Psychology, 2009, Vol. 30(2), 172–180

Dare, M., Schirmer, J. and Vanclay, F., *Community Engagement and Social Licence to Operate*, Impact Assessment and Project Appraisal, 2014, Vol. 32(3), 188–197

Darwall, S., *Sympathetic Liberalism: Recent Work on Adam Smith*, Philosophy and Public Affairs, 1999, Vol. 28(2), 139–164

Davidson, J., *Realising the benefits of purposeful leadership*, speech delivered at the CCTA 2018 Conference, Nottingham, 1 November 2018

Davis, G. F., *Managed by the Markets: How Finance Re-shaped America* (Oxford University Press 2009)

Dawes, R. M., van der Kragt, A. J. C. and Orbell, J. M., 'Cooperation for the Benefit of Us – Not Me, or My Conscience', in *Beyond Self-interest*, ed. Mansbridge, J. J. (University of Chicago Press 1990)

Dawkins, R., *The God Delusion* (Black Swan 2016)

Dawkins, R., *The Selfish Gene* (40th Anniversary edn, Oxford University Press 2016)

de Grauwe, P., *The Limits of the Market: The Pendulum Between Government and Market* (Oxford University Press 2017)

de Vignemont, F. and Singer, T., *The Empathic Brain: How, When and Why?* Trends in Cognitive Sciences, 2006, Vol. 10(10), 435–441

Debes, R., *Adam Smith on Dignity and Equality*, British Journal for the History of Philosophy, 2012, Vol. 20(1), 109–140

Debes, R., 'Introduction', in *Dignity: A History*, ed. Debes, R. (Oxford University Press 2017)

Delli Carpini, M. X., Lomax Cook, F. and Jacobs, L. R., *Public Deliberations, Discursive Participation and Citizen Engagement: A Review of the Empirical Literature*, Annual Review of Political Science, 2004, Vol. 7(1), 315–344

Delsen, L. and Lehr, A., *Value Matters or Values Matter? An Analysis of Heterogeneity in Preferences for Sustainable Investments*, Journal of Sustainable Finance and Investment, 2019, Vol. 9(3), 240–261

Demuijnck, G., and Fasterling, B., *The Social Licence to Operate*, Journal of Business Ethics, 2016, Vol. 136(4), 675–685

Denning, S., *The Secret Language of Leadership: How Leaders Inspire Action Through Narrative* (Jossey-Bass 2007)

Denning, S., *The Leader's Guide to Storytelling: Mastering the Art and Discipline of Business Narrative* (revised edn, Jossey-Bass 2011)

Department for Business, Innovation and Skills, *The Future of Narrative Reporting: Consulting on a New Reporting Framework*, September 2011

DeSteno, D., et al., *Gratitude as Moral Sentiment: Emotion-Guided Cooperation in Economic Exchange*, Emotion, 2010, Vol. 10(2), 289–293

Deutsch, M. and Gerrard, H. B., *A Study of Normative and Informational Social Influences Upon Individual Judgement*, Journal of Abnormal and Social Psychology, 1955, Vol. 51(3), 629–636

Dietrich, F. and List, C., *Where Do Preferences Come From?* International Journal of Game Theory, 2013, Vol. 42(3), 613–637

Dik, B. J. and Duffy, R. D., *Calling and Vocation at Work: Definitions and Prospects for Research and Practice*, The Counselling Psychologist, 2009, Vol. 37(3), 424–450

DiMaggio, P., *Culture and Cognition*, Annual Review of Psychology, 1997, Vol. 23, 263–287

Donne, J. and Raspa, A., *Devotions Upon Emergent Occasions* (Oxford University Press 1987)

Dorsey, D., *Adaptive Preferences Are a Red Herring*, Journal of the American Philosophical Association, 2017, Vol. 3(4), 465–484

Drucker, P., *Management: Tasks, Responsibilities, Practices* (Heinemann 1974)

Dudley, W. C., *The importance of incentives in ensuring a resilient and robust financial system*, remarks at the U.S. Chamber of Commerce, 26 March 2018

Dudley, W. C., *Strengthening culture for the long term*, speech at the Federal Reserve Bank of New York, 18 June 2018

Duffie, D., *Challenges to a Policy Treatment of Speculative Trading Motivated by Differences in Beliefs*, Journal of Legal Studies, 2014, Vol. 43, 173–182

Duffy, R. D. and Dik, B. J., *Research on Calling: What Have We Learned and Where are We Going?* Journal of Vocational Behaviour, 2013, Vol. 83(3), 428–436

Duffy, R. D., England, J. W. and Dik, B. J., 'Callings', in *The Oxford Handbook of Meaningful Work*, eds. Yeoman, R., et al. (Oxford University Press 2019)

Dufwenberg, M., Gächter, S. and Hennig-Schmidt, H., *The Framing of Games and the Psychology of Play*, Games and Economic Behavior, 2011, Vol. 73(2), 459–478

Dunfee, T. W. and Donaldson, T., *Ties That Bind: A Social Contracts Approach to Business Ethics* (Harvard Business School Press 1999)

Dur, R. and van Lent, M., *Socially Useless Jobs*, Industrial Relations, 2019, Vol. 58(1), 3–16

Dworkin, R., *The Model of Rules*, University of Chicago Law Review, 1967, Vol. 35(1), 14–46

Dworkin, R., *Law's Empire* (Belknap Press of Harvard University Press 1986)

Dworkin, R., *Justice for Hedgehogs* (Belknap Press of Harvard University Press 2011)

Economist Intelligence Unit, *A Crisis of Culture – valuing ethics and knowledge in financial services*, 2013

Edelman, Edelman Trust Barometer, available at https://www.edelman.com/research/edelman-trust-barometer-archive (accessed 14 October 2019)

Edmans, A., Gabaix, X. and Jenter, D., *Executive Compensation: A Survey of Theory and Evidence*, European Corporate Governance Institute Finance Working Paper No. 514/2017, July 2017

Edwards, P., et al., *Social Licence to Operate and Forestry – An Introduction*, Forestry, 2016, Vol. 89(5), 473–476

Edwards, P., et al., *Trust, Engagement, Information and Social Licence – Insights from New Zealand*, Environmental Research Letters, 2019, Vol. 14(2), 024010

Eisenberg, M. A., *Corporate Law and Social Norms*, Columbia Law Review, 1999, Vol. 99, 1253–1292

Ellingsen, T., et al., *Social Framing Effects: Preferences or Beliefs?* Games and Economic Behaviour, 2012, Vol. 76(1), 117–130

Emtairah, T. and Mont, O., *Gaining Legitimacy in Contemporary World: Environmental and Social Activities of Organisations*, International Journal of Sustainable Society, 2008, Vol. 1(2), 134–148

Ervasti, H., Kouvo, A. and Venetoklis, T., *Social and Institutional Trust in Times of Crisis: Greece 2002–2011*, Social Indicators Research, 2019, Vol. 141(3), 1207–1231

Escalas, J. E., *Narrative Processing: Building Consumer Connections to Brands*, Journal of Consumer Psychology, 2004, Vol. 14(1), 168–180

European Commission, *Action Plan: Financing Sustainable Growth*, Communication from the European Commission, COM (2018) 97 final

European Commission, *Communication from the Commission on Artificial Intelligence for Europe*, European Commission COM (2018) 237 final

European Systemic Risk Board, *Too Late, Too Sudden: Transition to a Low-Carbon Economy and Systemic Risk*, Reports of the Advisory Scientific Committee, No. 6/ February 2016

European Union Technical Group on Sustainable Finance, *Financing a Sustainable European Economy, Taxonomy Technical Report*, June 2019

Fair and Effective Markets Review, *How Fair and Effective are the Fixed Income, Foreign Exchange and Commodities Markets*, Consultation Document, HM Treasury, Bank of England and Financial Conduct Authority, October 2014

Fair and Effective Markets Review, *The Fair and Effective Markets Review*, Final Report, HM Treasury, Bank of England and Financial Conduct Authority, June 2015

Farrell, B., Cobbin, D. and Farrell H., *Codes of Ethics – Their Evolution, Development and Other Controversies*, Journal of Management Development, 2002, Vol. 21(2), 152–163

Faulhaber, G. and Baumol, W., *Economists as Innovators: Practical Products of Theoretical Research*, Journal of Economic Literature, 1988, Vol. 26, 577–600

Fehr, E. and Falk, A., *Psychological Foundations of Incentives*, Institute for Empirical Research in Economics, European Economic Review, 2002, Vol. 46(4), 687–724

Fehr, E. and Fischbacher, U., *Social Norms and Human Cooperation*, Cognitive Sciences, 2004, Vol. 8(4), 185–190

Fehr, E. and Gächter, S., *Fairness and Retaliation: The Economics of Reciprocity*, The Journal of Economic Perspectives, 2000, Vol. 14(3), 159–181

Fehr, E. and Gintis, H., *Human Motivation and Social Cooperation: Experimental and Analytical Foundations*, Annual Review of Sociology, 2007, Vol. 33, 43–64

Fehr, E., Kremhelmer, S. and Schmidt, K. M., *Fairness and the Optimal Allocation of Ownership Rights*, The Economic Journal, 2008, Vol. 118, 1262–1284

Feintuck, M., 'Regulatory Rationales Beyond the Economic: In Search of the Public Interest', in *The Oxford Handbook of Regulation*, eds. Baldwin, R., Cave, M. and Lodge, M. (Oxford University Press 2011)

Ferraro, F., Pfeffer, J. and Sutton, R. I., *Economics Language and Assumptions: How Theories Can Become Self-fulfilling*, Academy of Management Review, 2005, Vol. 30(1), 8–24

Festinger, L., *A Theory of Social Comparison Processes*, Human Relations, 1954, Vol. 7(2), 117–140

Festré, A. and Garrouste, P., *Theory and Evidence in Psychology and Economics About Motivation Crowding Out: A Possible Convergence?* Journal of Economic Surveys, 2015, Vol. 29(2), 339–356

Financial Conduct Authority, *Economics for Effective Regulation*, Occasional Paper 13, March 2016

Financial Conduct Authority, *Our Mission 2017: How We Regulate Financial Services*, 2017

Financial Conduct Authority, *How we Analyse the Costs and Benefits of our Policies*, July 2018

Financial Conduct Authority, *Industry Codes of Conduct and Feedback on Principle 5*, Policy Statement PS18/18, July 2018

Financial Conduct Authority, *FCA Mission: Approach to Supervision*, April 2019

Financial Conduct Authority, *FCA Mission: Approach to Enforcement*, April 2019

Financial Conduct Authority, *Climate Change and Green Finance: Summary of Responses and Next Steps, Feedback to DP 18/8*, Feedback Statement FS 19/6, October 2019

Financial Conduct Authority, *Business Plan 2019/20*

Financial Crisis Inquiry Commission, *The Financial Crisis Inquiry Report: Final Report of the National Commission on the Causes of the Financial and Economic Crisis in the United States*, January 2011

Financial Reporting Council, *The UK Corporate Governance Code*, 2018

Financial Reporting Council, *Guidance on the Strategic Report*, 2018

Financial Services Authority, *The Failure of the Royal Bank of Scotland*, Financial Services Authority Board Report, December 2011

Financial Stability Board, *Stocktake of Efforts to Strengthen Governance Frameworks to Mitigate Misconduct Risks*, May 2017

Financial Stability Board *Artificial Intelligence and Machine Learning in Financial Services: Market Developments and Financial Stability Implications*, 1 November 2017

Financial Stability Board, *Strengthening Governance Frameworks to Mitigate Misconduct Risk: A Toolkit for Firms and Supervisors*, 20 April 2018

Fine, G. A., 'The Storied Group: Social Movements as "Bundles of Narratives"', in *Stories of Change: Narrative and Social Movements*, ed. Davis, J. E. (State University of New York Press 2002)

Fink, L., *A Sense of Purpose*, 2018, and *Purpose & Profit*, 2019, annual letters to CEOs of companies in which Blackrock invests client funds, available at https://www.blackrock.com/corporate/investor-relations/larry-fink-ceo-letter (accessed 5 November 2019)

Fischbacher, U., Gächter, S. and Fehr, E., *Are People Conditionally Cooperative? Evidence From a Public Goods Experiment*, Economics Letters, 2001, Vol. 71(3), 397–404

Fisher, W. E., *Narration as a Human Communication Paradigm: The Case of Public Moral Argument*, Communication Monographs, 1984, Vol. 51(1), 1–22

Fisher, W. R., *Human Communication as Narration: Toward a Philosophy of Reason, Value, and Action* (University of South Carolina Press 1987)

Foreign Exchange Working Group *Report on Adherence to the Global FX Code*, May 2017

Foster, C. and Frieden, J., *Crisis of Trust: Socio-Economic Determinants of Europeans' Confidence in Government*, European Union Politics, 2017, Vol. 18(4), 511–535

Frank, B. and Schulze, G. G., *Does Economics Make Citizens Corrupt?*, Journal of Economic Behavior and Organization, 2000, Vol. 43(1), 101–113

Frank, R. H., Gilovich, T. and Regan, D. T., *Does Studying Economics Inhibit Cooperation?* The Journal of Economic Perspectives, 1993, Vol. 7(2), 159–171

Frankel, M. S., *Professional Codes: Why, How, and with What Impact*, Journal of Business Ethics, 1989, Vol. 8(2), 109–115

Freeman, E. R., *Strategic Management: A Stakeholder Approach* (Pitman 1984)

Frerichs, S., *Bounded Sociality: Behavioural Economists' Truncated Understanding of the Social and Its Implications for Politics*, Journal of Economic Methodology, 2019, Vol. 26(3), 243–258

Frey, B. S. and Meier, S., *Are Political Economists Selfish and Indoctrinated? Evidence From a Natural Experiment*, Economic Inquiry, 2003, Vol. 41(3), 448–462

Friedman, M., *Capitalism and Freedom* (40th anniversary edn, University of Chicago Press 2002)

Fukuyama, F., *Trust: The Social Virtues and the Creation of Prosperity* (Simon & Schuster 1995)

Fuller, L., *The Morality of Law* (Yale University Press 1964)

Gabriel, Y., *Storytelling in Organizations: Facts, Fictions and Fantasies* (Oxford University Press 2000)

Galizzi, M. M. and Navarro-Martínez, D., *On the External Validity of Social Preference Games: A Systematic Lab-Field Study*, Management Science, 2019, Vol. 65(3), 976–1002

Gallois, C., et al., *The Language of Science and Social Licence to Operate*, Journal of Language and Social Psychology, 2017, Vol. 36(1), 45–60

Gandal, N., et al., *Personal Value Priorities of Economists*, Human Relations, 2005, Vol. 58(10), 1227–1252

Ganz, M., 'Public Narrative, Collective Action, and Power', in *Accountability Through Public Opinion: From Inertia to Public Action*, eds. Odugbemi, S. and Lee, T. (World Bank 2011)

Geertz, C., *The Interpretation of Cultures* (Basic Books 1973)

Gehman, J., Lefsrud, L. M. and Fast, S., *Social License to Operate: Legitimacy by Another Name?* Canadian Public Administration, 2017, Vol. 60(2), 293–317

George, D., *Preference Pollution: How Markets Create the Desires We Dislike* (University of Michigan Press 2004)

Ghosh V. E. and Gilboa, A., *What is a Memory Schema? A Historical Perspective on Current Neuroscience Literature*, Neuropsychologia, 2014, Vol. 53, 104–114

Giddens, A. and Sutton, P. W., *Essential Concepts in Sociology* (Polity Press 2017)

Gintis, H., et al., 'Moral Sentiments and Material Interests: Origins, Evidence, and Consequences', in *Moral Sentiments and Material Interests: The Foundations of Cooperation in Economic Life*, eds. Gintis, H., et al. (MIT Press 2005)

Glaser, V. L., et al., 'Institutional Frame Switching: How Institutional Logics Shape Individual Action', in *How Institutions Matter!* Research in the Sociology of Organizations, eds. Gehman, J., Lounsbury, M. and Greenwood, R. (Emerald Group Publishing Limited 2017), Vol. 48A

Global Sustainable Investment Alliance, *2018 Global Sustainable Investment Review*, 2018

Gneezy, U., and Rustichini, A., *A Fine Is a Price*, Journal of Legal Studies, 2000, Vol. 29(1), 1–17

Gold, N., 'Trustworthiness and Motivations', in *Capital Failure*, eds. Morris, N. and Vines, D. (Oxford University Press 2014)

Gomez-Mejia, L. and Wiseman, R. M., *Reframing Executive Compensation: An Assessment and Outlook*, Journal of Management, 1997, Vol. 23(3), 291–374

Gowdy, J. and Seidl, I., *Economic Man and Selfish Genes: The Implications of Group Selection for Economic Valuation and Policy*, The Journal of Socio Economics, 2004, Vol. 33, 343–358

Gower, L. C. B., *The English Private Company*, Law and Contemporary Problems, 1953, Vol. 18, 535–545

Graham, J., et al., *Mapping the Moral Domain*, Journal of Personality and Social Psychology, 2011, Vol. 101(2), 366–385

Granovetter, M., *Economic Action and Social Structure: The Problem of Embeddedness*, American Journal of Sociology, 1985, Vol. 19(3), 481–510

Grant, A. M., *Relational Job Design and the Motivation to Make a Prosocial Difference*, Academy of Management Review, 2007, Vol. 32(2), 393–417

Grant, A. M., *The Significance of Task Significance: Job Performance Effects, Relational Mechanisms, and Boundary Conditions*, Journal of Applied Psychology, 2008, Vol. 93(1), 108–124

Grant, A. M., *Giving Time, Time After Time: Work Design and Sustained Employee Participation in Corporate Volunteering*, Academy of Management Review, 2012, Vol. 37(4), 589–615

Grant, A. M., *Leading With Meaning: Beneficiary Contact, Prosocial Impact, and the Performance Effects of Transformational Leadership*, Academy of Management Journal, 2012, Vol. 55(2), 458–476

Green, M. C. and Brock, T. C., *The Role of Transportation in the Persuasiveness of Public Narrative*, Journal of Personality and Social Psychology, 2000, Vol. 79(5), 701–721

342   **Bibliography**

Griswold, C. L., *Adam Smith and the Virtues of Enlightenment* (Cambridge University Press 1999)

Guiso, L., Sapienza, P. and Zingales, L., 'Civic Capital as the Missing Link', in *Handbook of Social Economics Vol. 1A*, eds. Benhabib, J., Bisin A. and Jackson M. O. (North-Holland 2011)

Gunningham, N. and Grabosky, P., *Smart Regulation: Designing Environmental Policy* (Clarendon Press Oxford 1998)

Gunningham, N., Kagan, R. A. and Thornton, D., *Social License and Environmental Protection: Why Businesses Go beyond Compliance*, Law and Social Enquiry, 2004, Vol. 29(2), 307–341

Gunster, S. and Neubauer, R., *From Public Relations to Mob Rule: Media Framing of Social Licence in Canada*, Canadian Journal of Communication, 2018, Vol. 43(1), 11–32

Gutsche, G. and Ziegler, A., *Which Private Investors Are Willing to Pay for Sustainable Investments? Empirical Evidence From Stated Choice Experiments*, Journal of Banking and Finance, 2019, Vol. 102, 193–214

Guzzo, R. A. and Dickson, M. W., *Teams in Organizations: Recent Research on Performance and Effectiveness*, Annual Review of Psychology, 1996, Vol. 47(1), 307–338

Hackenberg, T. D., *Token Reinforcement: Translational Research and Application*, Journal of Applied Behavior Analysis, 2018, Vol. 51(2), 393–435

Hafer, C. L. and Bègue, L., *Experimental Research on Just-world Theory: Problems, Developments, and Future Challenges*, Psychological Bulletin, 2005, Vol. 131(1), 128–167

Haldane, A., *The Great Divide*, speech at the New City Agenda Annual dinner, London, 18 May 2016

Hamilton, W. D., *The Genetical Theory of Social Behaviour*, Journal of Theoretical Biology, 1964, Vol. 7, 1–52

Hammack, P. L., *Narrative and the Politics of Meaning*, Narrative Inquiry, 2011, Vol. 21(2), 311–318

Hammack, P. L., 'Mind, Story and Society: The Political Psychology of Narrative', in *Warring With Words: Narrative and Metaphor in Politics*, eds. Hanne, M., Crano, W. D. and Mio, J. S. (Psychology Press 2015)

Hammack, P. L. and Pilecki, A., *Narrative as a Root Metaphor for Political Psychology*, Political Psychology, 2012, Vol. 33(1), 75–103

Hammer, S. *The Role of Narrative in Political Campaigning: An Analysis of Speeches by Barack Obama*, National Identities, 2010, Vol. 12(3), 269–290

Han, Y., *Is Public Service Motivation Changeable? Integrative Modeling with Goal-Setting Theory*, International Journal of Public Administration, 2018, Vol. 41(3), 216–225

Hanne, M. and Weisberg, R., *Narrative and Metaphor in the Law* (Cambridge University Press 2018)

Hanrahan, P., *Corporate Governance, Financial Institutions and the "Social Licence"*, Law and Financial Markets Review, 2016, Vol. 10(3), 123–126

Hansson, S. O. *Philosophical Problems in Cost-Benefit Analysis*, Economics and Philosophy, 2007, Vol. 23, 163–183

Hardy, C., 'Hysteresis', in *Pierre Bourdieu: Key Concepts*, ed. Grenfell, M. (2nd edn, Routledge 2014)

Hart, H. L. A., *The Concept of Law* (Clarendon Press Oxford 1963)

Hart, O., *Incomplete Contracts and Control*, American Economic Review, 2017, Vol. 107(7), 1731–1752

Hartzmark, S. and Sussman, A. B., *Do Investors Value Sustainability? A Natural Experiment Examining Ranking and Fund Flows*, forthcoming in the Journal of Finance

Harvard Business Review, *The Business Case for Purpose*, Harvard Business Review Analytic Services Report, (Harvard Business School Publishing 2015)

Hasnas, J., *The Normative Theories of Business Ethics: A Guide for the Perplexed*, Business Ethics Quarterly, 1998, Vol. 8(1), 19–42

Hass, J., *Economic Sociology: An Introduction* (Routledge 2007)

Hazard, G. C., *Legal Ethics: Legal Rules and Professional Aspirations*, Cleveland State Law Review, 1981, 571–576

Held, M., *The evolving first line of defense*, speech at the 1LoD Summit, New York City, 17 April 2018

Hellmich, S. N., *Are People Trained in Economics "Different," and If So, Why? A Literature Review*, The American Economist, 2019, Vol. 64(2), 246–268

Henrich, J., et al., *In Search of Homo Economicus: Behavioral Experiments in 15 Small-Scale Societies*, American Economic Review, 2001, Vol. 91(2), 73–78

Henrich J., et al., *Foundations of Human Sociality: Economic Experiments and Ethnographic Evidence From Fifteen Small-scale Societies* (Oxford University Press 2004)

Herzog, L., ed. *Just Financial Markets? Finance in a Just Society* (Oxford University Press 2017)

HM Treasury, *The Green Book: Central Government Guidance on Appraisal and Evaluation*, 2018

Hobbes, T., *On the Citizen*, edited and translated by Tuck, R. and Silverthorne, M. (Cambridge University Press 1998)

Hodson, R., *Dignity at Work* (Cambridge University Press 2001)

Hoff, K. and Stiglitz, J. E., *Striving For Balance in Economics: Towards a Theory of the Social Determination of Behavior*, Journal of Economic Behavior and Organization, 2016, Vol. 126, 25–57

Hoppit, J., *The Myths of the South Sea Bubble*, Transactions of the Royal Historical Society, 2002, Vol. 12, 141–165

House of Commons Treasury Committee, *The Run on the Rock*, fifth report of session 2007–08, HC 56–I

Howarth, D., *Law as Engineering: Thinking About What Lawyers Do* (Edward Elgar 2013)

Howell, S. T., Niessner, M. and Yermack, D., *Initial Coin Offerings: Financing Growth with Cryptocurrency Token Sales*, ECGI Finance Working Paper No. 564/2018, July 2018

Hühen, M. P., *You Reap What You Sow: How MBA Programs Undermine Ethics*, Journal of Business Ethics, 2014, Vol. 121(4), 527–541

Hume, D., *A Treatise of Human Nature*, eds. David Norton and Mary Norton (Oxford University Press 2001)

Hume, D., *The History of England* (Phillips, Sampson and Company 1856, Michigan Historical Reprint Society)

Hupé, J., *Shortcomings of Experimental Economics to Study Human Behavior: A Reanalysis of Cohn et al. 2014, Nature 516, 86–89, 'Business Culture and Dishonesty in the Banking Industry'* SocArXiv, 22 March 2018, https://doi.org/10.31235/osf.io/nt6xk

Hyll, W. and Schneider, L., *The Causal Effect of Watching TV on Material Aspirations: Evidence From the "Valley of the Innocent"*, Journal of Economic Behavior and Organization, 2013, Vol. 86, 37–51

Intergovernmental Panel on Climate Change, *Global Warming of 1.5 °C*, October 2018

International Integrated Reporting Council, *International <IR> Framework*, 2013

Isaksen, E. T., Brekke, K. A. and Richter, A., *Positive Framing Does Not Solve the Tragedy of the Commons*, Journal of Environmental Economics and Management, 2019, Vol. 95, 45–56

Janicik, G. A. and Bartel, C. A., *Talking About Time: Effects of Temporal Planning and Time Awareness Norms on Group Coordination and Performance*, Group Dynamics: Theory, Research, and Practice, 2003, Vol. 7(2), 122–134

Jensen, M. C. and Meckling, W. H., *Theory of the Firm: Managerial Behavior, Agency Costs and Ownership Structure*, Journal of Financial Economics, 1976, Vol. 3(4), 305–360

John, S., *In codes we trust – Redefining the social licence for financial markets*, speech to the Association of Corporate Treasurers, Bank of England, London, 13 June 2017

Jones, K., 'Distrusting the Trustworthy' in *Reading Onora O'Neill*, eds. Archard, D., et al., (Routledge 2013)

Kahneman, D., *Thinking Fast and Slow* (Allen Lane 2011)

Kant, I. *Groundwork of the Metaphysics of Morals*, translated and edited by Gregor. M and Timmermanm, J., revised edition (Cambridge University Press 2012)

Kaptein, M. and Mark S. Schwartz, *The Effectiveness of Business Codes: A Critical Examination of Existing Studies and the Development of an Integrated Research Model*, Journal of Business Ethics, 2008, Vol. 77(2), 111–127

Kay, J., *Other People's Money: Masters of the Universe or Servants of the People?* (Profile Books 2015)

Kay Review of UK Equity Markets and Long-Term Decision Making, *Final Report*, July 2012

Kennedy, G., *Adam Smith and the Invisible Hand: From Metaphor to Myth*, Econ Journal Watch, 2009, Vol. 6(2), 239–263

Keynes, J. M., *The General Theory of Employment, Interest and Money* (Royal Economic Society/Macmillan Press 1976 reprint)

Kindleberger, C. P. and Aliber, R. Z., *Manias, Panics and Crashes: A History of Financial Crises* (5th edn, Palgrave Macmillan 2005)

Koessler, A. and Engel, S., *Policies as Information Carriers: How Environmental Policies May Change Beliefs and Consequent Behaviour*, IDEAS Working Paper Series from RePEc, 2019

Krebs, D. L., *Empathy and Altruism*, Journal of Personality and Social Psychology, 1975, Vol. 32(6), 1134–1146

Kurzban, R., Burton-Chellew, M. N. and West, S. A., *The Evolution of Altruism in Humans*, Annual Review of Psychology, 2015, Vol. 66, 575–599

Kvaløy, O., Nieken, P. and Schöttner, A., *Hidden Benefits of Reward: A Field Experiment on Motivation and Monetary Incentives*, European Economic Review, 2015, Vol. 76, 188–199

Lacey, J., Edwards, P. and Lamont, J., *Social Licence as Contract: Procedural Fairness and Agreement-Making in Australia*, Forestry, 2016, Vol. 89(5), 489–499

Lagarde, C., *Ethics and finance – aligning financial incentives with societal objectives*, speech delivered at an Event hosted by the Institute for New Economic Thinking: Finance and Society, 6 May 2015

Lastra, R. M. and Brener, A. H., 'Justice, Financial Markets, and Human Rights', in *Just Financial Markets? Finance in a Just Society*, ed. Lisa Herzog (Oxford University Press 2017)

Law Commission of England and Wales, *Fiduciary Duties of Intermediaries Report*, 1 July 2014

Law Commission of England and Wales, *"Is it always about the money?" Pension trustees' duties when setting an investment strategy: Guidance from the Law Commission*, 1 July 2014

Lazarus, R., *Emotion and Adaptation* (Oxford University Press 1991)

Lewin, L., *Self-interest and Public Interest in Western Politics* (Oxford University Press 1991)

Lewis, M., *Flash Boys: A Wall Street Revolt* (W. W. Norton & Company 2014)

Liberman, V., Samuels, S. M. and Ross, L., *The Name of the Game: Predictive Power of Reputations Versus Situational Labels in Determining Prisoner's Dilemma Game Moves*, Personality and Social Psychology Bulletin, 2004, Vol. 30(9), 1175–1185

Lichtenberg, J., 'What Are Codes of Ethics For?', in *Codes of Ethics and the Professions*, eds. Coady, M. and Block, S. (Melbourne University Press 1996)

Lins, K. V., Servaes H. and Tamayo A., *Social Capital, Trust, and Firm Performance: The Value of Corporate Social Responsibility During the Financial Crisis*, Journal of Finance, 2017, Vol. 72(4), 1785–1824

Lodder, P., et al., *A Comprehensive Meta-Analysis of Money Priming*, Journal of Experimental Psychology: General, 2019, Vol. 148(4), 688–712

Lopes, H., *From Self-Interest Motives to Justice Motives: The Challenges of Some Experimental Results*, American Journal of Economics and Sociology, 2008, Vol. 67(2), 287–314

Lorenz, E., *Trust, Contract and Economic Cooperation*, Cambridge Journal of Economics, 1999, Vol. 23(3), 301–315

Lundquist, T., et al., *The Aversion to Lying*, Journal of Economic Behavior and Organization, 2009, Vol. 70(1–2), 81–92

MacIntyre, A., 'Utilitarianism and Cost-Benefit Analysis: An Essay on the Relevance of Moral Philosophy to Bureaucratic Theory', in *The Moral Dimensions of Public Policy Choice: Beyond the Market Paradigm*, eds. Gilroy, J. M. and Wade, M. (University of Pittsburgh Press 1992)

MacIntyre, A., *After Virtue: A Study in Moral Theory* (3rd edn, Bloomsbury 2007)

MacKenzie, D., *An Engine, Not a Camera: How Financial Models Shape Markets* (MIT Press 2006)

Macklem, T., *Law and Life in Common* (Oxford University Press 2015)

Macrory Review, *Regulatory Justice: Making Sanctions Effective*, Final Report of the Macrory Review (Cabinet Office, November 2006)

Maitland, I., 'How Insiders Abuse the Idea of Corporate Personality', in *The Moral Responsibility of Firms*, eds. Orts, E. W. and Smith, N. C. (Oxford University Press 2017)

Mansbridge, J. J., 'On the Relation of Altruism and Self-interest', in *Beyond Self-interest*, ed. Mansbridge, J. J. (University of Chicago Press 1990)

Mansell, S. F., *Capitalism, Corporations and the Social Contract: A Critique of Stakeholder Theory* (Cambridge University Press 2013)

Markus, H. R. and Kitayama, S., *Cultures and Selves: A Cycle of Mutual Constitution*, Perspectives on Psychological Science, 2010, Vol. 5(4), 420–430

Marshall, J. and Adamic, M., *The Story Is the Message: Shaping Corporate Culture*, Journal of Business Strategy, 2010, Vol. 31(2), 18–23

Marwell, G. and Ames, R. E., *Economists Free Ride, Does Anyone Else? Experiments on the Provision of Public Goods, IV* Journal of Public Economics, 1981, Vol. 15(3), 295–310

Maslow, A. H., *Motivation and Personality* (Harper & Row 1954)

Mather, C. and Fanning, L., *Social Licence and Aquaculture: Towards a Research Agenda*, Marine Policy, 2019, Vol. 99, 275–282

Mauss, M., Douglas, M. and Halls, W. D., *The Gift: The Form and Reason for Exchange in Archaic Societies* (Routledge Classics edn 2002)

Mayer, C. P., *Firm Commitment* (Oxford University Press 2013)

Mayer, C. P., *Prosperity: Better Business Makes the Greater Good* (Oxford University Press 2018)

Mayer, D. M., et al., *The Money or the Morals? When Moral Language Is More Effective for Selling Social Issues*, Journal of Applied Psychology, 2019, Vol. 104(8), 1058–1076

Mayer, R. C., Davis, J. H. and Shoorman, F. D., *An Integrative Model of Organizational Trust*, Academy of Management Review, 1995, Vol. 20(3), 709–734

McCrudden, C., 'In Pursuit of Human Dignity: An Introduction to Current Debates', in *Understanding Human Dignity*, ed. McCrudden, C. (published for the British Academy by Oxford University Press 2013)

McDonald, G., *An Anthology of Codes of Ethics*, European Business Review, 2009, Vol. 21(4), 344–372

McGilchrist, I., *The Master and His Emissary: The Divided Brain and the Making of the Western World* (Yale University Press 2012)

McLean, B. and Elkind, P., *The Smartest Guys in the Room: The Amazing Rise and Scandalous Fall of Enron* (Penguin 2004)

Milgram, S., *Behavioral Study of Obedience*, The Journal of Abnormal and Social Psychology, 1963, Vol. 67(4), 371–378

Milgram, S., *Obedience to Authority: An Experimental View* (Tavistock Publications 1974)

Miller, D. T., *The Norm of Self-interest*, American Psychologist, 1999, Vol. 54(12), 1053–1060

Moffat, K., et al., *The Social Licence to Operate: A Critical Review*, Forestry, 2016, Vol. 89(5), 477–488

Moffat, K. and Zhang, A., *The Paths to Social Licence to Operate: An Integrative Model Explaining Community Acceptance of Mining*, Resources Policy, 2014, Vol. 39(1), 61–70

Molinsky, A. L., Grant, A. M. and Margolis, J. D., *The Bedside Manner of Homo Economicus: How and Why Priming an Economic Schema Reduces Compassion*, Organizational Behavior and Human Decision Processes, 2012, Vol. 119(1), 27–37

Morgan, B. and Yeung, K, *An Introduction to Law and Regulation: Text and Materials* (Cambridge University Press 2007)

Morgan, M. S., *Economic Man as Model Man: Ideal Types, Idealization and Caricatures*, Journal of the History of Economic Thought, 2006, Vol. 28(1), 1–27

Morrison, J., *The Social License: How to Keep Your Organization Legitimate* (Palgrave Macmillan 2014)

Moulton, S. and Freeney, M. K., *Public Service in the Private Sector: Private Loan Originator Participation in a Public Mortgage Program*, The Journal of Public Administration Research and Theory, 2011, Vol. 21(3), 547–572

Muller, J. Z., *The Tyranny of Metrics* (Princeton University Press 2018)

Navarro-Carrillo, G., et al., *Do Economic Crises Always Undermine Trust in Others? The Case of Generalized, Interpersonal, and In-Group Trust*, Frontiers in Psychology, October 2018, Vol. 9, Article 1955

Nicholson, D., *Making Lawyers Moral? Ethical Codes and Moral Character*, Legal Studies, 2005, Vol. 25(4), 601–626

Norman, D. A. and Shallice, T., 'Attention to Action: Willed and Automatic Control of Behavior', in *Consciousness and Self-regulation, Vol. 4: Advances in Research and Theory*, eds. Davidson, R. A., Schwartz, G. E. and Shapiro, D. (Plenum Press 1986)

Norman, J. *Adam Smith: What He Thought and Why It Matters* (Allen Lane 2018)

Nowak, M. A., *Five Rules for the Evolution of Cooperation*, Science, 2006, Vol. 314, 1560–1563

O'Brien, J., et al., *Professional Standards and the Social Licence to Operate: A Panacea for Finance or an Exercise in Symbolism?* Law and Financial Markets Review, 2015, Vol. 9(4), 283–292

Oddie, G., 'Desire and the Good: In Search of the Right Fit', in *The Nature of Desire* eds. Lauria, F. and Deonna, J. A. (Oxford University Press 2017)

Offer, A., 'Regard for Others', in *Capital Failure: Rebuilding Trust in Financial Services*, eds. Morris, N. and Vines, D. (Oxford University Press 2014)

Omarova, S. T., *New Tech v. New Deal: Fintech as a Systemic Phenomenon*, Yale Journal on Regulation, 2019, Vol. 36(2), 735–793

O'Neill, O., *What is banking for?*, remarks at the Federal Reserve Bank of New York, 20 October 2016

Orlitzky, M., *The Politics of Corporate Social Responsibility or: Why Milton Friedman Has Been Right All Along*, Annals in Social Responsibility, 2015, Vol. 1(1), 5–29

Orwell, G., *Nineteen Eighty-Four* (Penguin Books reprint 1988)

Osterloh, M. and Frey, B. S., 'Motivation Governance', in *Handbook of Economic Organization: Integrating Economic and Organization Theory*, ed. Grandori, A. (Edward Elgar 2013)

Owen, J. R. and Kemp, D., *Social Licence and Mining: A Critical Perspective*, Resources Policy, 2013, Vol. 38(1), 29–35

Painter-Morland, M., *Triple Bottom-Line Reporting as Social Grammar: Integrating Corporate Social Responsibility and Corporate Codes of Conduct*, Business Ethics: A European Review, 2006, Vol. 15(4), 352–364

Parliamentary Commission on Banking Standards, '*An Accident Waiting to Happen': The Failure of HBOS*, fourth report of session 2012–13, 7 March 2013, HL Paper 144, HC 705

Parliamentary Commission on Banking Standards, *Changing Banking for Good*, First Report of Session 2013–2014, Volume I: Summary, and Conclusions and Recommendations, HL Paper 27-I, HC 175-I, June 2013

Parliamentary Commission on Banking Standards, *Changing Banking for Good*, First Report of Session 2013–14, Volume II: Chapters 1 to 11 and Annexes, together with formal minutes, HL Paper 27-II HC 175-II, June 2013

Parsons, R., Lacey, J. and Moffat, K., *Maintaining Legitimacy of a Contested Practice: How the Minerals Industry Understands Its Own 'Licence to Operate'*, Resources Policy, 2014, Vol. 41, 83–90

Parsons, R. and Moffat, K., *Constructing the Meaning of Social Licence*, Social Epistemology, 2014, Vol. 28(3–4), 340–363

Parsons, R. and Moffat, K., *Integrating Impact and Relational Dimensions of Social Licence and Social Impact Assessment*, Impact Assessment and Project Appraisal, 2014, Vol. 32(4), 273–282

Pasquale, F., *Two Narratives of Platform Capitalism*, Yale Law and Policy Review, 2016, Vol. 35(1), 309–318

Patil, I., et al., *Neuroanatomical Basis of Concern-based Altruism in Virtual Environment*, Neuropsychologia, 2018, Vol. 116, 34–43

Peters, E., 'The Functions of Affect in the Construction of Preferences', in *The Construction of Preference*, eds. Lichtenstein, S. and Slovic, P. (Cambridge University Press 2006)

Podsakoff, P. M., Mackenzie, S. B. and Podsakoff N. P. eds., *The Oxford Handbook of Organizational Citizenship Behavior* (Oxford University Press 2018)

Pogge, T., 'Dignity and Global Justice', in *The Cambridge Handbook of Human Dignity: Interdisciplinary Perspectives*, eds. Düwell, M., et al. (Cambridge University Press 2014)

Polkinghorne, D. E., *Narrative Knowing and the Human Sciences* (State University of New York Press 1988)

Polletta, F., 'Plotting Protest', in *Stories of Social Change: Narrative and Social Movements*, ed. Davis, J. E. (State University of New York Press 2002)

Polletta, F., et al., *The Sociology of Storytelling*, Annual Review of Sociology, 2011, Vol. 37, 109–130

Polletta, F. and Callahan, J., *Deep Stories, Nostalgia Narratives and Fake News: Storytelling in the Trump Era*, American Journal of Cultural Sociology, 2017, Vol. 5(3), 392–408

Portes, A., *Economic Sociology: A Systematic Enquiry* (Princeton University Press 2010)

Posner, E. A. and Adler, M. D., *Rethinking Cost-Benefit Analysis*, Yale Law Journal, 1999, Vol. 109, 165–247

Posner, E. A. and Weyl, E. G., *Cost-Benefit Analysis of Financial Regulations: A Response to Criticisms*, Yale Law Journal Forum, 2015, Vol. 124, 246–262

Prinz, J. J. and Nichols, S., 'Moral Emotions', in *The Moral Psychology Handbook*, eds. Doris, J. M., et al. (Oxford University Press 2010)

Pritchard, M. S., *Human Dignity and Justice*, Ethics, 1972, Vol. 82(4), 299–313

Prudential Regulation Authority, *The Prudential Regulation Authority's Approach to Banking Supervision*, October 2018

Purvis, B., Mao, Y. and Robinson, D., *Three Pillars of Sustainability: In Search of Conceptual Origins*, Sustainability Science, 2019, Vol. 14(3), 681–695

Putnam, R. D., *Bowling Alone: The Collapse and Revival of American Community* (Simon & Schuster 2001)

PWC, *Pay: What Motivates Financial Services Executives?*, 2012

PWC, *Codes of Conduct: A Barrier or a Breakthrough for Corporate Behaviour?*, 2013

PWC, *The Ethics of Pay in a Fair Society, What Do Executives Think?*, 2017

Railton, P., 'Learning as an Inherent Dynamic of Belief and Desire', in *The Nature of Desire*, eds. Lauria, F. and Deonna, J. A. (Oxford University Press 2017)

Rappaport, A., *Creating Shareholder Value: The New Standard for Business Performance* (The Free Press 1986)

Rawls, J., *A Theory of Justice* (original edn, Harvard University Press 1971)

Rawls, J. and Erin, K., *Justice as Fairness: A Restatement* (Harvard University Press 2001)

Rhee, R. J. *A Legal Theory of Shareholder Primacy*, Minnesota Law Review, 2018, Vol. 102, 1951–2017

Richerson, P. J., et al., *Cultural Group Selection Plays an Essential Role in Explaining Human Cooperation: A Sketch of the Evidence*, Behavioral and Brian Sciences, 2016, Vol. 39, 1–68

Rock, E. B. *Adapting to the New Shareholder-Centric Reality*, University of Pennsylvania Law Review, 2013, Vol. 161(7), 1907–1988

Rodell, J. B., *Finding Meaning Through Volunteering: Why Do Employees Volunteer and What Does It Mean for Their Jobs?* Academy of Management Journal, 2013, Vol. 56(5), 1274–1294

Rodell, J. B., et al., *Employee Volunteering: A Review and Framework for Future Research*, Journal of Management, 2016, Vol. 42(1), 55–84

Rogoff, B., *The Cultural Nature of Human Development* (Oxford University Press 2003)

Rohrer, D., Pashler, H. and Harris, C. R., *Discrepant Data and Improbable Results: An Examination of Vohs, Mead, and Goode* (2006), Basic and Applied Social Psychology, 2019, Vol. 41(4), 263–271

Rosen, M., *Dignity: Its History and Meaning* (Harvard University Press 2012)

Ross, D. and Miller, M. T. eds., *The Justice Motive in Everyday Life* (Cambridge University Press 2002)

Rosso, B. D., Dekas, K. H. and Wrzesniewski, A., *On the Meaning of Work: A Theoretical Integration and Review*, Research in Organizational Behavior, 2010, Vol. 30, 91–127

Rostbøll, C. F., *Preferences and Paternalism: On Freedom and Deliberative Democracy*, Political Theory, 2005, Vol. 33, 370–396

Roth, M. T., *Law Collections from Mesopotamia and Asia Minor* (Scholars Press, Atlanta, 1995)

Royal Commission into Misconduct in the Banking, Superannuation and Financial Services Industry, *Final Report*, Commonwealth of Australia, 2019

Rumelhart, D. and Ortony, A., 'The Representation of Knowledge in Memory', in *Schooling and the Acquisition of Knowledge*, eds. Anderson, R. C., Spiro, R. J. and Montague, W. E. (Lawrence Erlbaum Associates Inc. 1977)

Russo, B. D, Dekas, K. H. and Wrzesniewski, A., *On the Meaning of Work: A Theoretical Integration and Review*, Research in Organizational Behavior, 2010, Vol. 30, 91–127

Ryan, R. M. and Deci, E. L., *Self-determination Theory: Basic Psychological Needs in Motivation, Development and Wellness* (The Guilford Press 2017)

Sacconi, L., *The Social Contract of the Firm: Economics, Ethics and Organisation* (English edition, Springer 2000)

Salz, A., *Salz Review: An Independent Review of Barclays' Business Practices*, April 2013

Samuels, W. J., *Erasing the Invisible Hand: Essays on an Elusive and Misused Concept in Economics* (Cambridge University Press 2011)

Sandel, M. J., *Justice* (Farrar, Straus and Giroux 2009)

Sandel, M. J., *The Moral Economy of Speculation: Gambling, Finance and the Common Good*, The Tanner Lectures on Human Values, University of Utah, 2013

Sanderson, R., et al., *Strangers in a Strange Land: Relations Between Perceptions of Others' Values and Both Civic Engagement and Cultural Estrangement*, Frontiers in Psychology, 2019, Vol. 10, Article 559

Sapolsky, R., *Behave: The Biology of Humans at Our Best and Worst* (Bodley Head 2017)

Schank, R. C. and Abelson, R. P., *Scripts, Plans, Goals and Understanding: An Inquiry into Human Knowledge Structures* (Lawrence Erlbaum Associates 1977)

Schanzenbach, M. M. and Sitkoff, R. H., *The Law and Economics of Environmental, Social and Governance Investing by a Fiduciary*, Harvard Law School Discussion Paper 971, September 2018

Schechtman, M., 'The Narrative Self', in *The Oxford Handbook of the Self*, ed. Shaun Gallagher, S. (Oxford University Press 2011)

Schein, E. *Organizational Culture and Leadership* (4th edn, Jossey-Bass 2010)

Schmälzle, R., et al., *Engaged Listeners: Shared Neural Processing of Powerful Political Speeches*, Social Cognitive and Affective Neuroscience, 2015, Vol. 10(8), 1137–1143

Schmid, H. B., 'The Feeling of Being in a Group: Corporate Emotions and Collective Consciousness', in *Collective Emotions*, eds. von Scheve, C. and Salmela, M. (Oxford University Press 2014)

Scholten, W. W. and Ellemers, N., *Bad Apples or Corrupting Barrels? Preventing Traders' Misconduct*, Journal of Financial Regulation and Compliance, 2016, Vol. 24(4), 366–382

Schroeder, T., Roskies A. L. and Nichols, S., 'Moral Motivation', in *The Moral Psychology Handbook*, eds. Doris, J. M., et al. (Oxford University Press 2010)

Schwartz, S. H., *Les Valeurs de Base de la Personne: Théorie, Mesures et Applications*, Revue Française de Sociologie, 2006, Vol 47(4), 929–969

Schwartz, S. H. and Bardi, A., *Value Hierarchies Across Cultures: Taking a Similarities Perspective*, Journal of Cross-Cultural Psychology, 2001, Vol. 32(3), 268–290

Searle, J. R., *The Construction of Social Reality* (Free Press 1995)

Sedikides, C. and Gaertner, L., 'The Social Self: The Quest for Identity and the Motivational Primacy of the Individual Self', in *The Social Mind: Cognitive and Motivational Aspects of Interpersonal Behavior*, eds. Forgas, J. P., Williams, K. D. and Wheeler, L. (Cambridge University Press 2001)

Sen, A., *Rational Fools: A Critique of the Behavioral Foundations of Economic Theory*, Philosophy & Public Affairs, 1977, Vol. 6(4), 317–344

Sen, A., *The Idea of Justice* (Allen Lane 2009)

Servaes, H. and Tamayo, A., *The Role of Social Capital in Corporations: A Review*, Oxford Review of Economic Policy, 2017, Vol. 22(2), 201–220

Sharapov, K., *Understanding Public Knowledge and Attitudes Towards Trafficking in Human Beings*, Research Paper, Part 2. (Center for Policy Studies, Central European University 2015)

Sherif, M., *A Study of Some Social Factors in Perception*, Archives of Psychology, 1935, No. 187, 23–46

Sherwin, R. K., *The Narrative Construction of Legal Reality*, Vermont Law Review, 1994, Vol. 18, 681–719

Shiller, R. J., *Narrative Economics: How Stories Go Viral & Drive Major Economic Events* (Princeton University Press 2019)

Skonieczny, A., *Emotions and Political Narratives: Populism, Trump and Trade*, Politics and Governance, 2018, Vol 6(4), 62–72

Smith, A., *An Inquiry into the Nature and Causes of the Wealth of Nations* (Liberty Fund edn 1981)

Smith, A., *The Theory of Moral Sentiments* (Liberty Fund edn 1982)

Smith, K. S. and Graybiel, A. M., *Habit Formation*, Dialogues in Clinical Neuroscience, 2016, Vol. 18(1), 33–43

Smith, V. L., *Human Nature: An Economic Perspective*, Dædalus, 2004, Vol. 133(4), 67–76

Smyth, M. L. and Davis, J. R., *Perceptions of Dishonesty Among Two-Year College Students: Academic Versus Business Situations*, Journal of Business Ethics, 2004, Vol. 51(1), 63–73

Sobel, J. *Can We Trust Social Capital*, Journal of Economic Literature, 2002, Vol. 40, 139–154

Sobel, J., *Interdependent Preferences and Reciprocity*, Journal of Economic Literature, 2005, Vol. 43(2), 392–436

Sonenshein, S., *Crafting Social Issues at Work*, Academy of Management Journal, 2006, Vol. 49(6), 1158–1172

Steffen, W., et al., *The Trajectory of the Anthropocene: The Great Acceleration*, The Anthropocene Review 2015, Vol. 2(1), 81–98

Steger, M. F., 'Meaning in Life', in *The Oxford Handbook of Positive Psychology*, eds. Lopez S. J. and Snyder, C.R. (2nd edn, Oxford University Press 2009)

Stich, S., Doris, J. M. and Roedder, E., 'Altruism', in *The Moral Psychology Handbook*, eds. Doris, J. M., et al. (Oxford University Press 2010)

Stiroh, K. J., *Misconduct risk, culture and supervision*, speech at the Federal Reserve Bank of New York, 7 December 2017

Stiroh K. J., *The complexity of culture reform in finance*, speech at the 4th Annual Culture and Conduct Forum for the Financial Services Industry, London, 4 October 2018

Stiroh, K. J., *Reform of culture in finance from multiple perspectives*, speech at the GARP Risk Convention, New York City, 26 February 2019

Stout, L., *Cultivating Conscience: How Good Laws Make Good People* (Princeton University Press 2011)

Suchman, M. C., *Managing Legitimacy: Strategic and Institutional Approaches*, Academy of Management Review, 1995, Vol. 20(3), 571–610

Sunstein, C. R., *On the Expressive Function of Law*, University of Pennsylvania Law Review, 1995, Vol. 144(5), 2021–2053

Sunstein, C. R., *Financial Regulation and Cost-Benefit Analysis*, Yale Law Journal Forum, 2015, Vol. 124, 263–279

Sunstein, C. R., *The Ethics of Influence: Government in the Age of Behavioural Science* (Cambridge University Press 2016)

Tanis, M., and Postmes, T., *A Social Identity Approach to Trust: Interpersonal Perception, Group Membership and Trusting Behaviour*, European Journal of Social Psychology, 2005, Vol. 35(3), 413–424

Tartakovsky, E. and Cohen, E. *Values in the Bank: Value Preferences of Bank Frontline Workers and Branch Managers*, European Journal of Work and Organizational Psychology, 2014, Vol. 23(5), 769–782

Taylor, C., 'To Follow a Rule', in *Philosophical Arguments* (Harvard University Press 1995)

Taylor Review of Modern Working Practices, *Good Work: The Taylor Review of Modern Working Practices*, 2017

Thaler, R. H. and Sunstein, C. R., *Nudge: Improving Decisions About Health, Wealth, and Happiness* (Penguin Books 2009)

Thomas, C. A., *The Uses and Abuses of Legitimacy in International Law*, Oxford Journal of Legal Studies, 2014, Vol. 34(4), 729–758

Tirole, J., *Economics for the Common Good* (Princeton University Press 2017)

Tobin, J., *The Invisible Hand in Modern Macroeconomics*, Cowles Foundation Discussion Paper No. 966, Cowles Foundation for Research in Economics at Yale University, January 1991

Tooze, A., *Crashed: How a Decade of Financial Crises Changed the World* (Allen Lane 2018)

Trentmann, F., *The Empire of Things: How We Became a World of Consumers, From the Fifteenth Century to the Twenty-First* (Allen Lane 2016)

Treviño, L. K., den Niewenboer, N. A. and Kish-Gephart, J. J., *(Un)Ethical Behavior in Organizations*, Annual Review of Psychology, 2014, Vol. 65, 635–660

Trivers, R. L., *The Evolution of Reciprocal Altruism*, The Quarterly Review of Biology, 1971, Vol. 46(1), 35–57

Tucker, P., *Macro and microprudential supervision*, speech at the British Bankers' Association Annual International Banking Conference, London, 29 June 2011

Turner, A., *Between Debt and the Devil – Money, Credit and Fixing Global Finance* (Princeton University Press 2016)

Turner, J. D., *Banking in Crisis: The Rise and Fall of British Banking Stability, 1800 to the Present* (Cambridge University Press 2014)

Turner, J. D., 'The Development of English Company Law Before 1900', in *Research Handbook on the History of Corporate and Company Law*, ed. Wells, H. (Edward Elgar 2018)

Tyler, T. R., *Reducing Corporate Criminality: The Role of Values*, American Criminal Law Review, 2014, Vol. 51(1), 267–291

United Nations, *Guiding Principles on Human Rights: Implementing the United Nations 'Protect, Respect and Remedy' Framework*, 2 March 2011, A/HC/17/31

United Nations, *Transforming our World: The 2030 Agenda for Sustainable Development*, Resolution adopted by the General Assembly on 25 September 2015

United Nations Conference on Trade and Development, *World Investment Report 2014 – Investing in the SDGs: An Action Plan*

United Nations Environment Programme Finance Initiative, *Rethinking Impact to Finance the SDGs*, November 2018

United Nations Environment Programme Inquiry into the Design of a Sustainable Finance System, *Sustainable Finance Progress Report*, March 2019

United Nations Human Rights Council, *Protect, Respect and Remedy: a Framework for Business and Human Rights*, UN Human Rights Council A/HRC/8/5 7 April 2008

University of Cambridge Institute for Sustainability Leadership, *Walking the Talk: Understanding Consumer Demand for Sustainable Investing*, 2019

van der Cruijsen, C., de Haan, J. and Jansen, D., *Trust and Financial Crisis Experiences*, Social Indicators Research, 2016, Vol. 127(2), 577–600

Van Maanen, J. 'The Smile Factory: Work at Disneyland', in *Reframing Organizational Culture*, eds. Frost, P. J., et al. (Sage Publications 1991)

Van Ness, D. and Heetderks Strong, K., *Restoring Justice: An Introduction to Restorative Justice* (5th edn, Routledge 2014)

Vandenabeele, W., Ritz, A. and Neumann, O., 'Public Service Motivation: State of the Art and Conceptual Cleanup', in *The Palgrave Handbook of Public Administration and Management in Europe*, eds. Ongaro, E. and van Thiel, S. (Palgrave 2018)

Vogel, D., *Private Global Business Regulation*, Annual Review of Political Science, 2008, Vol. 11(1), 261–282

Vohs, K. D., *Money Priming Can Change People's Thoughts, Feelings, Motivations, and Behaviors: An Update on 10 Years of Experiments*, Journal of Experimental Psychology: General, 2015, Vol. 144(4), e86–e93

Vohs, K. D., Mead, N. L. and Goode, M. R., *Merely Activating the Concept of Money Changes Personal and Interpersonal Behavior*, Current Directions in Psychological Science, 2008, Vol. 17(3), 208–212

Vranka, M. A. and Houdek, P., *Many Faces of Bankers' Identity: How (Not) to Study Dishonesty*, Frontiers in Psychology, 2015, Vol. 6, Article 302

Wachtel, T., *Defining Restorative*, International Institute of Restorative Practices, 2013

Wade, J., O'Reilly, C. and Pollock, T., *Overpaid CEOs and Underpaid Managers: Fairness and Executive Compensation*, Organization Science, 2006, Vol. 17(5), 527–544

Wang, L., Malhotra, D. and Murnighan, J. K., *Economics Education and Greed*, Academy of Management Learning and Education, 2011, Vol. 10(4), 643–660

Wang, X., and Krumhuber, E. G., *The Love of Money Results in Objectification*, British Journal of Social Psychology, 2017, Vol. 56(2), 354–372

Warnick, B., *The Narrative Paradigm: Another Story*, Quarterly Journal of Speech, 1987, Vol. 73(2), 172–182

Westen, D., *The Political Brain: The Role of Emotion in Deciding the Fate of the Nation* (Public Affairs 2007)

Wexler, B. E., *Brain and Culture: Neurobiology, Ideology, and Social Change* (MIT Press 2006)

Wheeler, S., *Global Production, CSR and Human Rights: The Courts of Public Opinion and the Social License to Operate*, International Journal of Human Rights, 2015, Vol. 19(6), 757–778

Williams, J. C., *Banking culture: the path ahead*, speech at the Federal Reserve Bank of New York, 4 June 2019

Wilson, A. D. and Golonka, S., *Embodied Cognition Is Not What You Think It Is*, Frontiers in Psychology, 2013, Vol. 4, Article 58

Wilson, M., *The Re-tooled Mind: How Culture Re-engineers Cognition*, Social Cognitive and Affective Neuroscience, 2010, Vol. 5(2–3), 180–187

World Bank, *Mind, Society, and Behavior*, 2015

World Commission on Environment and Development, *Our Common Future: Report of the World Commission on Environment and Development* (Oxford University Press 1987)

Wright, B. E., *Public Service and Motivation: Does Mission Matter?* Public Administration Review, 2007, Vol. 67(1), 54–64

Wrzesniewski, A. 'Finding Positive Meaning in Work', in *Positive Organizational Scholarship: Foundations of a New Discipline*, eds. Cameron, K. S., Dutton, J. E. and Quinn, R. E. (Berrett-Koehler 2003)

Wrzesniewski, A., et al., *Jobs, Careers, and Callings: People's Relations to Their Work*, Journal of Research in Personality, 1997, Vol. 31(1), 21–33

Yeoman, R., et al., eds., *The Oxford Handbook of Meaningful Work* (Oxford University Press 2019)

Yezer, A. M., Goldfarb, R. S. and Poppen, P.J., *Does Studying Economics Discourage Cooperation? Watch What We Do, Not What We Say or How We Play*, Journal of Economic Perspectives, 1996, Vol. 10(1), 177–186

Zahavi, A., *Altruism as a Handicap – The Limitations of Kin Selection and Reciprocity*, Journal of Avian Biology, 1995, Vol. 26(1), 1–3

Zaki, J., Bolger, N. and Ochsner, K., *It Takes Two: The Interpersonal Nature of Empathic Accuracy*, Psychological Science, 2008, Vol. 19(4), 399–404

Zetzsche, D. A., Buckley, R. P. and Arner, D. W. *Regulating Libra: the Transformative Potential of Facebook's Cryptocurrency and Possible Regulatory Responses*, University of New South Wales Law Research Series [2019] UNSW Law Research Paper No. 47

Zhang, A., Measham, T. G. and Moffat, K., *Preconditions for Social Licence: The Importance of Information in Initial Engagement*, Journal of Cleaner Production, 2018, Vol. 172, 1559–1566

Ziqiang, X. and Guofang, L., *Homo Economicus Belief Inhibits Trust*, PLoS ONE, 2013, Vol. 8(10), E76671

Zucker, L., *The Role of Institutionalization in Cultural Persistence*, American Sociological Review, 1977, Vol. 42(5), 726–743

Index[1]

A

Altruism, 29n43, 70, 83–85, 88–90,
        93, 96–98, 108n122, 135, 224,
        235, 275, 302
Aristotle, 41, 96
Artificial intelligence, 7, 60, 63n9, 80
Aspiration, xxii, xxiii, 2, 3, 5, 8–10, 14,
        17–22, 42, 83, 114, 164,
        223, 273
Aspirational standards, 165, 168,
        179–181, 184–190, 216n42,
        247, 254–255, 278, 281, 282
Authority, 56, 58, 118, 130, 144,
        160–161n138, 233–234

B

Behaviour, viii, 2, 35, 37–62, 69, 111,
        114, 163, 221, 223–256, 273
Behavioural economics, 16
Beliefs, vii, viii, 9, 13, 25, 37–40,
        43–48, 50–52, 55, 56, 58, 61,
        63n9, 69, 70, 73, 78, 81, 84,
        116, 117, 127, 129, 141,
        160–161n138, 161n139, 163,
        223, 227, 229, 233, 235, 236,
        241–243, 245, 251, 252,
        256, 263n87
Bourdieu, Pierre, 244–246, 267n140,
        270n191, 281
Brand, 5, 77, 228

C

Character, 2, 40, 114, 125, 176, 186,
        221, 224, 227, 240–246, 275,
        276, 281, 291,
        294–296, 299–300
Codes of conduct, 114, 173, 185,
        187–190, 218n77, 249, 275, 288
Collateral Directive, 54
Common good, 11, 85
Companies
    behaviour, 58
    Companies Act 2006, 18, 58, 251
    directors' duties, 121, 149n24, 251
    purpose, 1, 13, 18, 19, 53, 283, 286

---

[1] Note: Page numbers followed by 'n' refer to notes.

© The Author(s) 2020
D. Rouch, *The Social Licence for Financial Markets*,
https://doi.org/10.1007/978-3-030-40220-4

Compliance, 24, 54–57, 146, 149n24,
   154n68, 165, 170, 174–176,
   182, 183, 186–188, 190,
   218n71, 218n77, 226, 253, 273,
   275, 291, 299–301
Cost-benefit analysis (CBA), xxiv, 14,
   274, 290–292
Crowding out, 186, 190, 217n60, 235,
   238–239, 299
Culture, xix, xx, xxiii, 2, 6, 9, 10, 14,
   16, 19, 20, 23–25, 33n98, 40,
   51, 62, 85, 129, 131, 137, 138,
   156n100, 176, 178, 188, 189,
   213n1, 224, 227, 231, 234, 238,
   240–246, 249, 254, 267n151,
   275–277, 280, 281, 285, 291,
   294–296, 299–300, 304

D

Desire
   instrumental, 37, 42, 61, 70, 83, 94,
      95, 133, 182, 265n115
   intrinsic, 37, 42, 61, 70, 83, 88, 94,
      95, 103n53, 133, 256
Dignity, viii, xxi, xxii, 70, 74, 84,
   91–96, 98, 99, 107n102,
   107n111, 114, 115, 134, 136,
   137, 140, 143, 146, 156n95,
   160n133, 169, 223, 226,
   230–232, 239, 256, 275,
   286, 300
Donne, John, 83, 96, 104n56

E

Economic man, xxi, 1, 9, 13, 15–19,
   226, 237, 246, 300
Emotion, 41, 43–44, 58, 61, 88, 127,
   135, 228
Empathy, 88, 89, 231, 234–235, 237
Ends, viii, ix, xxii, xxiii, xxv, 1–25, 35,
   37, 38, 41–43, 50, 51, 53, 55,
   59, 61, 62, 65n40, 69–99, 114,
   115, 128, 129, 136, 137,
   139–142, 163, 167, 172, 221,
   223, 226, 228, 232, 256,
   264n100, 267n148, 274, 280,
   286, 292, 293, 296, 299,
   303, 313–314
Enforcement, xxiv, 23, 107n108, 166,
   168, 170, 171, 182–190, 213n5,
   213n13, 214n17, 217n61,
   218n71, 249, 253, 275,
   281, 300–302
Environmental, Social and Governance
   (ESG), 77, 80, 81, 102n36,
   102n41, 102n42, 234, 250, 251
Ethics, 25, 163, 174, 181, 216n50,
   217n58, 218n73, 300
Evolution, 70, 224

F

Fair and Effective Markets Review, 6,
   75, 82, 188, 290, 302
Fiduciary duties, 171, 251
Finance, vii, ix, xx–xxiv, 1–3, 5–10, 12,
   14, 20–25, 35, 46–48, 55, 60,
   69, 74, 75, 77, 80–81, 94, 111,
   113–115, 119–122, 126, 131,
   139, 141, 143, 145, 163, 164,
   166, 168, 172, 174, 176, 177,
   187, 223, 225, 226, 231, 232,
   238, 241, 242, 246, 254, 274,
   276, 279–282, 285, 288, 289,
   293–299, 302, 314
Financial Services and Markets Act
   2000, 48, 64n33, 122, 215n40,
   248, 270n199, 308n59, 309n71
Formation, xxiii, 176, 186, 224, 225,
   240–246, 253, 255, 256,
   266n137, 275, 277, 278, 281,
   291, 298–300, 302
Framing, xxiii, 224, 225, 233,
   235–241, 247, 296

Freedom, xxii, 3, 4, 91, 114, 115, 118, 123, 139, 140, 142, 163, 169, 225, 227, 255–256, 276, 281
Friedman, Milton, 3–5, 10, 17, 18, 293
Friendship, 78, 96

G

Gambling, 275, 293–297, 309n71
Gift, xix, 70, 97, 113, 118, 142, 145, 232, 239
Goals, *see* Ends
Group behaviour, 40, 57, 60–62, 85

H

Habit, xxiii, 38, 40, 41, 49–51, 61, 146, 224, 227, 240, 243, 245, 246, 314
Habitus, 244–246, 252, 255, 267n140
Hobbes, Thomas, 86, 96, 144, 145
Homo economicus, *see* Economic man
Human rights, 91, 92, 125, 156n95, 169, 172, 214n17, 286
Hume, David, 41

I

Identity, 38, 50, 58, 95, 137, 142, 160n134, 180, 224, 227, 231, 234–235, 237, 243, 257n8
Incentives
negative, 164, 165, 175, 186–188, 275, 299, 300
positive, 164, 165, 182, 183, 186, 188, 247, 275, 299, 300
Incomplete contracts, 78–79, 97, 239, 249
Individual accountability, 66n44, 174, 176, 275, 299–300
Individual choice, *see* Freedom
Integrated reporting, 274, 278, 286, 287, 307n41, 307n42

International Swaps and Derivatives Association (ISDA), 69, 79, 82, 101n29, 171, 173, 187, 269n178
Investment, viii, xxiv, 3, 6, 18, 21–23, 43, 44, 48–50, 54, 58, 64n27, 76, 77, 80–81, 92, 95, 101n30, 113, 119, 125, 150n29, 153n62, 167, 174, 175, 177, 187, 215n33, 215n34, 215n37, 250, 251, 274, 275, 292–298
Invisible hand, xxi, 1, 9, 13, 14, 19–20, 58, 142, 145, 226, 228

J

Justice, xxii, 42, 43, 135–138, 169, 180–181, 231–232, 254–256
justice motivation, 90, 231
restorative justice, xxiv, 275, 300–302

K

Kant, Immanuel, 41, 91, 92
Keynes, John Maynard, 54, 294, 297

L

Language, xx, xxiv, 3, 10, 12, 20, 21, 23–25, 38, 45–48, 50, 51, 53, 54, 61, 62, 94, 95, 113, 121, 143, 166, 223, 224, 226, 244, 250, 280, 298, 299
Law, 48, 163–212, 246–255
international, 125, 151n38, 169
private, 171, 175, 183, 186, 214n16, 248, 249
public, 117, 171, 175, 248
Legal certainty, 278, 295
Legitimacy, vii, 56, 132, 142, 146, 148n11, 150n30, 155n92, 160–161n138, 161n139

Liberty, *see* Freedom
LIBOR, 71, 81–83, 87, 90, 98, 134,
    256, 299, 302

M
Markets
    behaviour, 2, 3, 40, 46, 48, 58, 62,
        73, 82, 86, 116, 175, 187, 224,
        227, 241, 248, 273, 277, 278
    meaning, 38, 46, 47, 69, 244
Markets in Financial Instruments
        Directive (MiFID), 248, 253
Meaning, xxiii, xxiv, 10, 37, 38, 42,
        44–55, 61, 62, 69, 72, 73, 84,
        86, 93–95, 99, 113, 115–117,
        119, 121, 122, 124, 141, 146,
        163, 164, 166, 167, 177, 178,
        182, 184, 223, 224, 227, 228,
        233, 235, 236, 239, 241, 243,
        246, 247, 249, 252, 253, 255,
        273, 276–278, 280–282, 287,
        288, 290–292, 294, 295, 299,
        300, 303, 314
Meaningfulness, 227, 232
Measurement, 303–305
Metaphor, xxi, 20, 84, 113, 116,
        123–124, 145, 146, 178
Models
    economic, xxi, 1, 2, 9, 13, 14, 20,
        22, 23, 43, 46, 51, 72, 74, 141,
        226, 241, 248
    mental, 8, 9, 13, 46, 62, 235,
        238, 240
Money, viii, xx, xxii, xxiv, 1–3, 7, 10,
        12, 17, 18, 37–42, 44–49, 51,
        54, 69, 70, 72–76, 93–95, 98,
        99, 113, 115, 119, 121, 122,
        141, 164, 166, 177, 178, 180,
        223, 226, 237, 239, 243, 244,
        283, 292, 293, 296, 303
Motivation
    extrinsic, 264n100
    intrinsic, 238, 239

Mutuality, 70, 71, 74, 91–94, 96, 97,
        115, 142, 144, 145, 230, 255,
        256, 277
    broad-based mutuality, 2, 71, 74,
        93, 96–98, 123, 134, 138, 143,
        145, 223, 226–227, 230, 276

N
Narrative, xxi, xxii, xxiv, 1, 2, 8–10,
        13–25, 38, 41, 43, 46–51, 55,
        61, 69, 71, 72, 74, 75, 82, 84,
        90, 99, 115, 116, 119, 122, 137,
        141, 145, 223–232, 235–237,
        240–250, 252, 255, 257n2, 276,
        279, 282, 283, 285, 287, 291,
        293, 294, 296, 299, 303
Neuroplasticity, 245, 246
Norms
    behavioural, 164, 168–169, 177,
        224, 240, 241, 245, 252
    written, 173

O
Other-regardingness, 19, 24, 25, 74,
        76, 77, 79, 82, 83, 87, 98, 182,
        233, 238, 243

P
Paris Climate Agreement, 172
Power, viii, 8, 10, 12, 20–22, 41,
        44–48, 51, 52, 56, 69, 73, 86, 89,
        94, 95, 116, 117, 119, 124, 125,
        133, 141, 152n51, 160–161n138,
        161n139, 165, 166, 171, 183,
        185, 186, 189, 190, 220n98, 223,
        224, 227–230, 232, 240,
        242–244, 294, 301
Preferences, 15, 16, 129, 133, 135,
        137, 145, 230, 236, 237, 240,
        255, 277, 299
    endogenous, 237, 277

Priming, 235, 237–238, 275
Public interest, 19, 24, 82, 130, 171,
    175, 240, 274, 279, 284, 289, 299
Public service motivation, 89, 90,
    231, 233
Purpose, vii, xxii, xxiv, 1, 5, 7–13, 15,
    16, 18, 19, 24, 25, 39, 43–45,
    50, 53, 58, 65n40, 72, 75–77,
    80, 86, 91, 95, 117, 121, 125,
    128–130, 170, 180, 184, 189,
    214n16, 227, 228, 231, 243,
    248, 249, 252, 253, 269n169,
    274, 275, 278, 282–286,
    288–290, 293–297, 309n71

R
Rawls, John, 144, 160n134
Reason, xxii, xxiii, 3, 11, 14, 17, 18,
    37, 40, 41, 44, 47, 49–51,
    53–55, 57, 58, 61, 62n5, 74, 76,
    84, 85, 88, 89, 92, 119, 124,
    126, 127, 129, 134, 140, 141,
    143, 159n118, 165, 225,
    227–229, 231, 232, 236, 238,
    241, 247, 249, 254–256,
    270n200, 279, 284, 292,
    293, 296
Reciprocity, xx, 2, 8, 71, 74, 78, 84,
    87, 96–98, 138, 139, 159n116,
    256, 304
    positive reciprocity, viii, xx, xxiii, 2,
    3, 8, 14, 39, 69, 71, 73, 96–99,
    134, 138, 143, 223, 224, 226,
    230, 236, 241, 273, 276, 277,
    279, 299, 314
Relational goods, xxiv, 84, 115, 134,
    136, 138, 140, 226, 274, 286,
    291, 314
Remuneration, 17, 47, 75, 76,
    87, 94, 99n3, 174, 178, 182,
    183, 186, 243, 275, 282,
    296, 299–300
Rule following, 252, 255, 270n191

S
Schemas, 28n32, 49–51, 55, 61,
    65n40, 235, 237
Self-interest, viii, xix, xxi, xxii, xxiv, 1,
    4, 9, 10, 13, 15–17, 19–22, 24,
    25, 29n43, 42, 70, 75, 83–90,
    93, 96–98, 102n31, 120, 131,
    135, 144, 145, 159n116,
    160n133, 160n134, 160n138,
    180, 182, 183, 186, 224, 230,
    235, 237, 238
    financial self-interest, xxii, 1, 10, 13,
    14, 16, 17, 22, 23, 41, 70, 71,
    73, 80, 81, 83, 87, 90, 94–95,
    134, 141, 224, 226, 230, 238,
    243, 292–293, 299, 313
Selfish gene, 14, 70, 84
Senior Managers Regime, 57, 219n88,
    284, 299
Settlement Finality Directive, 53–54
Shareholder value, xxi, 1, 9, 13, 14,
    17–19, 30n51, 31n65, 226, 243,
    251, 252
Short Selling Regulation, 295, 308n62
Social capital, vii–ix, 96, 109n124,
    109n131, 139–141, 304
Social contract, 115, 144–145
Social control, 255–256
Social licence for financial
    markets, xix, xxii, xxiv, 2, 3,
    7–13, 24, 25, 37, 39, 43,
    46, 48, 49, 51, 57, 62, 73, 83,
    92, 98, 99, 113–146, 163,
    164, 168, 169, 173, 177, 178,
    180, 190, 223, 224, 226–228,
    230, 234, 237, 247, 255,
    280, 287
Social licence to operate
    (SLO), 114, 116, 117,
    119–121, 125–127, 129,
    131–133, 137, 139, 143, 144,
    146, 147n2, 148n11, 148n12,
    152n50, 161n140, 172,
    279, 281

Society, vii–ix, xix, xxi–xxiv, 1–5,
8, 10, 13, 17–20, 24, 26n14,
46, 76, 77, 81, 82, 85, 86, 89,
92, 96, 97, 113–116, 118–131,
133–139, 141–145, 151n34,
151n37, 152n50, 163, 164,
166, 171, 185, 223, 225, 226,
230, 231, 239, 240, 247,
255, 256, 273, 275–277,
284, 287, 289, 294,
302–304, 314
Solidarity, xix, xx, xxii, 1, 2, 6, 8, 39,
70, 71, 73, 99, 107n108, 113,
114, 119, 122, 140–142, 145,
165, 167, 177, 178, 226,
279, 314
Speculation, 275, 293–298
Stakeholder theory, 18, 142
Structural written standards, 164, 178,
276, 288
Sustainability, xx, xxii, 1, 5, 6, 20–23,
80, 115, 131, 136, 163, 175,
274, 277, 279–281,
285–287, 303
Sustainable Development Goals
(SDGs), 21, 172

T
Technology, xx, 7, 40, 60–61, 80
Trust, vii–ix, xxi, xxii, xxiv, 4, 6, 14, 23,
39, 55, 69, 70, 73, 76, 78–80,
97, 114, 115, 122, 123, 130,
133, 139–141, 145, 146,
159n116, 188, 226, 234–235,
237, 248, 249, 256, 285, 287,
291, 298, 301–304

U
Universal Declaration of Human
Rights, 70, 84, 91, 156n95
Utilitarianism, 86

V
Values, vii, xx, xxi, xxv, 1, 5, 9, 10,
12–14, 16, 42, 70, 115, 137,
165, 180–181, 224, 276

W
Written standards, 115, 163–213, 224,
225, 227, 246–255, 281, 288

Druck:
Customized Business Services GmbH
im Auftrag der
KNV Zeitfracht GmbH
Ein Unternehmen der Zeitfracht - Gruppe
Ferdinand-Jühlke-Str. 7
99095 Erfurt